Group Politics and
Social Movements in Canada

Group Politics and

Social Movements in Canada

EDITED BY MIRIAM SMITH

broadview
press

Library and Archives Canada Cataloguing in Publication

Group politics and social movements in Canada / edited by Miriam Smith.

Includes bibliographical references and index.
ISBN 978-1-55111-771-3

1. Social movements—Political aspects—Canada. 2. Social movements—Political aspects—Canada—Case studies. I. Smith, Miriam Catherine

HM881.G76 2007   322.4'40971   C2007-905296-7

Broadview Press is an independent, international publishing house, incorporated in 1985. Broadview believes in shared ownership, both with its employees and with the general public; since the year 2000 Broadview shares have traded publicly on the Toronto Venture Exchange under the symbol BDP.

We welcome comments and suggestions regarding any aspect of our publications — please feel free to contact us at the addresses below or at broadview@broadviewpress.com.

www.broadviewpress.com

North America
Post Office Box 1243,
Peterborough, Ontario,
Canada K9J 7H5
Tel: (705) 743-8990
Fax: (705) 743-8353
customerservice
@broadviewpress.com

Post Office Box 1015,
3576 California Road,
Orchard Park, NY
USA 14127

UK, Ireland, and Continental Europe
NBN International
Estover Road
Plymouth PL6 7PY
United Kingdom
Tel: +44 (0) 1752 202300
Fax: +44 (0) 1752 202330
enquiries@nbninternational.com

Australia and New Zealand
UNIREPS
University of
New South Wales
Sydney, NSW, 2052
Tel: + 61296 640 999
Fax: + 61296 645 420
info.press@unsw.edu.au

Broadview Press acknowledges the financial support of the Government of Canada through the Book Publishing Industry Development Program (BPIDP) for our publishing activities.

Copy-edited by Betsy Struthers. Cover design, photograph, and typeset by Zack Taylor.

  This book is printed on paper containing 100% post-consumer fibre.

Printed in Canada

Contents

Acknowledgements

I would like to thank the contributors for their excellent work in producing chapters in a timely fashion and responding to my deadlines and requests; David Tough for assistance with editing and manuscript preparation; the manuscript reviewers who provided many useful suggestions for revision; Betsy Struthers for outstanding copy-editing; and Greg Yantz and Michael Harrison at Broadview Press for their continued assistance and support.

Preface

This book evolved from my own need for a teaching text that would provide a comprehensive overview of the recent evolution of social movement and group politics in Canada. The main challenge in developing this volume was to locate authors who could write about all of the movements that would ideally be included in such a text. With help from many colleagues and with suggestions from Broadview Press, I succeeded in developing a team to write on most of the main topics.

The book provides an introductory theoretical chapter, adapted with permission from my book *A Civil Society? Collective Actors in Canadian Political Life* (Broadview Press, 2005), and each contributor was asked to provide an overview of the main organizations and political issues for each group or movement and an evaluation of the success or failure of the group or movement in exercising influence in Canadian politics. Most of the chapters focus on the activities of groups and social movements in federal politics, and many of them provide an overview of trajectories of influence and political mobilization over time. All of the chapters were written by authors who have a long-standing interest in the area and, therefore, they reflect a broad and deep expertise and familiarity with the subject matter. Many of the movements and groups included here are relatively under-studied in the Canadian context (e.g., health and disability) while others are rarely approached through the lens of social movement mobilization (e.g., First Nations and Quebec nationalism). Other chapters deal with enduringly important areas such as the women's movement, the labour movement, and the environmental movement; they provide authoritative overviews that will be of interest in teaching and scholarship. As the volume extends to "group politics," I have included a chapter on business organizing as the business community in Canada has been very successful in using the tools of collective action and in exercising political influence. The result is a volume that provides a strong synthetic overview of a wide range of empirical material from different theoretical perspectives. The texts reflect the diverse theoretical interests and approaches of their authors. I believe that this theoretical pluralism best represents the state of the field and will prove most useful in providing an introduction and overview of this rich material. In addition, each contributor was asked to provide an extensive list of references to assist further reading on each group or movement.

All in all, I hope the book fills a gap in the existing literature in Canadian politics and that it focuses our interest and attention on the possibilities, potential, and pitfalls of political agency.

List of Acronyms

9/11	terrorist attacks in New York City and Washington, DC, on September 11, 2001
ACT UP	AIDS Coalition to Unleash Power
ADA	*Americans with Disabilities Act*
ADAPT	American Disabled for Attendant Programs Today
ADQ	*Action démocratique du Québec* (Quebec Democratic Action)
AFN	Assembly of First Nations
AISH	Assure Income for the Severely Handicapped-Alberta
ASK	Association for Social Knowledge
BQ	Bloc Québécois
BWA	boiled water advisory
CACL	Canadian Association for Community Living
CACSW	Canadian Advisory Council on the Status of Women
CAMR	The Canadian Association of Mental Retardation
CAP	Canada Assistance Plan
CATJO	Canadian Alliance for Trade and Job Opportunities
CAW	Canadian Auto Workers
CBA	Canadian Bankers Association
CBC	Canadian Broadcasting Corporation
CCC	Canadian Chamber of Commerce
CCCE	Canadian Council of Chief Executives
CCD	Council of Canadians with Disabilities
CCF	Cooperative Commonwealth Federation
CCJC	Cooperative Committee for Japanese Canadians
CCNC	Chinese Canadian National Council
CCSD	Canadian Council on Social Development
CDC	Centers for Disease Control (US)
CEC	Canadian Ethnocultural Council
CEN	Canadian Environmental Network
CEQ	*Centrale de l'enseignement du Québec* (Quebec Teachers' Union)
CFIB	Canadian Federation of Independent Business
CHP	Christian Heritage Party

CHST	Canada Health and Social Transfer
CLC	Canadian Labour Congress
CME	Canadian Manufacturers and Exporters Association
CNF	Canadian Nature Federation
CNIB	Canadian National Institute for the Blind
COPOH	Coalition of Provincial Organizations of the Handicapped
CPAWS	Canadian Parks and Wilderness Society
CPC	Communist Party of Canada
CRRF	Canadian Race Relations Foundation
CSN	*Confédération des syndicats nationaux* (Confederation of National Trade Unions)
CSQ	*Centrale des syndicats du Québec* (Quebec Central Labour Body)
CTF	Canadian Taxpayers Federation
CUFTA	Canada-US Free Trade Agreement
CUPE	Canadian Union of Public Employees
CUPW	Canadian Union of Postal Workers
CWC	Canadian Welfare Council
DAWN	DisAbled Women's Network of Ontario
DEM	deep ecology movement
DG	*Die Grünen* (German Green Party)
ECO	Environmental Commissioner of Ontario
EMO	environmental movement organization
FEUQ	*Fédération étudiante universitaire du Québec* (Quebec Federation of University Students)
FFQ	*Fédération des femmes du Québec* (Quebec Women's Federation)
FLQ	*Front de libération du Québec* (Front for the Liberation of Quebec)
FOL	Friends of the Lubicon
FQF	*Front du Québec français* (Front for a French Quebec)
FRAPRU	*Front d'action populaire en réaménagement urbain* (Popular Action Front in Urban Renewal)
FSIN	Federation of Saskatchewan Indian Nations
FTAA	Free Trade Area of the Americas
FTQ	*Fédération des travailleurs du Québec* (Workers' Federation of Quebec)
GPC	Green Party of Canada
HBC	Hudson Bay Company
HEU	Hospital Employees' Union (British Columbia)
HRDC	Human Resources Development Canada

HSM	health social movement
IAA	Indian Association of Alberta
IBC	Insurance Bureau of Canada
ILPs	Independent Labour Parties
IMF	International Monetary Fund
IREQ	*Institut de recherche sur l'économie du Québec* (Research Institute on Quebec's Economy)
LEAF	Women's Legal Education and Action Fund
LGBT	lesbians, gays, bisexuals, and transgendered persons
MCS	Multiple Chemical Sensitivity
MLA	member of [provincial] Legislature
MNC	Métis National Council
MNQ	*Mouvement national des Québécois* (National Movement of Quebeckers)
MP	member of Parliament
MSA	*Mouvement souveraineté-association* (Sovereignty-association Movement)
NAC	National Action Committee on the Status of Women
NAFTA	North American Free Trade Agreement
NAJC	National Association of Japanese Canadians
NAPO	National Anti-Poverty Organization
NCC	National Citizens Coalition
NCC	Native Council of Canada
NCW	National Council of Welfare
NDP	New Democratic Party
NGO	non-governmental organization
NHHN	National Housing and Homelessness Network
NIB	National Indian Brotherhood
NRPR	New Religious Political Right
NSM	new social movement
NUPGE	National Union of Public and General Employees
OCAP	Ontario Coalition Against Poverty
ODA	*Ontarians with Disabilities Act*
ODSP	Ontario Disability Support Program
OECD	Organization for Economic Development
PQ	Parti Québécois
PWA	people with AIDS
QS	*Québec solidaire* (Quebec Solidarity)
RCMP	Royal Canadian Mounted Police
REAL	Real, Equal, and Active for Life (Women of Canada)

RIN   *Rassemblement pour l'indépendance nationale* (National Independence Movement)
RMT   Resource Mobilization Theory
RN   *Ralliement national* (National Movement)
SARC   Social Assistance Review Committee
SCC   Sierra Club of Canada
SDP   Social Democratic Party of Canada
SLAPPs   Strategic Lawsuits Against Public Participation
SPC   Socialist Party of Canada
SSJB   *Société Saint-Jean-Baptiste* (Saint-Jean-Baptiste Society)
TCAH   Toronto Coalition Against Homelessness
TDRC   Toronto Disaster Relief Committee
UAW   United Auto Workers of America
UDA   *Union des artistes* (Artists' Union)
UFP   *Union des forces progressistes* (Union of Progressive Forces)
UK   United Kingdom
UN   United Nations
UNCESCR   United Nations Committee on Economic, Social, and Cultural Rights
US   United States of America
USWA   United Steelworkers of America
WCAR   World Conference on Racism, Racial Discrimination, Xenophobia, and Related Intolerance
WTO   World Trade Organization
WWF   World Wildlife Fund Canada

INTRODUCTION

Theories of Group and Movement Organizing[1]

Miriam Smith

This book provides a set of case studies of the role of social movements and interest groups in Canadian politics. Such groups provide a vehicle for public participation in collective decision-making in a democratic society. Collective action is an alternative to voting and participating in the electoral system and enables people to pursue and express a broad range of political interests and identities. Participation in collective action is central to democratic political life. The right to assemble freely was one of the first freedoms of the democratic revolution and remains a core element in democratic practice. The most recent wave of contestation and contention, centred in the anti-globalization movement, may convey the impression that the global era is one in which groups have more power than ever in the political process. The declining role of states may lead to the decoupling of democratic rights from the framework of the nation-state (Held, 1995). Historically, the central framework of democratic group politics has been provided by the nation-state. While transnational and global organizing are important forms of collective action, there are a broad range of issues on which the domestic nation-state is still central to decision-making and to political outcomes.

The chapters in this volume cover a broad range of organized group and movement activity, ranging from business and labour through to health and disability. The authors deploy a broad range of theoretical perspectives in describing the evolution of organized groups and movements in their sector and in evaluating the success of organized groups in exercising influence in Canadian politics. The diversity of approaches is one of the strengths of the volume as the chapters provide concrete examples of groups and movements in action in the Canadian context. Some chapters evaluate a number of approaches to understanding the sources and effectiveness of group political mobilization. For example, Peter Clancy's chapter on business organizing includes discussion of Canadian political economy as well as neopluralist approaches to understanding the role of business in Canadian politics. Trevor Harrison's chapter on populism and Christian evangelical organizing evaluates different explanations of the evolution of populist movements. Other chapters concentrate on developing a particular theoretical perspective. For example, Alexandra Dobrowolsky's chapter on the women's movement argues for specific developments in social movement theory while David Camfield's chapter is situated squarely within a neo-Marxist perspective.

The purpose of this introduction is to set the stage for these case studies by providing an overview of the main theoretical approaches to explaining and understanding the role of interest groups and social movements in Canada. There is no agreement among political scientists specifically or social scientists in general about the best ways to study group and social movement politics. Rather, there are a plethora of theories that draw our attention to different facets of collective action (Baumgartner and Leech, 1998). Each of these theories have clear normative and ideological implications. Some tend to legitimate the existing political system while others provide a critical stance toward existing democratic institutions. In the sections to follow, we will canvass a number of these theoretical approaches for studying social movements and groups in comparative and Canadian politics and explore their normative implications. The main approaches that will be explored are pluralism, Marxism, political economy, historical institutionalism, social movement theory, and rational choice theory.

Pluralism

For pluralists, society is composed of individuals. This may not seem like a controversial assertion; however, there is a key difference between pluralism and rational choice theory, which gives methodological primacy to the role of the individual in politics, and Marxism or Canadian political economy, which emphasizes the importance of groups and structures of power. Pluralists begin with the individual, who, in their view, has multiple loyalties, representing his or her diverse interests and preferences. Any of the individual's interests may form the basis for participation in a group that seeks to influence politics.

In Canadian society, for example, class, language, religion, region, socio-economic status, gender, and ethnicity might all be considered important lines of political cleavage. Groups form when like-minded individuals join together in pursuit of their common interests and pressure or lobby government for policies that will favour their group. Pluralists usually describe such groups as interest groups or pressure groups. Many of the groups discussed in this volume might be categorized as interest groups, ranging from the Canadian Council of Chief Executives described in Peter Clancy's chapter to the environmental organizations discussed by Judith McKenzie. Because there are many potential political cleavages in complex societies, pluralist theory argues that no one group ever dominates politics for long. If one group becomes too powerful, another will often rise to counterbalance its power (Bentley, 1908). The multiple interests of individuals mean that there are many possible groups and that society is characterized by cross-cutting cleavages along different lines. However, society is not divided by class cleavages alone, but is also characterized by cleavages based on other definitions of the interests of the individual. Because of this, it is not likely that one cleavage will become dominant or that strong groups will go unchallenged.

According to pluralist theory, political scientists should be interested in group politics because public policy is a reflection of the struggle between groups to secure advantage (Dahl, 1961; Polsby, 1963). For pluralists, manifest and open conflict between groups is the key to political conflict; cases in which conflicts are submerged or marginalized or in which power is exercised by structural forces cannot be subsumed under the rubric of pluralism (Gaventa, 1982; Lukes, 1974). In this respect, state actors, such as politicians and bureaucrats, do not play an independent role in the development of public policy as they are influenced by the contestation of groups (although see Almond, 1988). Pluralist theory is analogous to Adam Smith's idea of the "invisible hand" of the market economy in which economic growth for the good of all is the end result of the self-interested struggle of individuals. Pluralist theory suggests that there are multiple access points to the political system for all citizens through group politics.

However, in the 1960s and after, pluralist theory was found wanting on several fronts. The social conflicts of the period suggested that not everyone has access to the political system. Some groups may be permanently marginalized, and some may indeed have more power than others. This point was brought home forcefully by the race riots of the 1960s, the anti-war movement, and the student movement in the US. In Canada, the rise of more powerful Quebec and Aboriginal nationalisms and the resurgence of anti-Americanism among youth in English-speaking Canada deepened the critique of a happy and benign group politics. Developments in these movements are discussed in the chapters by David Camfield and Charlotte Yates on the evolution of the working class and trade union movements in Canada, Kiera Ladner on Aboriginal politics, Pascale Dufour and Christophe Traisnel on the evolution of Quebec nationalism as a social movement, Miriam Smith on the lesbian and gay movement, and Alexandra Dobrowolsky on the women's movement. These movements and the accompanying counterculture of the period suggested a more profound appraisal of democratic capitalism and called attention to structures of power in society such as racism and sexism. Just as the US was under internal siege from within during the late 1960s and early 1970s, so too the dominant pluralist approach in political science came under fire. The response to these critiques was the development and revival of other approaches including neo-Marxism, Canadian political economy, and neopluralism. The neo-Marxist critiques of pluralist theory in political science helped to spawn the neopluralist amendments of the original theory. Therefore, it is to neo-Marxism that we will now turn.

Marxism and Neo-Marxism

In contrast to pluralism, structural theories of the role of social forces in the political process stress that power relations are not the result of individual choices but of socially patterned behaviour, collective action, and institutional and organizational configurations. Individual choices are overwhelmed by the structural forces that shape behaviour. The pattern of group formation is affected by economic and social inequality, which create systemic obstacles for marginalized groups in the political system. While there are a number of such structural theories, the most elaborated by far is Marxism and its neo-Marxist variants (Seidman, 2004).

Unlike the pluralists and neopluralists who see social forces as individuals organized into groups or interest groups, Marxists understand social forces as organized into classes. Classes are not merely socioeconomic groupings, such as "middle class" or "lower class," but are specifically defined by their relationship to the means of production. David Camfield extensively discusses the evolution of the term "working class" in Canadian politics; Charlotte Yates discusses the evolution of organized labour in Canadian politics in relation to the socialist political project; and Trevor Harrison considers class as a factor in the rise of right-wing populist movements. These chapters provide concrete examples of the use of class analysis in understanding political mobilization in Canada.

For Marxists, the economic organization of society determines class relationships. In a capitalist economic system like Canada's in which property is privately owned, the means of production (land, labour, and capital) are owned by the capitalist class or bourgeoisie, and the working class or proletariat, which does not own the means of production, is forced to work in order to live. The capitalist class attempts to extract as much value from the labour of the working class as possible, and the working class, in turn, struggles to resist this exploitation. The conflict between capitalists and workers in a capitalist economy is termed the class struggle. In the Marxist view, political conflict centres on the class struggle between workers and capitalists (Panitch, 1995). This perspective constitutes a profound critique of the pluralist idea of the role of interest groups. It suggests that the main cleavages in society are not based on multiple group memberships but on economic divisions rooted in the capitalist economic system. Groups are not all able to access the political system; rather, the system is profoundly unequal, and the subordinated classes face structural barriers to political influence and participation.

In the analysis of collective actors in the political process, then, neo-Marxism and pluralism begin at very different starting points. Pluralists view society as composed of individuals who have multiple interests that give rise to cross-cutting cleavages. Neo-Marxists view society as composed of classes in which the dominant class exploits the subordinated class, thus giving rise to class struggle. Pluralists have a benign interpretation of the ends of power; in the long run, the struggle between groups will even itself out, and no group will dominate politics in a democratic political system. The neo-Marxist views democratic political institutions as a cover or tool for capitalist class power and as an arena of class struggle. The pluralist does not inquire into the source of the individual's interests and preferences, while the neo-Marxist emphasizes the ways in which the common sense consciousness of everyday life is shaped by the class system. What these two perspectives do have in common, though, is their view of the state and of state institutions as relatively passive in relation to organized collective actors. While there are many different interpretations of the role of the state within Marxist theory and within the middle-range empirical studies of the pluralists, both perspectives tend to downplay political institutions and their effects on group politics and policy development. The pluralist sees the state as vulnerable to group influence, an unsurprising conclusion given that pluralist analysis has most often been applied to the American political system, a system that provides multiple points for group access. The neo-Marxist sees the state as fundamentally capitalist and thus sees its actions as structurally circumscribed by class power, the capitalist economic system, and even the consciousness of citizens, who may be taught to consent to their own exploitation.

Canadian Political Economy

While pluralist approaches to the study of pressure groups existed in Canada during the 1960s, the approach was not as dominant as it was in the US. Nonetheless, its benign assumptions about the nature of political power in capitalist democracies also came under fire in this country. However, the Canadian critique took on a particular flavour. As Peter Clancy discusses in his chapter on business organization, students of Canadian politics of this period were influenced by the political economy tradition. During the 1970s, political economy approaches were revived by a new generation of political economists, led by Mel Watkins (1977). The new political economy took up the theme of colonialism, specifically, the colonial position of Canada in relation to American political and economic power. However, it had an ambiguous relationship to capitalist class power. Some analysts in this tradition, such as Tom Naylor, viewed the Canadian state as the instrument of capitalist class power, much as in the instrumentalist Marxist view outlined in the previous section. Others bemoaned the weak position of Canadian capital as undermining Canadian sovereignty and economic independence (Levitt, 1970). Much of the new political economy was concerned with structures of economic power in Canada and Canada's position of relative underdevelopment, compared to other similar political systems (e.g., Laxer, 1989; Marchak, 1985), and did not have much to say about collective actors in politics. For example, a new political economy analysis of why Canada adopted free trade would focus on the position of Canada as a region or series of regions in the North American political economy and the role of the Canadian state in reinforcing north-south economic linkages following the demise of the Keynesian welfare state. Similarly, recent attempts to bring gender and race into Canadian political economy explore such issues as the ways in which the labour market is gendered or racialized but not the role of collective actors as agents in the political process (Vosko, 2000; Abele and Stasiulis, 1989). The new Canadian political economy then, is mainly a structural approach that focuses on the social and economic forces that limit the actions of political actors, but does not suggest an approach to the study of such actors.

Historical Institutionalism

Historical institutionalists argue that the main problem with both pluralist and neo-Marxist theories of state-society relations was that both assumed that the state's actions were driven by social forces, that state decisions reflected the power of the dominant forces in society, and that political institutions played almost no independent role in shaping policy and political outcomes. Pluralists and neo-Marxists disagreed over the nature of society and over the nature of the collective actors or groups that comprised the social forces driving the state. As we have seen, for pluralists, groups are the most important social actors, and their conflicts drive politics. For neo-Marxists, the pluralist emphasis on the group is an ideology that masks the importance of classes, whose conflicts drive politics. Pluralist analyses tended to legitimate American democracy (and, hence, indirectly, American power in the world), while neo-Marxist analyses tended to de-legitimate American democracy and power. But, despite the profound theoretical, normative, and ideological differences between pluralists and neo-Marxists, they shared an important theoretical similarity in their lack of attention to the independent causal power of states and state institutions (Skocpol, 1979).

In contrast, historical institutionalists argue for a return to the Weberian tradition in social science, meaning a return to the work of German sociologist Max Weber who pioneered the study of the rationalities of a variety of large-scale social institutions such as religion, bureaucracy, and the state. Weber developed a critique of bureaucracy as the "iron cage" of modern industrial society as well as taxonomies of states and the implications of their differences for political styles and outcomes (Seidman, 2004). Weber's importance rests on his systematic attention to the understanding of states as independent and internally differentiated, an attention that institutionalist critics found to be lacking in American political science scholarship during the pluralist period. As we have seen, pluralists largely viewed the state in terms of government, hence neglecting the state's permanent apparatus, most importantly, the bureaucracy. According to the institutionalist critique, pluralists tended to view government as the "cash register of group demands" rather than an independent player, while the neo-Marxists were unable to offer any explanation of the capitalist state beyond their claim that it *was* capitalist and that it would enact policies that protected the capitalist system. As historical institutionalists rightly pointed out, a theory of the capitalist state that rests on the assertion that such a state will always protect capitalism and/or capitalists cannot explain the myriad of interesting differences between capitalist states, such as the low rate of American social spending compared to other capitalist democracies (Skocpol, 1985).

Compared to the other approaches that have been described so far, historical institutionalists share with neo-Marxists the idea that the beliefs and values of collective actors are shaped through social processes. Unlike neo-Marxists, however, historical institutionalists open up the possibility that the values and preferences of collective actors are shaped by contingent policy processes (policy legacies) as much as by macro social forces (the capitalist economic system). While a neo-Marxist might ask why workers believe in and consent to a capitalist economic system, the historical institutionalist would explore why workers in one context argued for industrial policies while workers in another ignored industrial policies and demanded Keynesian macroeconomic stabilization (e.g., Hattam, 1993). Precisely because historical institutionalism focuses on the mid-range level, it does not have a theory of history or an overall theory of social power. Therefore, in historical institutionalist analyses, class-based politics arising from capitalist exploitation may be acknowledged at the same time as group-based interests are also recognized.

Neopluralism

In response to the critiques of their approach by both neo-Marxists and historical institutionalists, pluralists amended their theory. They developed a new perspective, often called neopluralism (Lukes, 1974). In this approach, more attention was paid to the idea that government may influence the public agenda. The neopluralists conceded two important points to critics of the original pluralist theory. First, they acknowledged that democratic capitalist societies, such as Canada, might be characterized by persistent social inequality that would create barriers to the formation and influence of interest groups. For example, poor people are unlikely to have the economic and social resources to form effective interest groups, and their interests will not be reflected in the political system. Jonathan Greene's chapter on the anti-poverty movement (Chapter 4) emphasizes the ways in which anti-poverty organizations do not have the resources to exercise substantial influence. The political system itself may mobilize bias; that is, certain types of political issues may be mobilized out of political consideration and debate. Another example is that of race. Until recently, the idea that Canadian society might be characterized by pervasive racism was not a subject of political debate. As Audrey Kobayashi's chapter discusses, until recently, political debate was biased against consideration of the problem of racism in Canadian society and of how public policies could be designed to address it (Chapter 5).

Second, in a variant of institutionalist analysis, neopluralists recognized that governments themselves could play an important role in the development of public policy. Governments were not simply carrying out the wishes of the strongest group; instead, politicians and bureaucrats were actively involved in the development of public policy and often used groups to communicate with particular constituencies of citizens to legitimate these policies. Groups might advocate their interests to government, but the bureaucracy also might develop institutionalized links with key groups and consult them regularly on the formation of policy. This type of analysis draws on historical institutionalism but is less theoretically ambitious and relies more on public policy analysis than on the grand questions of comparative politics. Studies of policy communities and policy networks are important in the studies of Canadian public policy.

Social Movement Theory

Another approach to the analysis of groups in the political process is provided by social movement theory, which was mainly developed by sociologists. In part, it is based on the experiences of the 1960s when a number of new movements arose that posed profound challenges to the status quo. The women's, environmental, gay liberation, peace, student, and civil rights movements suggested that all was not well with capitalist democracies. New left movements, as they were sometimes termed, engaged in mass protests and demonstrations and generated a culture of transformative and liberation politics. These spontaneous mass protests seemed to be fundamentally different from the well-organized and institutionalized interest groups of pluralist theory and from the class politics of neo-Marxist theories.

New social movement theory, developed mainly in Europe, and resource mobilization theory, developed mainly in the US, evolved to explain the rise of the social movements of the 1960s and after. A third approach—the political process model—synthesizes these two theories (Della Porta and Diani, 1999). The political process model deals with many of the same issues as political science models of group behaviour, as we will see below.

We will begin by looking at some of the common elements in the analysis of social movements across the three most recent theories—new social movement theory, resource mobilization, and the political process model—followed by a look at some of the distinctive features of each of the three approaches in the order in which they arose.

What is a social movement? The broadest definition, offered by Manuel Castells, is: "purposive collective actions whose outcome, in victory as in defeat, transforms the values and institutions of society" (Castells, 1997: 3). For political scientists and sociologists who encountered the social movements of the 1960s, a series of traits was thought to distinguish the "new" social movements from organized interest and advocacy groups. First, social movements challenge the traditional boundary between state and society, public and private. In pluralist and neopluralist theory, there is a clear distinction between state and society; societal groups form and then attempt to influence government. Although groups may develop institutionalized links to government, there is still a clear distinction between public and private. Social movements challenge this distinction, arguing that "the personal is political" and bringing issues that were once defined as private into the sphere of public debate. Social movements may also challenge the public/private divide by demonstrating how the private sphere is imbued with power relationships or politics. Chapters by Alexandra Dobrowolsky on the women's movement, Sally Chivers on the disability movement, Michael Orsini on health social movements, Miriam Smith on the lesbian and gay rights movement, and Judith McKenzie on the environmental movement exemplify this challenge to the conception and definition of the private sphere.

Second, social movements may emphasize the creation and reinforcement of identity and the promotion of certain values over the pursuit of material interests. As such, social movement goals may be primarily aimed at society rather than the state. Alexandra Dobrowolsky provides a strong discussion of the role of identity in the women's movement and the ways in which its claims are framed. The second wave of the women's movement often engaged in consciousness-raising in which small groups of women would meet to share their experiences. In the process, women realized that their problems and experiences were not unique, that many women had had similar experiences, and that their problems had social and political causes. In this way, a common bond of solidarity was created among feminist women, and a new identity was formed which, in turn, provided the base for women's mobilizing. Sally Chivers highlights the social construction of "disability" and points to the role of disability activism in challenging the dominant constructions of ability and disability. Similarly, Michael Orsini demonstrates how social movements may challenge dominant definitions of knowledge and science in the health care field. In this way, as Alberto Melucci has put it, social movements challenge the dominant "codes" of society (Melucci, 1996). Although state policies may also be targeted, state policy alone cannot effect changes in social behaviour. Movements aim to achieve cultural and knowledge shifts and not just shifts in policy.

Third, social movements are often said to engage in strategies and tactics that are more radical than those used by interest groups. While interest groups may attempt to influence government policy through the conventional means of lobbying in one form or another, social movements often engage in direct action tactics. For example, the environmental movement has often chosen to confront its opponents directly rather than to work with government. For example, environmentalists have spiked trees and chained themselves to trees to prevent clear-cut logging. Such direct action tactics are often particularly useful because they create dramatic media footage that can be used to promote the values of the movement. Large-scale disruptive demonstrations and protests may also be used to force government action and to capture media attention, as Jonathan Greene discusses in his chapter on anti-poverty organizing in Canada.

Social movements are also said to have a more decentralized and democratic organization than interest groups. They often form as networks of activists, with little formal organization, and even where formal organizations exist, they are often highly decentralized. The new left explicitly rejected bureaucratization and majority rule as oppressive and often operated by direct democracy, task rotation, and consensus decision-making in which each member of the group could veto group decisions and in which tasks were rotated among members.

In reality, social movements may not conform to this ideal typical picture. Some have been quite well-organized, at least during certain periods, and may seek to influence government through participation in consultative exercises or policy communities. Unlike traditional interest groups, social movements usually form networks of smaller groups instead of well-organized and hegemonic organizations. Rather than conforming to the ideal type of social movement political behaviour, many may follow a dual strategy of influencing the state and influencing society. For example, environmental groups may lobby government while engaging in activities that are designed to influence public opinion and to change social attitudes (Wilson, 1992). In practice, social movements pursue diverse strategies. Further, distinguishing collective actors on the basis of their regard for their own material interests is also problematic. As we shall see, the tools of social movement analysis work well for understanding the business militancy of the 1980s and 1990s, despite the fact that such groups pursue the material interests of their members. Social movements that are thought to be part of identity politics—ethnocultural groups, gay and lesbian groups, or women's groups—may also have important material interests at stake in their organizing.

Why do social movements arise, and what are the most important factors that influence their success and failure? The three theories of social movements have different answers to these questions. According to resource mobilization theory, social movements mobilize pre-existing grievances. For example, African Americans living under segregation evidently had grievances; however, systematic political mobilization around these grievances did not emerge until the 1950s. Thus, according to resource mobilization theory, it is not the grievances that are new but the resources that movements can bring to bear to press their demands (Jenkins, 1993). Audrey Kobayashi's article on ethnocultural organizing also highlights the historical and material obstacles and barriers to organizing. According to resource mobilization theory, the success and failure of social movements is determined by their ability to bring diverse resources—money, organization, sympathetic allies, and expertise—to bear in their struggles. Resource mobilization is analogous to pluralist theory in political science because it focuses on organized groups that attempt to influence government and that are viewed as competing on a relatively level playing field (Mayer, 1995). In fact, many of the same critiques that were made of pluralist theory have been made of resource mobilization, particularly with respect to the extent to which the theory ignores both preference and value formation and structural sources of social power.

The new social movement approach argues that social movements are increasingly a feature of developed capitalist democracies as the older class-based politics has declined. According to this view, the developed democracies are increasingly post-materialist, that is, their political cultures are increasingly oriented around non-material political issues such as identities and values. Post-materialist values emphasize issues like quality of life and political participation rather than the material questions of who gets what, when, where, and how. This political cultural change sets the stage for the rise of movements that stress identity and non-material goals (Inglehart, 1997),which are associated with a particular class politics. The new social movement approach is post-Marxist in that it argues that the traditional class struggle is no longer dominant in the politics of advanced capitalist societies; instead, it stresses the rise of the new middle class of professional knowledge workers, who break with the old division between worker and capitalist and who are carriers of post-materialist values. Michael Orsini's chapter on health social movements in Canada illustrates another theme in this debate by pointing to the ways in which health and risk have become increasingly important markers of political mobilization and identity.

The political process model brings together elements of resource mobilization and the new social movement approach, drawing from the former a focus on the social movement organization and the organizational networks that underpin such groups and from the latter the focus on identity and on the cultural processes through which movements construct their activism. However, in addition to this, the political process model, found in the work of scholars such as Sidney Tarrow (1998), brings together these elements with a focus on the broader political environment within which social movements operate. The broad context of politics in relation to the goals of the social movement is what Tarrow terms the "political opportunity structure," which he defines as "consistent—but not necessarily formal, permanent or national—dimensions of the political environment which either encourage or discourage people from using collective action. The concept of political opportunity structure emphasizes resources external to the group" (Tarrow, 1998: 18). The concept of political opportunity encompasses the institutions of the state and the ways in which political institutions provide points of access to social movements or block them. For instance, Audrey Kobayashi includes a case study of the Japanese-Canadian redress movement, emphasizing the ways in which a constellation of political opportunity external to the movement helped facilitate success for redress claims at a particular historical moment. Similarly, Miriam Smith's chapter on the lesbian and gay movement emphasizes the opportunities provided by the *Charter of Rights and Freedoms* as influencing the direction of the movement and its recent successes in securing public policy change.

Rational Choice Theory

The contributors to this volume largely reflect the lack of interest in Canadian scholarship in the area of rational choice theory. However, this approach is worth mentioning because it has become one of the dominant approaches to the study of collective action outside this country. To date, there have been very few works that have attempted to apply this perspective to the study of group behaviour in the Canadian context, and those that have appeared are not the strongest exemplars of the rational choice tradition (e.g., Flanagan, 1998). Despite the weaknesses of Canadian work on rational choice, the approach has important implications for the study of group politics.

The seminal work in the development of rational choice theory and group politics is Mancur Olson's *Logic of Collective Action* (1971 [1965]). Drawing from economics, Olson based his theory on the individual as a rational self-maximizer. Each individual seeks to maximize their own "utility" or seeks benefits for themselves. Economic theory is based on the assumption that the individual—whether a consumer or a firm—will seek to maximize utility. For example, a consumer is more likely to make a purchase if the price of the desired item drops. Firms are less likely to hire if the price of labour increases. Rational choice theory, then, is based on the idea that society is composed of individuals who seek their own advantage. Moreover, they seek advantage based on rationality, that is, there is a logical relationship between the ends sought and the means used to reach the ends. The ends sought by the individual are labelled "preferences" by rational choice theorists. Preferences are rank ordered, meaning that some are considered to be more important than others. The focus on the collective as the sum of the individual is quite different from the neo-Marxist, political economy, and institutionalist traditions, which are structuralist in their interpretation of individual action.

The individual's pursuit of her own best interests through rational self-maximizing behaviour makes collective action difficult. A goal or a "good" (in rational choice parlance) may be such that the benefit cannot be restricted to the individual. One example of such a good would be clean air: the benefit of clean air cannot be restricted to a single individual. The same applies to many other types of goods, which, by definition, benefit a group of individuals. Higher wages, for example, benefit all workers in a given workplace. Resources for student activities and clubs on a university campus benefit all students. Rational choice theory labels these types of goods "public goods." In contrast, "private goods" are the property of the individual and the benefit accrues to the individual alone.

Much of politics is about the pursuit of public goods. According to Olson, the problem of collective action arises from the fact that the individual has no incentive to pursue a public good. The individual will benefit from the achievement of the goal (cleaner air, higher wages, better student activities on campus) as long as she is a member of the class affected by the public good (human beings, workers, students). Therefore, why should the individual waste her time in pursuing these public goods? Why should the individual join together with other individuals in pursuit of the goal? Why should workers join a union to push for higher wages when they will receive the benefit of the higher wages regardless of their contribution to the collective effort? Why should students push for better student activities or student services when all students will benefit from any gains that are made? Why not let someone else do the work and run any risks that may be entailed? This behaviour is called "free riding" in rational choice parlance. According to Olson, the rational self-maximizing individual will tend to free ride on the efforts of others in the pursuit of public goods. This, for Olson, is the "problem of collective action," which is the central contribution of rational choice theory to the study of group politics. According to this view, individuals are not naturally inclined to sociability and group life. Such behaviour must be explained, rather than assumed, by the analyst. Here, rational choice theory parts ways very fundamentally with pluralist analysis. The pluralists saw society as composed of groups, which, in turn, were made up of individuals with diverse interests. Rational choice theory views society as composed of individuals with diverse interests. The pluralists never gave a thought to the process by which groups form. They assumed that, by default, people with common interests would form groups. Rational choice theory assumes that, by default, individuals will not form groups.

How then do groups come into being in society, according to rational choice theory? The solution of the problem of collective action is "selective incentives"—benefits that are restricted to members of the group. You must join the group in order to receive information from the group, to receive access to governmental decision-makers who may affect your business, or to receive insurance benefits through a group scheme. All of these are examples of selective incentives.

According to rational choice theory, the groups that are most likely to be able to offer selective incentives are those that are most likely to form. These will be groups that are able to offer economic incentives of some kind. Some rational choice theorists (including Olson) argue that politics will tend to be dominated by narrowly defined group interests because these are the groups that will be able to organize themselves successfully by using selective incentives (Olson, 1982). Rational choice theory is particularly concerned about groups that are very large, such as taxpayers and consumers. It is difficult for such broad groups to form because of the problem of offering selective incentives to encourage organization. In the view of rational choice theory, all taxpayers would benefit from lower taxes, but it is unlikely that taxpayers will be able to organize to achieve this because of the problem of collective action. Similarly, although consumers would benefit from lower food prices, it is unlikely that consumer interests will be represented in debates over farm policy. Farmers' groups are much better able to organize and to offer selective incentives. In Europe, Canada, and the US, farmers' organizations have succeeded in negotiating important subsidies and tax breaks that greatly enhance profitability at the expense of consumers.

Just as pluralist theory implies liberalism and neo-Marxist theory implies socialism, so too there are important ideological implications to rational choice theory. It tends to lend very strong support to the neoliberal political project, that is, the restructuring of state-society relations around the rolled-back state, the retrenchment of social programs and social obligation, and the primacy of the choice and responsibility of the individual. By placing the self-maximizing individual at the heart of the analysis, rational choice theory supports the central tenet of neoliberalism—the primacy of the individual in the market. Rational choice theory's pessimistic view of collective action mirrors the neoliberal distaste for groups and provides a justification for skepticism toward group claims. Rational choice theories suggest that group claims are undemocratic. Because groups comprised of most of society's citizens (e.g., taxpayers) are unlikely to be able to provide selective incentives, the groups that do form will tend to represent narrow and selfish interests. In this way, rational choice theory provides a theoretical justification for neoliberalism.

New Theoretical Directions

Other chapters in this volume also point to themes that are underdeveloped in the literatures on group politics and social movements in Canada as well as to the ways in which existing approaches need to be expanded to take account of new forms of collective action. Two of the chapters offer original explorations of the links between nationalism and social movement politics in Canada. Pascale Dufour and Christophe Traisnel provide an ambitious overview of the sovereignist movement in Quebec and demonstrate the ways in which it has been based in a broad range of networks and organizations, including political parties but also the trade union movement, the women's movement, artistic and cultural networks, and other organizations. Kiera Ladner tells the stories of Aboriginal resistance to colonialism in Canada over time and provides a useful corrective to the view that Aboriginal movements only emerged in the 1960s. Audrey Kobayashi explores the evolution of organizing among racialized minorities in Canadian politics and, especially, the emergence of "third force" and ethnocultural organizing in Canada in response to the constitutional politics of the 1970s and 1980s. Kobayashi's case study of the redress movement of Japanese Canadians demonstrates both the importance of racialization in Canadian social movement politics and the emergence of collective action around new issues. For example, the idea of redress or compensation for past state actions has emerged relatively recently and extends to other cases of ethnocultural organizing such as the Chinese-Canadian head tax case as well as to cases of compensation for medical injury and "natural" disasters such as hurricanes (James, 2007). These chapters suggest that existing frameworks on collective action and political mobilization in Canadian politics have not paid sufficient attention to the structuring impact of colonialism and racialized power relations in Canadian society. A next step from these analyses would explore the ways in which other forms of organized political action, such as business organizing, or other social movements, such as the environmental movement or the lesbian and gay rights movement, enact, reinforce, or challenge existing structures of gendered and racialized power.

Finally, many of the contributors point to the emergence of new political cleavages in Canadian society that have not traditionally been the focus of attention by political scientists and sociologists who have studied interest groups and social movements. It is only very recently that scholars in Canada have even paid serous scholarly attention to the women's movement or to the emergence of movements and groups that politicize gender relations and sexuality such as the lesbian and gay rights movement. The study of disability movements and health social movements in Canada is in its infancy. These themes in the study of collective action indicate that a new set of political actors has arrived on the scene, emphasizing a new set of issues in the process of political mobilization.

Taken together, the chapters in this volume highlight both the traditional political actors such as business and labour but also the new political actors such as the disability movement and health social movements. In doing so, *Group Politics and Social Movements in Canada* draws attention to the question of how these movements interact and how they reflect the structuring of economic, social, and political power in Canada in the global era. It does not provide a systematic answer to the question of which theory or theoretical approach best helps us to make sense of social movement and organized group politics in Canada. However, it does provide an indication of the broad range of civil society activity that must be taken into consideration in thinking about and theorizing about the role of collective actors in Canadian political life.

Note

1. This is an adapted and abridged version of the first chapter of my book, *A Civil Society? Collective Actors in Canadian Political Life* (Peterborough: Broadview Press, 2005).

References and Further Reading

Abele, Frances, and Daiva Stasiulis. 1989. "Canada as a White Settler Colony: What About Natives and Immigrants?" In Wallace Clement and Glen Williams (eds.), *The New Canadian Political Economy*. Montreal and Kingston: McGill-Queen's University Press. 240–77.

Almond, Gabriel. 1988. "The Return to the State." *American Political Science Review* 82(3): 853–74.

Baumgartner, Frank R., and Beth L. Leech. 1998. *Basic Interests: The Importance of Groups in Politics and in Political Science*. Princeton: Princeton University Press.

Bentley, Arthur F. 1908. *The Process of Government*. Chicago: University of Chicago Press.

Castells, Manuel. 1997. *The Power of Identity*. Oxford: Blackwell.

Dahl, Robert A. 1961. *Who Governs? Democracy and Power in an American City*. New Haven: Yale University Press.

Della Porta, Donatella, and Mario Diani. 1999. *Social Movements: An Introduction*. Oxford: Blackwell.

Flanagan, Thomas. 1998. *Game Theory and Canadian Politics*. Toronto: University of Toronto Press.

Gaventa, John. 1982. *Power and Powerlessness*. Urbana and Chicago: University of Illinois Press.

Hattam, Victoria C. 1993. *Labor Visions and State Power: The Origins of Business Unionism in the United States*. Princeton: Princeton University Press.

Held, David. 1995. *Democracy and the Global Order: From the Modern State to Cosmopolitan Governance*. Stanford: Stanford University Press.

Inglehart, Ronald. 1997. *Modernization and Postmodernization: Cultural, Economic, and Political Change in Forty-Three Societies*. Princeton: Princeton University Press.

James, Matt. 2007. "The Permanent-Emergency Compensation State: A 'Postsocialist' Tale of Political Dystopia." In Michael Orsini and Miriam Smith (eds.), *Critical Policy Studies*. Vancouver: University of British Columbia Press. 321–46.

Jenkins, J. Craig. 1993. "Resource Mobilization Theory and the Study of Social Movements." *American Review of Sociology* 9: 527–53.

Laxer, James L. 1989. *Open for Business: The Roots of Foreign Ownership in Canada*. Toronto: Oxford University Press.

Levitt, Kari. 1970. *Silent Surrender: The Multinational Corporation in Canada*. Toronto: Macmillan.

Lukes, Stephen. 1974. *Power: A Radical View*. London: Macmillan.

Marchak, Patricia. 1985. "Canadian Political Economy." *Canadian Review of Sociology and Anthropology* 22(5): 673–709.

Mayer, Margit. 1995. "Social Movement Research in the United States: A European Perspective." In Stanford M. Lyman (ed.), *Social Movements: Critiques, Concepts, Case-Studies*. London: Macmillan. 168–95.

Melucci, Alberto. 1996. *Challenging Codes: Collective Action in the Information Age*. Cambridge: Cambridge University Press.

Olson, Mancur. 1971 [1965]. *The Logic of Collective Action: Public Goods and the Theory of Groups*. Cambridge, MA: Harvard University Press.

Olson, Mancur. 1982. *The Rise and Decline of Nations: Economic Growth, Stagflation, and Structural Rigidities*. New Haven: Yale University Press.

Panitch, Leo. 1995. "Elites, Classes, and Power in Canada." In Michael S. Whittington and Glen Williams (eds.), *Canadian Politics in the 1990s*. Toronto: Nelson. 152–75.

Polsby, Nelson W. 1963. *Community Power and Political Theory*. New Haven: Yale University Press.

Seidman, Steven. 2004. *Contested Knowledge: Social Theory Today*. 3rd ed. Oxford: Blackwell.

Skocpol, Theda. 1979. *States and Social Revolutions: A Comparative Analysis of France, Russia, and China*. Cambridge: Cambridge University Press.

Skocpol, Theda. 1985. "Bringing the State Back In: Strategies of Analysis in Current Research." In Peter B. Evans, Dietrich Rueschmeyer, and Theda Skocpol (eds.), *Bringing the State Back In*. Cambridge: Cambridge University Press. 3–37.

Tarrow, Sidney. 1998. *Power in Movement: Social Movements, Collective Action, and Politics*. 2nd ed. Cambridge: Cambridge University Press.

Vosko, Leah. 2000. *Temporary Work: The Gendered Rise of a Precarious Employment Relationship*. Toronto: University of Toronto Press.

Watkins, Mel. 1977. "The Staples Theory Revisited." *Journal of Canadian Studies* 12(5): 83–95.

Wilson, Jeremy. 1992. "Green Lobbies: Pressure Groups and Environmental Policy." In Robert Boardman (ed.), *Canadian Environmental Policy: Ecosystems, Politics, and Process*. Toronto: Oxford University Press. 109–25.

PART ONE
Political Economy

ONE

Business Interests and Civil Society in Canada

Peter Clancy

This chapter explores the many shapes of business influence in Canadian civil society. In the pages below we consider the structure of capitalist interests, their organizational expressions, the political issues that top the business agenda today, the processes and instruments of exercising power, and the ramifications for group and movement theory. This discussion will show that there is a striking variability in the political orders and relationships involving capital, which vary over time, space, and function. The structure of markets makes a difference here, as does the structure of state institutions. Thus there is a value to distinguishing periods—and generic "types" and "styles"—of political representation and intervention. A central question in this chapter is how does organized capital relate, within itself and to other social interests, in the democratic context? This theme figures strongly in contemporary political debate, where the power of national and international capital is widely considered as hostile to both public interests and popular politics. A corollary question, of more than passing interest, is whether business and market players should be conceptualized as a part of civil society or outside of it. This is a matter of theoretical and also tactical significance. The discussion below suggests some difficulties in demarcating a firm boundary between market and civil space.

There is a tendency to see capital as a powerful but "traditional" block of interests in politics, the prime beneficiaries and the great defenders of the processes of capitalist democracy. It is certainly true that firms and trade associations have functioned as the interest groups of the marketplace. The same qualities enabled the business bloc to penetrate centrist and rightist political parties by furnishing leadership talent and financial resources critical to the ministerial, parliamentary, and electoral processes. It would be a mistake, however, to assume that business power starts and ends in this way. Given the extraordinary financial and informational resources that are controlled by business firms, they can wield power in many domains. This capability has been applied to new and innovative effect in recent decades.

Historical Considerations

A number of preliminary points can be made. First, as a capitalist economy expands, the range of business interests diversifies, and the political structure of business interests tends to be cumulative. Over time this creates complex fields, revealing considerable variation. This opens the way for political difference and tension as well as a potential for cooperative or collective action. The understanding of these webs of class and group alignments will of course vary, according to the theoretical perspective that underpins the analysis. As the Introduction points out, each framework highlights a particular set of relationships.

In Canada, business politics has shaped public life from the historical outset. It started in the 1500s, when European merchant syndicates encountered Aboriginal peoples in the New World. As colonial settlement progressed, the range of staple commodities broadened, and French and English export networks for fur, fish, timber, and grains dominated business politics. Imperial trade policy was, in many ways, the wellspring of business viability, and decisions made in London (and later Washington) could create or destroy the prospects for profitable accumulation. In addition, the local markets that sprang up along transport corridors—first the rivers and ports and later the railways—made possible new domestic business sectors that were ultimately consolidated in the post-Confederation market. Pioneer manufacturing was followed by factory production under the National Policy protective tariff regime installed in Ottawa in 1879 (Williams, 1983). Advancing technologies made possible successive waves of new industries: from textiles and food processing to coal, rail, and steam; steel and autos; electricity and petroleum; aeronautics and chemicals. The most recent innovations derive from microelectronics, telecommunications, and bio-technology. The rise of the service business sector marked another historic shift. The traditional services in the legal, financial, and transport sectors were joined, in the second half of the twentieth century, by a burgeoning public or government service sector including medical, hospital, education, and social services.

This diversification of business interests by sector, industry, and geography means that affinities and rivalries within the capitalist bloc can be pivotal in determining its power. Pluralist perspectives view this principally as a problem of representation, or the distillation of pressure vectors within issue areas. Neo-Marxists have been particularly sensitive to the impact of fractional tensions on the overall coherence of capital in politics.

A second point refers to the relationships between capital and the state. It is not simply a matter for the business bloc to manage its own differences. State authorities can play crucial roles in ordering priorities, fashioning compromises, and securing coherence among the disparate political tendencies of capital. This is not to say that government could or would satisfy all business demands. The state does, however, have the capacity to shape the playing field of the market through political intervention, sometimes in decisive ways. This is acknowledged in both neo-Marxist and neopluralist paradigms. The former view the state as playing crucial roles in ordering the relationships between classes and within them, thus formalizing and stabilizing hierarchies of class power. This can be achieved, for example, by implementing policy strategies to underwrite long-term investment and profitability. Neopluralists also acknowledge the complexity of business-state relations, though they tend to concentrate on the importance of linkage processes in shaping outcomes.

In Canada, a number of crucial public policy bargains were struck over the years. So fundamental were some of these that they underwrote normal politics for generations at a time. The mercantile colonial era of staple resource exports was the first such framework regime. The National Policy tariff, already mentioned, was another. By simultaneously facilitating natural resource exports (at low or zero tariff rates) and domestic manufacturing (at medium to high tariff rates), the 1879 system anchored Canadian economic growth (and business prosperity) for the next half century. Following the upheaval of the 1930s Depression and World War II, the federal government fashioned a new political settlement. This involved the application of fiscal (budgetary) policy along Keynesian lines to promote full employment and economic growth, together with the income redistribution measures of the welfare state. This post-war settlement flourished for a generation, but came under significant political pressure by 1975. Yet another basic policy bargain has emerged in the decades since (McBride, 2001). Known as neoliberalism, its hallmarks include continental free trade, budget constraints, and deregulation of financial markets. In pursuing these aims, Western states have, once again, had to alter some basic operational contours. The new governing challenge is to stabilize national societies against global pressures while operating on neoliberal foundations.

A third and final point here is a caution against easy assumptions about business power. Business interests seldom enjoy absolute dominance, particularly in contexts of democratic politics. Issues are almost invariably contested by non-business interests, which frequently prevail. While politicians can be disciplined by market forces—such as currency runs, capital strikes, and adverse bond ratings—corporations also can be disciplined by commercial scandals, populist electoral outcomes, and consumer boycotts. On another level, existing state institutions and policies may be regarded as the distillation of past political struggles, exerting an independent impact on the shape and prospects for politics today. The neo-institutional concept of path-dependence (the notion that historically earlier choices serve to shape the range of available opportunities and choices in the future) is insightful here as well. Not only can it explain how state agencies and programs can enjoy significant political autonomy but also how state-based actors can acquire an independent standing as "interests of state" (Pal, 1995).

The Gramscian concept of hegemony, or dominance, also provides helpful insights. If the constellation of organized interests is considered as a hierarchy of power, then those who occupy the highest echelons, over time, can be thought of as hegemonic. This does not mean that they will prevail on every issue; however, they will very likely prevail on the issues that most matter, and furthermore they may assist in politically resolving other matters. In this sense, business can be considered hegemonic in capitalist systems.

Canadian researchers in the political economy school have long debated the range and ordering of capitalist class fractions and the seat of business dominance. Not surprisingly, the answers have varied over time. One influential interpretation, put forward by R.T. Naylor, held that an alliance of merchant and finance capitalists, rooted in the colonial era, managed to subordinate indigenous (Canadian) manufacturing following Confederation (Naylor, 1972). According to this argument, the profit terms of commercial capital (short investment horizons, low fixed capital, open borders) were incompatible with those of domestic manufacturing (long-term horizons, high fixed investment, tariff protection). Consequently, the primacy of commercial capital served to relegate the manufacturing fraction to a subordinate and truncated form. Wallace Clement took a somewhat different line. Emphasizing compatibility rather than antagonism, he argued that the indigenous or Canadian-owned fraction of finance capital anchored an alliance with a comprador or foreign-dominated industrial fraction, particularly by underwriting the expansion in Canada of US corporate capital (Clement, 1983).

Rianne Mahon drew attention to the critical role of state institutions in ordering and adjusting the hierarchies of business interest. For Mahon, the alliance of indigenous finance and staple resource export fractions was anchored by the federal Department of Finance. Its strategic place atop Ottawa's bureaucratic state, and commitments to liberal trade and investment flows as prerequisites for Canadian economic growth, allowed the department to indirectly "represent" the core fraction's interests in strategic policy. Indeed a more elaborate inter-agency "structure" of representation provided voices for all significant factions and classes. Mahon's study of strategic efforts to revive the declining textile manufacturing sector illustrated both the constraints and opportunities available within the larger structured state (Mahon, 1984).

There are further questions to consider. For example, does capital benefit from a number of structural mechanisms that confer privileged political leverage on business interests? Structural dependence points to mechanisms that enable business to entrench its interests despite government opposition. These must be fixed relationships and mechanisms that routinely prevent anti-business policies or activities from taking place. Charles Lindblom describes this as the market behaving as a "prison." Formally, of course, governments remain free to enact any policy they see fit. However, they discover that certain types of non-business or anti-business initiatives result in an automatic "recoil" effect, a dramatic reaction from the business system that punishes the political authors of the offending policy. Repeated experience with the recoil tends to discourage politicians from pursuing such policy initiatives. Since no other social institution enjoys similar power to the market in this respect, the capitalist interest is said to enjoy a privileged position (Lindblom, 1982).

A powerful example of this is the mechanism of modern global finance. In recent decades, capital has become highly mobile and volatile. Trading takes place around the clock and around the globe, in currencies, commodities, bonds, and shares. Extraordinary amounts of money are at stake, and one of the key stimulants of speculative business moves is political. Put simply, the markets can "vote" with their wallets, expressing approval or hostility to government policy by deciding to invest or disinvest. While this business "confidence" is an elusive notion, its effects are clear to see.

When left-of-centre parties take power, the financial markets slump as a signal of suspicion or disapproval. When tax rates are raised, or budget deficits increased, the markets give out negative signals. In extreme cases, currencies go into free fall, capital strikes occur, and business shifts its operations elsewhere. Even right-of-centre governments can be affected. In 1974, the Alberta oil industry was so enraged by Progressive Conservative Premier Peter Lougheed's new tax and royalty policies that exploration activity dried up (Richards and Pratt, 1979: 227). Companies hauled their rigs into Saskatchewan or neighbouring Montana, where they sat idle as pressure built on Lougheed to revise his position.

Another powerful mechanism is the debt relationship between private lenders and government borrowers when budget shortfalls occur. After 1980, Western governments were swept up in a fiscal crisis that left them facing persistent budget deficits. These could only be met by borrowing from private sources in financial centres such as New York, London, and Toronto. Corporate lenders acquired leverage over prospective borrowers, and differing levels of risk were reflected in interest rates. Bond rating services like Moody's Investor Services, Standard and Poor's, and the Dominion Bond Rating Service weighed government fiscal policies and graded them on a scale of credit worthiness. Finance ministers made annual treks to New York to outline their fiscal plans and pitch for positive ratings. In effect, the financial markets became a key arbiter of government policy choice.

Main Organizations and Networks

Any exploration of business politics involves knowledge of the actors. The literature on political conflict (and the chapters in this book) utilize a variety of terms in identifying the political players: interest groups, organizations, associations, social movements, coalitions, and networks. Such terms tend to be associated with different theoretical traditions and derive some of their core properties from these traditions. Interest or pressure groups, for example, are the preferred analytic unit of pluralism, which holds that decisions in any policy field or issue area will be determined by the balance of forces among organized groups that are policy-specific. This was later reformulated as "post"- or "neo"-pluralism, with the recognition that state authorities were normally entangled with groups in policy networks that jointly shaped decisional outcomes. Organizations and associations have been treated, at times, as synonyms for interest groups, acknowledging, for example, that groups must achieve a level of "organization" to achieve longevity or that most groups involve a membership that is "associated" with a particular interest. On the other hand, there are many organizations in modern life (formally structured social bodies such as churches, corporations, and universities) that are not, first and foremost, dedicated to political intervention. They do, however, assume political roles when their underlying interests are at stake in the policy process. Social movements refer to political bodies that are based often on shared identities (as opposed to material interests) and that promote both social and political change.

In this chapter, we will consider the full range of prospective business actors described above. First, though, it is useful to survey the bloc of business interests as an action universe. How can business interests organize politically? This reveals a continuum of levels on which interests can be mobilized. At the most general level, there are certain common interests of capital that are shared by virtually all commercial enterprise. Somewhat less inclusive, but still expansive, is the sectoral political interest, where firms sharing some decisive property (big or small scale, manufacturing or service activity, national or global operations) come together on that basis. On the next scale we find that each industry, or even sub-industry, constitutes a shared interest that member firms must advance or defend politically. Finally, there are the political interests of the specific firm, which are asserted against those of business rivals. This continuum is illustrated in Table 1.1 below.

Table 1.1: Levels of Political Representation of Business

Level of Interest	Organizational Form	Defined Against
Business as a Whole	Structural Pressures Market Reflexes (e.g., currency, equity, credit)	Other Social Classes (e.g., Labour, Farmers, Consumers)
Economic Sectors	Peak Associations (CCCE, CME, CCC, CFIB)	Other Sectors
Industries & Sub-Industries	Trade Associations (national or provincial)	Backward and Forward Linked Industries, or Substitute Product Industries
Firms	Company-based Government Relations (In-house or Consultant)	Rival Firms in industry, or Backward/Forward Linked Firms

If political interests can spring from such distinct levels, then we can expect organizations to be formed to articulate each in turn. At the most general level, it is often the market mechanism itself that exerts pressure, through the "automatic recoil" mechanism described by Lindblom. Here currency, commodity, or share markets react adversely to state policies deemed negative to "business," signalling their opposition and bringing pressure to bear on the political class. In the 1963 budget, federal Finance Minister Walter Gordon announced a new "takeover tax" to discourage foreign acquisitions of Canadian firms. This triggered a major sell-off on the stock markets and the proposal was subsequently dropped. The very prospect of such policy recoil by markets, and their subsequent political costs, can be sufficient to nullify policy choices in advance.

A series of studies have highlighted the multidimensional spectrum of business interest groups or associations. Some of these operate at the peak association level, where particular capitals and industries are gathered together. In some nations, a comprehensive umbrella voice speaks for propertied interests on general issues. In Canada, there is no single peak business group, but several contenders with impressive though less than comprehensive scope. For example, the Canadian Council of Chief Executives (CCCE; formerly, the Business Council on National Issues) speaks for big corporate capital and the staple resource faction, drawing its membership from the 150 largest firms (Langille, 1987). The Canadian Manufacturers and Exporters Association (CME) represents secondary industry, much of it made up of foreign-owned subsidiaries. The increasing export orientation of this faction during the 1970s and 1980s culminated in the amalgamation of the hitherto separate voices of manufacturers and exporters. The Canadian Chamber of Commerce (CCC), a federation of local and provincial bodies, tends to reflect the concerns of small and medium sized business, including service and retail capital. Finally, the Canadian Federation of Independent Business (CFIB) claims 100,000 small and often independent operators and proprietors as members. Despite this institutional separation, the peak voices of Canadian business are not necessarily at odds on important issues. In some situations, such as the continental free trade campaigns of 1985–93, the peak groups have been known to form issue-based alliances in order to extend their leverage.

At the industry and sub-industry level, hundreds of national "trade associations" represent member firms for political advocacy at a more restrictive level (Coleman, 1988; Atkinson and Coleman, 1989). By contrast to the visibility of the peak lobby groups, which tend to assume a high media profile, trade associations operate more commonly within the policy orbits of government bureaus and agencies where information exchange and clientelistic access can translate into policy leverage (Litvak, 1984). Indeed, the micropolitics of business is a fertile field for industry and sub-industry advocates (Clancy, 2004).

In one sense, business power is constituted by the continuing networks of interest operating within and between such associations. There are moments, however, when the extraordinary scope and depth of these formations is evident in campaigns of joint action. During the 1970s, for example, the federal government launched a comprehensive revision of Canada's competition policy. There was widespread recognition that this long-standing statutory framework to enforce competitive market behaviour suffered from fundamental flaws. In response, the federal government commissioned a series of technical reviews aimed at renewing the competition regime, and new draft legislation was tabled. The negative reaction from the corporate sector was overwhelming, and a decade-long struggle ensued between successive Ottawa governments advancing policy renewal and the corporate opponents (and potential targets) of an invigorated competition mechanism (Stanbury, 1977).

Finally, there is the situation where specific firms define and advance political interests against their rivals in a shared marketplace and lobby accordingly. This is the most fine-grained level of business politics. What is the place of individual firms in this political environment? Do they possess irreducible interests that cannot be merged with rivals or realized through collective association? In fact there are many respects in which adroit political intervention can confer strategic advantage on the single firm. Government procurement, in which rival firms bid competitively for public tenders, is one such field. Regulated industry politics, in which statutory agencies control key business variables by license or permit, is another. Defensive trade tactics, aimed at blocking import competition or dumping by offshore rivals, is a third example.

Operationally, such firm-specific advocacy can be handled by in-house government relations specialists (often the case for top-tier corporations). It may also be handled by political affairs consultants for hire, a more viable option for small and medium sized firms (Gollner, 1983).

Main Political Issues Today

Is there a consensual business policy agenda in contemporary Canada? Or are there rival agendas, advanced by separate coalitions, vying for the limited attention of executive political elites? Part of the literature on business politics holds that a tight core of market-centred values propels a largely unified business political agenda (Clarke, 1997; Dobbin, 1998). This right-wing agenda is seen as deeply rooted in the shifting international economy following 1980. Sometimes known as the "Washington consensus" and also labelled the "neo-liberal agenda" or "market-driven politics," it includes initiatives to curtail state spending, privatize state enterprise, deregulate markets and industries (including the labour market), and promote a culture of individual as opposed to collective interest (Leys, 2001). Underlying such actions is a theory or philosophy of economic rationality (the rational choice theory discussed in the Introduction). Either way, however, it unleashes a blistering logic of programmatic change (Edwards, 2002). However, while the neoliberal consensus might offer a template or wish-list for business-friendly governance, there is no guarantee that any right-of-centre government will fully subscribe. Even if it did, there is no further guarantee that the measures will emerge intact from the issue definition and agenda-setting stages of the policy process.

In sorting out these difficulties, one useful distinction is between a category of fundamental policies that define a generalized framework or regime and a category of normal or routine policies that can be addressed from within the regime. Stephen McBride elaborates on the notion of the "conditioning framework"—a set of institutions (often embedded by international agreement) whose "provisions foreclose certain options that the populations of nation-states may want to preserve or adopt in the future" (McBride, 2001: 103).

An interesting aspect of framework-setting policies is that they impose, either through their design logic or their operational biases, powerful consequences for future action. The Canada-US Free Trade Agreement (CUFTA) and the North American Free Trade Agreement (NAFTA), embedded in international agreement, are no longer under the strict control of a national legislature to alter. The ill-fated Multilateral Agreement on Investment, sponsored by the Organization for Economic Development (OECD) is another example (Jackson and Sanger, 1998). When the agreement further restricts the unilateral capacity of either partner to act, by prohibiting lines of policy action that were hitherto utilized, the follow-on consequences are evident. A conditioning framework sets the rules for future exercise of normal policy and the more basic the constraints, the more significant the framework policy.

Another example of an emerging framework policy, this time in the domestic setting, is Ottawa's war on the deficit in the 1990s. Curiously, meaningful "fiscal restraint" had been central to the business agenda for a decade or more. Yet, despite their neoliberal credentials on other issues, ranging from continental trade to financial deregulation to tight monetary policy, the Mulroney Progressive Conservatives were unable to deliver results on the fiscal front. This contrasts with the record of the Chrétien-Martin Liberals after 1993. Despite campaigning for a roll-back of the Mulroney agenda, the Liberals managed to consolidate this program in almost all key respects. Indeed, when it came to budget balancing, Finance Minister Paul Martin was able to achieve in four years what Mulroney had failed to deliver in eight. Ottawa's "program review" exercise, which aimed to roll back federal expenditures by an average of 19 per cent, imposed draconian cuts on national programs and intergovernmental transfers (Lewis, 2003). In the process, Martin successfully presented the drive for fiscal surplus as a public virtue, which was confirmed in two subsequent elections. So deeply embedded is this standard, after nine successive budget surpluses (at time of writing), that a market recoil and perhaps even a popular recoil can be expected to attend any significant return to deficit.

For Canadian business, the notion of the continuum of priorities arises again. If business seldom speaks with one voice, we would not expect an easy or spontaneous consensus to emerge. Still, certain issues may, by their scope, extent of support, or persistence, come to typify an era. For Canadian business, the 1985–95 period was dominated by engagement on two overriding issues—continental trade ties with the US and Mexico and fiscal deficit elimination at home. In the decade that followed, there was less focus. Issues rose and fell. Quebec sovereignty has moved on and off the agenda. Canada-US sectoral trade disputes—in softwood lumber, cattle exports, wheat, steel, and others—rotate through the action list. The corporate sector advanced a productivity agenda that has attracted rhetorical support from ministers of finance and industry in the last two national governments. However, the concrete policy outputs remain thin. A round of tax cuts preceded the November 2000 election, but expenditure priorities have absorbed the lion's share of the fiscal dividend in the period since. Part of this was directed to security and border policing upgrades following the 9/11 terrorist attacks. Indeed, for the Canadian business sector, the threat of draconian post-9/11 security measures from Washington constitutes the greatest single threat to continental trade.

Some measure of the degree of business policy consensus can be found by examining the policy priorities advanced by the Canadian peak associations in 2005. Based upon an analysis of the central policy statements of the respective groups, this is captured in Table 1.2 below. The overriding shared sentiment is one of resigned anxiety. All four groups stress the dangers posed by Canada's declining competitiveness since 2000 in the face of the new Asian trade challenge, and several groups highlight the widening productivity gap between Canada and the US. There is also a clear sense that Ottawa's appetite for fiscal change slowed dramatically after victory was declared in the deficit war. Record budget surpluses, possibly a once-in-a-lifetime opportunity, have not been applied to debt or tax relief so much as renewed public expenditure. Skilled labour shortages, which threaten future investment in Canada, are not being systematically addressed, nor is necessary commercial infrastructure. Also drawing attention is the "standstill" character of the minority governments elected since 2004. From a market perspective, as these governments are constantly threatened with defeat in Parliament, there is a lack of stability and a sense that the decisions of one government could be reversed by election defeat.

Means of Action

Given the multiple dimensions of business interests, and the varying forms of political representation, it is not surprising that a wide choice of mechanisms is available for political action. Well-resourced organizations have access to a range of political weapons. This section explores some of the most prominent forms: the businessman-politician, the party system, the business interest group, the coalition or alliance of groups, the populist movement, the policy think tank, judicial litigation, and public propaganda. Each form is illustrated by a brief case study. It is important to remember that issue conflicts will normally include more than one line of action. Part of the art of issue campaigning is to recognize the strengths and weaknesses and the optimal applications for these respective techniques.

BUSINESSMAN-POLITICIAN

The phenomenon of the politically engaged businessman is as old as Western commercial society. It refers to the migration of capitalists into government, as an extension of their market interests. By this logic, the best way to influence critical decisions of state is from the inside. There are many examples in Canadian history. For example, Prime Minister R.B. Bennett (1930–35) came to politics from a dense world of corporate directorships (Finkel, 1979). Liberal minister C.D. Howe (1935–57) enjoyed perhaps the widest-ever network of Canadian business contacts, dating from his responsibilities for wartime production (Bothwell and Kilbourn, 1979).

Table 1.2: Peak Association Policy Priorities, 2005

	CCCE	CME	CCC	CFIB
1	Redesign federal tax mix	Danger of rising value of Cdn$	Workforce skills: new post-secondary investment	Personal income tax cut
2	Eliminate tax biases against investment	Strategy to deal with China competition	Streamlined rules for skilled immigrants	Small/medium business tax cut
3	Lift regulatory burdens—smart agenda	Looming shortage of skilled workers	Personal tax cuts in all brackets	Gasoline tax reductions
4	Strategy for China and LDC competition	Secure reliable/ competitive Ontario power supply	Fiscal policies: corporate tax cut	Accelerated debt reduction
5	Enhanced skills by immigration and training	Investment in border infrastructure	Accelerated debt reduction	Opposes new municipal tax and regulatory power (ON)
6	Enhanced R&D support	Incentives to commercialize new products	Limit program spending growth to 3% per year	Freeze or cut to employer WSIB rates (ON)
7	Strengthened intellectual property rules	Business tax relief	Accelerate smart regulation reforms	Amendments to Labour Relations Act (ON)
8	Investment in border infrastructure	Accelerated smart regulation reforms	Expanded R&D incentives	
9	Resist short-term pressures of minority government	Incentives for capital inflow	Renewed free trade initiatives	
10	Public governance reforms		Infrastructure upgrades urgent	

Source: CCCE, *Canada First! Taking the Lead in Transforming the Global Economy*, 2005; CME, *Manufacturing 20/20*, 2005; CCC, *Promoting Productivity, Pursuing Prosperity*, 2005; CFIB, *www.cfib.ca*, 2006.

While no cabinet is entirely without business-affiliated ministers, their prominence declined after the 1950s. This became a cause for concern in business circles, where it was argued that a lack of champions around the cabinet table left corporate Canada in a politically vulnerable position (Gillies, 1981). In the Mulroney and Chrétien eras, there was no shortage of businessman-politicians. Mulroney himself sprang from the Montreal corporate network while Chrétien's cabinet included the Three Ms—Paul Martin, Roy MacLaren, and John Manley. Indeed Martin, who became prime minister in 2003, sported the strongest business credentials since Howe, even to the point of his alumnus status with the CCCE. Yet, there are grounds to question the assumption that career businessmen ensure effective cabinet representation. At senior levels of influence, politicians speaking for only Bay Street have extremely limited potential. Besides, a variety of ancillary channels provide means of political leverage.

PARTY SYSTEM

When elite social connections no longer sufficed to guarantee access to state power, new channels rose to prominence. The nineteenth-century emergence of elected legislatures and responsible government marked a new stage in liberal politics. Political parties, first as legislative caucuses made up of like-minded representatives and later as mass membership associations grouped around shared values, ideology, or patron-client networks, began to play a crucial linkage role.

Jesse Unruh, the speaker of the California Assembly in the 1960s, made the famous observation that "money is the mother's milk of politics." Nowhere is this more true than in the case of political parties. While business leaders seldom make the most effective politicians, business interests have recognized the need to have an influence at the party and electoral levels. One way of making meaningful contacts, and ensuring access when necessary, is through financial contributions. In the lore of party politics, an omnipresent figure is the party "bagman," the broker who approaches wealthy firms and businessmen for voluntary donations to electoral war chests. In times past, political leaders might have served as their own fundraisers, though this was not without serious risk. In the years immediately following Confederation, Conservative leader John A. Macdonald was often in this position. In an ill-considered moment in the heat of the 1872 election, Macdonald wired Sir John Abbott, the legal advisor to the Canadian Pacific Railway, stating "I must have another ten thousand: will be the last time of calling; do not fail me; answer today." Abbott's reply ("Draw on me for another ten thousand dollars") was later publicly revealed, and Macdonald was forced from office by the so-called "Pacific Scandal." In more modern times, leaders have sought to distance themselves from direct fundraising. Nonetheless, the "$5,000-a-plate" dinner or cocktail party is a familiar modern fixture, where donors are invited to a social evening with elite leaders.

Business interests often adopted hedging financial strategies to manage the uncertainty of voter choice. It has been common for corporate donors, as a matter of formal policy, to split their party contributions between the leading contenders advancing business-oriented agendas. For example, the party of government might win a 60 per cent share while the leading opposition party receives the remaining 40 per cent. More generally, the party system alignment may work to the benefit of vested commercial interests. Canada's party system has long been described as a "brokerage system" in which the leading parties (Liberal and Conservative) follow strategies that appeal across major social cleavages in efforts to defuse potential tensions. This is best done through a pragmatic form of decision-making, often aimed at accommodating group elites and avoiding firm doctrinal or ideological commitments. Such brokerage politics often leads to a convergence between the contending parties as they compete to build the largest voter coalitions. Whether campaigning or governing, this can result in rather shallow differences between the competitors. Populist democrats have long condemned such arrangements as a democratic sham, depriving voters of real choice and protecting vested interests by the faux displacement of "tweedledum" by "tweedledee."

In 2003, the federal laws governing national campaign finance were revised, with potentially significant consequences for corporate participation. Effective the following year, a ban took effect on contributions by corporations, associations, and trade unions to registered political parties and party leadership campaigns. (Individuals may contribute up to $5,000 annually.) This was part of a new electoral finance regime that saw expanded public (state) financial support to parties. Corporations and unions may still contribute a maximum of $1,000 per year to constituency associations and nomination contestants (combined) and to non-registered candidates for election. Furthermore, so-called "third parties" (which refers, somewhat paradoxically, to non-political party actors) can sponsor election advertisements up to almost $170,000 in total, thereby providing a significant continuing outlet for corporate and union interests. The constitutionality of regulating "third-party" participation was itself politically contested and was confirmed by the Supreme Court of Canada in 2004 in the *Harper* case. How seriously the new finance regime will curtail corporate influence, or advocacy, remains to be seen.

Thomas Ferguson offers an alternative perspective on business involvement in politics. He contends that electoral contributions can be viewed as investments, by firms and industries, in the party that offers the greatest policy fit with corporate interests. Even in brokerage systems, it is argued, key issues will arise (often in crisis conditions) that will polarize the business sector and differentiate the contending parties. Corporate coalitions gather behind the respective parties at such moments. Once a crisis passes, new business coalitions can enjoy dominance within the party system for an extended time (Ferguson, 1995). There have been many arguments about the decline of political parties as policy engines in the face of contemporary rivals: the bureaucratic state, the new mass media, and the deepening networks of civil interests. While this may indeed be the case, it does not invalidate Ferguson's notion of parties as vehicles for business strategy, under particular conditions.

BUSINESS ASSOCIATIONS

There have always been business lobbies in Canada. The Canadian Manufacturers and Exporters Association and the Chambers of Commerce trace their roots to the pre-Confederation period (Clark, 1939). With industrialization, trade associations grew in number to represent member firms in policy matters involving trade, employment, and transport. Following World War II, however, and the rise of the bureaucratic state, business groups further proliferated as instruments of influence with the administrative state. One study identified more than 750 national associations in the modern period (Litvak, 1984). Another study reports that the majority of these originated in the post-World War II era (Coleman, 1988). It is not by coincidence that the rising profile of trade group representation paralleled the expanding reach of the state.

The target of business influence shifted from legislatures (and to some degree, cabinets) to the professional civil service. It was here that policy problems were being identified and policy responses were being formulated. Effective group influence depended upon early involvement. This, in turn, required new forms of advance scanning, deliberation, and intervention. The technical and professional expertise that business lobbies bring to the table is a valued policy commodity, which can open the way to the inner reaches of many consultative networks.

None of this can guarantee success, of course, in particular political battles. While the classic confrontations are often seen between financiers and farmers, or between manufacturers and workers, a surprisingly high proportion of business political encounters pit one industry or block of industries against another. In such situations, a number of additional determinants arise. For one, the respective mobilizing capacities of the rivals are put to the test. For another, the wider coalitions of interest attached to the principals can play a decisive role. In addition, the protagonists may be aligned with separate parts of the state, which can be drawn into the struggle as proxies.

Consider the following situation. Until recently, the four "pillars" of Canadian finance were defined as separate sectors: the chartered banks, insurance companies, trust companies, and stock brokers. Each was separately regulated in law, with rules against operating in more than one sector. The walls between these pillars began to dissolve in the 1980s, as finance was progressively deregulated around the Western world. In 1995, the federal government turned its attention to new rules for the insurance market, and two rival business associations appeared before the Liberal Party caucus (the body of Liberal members of Parliament and senators) in Ottawa to make their case.

Representing the chartered banks, the Canadian Bankers Association (CBA) mounted an aggressive argument for gaining access to insurance sales. For its part, the Insurance Bureau of Canada (IBC) pushed strongly for the status quo, fearing that the huge banks would carve up the insurance market through mergers and takeovers. At the Liberal caucus meetings, the CBA received a cold and critical reception. Reflecting the public's resentment of the chartered banks, which were reporting record profits despite a poor record of lending to small business, parliamentarians responded in kind. By contrast, and perhaps surprisingly, the IBC gained a sympathetic ear in the caucus. One key factor flowed from the contrast in the membership structures of the two industry groups. The highly centralized banks spoke from their corporate headquarters, with little local input to their campaign. In contrast, the insurance sector mobilized thousands of affiliated brokers in towns and cities across the nation. This registered strongly on Liberal members of Parliament (MPs) and was instrumental in swinging government opinion. In the end, the IBC prevailed (Howlett *et al.*, 1996).

ALLIANCES

In some cases, formal coalitions of groups are marshalled behind an advocacy campaign. Here the logic is that a broad common front can signal a virtual consensus position on an issue. Not surprisingly, such interest group alliances are likely on issues of general business salience, which affect firms and industries regardless of size or product. For example, in the late 1960s, corporate Canada mobilized with determination to oppose a proposed revision of the income tax regime that stood to increase business exposure and burden. Acknowledging a business *force majeure*, Ottawa backed away from corporate tax reform. Less than a decade later, another broad front was forged to resist revisions to the competition policy law, whose effects would stiffen the policing of collusive behaviour and mergers. For months, business representatives deluged a parliamentary committee with criticism and prognostications, until the Trudeau government buckled under the pressure.

More recently, three dramatic instances of broad scale corporate advocacy coalitions come to mind. The first of these coalesced in 1987, as the Canadian

Alliance for Trade and Job Opportunities (CATJO). In its first year of operation, CATJO advertised extensively in newspapers across the country and participated in over 500 conferences, meetings, and press conferences to the tune of $3 million (Doern and Tomlin, 1991). However it was during the 1988 federal election campaign, when support for the Mulroney Progressive Conservatives (and the free trade agreement) plummeted, that CATJO made its most forceful impact. Mounting the largest third-party advertising campaign in modern Canadian history, the pro-free trade CATJO spent more than $2.3 million during the election period (Hiebert, 1991: 20). Given that this was directed toward a single issue in a nation-wide context, it has been credited with staunching the Tory decline and, ultimately, contributing to the rescue of the free trade agreement.

The second example involves the business campaign to secure broad-scale tax cuts in the wake of Ottawa's 1998 balanced budget achievement. This marked the beginning of a new political era and a new political debate over how to dispose of Ottawa's mounting "fiscal dividend." Almost immediately, advocates for restored public expenditures (to fill the voids left by the program review) squared off against proponents of continued debt pay-down and champions of tax relief. In the February 1999 budget, Finance Minister Martin set out a formula for a 50/50 "balance" of expenditure and tax cut measures within the envelope of fiscal surplus. For the first time since the free trade campaign, more than a decade earlier, the CCCE, CCC, and CME joined together in the autumn of 1999 to emphasize their conviction. While their specific tax agendas varied, the three peak associations made common cause out of fear that tax relief was losing out (Toulin, 1999).

The third and most recent case arose after 9/11, when the US undertook an urgent review of its border security arrangements. There were serious prospects that, in its bid to clamp down on cross-border terrorist movements, Washington would impose a chokehold on Canadian exports to the south. With more than 80 per cent of its exports taking this route, Canadian business struck a Coalition for Secure and Trade-Efficient Borders. Directed by the four peak business associations, this encompassed more than 45 trade associations and companies. Its first statement was released less than two months after 9/11 and was followed by four years of work aimed at protecting the border passage of low-risk goods, strengthening Canadian border management, and ensuring border cooperation in the future (Coalition, 2001).

PROPERTY RIGHTS POPULISM
Social movement politics is not often associated with business campaigns. However business populism, once triggered, can be a formidable force. The identity at the root of many such campaigns is that of property-owner or

middle-class taxpayer, whose hard-won assets and earnings are vulnerable to the reckless appetites of the state. Sometimes these are labelled the "blue" movements to distinguish them from the green (environmental) and the red (socialist) social movements (see also the discussion of populism in Chapter 8).

Perhaps the most graphic modern example of such a movement is the California property tax revolt of the late 1970s (Sears and Citrin, 1985). In a series of citizen-driven referendum initiatives, state voters decisively reined in California budget leaders. The first of these, Proposition 13, was approved by a two-to-one margin and required property tax cuts together with limits on their future growth. A new era of "plebiscitary budgeting" had begun, and the tactics spread to new arenas, including Canada.

A number of groups have driven the Canadian experience with grass roots tax protest. A right-wing think tank, the Fraser Institute, has been highlighting tax trends for 30 years or more. This began with the calculation of a Canadian consumer tax index, after the fashion of the consumer price index and intending to highlight the inexorable growth of average family tax burdens. Several years later, the Fraser Institute launched a simpler but more visceral campaign. Following the lead of the US Tax Foundation, it began to calculate an annual calendar setting of "tax freedom day." This aimed to capture the point when the average family had earned sufficient income to pay its tax dues and could thereby begin to earn for themselves. For example, in 1981 the national tax freedom day was 30 May. By 2005 it had retreated to 26 June (Veldhuis, 2005). While tax freedom day, as applied by the Fraser Institute, may indeed amount to a "flawed, incoherent and pernicious concept" (Brooks, 2005), it nevertheless offers a ready frame of reference for resentful taxpayers.

The organizational catalyst for taxpayer resistance lies elsewhere, however, with the Canadian Taxpayers Federation (CTF). With roots going back to 1989 and the appearance of the Association of Saskatchewan Taxpayers, this group advanced the cause through newsletters and field representatives across Western Canada (Lanigan, 2000). Its energy level and organizational acumen jumped in 1991, when Jason Kenney (later a Reform MP and later still a Conservative MP) came on the scene. The CTF combined attacks on legislator perks (benefits and pensions for members of provincial legislatures), protests on the GST, and petitions for referendums on balanced budget laws. By 1993, offices were open in all four western provinces. Another turning point was the national "tax alert" campaign opposing revenue hikes as part of the federal Liberal Party's war on the deficit. In 1995, a petition bearing a quarter million signatures was presented to Finance Minister Martin.

Perhaps the CTF's most original and lasting policy contribution was its campaign for balanced budget laws. The model statute called for a requirement to balance the budget, a salary penalty on legislators who failed to achieve it, and plebiscitary approval for any new or increased tax measure. The first major success came in Manitoba, where Progressive Conservative Premier Gary Filmon put in place a *Taxpayer Protection Act* following the 1995 election. The remaining three western provinces followed, in varying degrees, as did Ontario Progressive Conservative Mike Harris in 1999. Today, this taxpayer advocacy group claims 65,000 members (Canadian Taxpayers Federation).

While there has been no Canadian taxpayer revolt along American lines, a distinct discourse of small property rights runs through the past several decades. Occasionally it intersects with another vector that stresses corporate tax cuts as part of big business's productivity agenda. Interestingly, it is at the provincial level that CTF-style advocacy has drawn greatest response.

LITIGATION

In the era of the *Charter of Rights and Freedoms* (the Charter), the judicial system is an increasingly prominent avenue of political dispute. For business, however, this was the case long before the entrenchment of the Charter in 1982. Indeed, capital has resorted to the courts to resist unfavourable state policies throughout Canadian history. A biting aphorism, attributed to Justice Darling, holds that "the law-courts of England are open to all men, like the doors of the Ritz Hotel." Not all, of course, enjoy the means to take advantage of that open door, and so it has been in politics.

Litigation is the process of contesting a claim in law. As a political weapon, it plays several functions. In the early stages of a policy process, when issues are still being defined, a favourable judicial ruling can set the limits of substantive content. Rulings can also re-order the political agendas of ruling governments, either elevating or diminishing the priority of an issue. In this way, courts can either block or facilitate government intentions. Litigation may also be effective in the latter stages of policy-making, when formal decisions have been made and attention turns to implementation. Here we consider three bases for strategic litigation in corporate politics.

For Canada's first century, the most important of these was the challenge based on federalism, which means challenging the constitutional competence of the originating jurisdiction. If a statute posed a threat to a powerful interest, it could be resisted by asking the court to declare the law *ultra vires*, or beyond the powers of the sponsoring legislature. Since the Constitution sets out a division of jurisdictions between federal and provincial authorities, judges are asked to consider the disputed subject against the constitutional division of federal and provincial powers and determine whether the sponsoring legislature had exceeded its authorized powers. For example, when the government of Ontario prohibited the export of raw pulp logs to the US in order to build up a forest processing industry within the province, log exporting firms challenged this measure by arguing that only the government of Canada could regulate such matters of international trade.

Notice the distinctive logic of a federalism challenge: a statute or program is questioned only for being enacted by the "wrong" government. If the appeal courts agree, that law is struck down, creating a policy vacuum. However, there is nothing to prevent the other level of government from enacting the identical measure, in complete constitutional propriety. (Nothing except the vigorous lobby that would undoubtedly be mounted by the judicial victors.) In the pulpwood case, the courts upheld the Ontario regulation (Armstrong, 1981).

A second basis of challenge involves procedural grounds. An important part of English common law is the notion of due process, which holds that state authorities must follow fair and proper channels as they conduct their business. Due process is particularly important in relations between citizens and the police and courts and to the field of administrative law, which involves relations between citizens and state bureaucracies. The need to follow fair procedure is central to this. Has there been adequate public notice where the law requires? Are officials free of bias or conflict of interest when they rule on important allocations? These are the staples of procedural challenge, since serious defects of process are sufficient to invalidate the results.

This provides interest holders with another potential lever for avoiding or evading adverse measures. In fields where government moves to regulate industry, it is common for the regulated firms to spend years in the courts testing the mandate, procedures, and personnel of newly established regulators. Even if the substance of such challenges fails, advantages are gained by postponing the application of the adverse policies for years. Quite apart from the time gains, political will may ebb in the face of persistent litigation and policy regimes may be transformed as a result. When the government of Nova Scotia created a Pulpwood Marketing Board in 1970, against unanimous opposition from the pulp and paper industry, the lead firms engaged in procedural challenges to delay agreement on the first supply contract for a full decade (Clancy, 1992).

A third type of challenge is based upon possible violation of constitutional rights. Prior to 1982 this was not a significant option. However, the enactment that year of the Charter opened a dramatic new field of rights-based judicial review of legislation. The Charter sets out categories of fundamental freedoms, democratic rights, legal rights, equality rights, language rights, and others. It is fair to say that it has revolutionized the practice of strategic litigation. The past 20 years have brought new prominence to the Supreme Court and heightened the "rights holding" theme in Canadian political culture. The National Citizens Coalition case on third-party electoral advertising, discussed below, is a case in point.

CIVIC PROPAGANDA

In essence, propaganda connotes schemes to propagate a doctrine or idea to a mass public. This becomes especially salient in democratic societies where the mass public plays an active political role. Not by accident, modern propaganda coincides with the emergence of electoral democracy, which occurred in the period 1880–1920. During this time, the extent of the franchise grew from 10–15 per cent to 40–50 per cent of liberal societies.

For capitalist interests, this was a transition fraught with danger. Under far more intense pressure from populist and working-class interests, the state more assertively challenged market prerogatives. Alex Carey argues that American corporate interests pioneered a most effective response, refining a set of propaganda techniques to shape public and cultural values in favour of private property and markets and thereby "taking the risk out of democracy" (Carey, 1995). This involved a convergence of new advertising and public relations techniques, new media of dissemination (in print and electronic forms), and a firm will on the part of organized business to use them. These are indirect techniques of political influence in that they seek to shape underlying social expectations and perceptions, largely through the manipulation of powerful symbols—religious, national, and patriotic. In the twentieth century, this included sustained efforts aimed at the assimilation of immigrants, the prospects for trade unions and social democratic parties, and the contours of the anti-Soviet Cold War alliance. The most recent cultural discourse to be promoted in this way is that of neoliberalism.

Carey contends that business propaganda efforts can function on parallel tracks, for "tree-tops" influence (with political elites) and mass influence (with the public at large). The first is the domain of the think tanks and peak associations. Policy research institutes or think tanks have become an increasingly prominent part of the policy landscape over the last quarter-century or so. Prior to 1970 there were few stand-alone research and advocacy centres in Canada. Since then, however, a series of primarily business-sponsored voices, such as the C.D. Howe Institute, the Fraser Institute, and the Atlantic Institute for Market Studies, have assumed public prominence. William Carroll points out that a series of shared directors link these groups into a corporate-sponsored network. Together, they advance a comprehensive neoliberal policy discourse while displaying a division of labour that "offers possibilities for a nuanced debate and diverse action repertoires, all within the perimeter of neoliberal discourse" (Carroll, 2004: 170).

The second, or mass influence strategy, aims directly at the civic public by means of alternative communications campaigns. This is the domain of the CTF, for example, whose creative publicity and grassroots networking was noted in sections above. The National Citizens Coalition (NCC) is interesting in this regard. Founded in the 1970s by right-wing businessman Colin Brown, it is funded by anonymous donors and is directed by a select group of voting members and a core staff group. Murray Dobbin sees a leit-motif in the generalized attack on publicly delivered programs and a corresponding preference for the personal and the private. Conservative Prime Minister Stephen Harper served briefly as president of the Coalition in the 1990s, between stints in Ottawa. Despite the grassroots nomenclature, the operative style is more commercial lobby than citizen democracy. "What the NCC does do ... is commission opinion polls, try to generate public pressure on politicians through opinion pieces and mass media advertising, cultivate political friends who will push its policies to the forefront, and make submissions to governments" (Dobbin, 1998: 205).

The breakthrough event for the Coalition came in 1984, when it won a court challenge to Ottawa's third-party advertising ban during election campaigns. The Alberta Supreme Court held that, short of evidence that it undermined the democratic process, any ban on third-party interventions violated the Charter right of freedom of expression. The practical consequences of this victory became clear four years later with the unprecedented third-party business intervention in the free trade election of 1988. This case captures the continuing dimensions of political victory on such framework-setting issues. Once objectives are achieved, they are embedded in the values or procedures by which future politics will be waged.

Theoretical Implications

In the discussion above, we have seen that capital can mobilize politically across a wide range of issues and act within a variety of arenas. These include embedded structures such as market recoil, active agents such as trade associations, formative mechanisms for mass beliefs and values, and populist movements. There are no grounds, theoretically or empirically, to expect universal business hegemony. Nonetheless, a pronounced tilt may affect the business-government relationship within national or local, sector or industry settings. To conclude, we will return to the question posed early in this chapter, as to whether business politics should be considered within or outside of civil society proper. That this question is posed at all reflects diverging perspectives on the constitution of society.

The very notion of civil society springs from the recognition of an autonomous political space that is outside of the state while related to it. It parallels the historical processes in the West that established first the liberal state and later the democratic state. While the liberal state emerged as a limited authority that guaranteed not only a private social space but also a public social space outside of its immediate control, the democratic state acknowledged that its authority sprang from a mass political mandate conferred and renewed by public consent. This involved citizens in a dual fashion, as voters in elections and as activists between them. Not only is the state-society dichotomy fundamental, but the quality of societal autonomy is critical. If organized capital furthers the cause of holding accountable the burgeoning modern state, it enhances the quality of civil society. Even while acting in defence of its immediate interests, the institutions of capital may contribute to the maintenance of that vital public space outside of the state where civil politics can be realized.

The alternate perspective, however, focuses on the capacities of these powerful market interests not to enhance but to erode civil society. It seems to prefer a more restricted version of civil society that would leave capitalist market interests on the outside, for the most part. It begins with the recognition that commercial markets constitute immensely powerful allocative systems. Not only are they capable of standing on their own for purposes of material production and exchange, they can also rival and even predominate over state systems (the only other allocative system of comparable scale). It is true that markets involve social relationships at various levels—buyers and sellers, employers and employees, lenders and borrowers. Furthermore, these relationships have given rise to collective bodies in the form of groups and movements to represent these commercial interests. Just as the institutions of the market depend on political authorities for validation and sanction, the social interests created by markets look to politics as a means of fulfilling their needs. However capitalist interests differ from other civil interests in their capacity to eclipse the public realm (Bakan, 2004).

This question of whether a preponderance of capitalist power serves to distort the shape and capacities of a civil society is another question entirely and has taken on growing urgency as capitalism matures. Indeed, it is the latter concern that underlies the civil sector's challenge to neoliberal politics and globalization, whether at World Trade Organization (WTO) conference sites, International Monetary Fund (IMF) governing meetings, United Nations (UN) Conferences on Sustainable Development, or G-7 summits. These battles will continue to shape the contexts of business politics for years to come.

References and Further Reading

Armstrong, Christopher. 1981. *The Politics of Federalism: Ontario's Relations with the Federal Government*. Toronto: University of Toronto Press.

Atkinson, Michael M., and William D. Coleman. 1989. *The State, Business, and Industrial Change in Canada*. Toronto: University of Toronto Press.

Bakan, Joel. 2004. *The Corporation: The Pathological Pursuit of Profit and Power*. Toronto: Penguin Canada.

Bothwell, Robert, and William Kilbourn. 1979. *C.D. Howe: A Biography*. Toronto: McClelland and Stewart.

Brooks, Neil. 2005. *Tax Freedom Day: A Flawed, Incoherent, and Pernicious Concept*. Ottawa: Canadian Centre for Policy Alternatives. June.

Canadian Chamber of Commerce. 2005. *Promoting Productivity, Pursuing Prosperity*. Ottawa.

Canadian Council of Chief Executives. 2005. *Canada First! Taking the Lead in Transforming the Global Economy*. Ottawa.

Canadian Federation of Independent Business. 2006. *About CFIB*. <http://www.cfib.ca/info/default_e.asp>.

Canadian Manufacturers and Exporters Association. 2005. *Manufacturing 20/20*. Ottawa.

Canadian Taxpayers Federation. <http://www.taxpayer.com>.

Carey, Alex. 1995. *Taking the Risk Out of Democracy*. Ed. Andrew Lohrey. Sydney: University of New South Wales Press.

Carroll, William K. 2004. *Corporate Power in a Globalizing World*. Don Mills: Oxford University Press.

Clancy, Peter. 1992. "The Politics of Pulpwood Marketing in Nova Scotia." In L. Anders Sandberg (ed.), *Trouble in the Woods*. Fredericton: Acadiensis Press.

Clancy, Peter. 2004. *Micropolitics and Canadian Business: Paper, Steel, and the Airlines*. Peterborough: Broadview.

Clark, S.D. 1939. *The Canadian Manufacturers Association: A Study in Collective Pressure and Political Action*. Toronto: University of Toronto Press.

Clarke, Tony. 1997. *Silent Coup: Confronting the Big Business Takeover of Canada*. Toronto: James Lorimer.

Clement, Wallace. 1983. *Class, Power, and Property: Essays on Canadian Society*. Toronto: Methuen.

Coalition for Secure and Trade-Efficient Borders. 2001. *Rethinking Our Borders: A Plan for Action*. (December). <http://www.cme-mec.ca/>.

Coleman, William. 1988. *Business and Politics: A Study of Collective Action*. Montreal and Kingston: McGill-Queen's University Press.

Dobbin, Murray. 1998. *The Myth of the Good Corporate Citizen*. Toronto: Stoddart.

Doern, G. Bruce, and Brian W. Tomlin. 1991. *Faith and Fear: The Free Trade Story*. Toronto: Stoddart.

Edwards, Lindy. 2002. *How to Argue with an Economist*. Cambridge: Cambridge University Press.

Ferguson, Thomas. 1995. *Golden Rule: The Investment Theory of Party Competition and the Logic of Money-Driven Political Systems*. Chicago: University of Chicago Press.

Finkel, Alvin. 1979. *Business and Social Reform in the Thirties*. Toronto: James Lorimer.

Gillies, James. 1981. *Where Business Fails*. Montreal: Institute for Research on Public Policy.

Gollner, Andrew. 1983. *Social Change and Corporate Strategy: The Expanding Role of Public Affairs*. Stamford: Issue Action Publishers.

Hiebert, Janet. 1991. "Interest Groups and Canadian Federal Elections." In F. Leslie Seidle (ed.), *Interest Groups and Elections in Canada*. Toronto: Dundurn Press.

Howlett, Karen, Barrie McKenna, and John Partridge. 1996. "How the Banks Lost Big." *Globe and Mail*, 9 March: B1.

Jackson, Andrew, and Matthew Sanger. 1998. *Dismantling Democracy: The Multilateral Agreement on Investment (MAI) and Its Impact*. Toronto: Canadian Centre for Policy Alternatives.

Langille, David. 1987. "The BCNI and the Canadian State." *Studies in Political Economy* (Autumn): 41–85.

Lanigan, Troy. 2000. *The Canadian Taxpayers Federation: A Ten Year Retrospective (1989–2000)*. <http://www.taxpayer.com>.

Lewis, Timothy. 2003. *In the Long Run We're All Dead*. Vancouver: University of British Columbia Press.

Leys, Colin. 2001. *Market-driven Politics: Neoliberal Democracy and the Public Interest*. London: Verso.

Lindblom, Charles. 1982. "The Market as Prison." *Journal of Politics* 44(2): 324–36.

Litvak, Isaiah. 1984. "National Trade Associations: Business-Government Intermediaries." *Business Quarterly*.

Mahon, Rianne. 1984. *The Politics of Industrial Restructuring: Canadian Textiles*. Toronto: University of Toronto Press.

McBride, Stephen. 2001. *Paradigm Shift: Globalization and the Canadian State*. Halifax: Fernwood.

Naylor, R.T. 1972. "The Rise and Fall of the Third Commercial Empire of the St. Lawrence." In Gary Teeple (ed.), *Capitalism and the National Question in Canada*. Toronto: University of Toronto Press. 1–36.

Niosi, Jorge. 1985. "Continental Nationalism: The Strategy of the Canadian Bourgeoisie." In Robert J. Brym (ed.), *The Structure of the Canadian Capitalist Class*. Toronto: Garamond Press.

Pal, Leslie A. 1995. *Interests of State: The Politics of Language, Multiculturalism, and Feminism in Canada*. Montreal and Kingston: McGill-Queen's University Press.

Richards, John, and Larry Pratt. 1979. *Prairie Capitalism: Power and Influence in the New West*. Toronto: McClelland and Stewart.

Sears, David O., and Jack Citrin. 1985. *Tax Revolt: Something For Nothing in California*. Cambridge, MA: Harvard University Press.

Stanbury, W.T. 1977. *Business Interests and the Reform of Competition Policy in Canada*. Toronto: Methuen.

Toulin, Alan. 1999. "Business Groups Unite to Battle for Tax Relief." *National Post*, 28 September.

Veldhuis, Niels. 2005. "Canadians Celebrate Tax Freedom Day on June 26." *Fraser Forum* (July-August): 4–10.

Williams, Glen. 1983. *Not For Export: Toward a Political Economy of Canada's Arrested Development*. Toronto: McClelland and Stewart.

Young, Brian. 1981. *George-Etienne Cartier: Montreal Bourgeois*. Montreal and Kingston: McGill-Queen's University Press.

TWO

The Working-Class Movement in Canada: An Overview[1]

David Camfield

Most people in Canada assume that they are part of the middle class—people "in the middle," in between the small wealthy elite and the minority that lives in poverty. But there is a different way of looking at class. From this perspective, most people are part of the working class: the class made up of all people who sell their ability to work to employers in exchange for a wage (whether paid by the hour or as a salary) and who do not exercise significant managerial authority plus unemployed wage-workers and unwaged people (for example, people working full-time as unpaid caregivers) who live in the households of wage-earners. All such people are the working class because they share a common relationship both to the way that society is organized to produce goods and services and to other social classes (especially the class of employers). The working class in this sense is extremely diverse: in Canada today, it includes both highly paid miners and minimum-wage retail staff, computer game designers (mostly white men) and health care workers (mostly female, many of them women of colour), citizens and non-citizens, people who work extremely long hours at one job and others who work part-time for pay on top of long hours of unpaid work taking care of children in the home. This chapter uses the term "worker" to refer to any member of the working class, waged or unwaged.

"Working-class movements" are made up of all the organizations, both formal (such as unions and political parties) and informal (such as workplace and community networks) through which workers collectively resist the exploitation and oppression they experience in capitalist societies. As we shall see, in Canada today the working-class movement is chiefly made up of unions. For this reason, most people who write about the "labour movement," as it is most often called, think only about unions. However, it would be a mistake to assume that working-class movements are only composed of unions or to think that unions past and present have all been the same kind of organization.

It might seem unnecessary to discuss what "politics" is, since most people, whether they think politics is boring and irrelevant or interesting and important, generally understand politics as matters concerning government or the state. But that is not all there is to it. There are also broader understandings of what politics is. One such view is nicely expressed in a document, "Working-Class Politics in the 21st Century," that provided an overview for a task-force created in 1999 by one of the largest unions in Canada, the Canadian Auto Workers (CAW):

> We generally think of politics as being about who gets elected and what they do—that is, about governments. But even though this is how it's normally expressed, the essence of politics is really about power and change: whose interests and values get attention and results, and how people organize to affect that. So politics is really about society and not just government. No matter who gets elected, as long as power in society remains basically in the hands of a minority, our lives are shaped and limited by that minority's control (power) over production, investment, finances, and communications. (CAW, n.d.)

It is this kind of broader understanding—that politics is about power in society—that informs this chapter. What elected governments do is part of politics, but so too is what unelected state authorities like central banks, courts, labour boards, and police forces do. More unusually, this chapter also considers what happens in workplaces as political; every day many people's lives are touched by the way that power is exercised and contested in the places where they work for pay (Rinehart, 2005).[2]

From this perspective, we can see that the working-class movement in Canada regularly contends with power and politics in two forms. The first is that of employers in the workplace. In the words of the CAW document quoted above, "Workers formed unions as a response to the imbalance of power in the workplace." It is this workplace power of employers that workers and unions must deal with daily. As the CAW document goes on to say, working-class movements are not only concerned with power and politics in the workplace: "If, however, we actually want to influence all dimensions of our lives, we can't restrict ourselves to workplace relations and collective bargaining" (CAW, n.d.). So the other form of power and politics that working-class movements frequently confront is that of government and the state.

Theoretical Perspectives

Which theoretical perspective one uses to understand the subject of this chapter is extremely important. For example, rational choice theory assumes that "free markets" are best (rational) and will therefore see workers' collective action that challenges the "free market" as irrational. A rational choice theorist would present a *very* different interpretation than the one I am putting forward.[3] Pluralists, neopluralists, and others who do not see class as a relationship of production and power at the heart of capitalist societies would also write this chapter very differently.

The theoretical perspective used here is Marxist. It sees politics as about power and change in society, not just government or the state. It understands conflicts between workers, employers, and governments not as moments of friction between interest groups but as part of a pattern of class struggle that happens because of the way capitalism is organized. Capitalism's fundamental priority—corporate profit—inevitably clashes with workers' needs. Workers are subjected to employer control in the workplace, must sell their ability to work to employers to get income, and live in households and communities that are affected by what corporations do. What states do and how they do it are shaped by the way that state power exists in a specifically capitalist form. All this makes class struggle inevitable; what course class struggle takes is most definitely not predetermined.

The Marxism of this chapter differs from most other Marxist/neo-Marxist perspectives in a number of ways. It is an anti-racist feminist Marxism that sees capitalist societies as organized by gender, race, sexuality, and other social relations as well as by class. It views these social relations as never existing independently of one another, but only in and through each other. This means that political actors do not just arise out of classes. Similarly, classes, like other social groups, are always shaped by many social relations. The theory used here takes seriously the idea that Marxism is *historical materialism*; that is, society is made up of structured processes that take place in time, in which people make their own history but not in circumstances of their own choosing. Thus, a social movement must be studied concretely and explained as an historical phenomenon in an historically specific social context; it cannot be deduced from abstract structures (see also McNally, 2002; and Wilmot, 2005).

Historical Overview

The working-class movement has had an important influence on how we live now. Its efforts helped to achieve laws that give workers at least a few rights and some health and safety protection on the job, unemployment insurance and other social programs, and more. Looking at the movement's history allows us to appreciate this and to understand how this movement became what it is today (see Heron, 1996; and Palmer, 1992).

BEGINNING TO ORGANIZE

As industrial capitalism took hold in Canada in the mid-1800s, skilled wage-earners increasingly found themselves facing employers intent on reducing their traditional control over how they did their jobs. Their distinct skills gave them power because employers could not easily replace them. By creating craft unions, they sought to defend their wage rates, control on the job, and status as skilled, white, male "breadwinners." As the main form of working-class movement organization in the second half of the 1800s, each craft union united practitioners of one specific craft or trade, often on an "international" (Canada and the US) basis. These unions only aimed to organize the small minority of workers who had skilled status and excluded all other workers—men who were less-skilled or not of Anglo-Celtic origin and women. Not surprisingly, even at their height they enrolled less than 10 per cent of all wage-workers in Canada.

The 1880s saw the rise and fall of the Knights of Labour, a hybrid organization that combined features of a union, religious association, political party, and fraternal order. Unlike the craft unions, they sought to organize both skilled and less-skilled workers. They admitted women as well as men and were open to African Canadians (but not Chinese Canadians). Although short-lived, the Knights briefly had a mass membership. They showed in practice that an alternative to craft unionism was possible, demonstrated a remarkable degree of working-class unity, and advanced a "labour reform" vision of a different society.

With the partial exception of the Knights of Labour, the early working-class movement had no independent perspective on issues outside the workplace. Nor did it have a political party of its own (many male workers did not have the right to vote due to property restrictions on the franchise, and no women could vote). At election time, craft unionists tended to back Conservatives in the 1870s and Liberals after that. If unionists ran for political office, it was as candidates of one of the two parties of the dominant class; some ran under the banner "Liberal-Labour." Later, some unionists concluded that it was impossible to make either of the parties of capital address workers' interests and launched local Independent Labour Parties (ILPs), which sought to use the existing institutions of government to bring in social reforms.

INDUSTRIAL UNIONISM AND NEW PARTIES

By the end of the 1800s, it was clear that craft unionism was incapable of responding to the needs of the majority of the working class who toiled in factories, mines, and other industrial capitalist workplaces where wages were low, conditions were awful, and workers vulnerable to the arbitrary decisions of managers and supervisors who wielded autocratic power. Craft union power was itself being weakened by employers' efforts to reorganize work and bring in machinery so that fewer skilled workers were needed.

Some activists began to build an alternative: industrial unionism. Industrial unionism aimed to organize all the workers in an industry into one union instead of organizing each craft or trade separately. It set out to organize the less-skilled majority of wage-earners no matter who they were or where they came from, using militant, democratic mass organization and action. However, employer hostility and state repression kept industrial unions from making much headway.

Many of the activists who saw industrial unions as the kind of organization workers needed to defend themselves in the workplace also believed that the working class would never achieve freedom and a good life under capitalism. For this reason, they saw the ILP goal of reforms within capitalism as utterly inadequate. Instead, they advocated the replacement of capitalism with a socialist society based on collective ownership of society's wealth. Both the Socialist Party of Canada (SPC, founded in 1904) and the Social Democratic Party of Canada (SDP, formed in 1911) were part of the working-class movement, conducting education and running candidates in elections.

Hardship at home and slaughter abroad during World War I and the inspiration that the 1917 Russian Revolution gave to working-class movements internationally led in Canada to an upsurge of struggle, the "Workers' Revolt," whose peak was the Winnipeg General Strike (1919). Workers rushed to join unions (including the conservative Roman Catholic unions in Quebec) and hoped for real social change. But this wave broke against the barriers of repression, an orchestrated anti-immigrant campaign, and the divisions between craft and industrial unions. Supporters of the politics of the Bolshevik Party that had led the Russian Revolution to victory formed the Communist Party of Canada (CPC) in 1921, greatly weakening the SPC and SDP. The CPC's original revolutionary and internationalist socialism was soon replaced by politics laid down by the bureaucratic dictatorship in the USSR that remade the Communist movement in its own interests.

The 1920s were hard years for the working-class movement. The Depression (1929–39) was even worse. Mass unemployment was a blow to already weak unions. However, it also gave rise to organizations of unemployed workers. Proclaiming "we refuse to starve in silence," these associations campaigned against evictions and for relief, jobs, and unemployment insurance (which was finally established in 1940). The Depression also prompted the formation of a new left-wing party, the Cooperative Commonwealth Federation (CCF), pledged to a program of major reforms to be achieved by electing it to office. Initially, the CCF had a weaker presence in the working-class movement than the CPC, and most craft unionists still backed the Liberals.

TURNING POINT

The breakthrough for the movement came during and after World War II. With mass unemployment replaced by full employment, fear evaporated. Many thousands of less-skilled workers rushed to join unions to press for higher wages, an end to authoritarian management, and better working conditions. A massive wave of strike ensued, followed by another at the war's end. CCF support grew. To prevent another workers' revolt, the federal government yielded and granted unions a legal procedure that allowed those with majority support in a workplace to be formally recognized (certified) and that compelled employers to negotiate with these certified unions.

This helped unions to win workplace rights, such as seniority rules, that improved conditions on the job by limiting the arbitrary power of managers and supervisors. Unions also won wage increases, pensions, paid vacations, and other benefits for the significant minority of workers (mostly men) who were now their members. In industries where unions were strong, their gains pushed non-unionized firms to improve wages and benefits too.

But along with unions' new rights came restrictions. Strikes for recognition were prohibited. All strikes were banned during the term of a collective agreement (contract between union and employer); workplace disputes were now to be addressed through bureaucratic grievance procedures instead of by direct action on the job. Union officials were required to uphold these rules and police their members.

These rights and restrictions, together with the crushing of the CPC-led left wing of the movement by the CCF-led right wing after the outbreak in 1946 of the Cold War between the Western alliance led by the US and the USSR, led to an historic shift in the nature of unionism in Canada. Most unions now accepted management's right to control the workplace and fully endorsed capitalism in exchange for union rights and economic gains for unionized workers (again, mostly male breadwinners). Unions became more stable but less democratic institutions, run by full-time officials and staff with a "leave it to us" attitude. The union officialdom grew more detached from workers than before, in part because of the spreading practice of employers automatically deducting union dues from the pay cheques of all workers in unionized workplaces on behalf of the union (the Rand Formula). The range of union concerns narrowed to enforcing collective agreement rights and negotiating better wages and benefits.

Most other issues were seen as the responsibility of the "political arm" of the movement—the CCF and its successor, the New Democratic Party (NDP), formed in 1961 as a moderate social democratic party. Launched in conservative times, the NDP had strong support among union officials and activists (although some continued to back the Liberals), but it never succeeded in winning the allegiance of more than a minority of workers in English-speaking Canada. The NDP's poor understanding of Quebec and support for a strong federal state prevented it from sinking roots in that province.

From 1960s' Militancy to Neoliberalism

In Quebec, a new nationalism and working-class militancy combined to create a climate of radicalism that infused unions and working-class community organizing from the mid-1960s through the 1970s. Outside Quebec, low unemployment and steady economic growth fostered militancy among unionized workers and a rapid growth of unions in the public sector, which brought many more women into unions. In English-speaking Canada, the youth-based New Left was largely outside the working-class movement.

The end of the long postwar economic boom in the mid-1970s was followed by the beginnings of an offensive by governments and employers against the working class that continues to this day. Most of the movement was ill-prepared to challenge the restructuring of workplaces, state, and society by corporations and governments that over time has led to neoliberalism (Harvey, 2005), a particular organization of capitalism whose "most basic feature ... is the systematic use of state power to impose (financial) market imperatives" (Saad-Filho and Johnston, 2005: 3). Lay-offs, work intensification, the spread of precarious employment, cuts to social programs, privatization, deregulation, and anti-union changes to labour law have pummelled unions. The NDP has moved rightwards and distanced itself from unions while continuing to draw on union support. Much working-class resistance has taken place in workplaces and communities, along with a number of major struggles against neoliberal governments (on four of these, see Palmer, 1987; Rapaport, 1999; Camfield, 2000; Camfield, 2006), but there have been few victories. The neoliberal offensive, resistance to it, and the efforts within unions of feminists, anti-racists, and supporters of the rights of lesbians, gays, bisexuals, and transgendered people (LGBT) have broadened the political consciousness of some unionized workers, some of whom have been drawn to the global justice and anti-poverty movements. Overall, though, the movement is battered, lacks a clear strategic direction, and is very much on the defensive.

THE WORKING-CLASS MOVEMENT TODAY

Because unions are the main organizations of the working-class movement in Canada today, we will now look at unions and their relations with political parties before glancing briefly at other movement organizations. Some working people think that unions are obsolete, irrelevant, or worse. For example, young part-time workers who get little attention from union officials may ask why they have to pay union dues, while non-union workers may resent the relatively better pay and working conditions of unionized workers. There is no doubt that unions in their current form have many weaknesses. Nevertheless, it is clear that they improve workers' wages and benefits (Jackson, 2005). Union collective agreements place some limits on the arbitrary power of employers and usually give workers stronger rights than those found in Canadian employment legislation, which offers workers little protection. Unions also have the potential to be a powerful force for social change.

UNIONS

As of the beginning of 2005, there were 4.381 million union members in Canada. This represents 30.7 per cent of the non-agricultural paid workforce (the usual measure of the portion of the workforce in unions, referred to as the union density rate), and 25.5 per cent of the total civilian labour force (Bédard, 2005).[4] Although the percentage of workers in unions in 2005 was up very slightly (.3 per cent) over 2004, the density rate has been slowly falling from a peak of 37 per cent two decades ago.

However, this overall measurement masks a stark contrast between the private sector and the public sector. Private sector union density has steadily fallen, reaching 17.5 per cent in 2005, while the rate in the public sector has remained much higher, now 71.3 per cent (Akyeampong, 2005). Workers in the public sector, whose share of total employment is shrinking, are now four times more likely to be union members than are workers in the private sector, where most people work and where most new jobs are being created. More than half of all union members are now public sector workers—a reflection of the weakening of unionization among people who work for private firms. The two largest unions in Canada, the Canadian Union of Public Employees (CUPE) and the National Union of Public and General Employees (NUPGE), are both public sector unions.

Another notable change over recent decades has been the growing percentage of union members who are women. Only 12 per cent of union members were women in the late 1970s, but today they make up just under half of the total membership. Employed women are now very slightly more likely than men to be union members (Akyeampong, 2004). Behind this change are two facts: a clear majority of public sector workers are women, and since the mid-

1970s many unionized jobs have been lost in manufacturing and other parts of the private sector where most workers are men. Young workers (ages 15 to 24), who are often employed in part-time and/or temporary private sector jobs, are the least likely to be union members, at 14.1 per cent, while workers aged 45 to 54 are the most likely members, 39.7 per cent (Akyeampong, 2005).

Most union members belong to unions that are formally structured as national (sometimes called "parent") organizations. Such unions are divided up into many local branches (often referred to simply as "locals"). Some unions are "internationals"; that is, they are American-based unions also active in Canada. The United Steelworkers of America (USWA), the third largest union in Canada, is one such union.

Some unions, such as CUPE and the unions that make up NUPGE, organize almost exclusively in the public sector. Others, like the USWA and the CAW, are based mainly in the private sector but now organize in the public sector too. In recent years, some unions that used to be overwhelmingly made up of workers in one industry have expanded to include many different kinds of workers; this is true of both the USWA and CAW.

The Canadian Labour Congress (CLC) is the main pan-Canadian union central or federation; most union members (72 per cent in 2005) belong to unions affiliated with the CLC. The CLC also has provincial federations of labour and, at the city or regional level, labour councils. In Quebec, in addition to the CLC-affiliated Quebec Federation of Labour there are three Quebec-based union centrals, the largest of which are the *Confédération des syndicats nationaux* and the *Centrale des syndicats du Québec*.

This sketch of the size and structure of the movement does not tell us anything about what unions *do*—a central question for understanding the working-class movement in Canada today—or what kinds of organizations today's unions are. A few words of caution are in order here. We often talk about what unions (or other organizations) do, but "trade unionism provides a good example of the way in which a purely institutional perspective can be dangerous and misleading ... what does it mean to say that 'the union' adopts a particular policy or carries out a certain action? This is a clear instance of ... reification: treating an impersonal abstraction as a social agent, when it is really only people who act" (Hyman, 1975: 16).

With this in mind, we should begin by noting that most unionized workers are not active union members most of the time. Only when union activity affects them very directly—such as when a tentative collective agreement has been negotiated by union and employer representatives and the members have their chance to vote to ratify or reject it, or when a strike or lock-out seems likely—will most workers become personally involved. Outside of such situations, union activity is carried out by union members elected or in some cases appointed to executive boards, committees, and other positions such as shop steward (workplace stewards are the lowest rank in the union officialdom) by union staff and by members of the rank and file (the majority of union members, who hold no union office). Most unions hire their staff, sometimes from outside their own ranks; the Canadian Union of Postal Workers (CUPW) is an exception as some CUPW staff are elected. Most union officials, such as local executive members and stewards, are volunteers; some get some paid time off work to carry out union activity. A minority of officials are full-time officers; that is, they perform union business on a paid full-time basis. Although top full-time officers and staff generally act as key leaders in unions, we should remember the many thousands of members who regularly carry out union activity in the workplace. What these volunteers do usually goes unnoticed by outside observers, but it is absolutely vital for unions. They are also a much larger group than the activist base of any other social movement in Canada.

What do all these people do? The bulk of union activity today is devoted to negotiating and then administering collective agreements, contracts that specify workers' pay and benefits and spell out in detail (often in difficult legalistic language) the workplace rights and obligations of employers, union members, and union officials. The contents of a collective agreement will reflect the relative power of union and employer. Unions also conduct educational workshops and courses for their members. Many unions involve themselves in some kind of political action outside the workplace sphere. Union activity is financed by the dues paid by workers covered by collective agreements.

The approach that unions take to what they do varies considerably between and within unions. However, in broad terms we can identify four different kinds of unionism:

- *Business unionism* is narrowly focused on collective bargaining, basically accepts neoliberalism, takes a cooperative approach with employers that includes a willingness to give up past gains, and assumes that unions should be run from the top down by small numbers of officials and staff rather than democratically by an active membership.
- *Social unionism* is more critical of neoliberalism and more concerned with social issues outside the workplace than business unionism, while still often non-confrontational and wary of greater militancy or democratic membership control. This is the most common form of unionism in Canada today.
- *Mobilization unionism* differs from social unionism in its willingness to use more militant means to defend and build the union movement and fight for

workers' rights. It encourages member involvement but does not challenge the running of unions primarily by staff and top officials.

- *Social movement unionism* puts democratic control of the union by an active membership at the heart of its approach to building unions that are militant and solidaristic. It clearly rejects neoliberalism and aims to build a broad movement of unions and community-based organizations to change society. It is anti-bureaucratic; that is, it seeks to undermine the dependence of most members on the activity and knowledge of a small number of leaders (usually union officials) by developing members' capacities. This is the least common kind of unionism in Canada.[5]

Like the rest of the society to which they belong, unions have long been shaped by male domination, white supremacy and heterosexism. However, the shift from women workers being a small minority of union members to almost half along with the efforts of women unionists to combat sexism have changed the culture of many unions. LGBT activists and their allies have also achieved changes in some unions, as have workers of colour and white anti-racists. Nevertheless, there is still a great deal to be done to make unions more anti-racist, anti-sexist, and anti-heterosexist (Briskin, 2003).

To close this overview of unions in Canada today, it is worth underlining what distinguishes them as social movement organizations:

1. Unions have a truly mass membership, much larger than the membership of any other movement.
2. Unions have the potential to be democratic organizations through which many workers engage in collective action. Usually, most union members are inactive: "most workers still view their unions as distant, though vital, service organizations" (Heron, 1996: 163). However, because most unions have local membership meetings and other structures, it is possible for them to become the organizational vehicle for large-scale collective action, such as strikes. Despite their many limitations, unions are the most democratic mass membership organization in Canadian society (which highlights how very little democracy there is in this society).
3. This potential to be the organizational framework for large-scale collective action simply does not exist in campaigning organizations (such as Greenpeace or the Council of Canadians) whose "members" are people who donate money and who lack any way of coming together to act collectively or exercise democratic control over the staff and board members who carry out all or most of such organizations' activity. Nor does this potential exist when social movement organizations are groups of activists

who do not have a structured relationship to a mass base of the people for whose interests they fight (as is true for most anti-poverty groups).

4. Unions can tap a unique source of power: the ability of workers to stop working for their employers by going on strike. Strikes by workers in private firms cost employers profits; strikes by public sector workers block the supply of services and can disrupt the functioning of the state. This power is more than just a matter of numbers; it is the power of the working class to bring capitalist society grinding to a halt.

UNIONS AND THE NDP

From its creation in 1961, the NDP was a social democratic party in which top union leaders from English-speaking Canada played a central role, along with middle-class professionals and university-trained white-collar workers. Unions were a vital source of money and volunteers for NDP election campaigns. Officials and activists from international unions like those based in the auto and steel industries were particularly active in the party. The NDP was the "political arm" of the working-class movement; its union supporters saw it as the way to achieve the social reforms that could not be achieved through collective bargaining with employers. The NDP's demands were modest and completely within the framework of capitalist society. These politics and the decisive influence of top union officials in the party were both confirmed in 1972 when union leaders insisted on the expulsion from the party of the Waffle, a group of New Left activists who sought to turn the NDP to more radical and nationalist politics and who had criticized the labour leadership's conservatism (for more on unions, politics, and the NDP, see Chapter 3 in this book).

The traditional relationship between unions and the NDP was shaken during the 1990s. The most important cause of this was the actions of the Ontario NDP government headed by Bob Rae (1990–95). Faced with pressure from Bay Street to follow the rules of neoliberal discipline that all governments were now expected to obey, the Rae government passed legislation that opened up public sector collective agreements and imposed unpaid days off. This sparked sharp debate within the union movement. In Ontario, public sector unions and the CAW opposed this attack and gave the NDP little or no support in the 1995 provincial election, while other unions offered only token objections to the government's actions and gave uncritical support. After the Progressive Conservatives won the 1995 election, debate continued in the province. The CAW and public sector unions championed a series of city-wide labour-community protests (including some political strikes) that became known as the Days of Action. However, before long, the heads of other unions came out in opposition, arguing that unions should put all their efforts into preparing to back the NDP in the next election.

Since the early 1990s, NDP governments in Saskatchewan, British Columbia, and Manitoba have acted like conventional neoliberal governments, disappointing many union supporters by not even trying to enact the kind of small pro-worker reforms that the Rae government had initially attempted. At the federal level, the low levels of voter support for the NDP in the 1993, 1997, and 2000 elections and the leadership's moves to openly adopt "Third Way" neoliberal policies like those of "New Labour" leader Tony Blair in the UK kept debate going about the union-NDP relationship. In British Columbia, the provincial NDP's embrace of Third Way policies and distancing from unionized workers' struggles in the belief that this will boost its chances of re-election has infuriated some of its union supporters.

Although in the 1990s there was considerable formal and informal critical discussion about the NDP among union activists, especially in public sector unions and the CAW, this did not lead to any attempt by unions to work with others to build a well-organized left current inside the NDP to try to change the party or to create a new political movement or party (the New Politics Initiative, which in 2001 failed in its effort to win the federal NDP to back the idea of creating a new party of the Left, did receive a small amount of support from the CAW). However, CUPE and the CAW are now more likely to act on their own on issues that two decades ago would have been more likely left to the NDP.

Since the defeat of the New Politics Initiative, the election of Jack Layton as federal NDP leader, and the recovery of voter support for the NDP in the 2004 and 2006 federal elections there has been a significant degree of reconciliation between the federal NDP leadership and unionists who had been critical of its political direction. One reason for this is that the sense of hope and the opening for new initiatives on the left in Canada, which had been created by the global justice movement with its mass protests in Seattle in November 1999 and Quebec City in April 2001, were swept away by the right-wing "War on Terror" backlash that followed 9/11. The reconciliation was clear in the 2006 federal election when most unions supported the NDP. The most notable exception was the CAW, which adopted a policy of backing the NDP in "winnable" ridings, the Liberals elsewhere in English-speaking Canada, and the Bloc Québécois (BQ) in Quebec. As punishment for openly backing the Liberals, CAW President Buzz Hargrove was expelled from the NDP.

UNIONS AND OTHER PARTIES
Although the NDP has been the party backed by most unions in English-speaking Canada, it is important to note that some unions have supported other parties that have never been part of the working-class movement. Some building trades and craft unions have a history of making financial contributions

to the federal Liberal Party. A number have backed provincial Liberals. Less well-known are donations made by labour leaders to individual politicians from parties other than the NDP, such as the attendance of the president of the British Columbia Federation of Labour and several other of that province's union leaders at a 2005 fundraising dinner for David Emerson, the federal Liberal minister of industry who in 2006 gained attention when he joined the cabinet of the newly elected Conservative government. In municipal elections, which are rarely fought along party lines, unions often back candidates who are not NDP members.

In Quebec, most unions have long backed the Parti Québécois (PQ) in provincial politics and the BQ at the federal level. The PQ and the BQ have never been the social democratic political arm of the working-class movement in the way that the NDP has been outside Quebec. Nevertheless, leaders of both these parties have built and maintained a close relationship with union officialdom. Many unionists support the PQ and BQ because they see them as more labour-friendly than the Liberals and because they support Quebec sovereignty as a step towards creating the kind of society they seek. Today many unionists are unhappy with the PQ's adoption of neoliberalism. How many of them will join or vote for *Québec solidaire*, the left-wing pro-independence party formed in February 2006, remains to be seen.

Other Organizations

Unions and the NDP have been by far the most important organizations of the working-class movement in Canada for many years. Yet they have never been its only components. Small community-based advocacy and activist groups, such as workers' centres that fight for the rights of non-unionized workers (Cranford and Ladd, 2003) and groups formed by unemployed workers and injured workers, are also part of the movement. A case can be made that the anti-poverty movement (see Chapter 4) is part of the working-class movement, at least insofar as it involves unemployed wage-earners. Although most distinct working-class neighbourhoods were profoundly disrupted by migration to growing suburbs and mass consumer culture during the years of the economic boom after World War II, there are still a few urban neighbourhoods where community associations and informal networks should be seen as belonging to the working-class movement. Informal and formal networks of activists exist to promote militancy and democracy and/or left-wing policies within unions; the Solidarity Caucus in British Columbia is the best contemporary example. "Flying squads"—groups of union members who engage in solidarity action to support workers on strike and other social justice struggles—have sometimes been distinct from unions themselves (Kuhling and Levant, 2006).

Main Political Issues Today

Today the working-class movement faces extraordinary challenges. The working class in Canada, as in other countries, has been under assault from the ruling class since the mid-1970s. Attacks by employers and governments shape this movement's political agenda.

THE EMPLOYERS' OFFENSIVE AND THE MOVEMENT

Beginning in the mid-1970s, employers went on the offensive to boost their profits and shift the balance of power in the workplace further in their favour. They have been quite successful in both the private sector and the public sector. Work has been extensively reorganized in ways that reduce the minimal degree of control that workers have over their jobs (Rinehart, 2005; Moody, 1997). Many workers have lost their jobs to "downsizing" and outsourcing. Real wages are stagnant. Employers are shifting away from offering full-time permanent jobs towards forms of precarious employment (such as fixed-term contracts and temporary positions) that rarely come with pensions or medical or dental benefits. Privatization and contracting-out have shrunk the percentage of workers employed in the public sector. It is not surprising, then, that the average rate of profit at the beginning of the twenty-first century actually surpassed the level of the boom years of the 1960s and early 1970s.

The working-class movement's key issues in the politics of the workplace arise in response to the employers' offensive. Some unions have accommodated to employers' demands and agreed to accept wage cuts and the loss of benefits or workplace rights in the hope that such concessions would save members' jobs—a top priority for all unions. Other unions have resisted demands for concessions, with varying degrees of success;[6] in some cases opposition to concessions has been a key union priority. For public sector unions, preventing further privatization, deregulation, and contracting-out of public services is paramount. For its part, the NDP leadership pays little attention to what employers do, since it, like most union leaders, accepts the classic social democratic division of labour between workplace politics (the domain of unions) and politics outside the workplace (the party's responsibility).

THE STATE AND THE MOVEMENT

State power has been central to the ruling class's efforts to reshape Canadian society along neoliberal lines (McBride and Shields, 1997). Governments at all levels have carried out neoliberal "reforms" to social policy (unemployment insurance, social assistance, health care, education, and other social services) and steered a neoliberal course with respect to labour and employment law and economic policy (monetary and fiscal policy, trade, and investment). State power has also been used extensively against unions, particularly in the public sector, in the form of legislated wage freezes or cuts, imposed contracts, and legislation that restricts the right to strike (Panitch and Swartz, 2003).

On this front, unions have made the defence of public health care a top priority. Recently, the protection of pensions from corporate attempts to reduce obligations to workers has become a key concern. Other priority issues include improvements to Employment Insurance; pay equity for women wage-earners; anti-scab legislation to prevent employers from using replacement workers (strike-breakers) during strikes and lockouts; opposition to state attacks on union rights; and stemming the tide of privatization, contracting-out, and deregulation in the public sector. Quebec sovereignty is a priority for many unions in Quebec.

OTHER ISSUES

In addition to the issues which become priorities, unions take positions on virtually every political issue of the day, from violence against women to climate change to war and foreign policy. However, it is easier for members concerned about an issue to get their union to adopt a policy on the subject than it is to make the union act on an issue, let alone make it a priority. Issues are most likely to become priorities for a union when they directly affect the union officialdom in a significant way (for example, a threat to remove the Rand Formula from labour law) than when they do not (such as the weakening of employment standards).[7]

Strategies

In taking action on issues of concern, the working-class movement uses a range of methods.

COLLECTIVE BARGAINING

Unions use the collective bargaining process to place demands on employers. The issues addressed in collective bargaining do not have to be limited to wages, paid vacations, hours of work, and the like. To give just a few examples, unionized university students who work on campuses as teaching assistants, research assistants, and lecturers have responded to rising tuition fees by bringing demands for fee rebates to the bargaining table; unions have won equal access to benefits for same-gender partners; and some unions have tabled demands for their employers to convert precarious and/or part-time jobs into permanent full-time positions. A critical factor affecting the ability of a union to force an employer to agree to union demands in collective bargaining is its power to strike (or at least credibly threaten to go on strike); recall that since the 1940s labour law has said that strikes are legal only as part of the collective bargaining process.

PARLIAMENTARY POLITICAL ACTION

Unions often put considerable effort into supporting a political party at election time. Changes to federal party finance legislation that took effect in 2004 have altered how unions support parties, above all the NDP, which no longer accepts donations by unions to its candidates, campaigns, or riding associations. What has not changed is union reliance on parliamentary politics as the main way to influence government. Union staff can take unpaid leave to work on an election campaign and union members can volunteer; many unions encourage their members and staff to devote time to the party supported by the union. Unions produce flyers, advertisements, websites, and other material designed to persuade unionists and members of their families to vote for a particular party, although the party may not be named explicitly. For example, in the 2006 federal election the CLC ran a campaign under the slogan "Better Choices." Its brochure did not explicitly name any party, while CUPE's "Vote Positive, Vote Public" brochure criticized the Liberals and Conservatives and praised the NDP.

Outside of election campaigns, the CLC, its provincial and local bodies, other labour centrals, and many unions use the conventional channels for attempting to influence governments, including lobbying, presenting briefs to committees, postcard campaigns, and the like. In Quebec, most of the labour officialdom believes that its close ties with the leadership of the PQ allow labour to advance its interests; when in government, the PQ has engaged in formal *concertation* (collaboration) with the leaders of unions and community organizations. Unions sometimes mount court challenges to pieces of legislation they oppose. Union financial support is a crucial source of funding for the Canadian Centre for Policy Alternatives, a think tank critical of neoliberal policies.

EXTRA-PARLIAMENTARY POLITICAL ACTION

The attacks by governments on workers and unions and the inability of the established methods of parliamentary political action to stop them have over the past three decades pushed the working-class movement to use methods that (except in Quebec) had all but vanished between the late 1940s and the mid-1970s.

The most common one is public protest in the streets: demonstrations, rallies, and marches. Often these are one-time-only affairs rather than part of escalating campaigns of action, and as such they represent a kind of highly visible mass lobbying of government. Protests of this type can also be a way for union officials to signal to their members that they are taking an issue seriously. Less often, such actions are undertaken as part of an ongoing mobilization, as in the case of the mass demonstrations that were part of the Ontario Days of Action of 1995–99. Public protest can also take place in support of an ongoing strike to express solidarity with the strikers and pressure a government or private employer to meet the strike's demands; for example, actions of this kind took place in support of the teachers' strike in British Columbia in October 2005. Unions have also mobilized members for demonstrations that they have organized in conjunction with other groups, or which they support, including global justice protests, student rallies against tuition increases, and anti-poverty actions. Symbolic action by unions (such as a rally or tightly regulated march) is much more common than militant mass direct action (such as taking to the streets without a permit or occupying a building).

Unions may also go on strike outside of collective bargaining to protest government actions. The CLC held a one-day general strike in 1976 against the federal government's wage control policy. Ontario teachers walked off the job for two weeks in 1997 in opposition to provincial legislation. Many of the Days of Action in Ontario involved work stoppages and protests on a Friday followed by large marches and rallies the following day. Quebec unions held a "Day of Disruption" in December 2003 that saw many workers strike. In British Columbia, strikes in solidarity with striking health care workers in 2004 and striking teachers in 2005 were also directed against the provincial Liberal government whose legislation led to both confrontations.

Evaluating the Movement's Efforts

Since the end of the long postwar economic boom in the mid-1970s and the beginning of the offensive by employers and governments against the working class—an offensive that has had particularly negative implications for women, people of colour, and others who face oppression distinct from the alienation and exploitation experienced by all wage-workers—the working-class movement's goals have been mainly defensive. The movement has generally opposed actions by employers and governments that would have negative effects on the working class. Although this resistance has been paramount, the movement has also sought to make some gains.

If we judge the movement in terms of its success in blocking the employers' agenda in the workplace and stopping neoliberalism (including CUFTA, NAFTA, and changes to unemployment insurance, social assistance, health care, education, employment legislation, and labour law), it clearly has not succeeded. Over time, employers and governments in Canada have been able to obtain most of their key objectives, spurring them to seek new, more ambitious goals. Neoliberal ideas—the private sector is better than the public sector, corporations should pay less tax, people should think of themselves as individual taxpayers rather than as citizens entitled to public services or members of the working class, to name only a few—have redefined "common sense" in Canadian society. This failure is not unique to Canada, but is shared—to significantly varying degrees—by working-class movements across the advanced capitalist countries of Europe, North America, and Asia.

That said, the movement's resistance has certainly not been futile, since sometimes it has fended off specific attacks or slowed the ruling-class offensive. For example, union opposition has made it more difficult for governments to shift the delivery of more health care services from the public sector to for-profit private firms. Resistance has inspired some people to refuse the neoliberal vision of how society should be organized and how people should live. Some unions have been able to make small gains in collective bargaining despite the unfavourable balance of forces they confront.

It is important to analyse why the movement has been relatively unsuccessful. A number of factors can be identified that, taken together, explain this record:

- A basic feature of capitalist societies is that the ruling class rules. Most of society's wealth and productive power is the private property of capitalists, and state power, including the law, operates in ways that serve to reproduce capitalism regardless of what political party holds office. As a result, the balance of power in society is more or less unfavourable to the working class, except in times of revolt or revolution.
- Since the end of the postwar boom in the mid-1970s, capitalists have been driven by falling profits and, even when profits are high, by the intensification of competitive pressures to act with determination in pursuit of their interests.
- Government in Canada is, at all levels, usually in the hands of politicians who not only accept the existing capitalist social order but are closely aligned with corporate interests. NDP governments have sometimes been less closely aligned than other governments, but they have never challenged neoliberalism.
- During the postwar boom, the working-class movement became permeated by complacency and bureaucratic conservatism. These were fostered by the relative ease of making economic gains for workers during the long boom years and the acceptance of "responsible" unions by most employers and governments. Critical perspectives on capitalism were marginalized. As a result, the movement was ill-prepared to understand the ruling-class offensive and neoliberalism, let alone develop adequate responses and an alternative vision.

- The changes in workplaces, communities, and households that have taken place over the past three decades as a result of the restructuring of society have further fragmented the working class, sapping the solidarity and unity on which the working-class movement depends (see Chapter 3 for more on the growing divide within the movement). Some examples: employees of one company often see the employees of another company in the same industry as competitors, not potential allies; better-off workers often look down on poorer workers, who in turn often resent them; people with jobs may treat the unemployed as responsible for their own fate; citizens often see new immigrants not as fellow workers but as a burden on taxpayers, even though this is factually incorrect.
- Since the mid-1970s, most of the movement has not done everything possible within the difficult circumstances in which it has found itself to resist hostile employers and governments. For example, the stubborn acceptance by unions of legal restrictions on when and how workers are allowed to go on strike has weakened the effectiveness of strikes; mass picketing and sympathy strikes (strikes in support of another strike), which helped win union victories in the 1940s, are now rare. Reliance on parliamentary politics in general and the NDP in particular has also been a barrier to mobilizing the most effective resistance possible.

The last of these factors raises another question: why has the movement so often stuck with strategies and tactics that have proven to be ineffective? One reason is that the union officialdom (especially full-time officials) usually opposes methods of action that fall outside the law. This is not just a matter of the ideology of those who lead the movement. The officialdom is a distinct social layer or group whose ultimate priority is preserving stable union institutions and bargaining relationships with employers. Officials face sanctions (which can include fines or imprisonment) when they or the members they represent violate labour law. Another reason for the persistence of ineffective methods is that there are few activists promoting an alternative approach for the movement that recognizes that mass direct action, working-class solidarity, and grassroots participatory democracy are key to winning victories.[8]

Nevertheless, many activists do feel the movement needs change. One indication of this came at the 2005 CLC convention, where outsider Carol Wall—who argued that "Lobbying government is important but we need to mobilize our members if we want to be a force for change in society"—won 37 per cent of delegates' votes when she ran against incumbent president Ken Georgetti, who was backed by the leaders of all major unions except the CUPW (Levant, 2005). Whether or not supporters of change grow stronger and become organized will influence the future of the working-class movement—something that matters a great deal to most people in Canada, whether or not they appreciate it.

Notes

1. Thanks to Alan Sears for comments on a draft of this chapter.

2. What goes on in households, where people do unpaid work, is also political, as feminists have long argued. However, the politics of the family and unpaid work in the home are beyond the scope of this chapter.

3. Rational choice theory is arguably a conservative theoretical perspective that "has sought to replicate the version of the scientific method (mathematical models and all) that it sees at work within economics" (Ollman: 2000, 555). Economics is the most conservative of social science disciplines, completely dominated by one perspective, neoclassical theory. The most notable attempt by left-wing scholars to use rational choice theory is "Analytical Marxism" (for a sampling, see Roemer, 1986; for a critique, see Roberts, 1996).

4. Neither of these statistics is an exact measurement of the percentage of workers in paid employment who are in unions. The non-agricultural paid workforce excludes wage-earners in agriculture (who are barred from unionizing in many provinces). The total civilian labour force includes higher level managers and others who are not part of the working class.

5. This use of the concept of social movement unionism differs from that of many writers on unions, who use it to refer to what I call mobilization unionism.

6. For examples, see Beck *et al.*, 2005; Camfield, 2006; and Kuhling, 2002.

7. It is arguable that the movement's priorities have neglected some issues of vital importance to workers (for example, the reorganization of workplaces and racism).

8. See Camfield, 2000 and 2006; and Brennan, 2005. The Solidarity Caucus in British Columbia is a rare example of an organized group of activists that promotes social movement unionism—see <http://www.solidaritycaucus.org>.

References and Further Reading

Akyeampong, Ernest B. 2004. "The Union Movement in Transition." *Perspectives on Labour and Income*. Statistics Canada Catalogue no. 75-001-XIE 5.8 (August): 5–13.

Akyeampong, Ernest B. 2005. "Fact Sheet on Unionization." *Perspectives on Labour and Income*. Statistics Canada Catalogue no. 75-001-XIE 6.8 (August): 18–42.

Allen, Bruce. 2006. "Inside the CAW Jacket." *New Socialist* 57 (July–August): 18–20. <http://www.newsocialist.org/mag-pdfs/NewSocialist-Issue57.pdf>.

Beck, Kaili, *et al.* 2005. *Mine Mill Fights Back: Mine Mill/CAW Local 598 Strike 2000–2001 Sudbury*. Sudbury: Mine Mill/CAW Local 598.

Bédard, Marie-Ève. 2005. "Union Membership in Canada—January 1, 2005." <http://www.hrsdc.gc.ca/en/lp/wid/union_membership.shtml>.

Black, Errol, and Jim Silver. 2001. *Building a Better World: An Introduction to Trade Unionism in Canada*. Halifax: Fernwood.

Brennan, Barry. 2005. "Canadian Labour Today: Partial Successes, Real Challenges." *Monthly Review* 57(2): 46–61.

Briskin, Linda. 2003. "The Equity Project in Canadian Unions: Confronting the Challenge of Restructuring and Globalisation." In Fiona Colgan and Sue Ledwith (eds.), *Gender, Diversity and Trade Unions: International Perspectives*. New York: Taylor and Francis. 28–47.

Camfield, David. 2000. "Assessing Resistance in Harris's Ontario, 1995–1999." In Mike Burke, Colin Mooers, and John Shields (eds.), *Restructuring and Resistance: Canadian Public Policy in an Age of Global Capitalism*. Halifax: Fernwood. 306–17.

Camfield, David. 2006. "Neoliberalism and Working-Class Resistance in British Columbia: The Hospital Employees' Union Struggle, 2002–2004." *Labour/Le Travail* 57 (Spring): 9–41.

Camfield, David. Forthcoming. "Renewal in Canadian Public Sector Unions: Neoliberalism and Union Praxis." *Relations industrielles/Industrial Relations.*

CAW (Canadian Auto Workers). "Working-Class Politics in the 21st Century: CAW Taskforce Overview." n.d. [1999]. <http://www.caw.ca/crisis1/index.asp>.

Cranford, Cynthia J., and Deena Ladd. 2003. "Community Unionism: Organizing for Fair Employment in Canada." *Just Labour* 3: 46–59. <http://www.justlabour.yorku.ca/volume3/pdfs/cranford.pdf>.

Gindin, Sam. 1995. *The Canadian Auto Workers: The Birth and Transformation of a Union*. Toronto: James Lorimer.

Gindin, Sam, and Jim Stanford. 2003. "Canadian Labour and the Political Economy of Transformation." In Wallace Clement and Leah F. Vosko (eds.), *Changing Canada: Political Economy as Transformation*. Montreal and Kingston: McGill-Queen's University Press. 422–42.

Harvey, David. 2005. *A Brief History of Neoliberalism*. Oxford: Oxford University Press.

Heron, Craig. 1996. *The Canadian Labour Movement: A Short History*. 2nd ed. Toronto: James Lorimer.

Hyman, Richard. 1975. *Industrial Relations: A Marxist Introduction*. London: Macmillan.

Jackson, Andrew. 2005. *Work and Labour in Canada: Critical Issues*. Toronto: Canadian Scholars' Press.

Kuhling, Clarice. 2002. "How CUPE 3903 Struck and Won." *Just Labour* 1: 77–85. <http://www.justlabour.yorku.ca/volume1/pdfs/jl_kuhling.pdf>.

Kuhling, Clarice, and Alex Levant. 2006. "Political Deskilling/Reskilling: Flying Squads and the Crisis of Working Class Consciousness/Self-Organization." In Caelie Frampton, Gary Kinsman, Andrew Thompson and Kate Tilleczek (eds.), *Sociology for Changing the World*. Halifax: Fernwood. 209–29.

Kumar, Pradeep, and Christopher Schenk. 2006. *Paths to Union Renewal: Canadian Experiences*. Peterborough: Broadview, Garamond, and the Canadian Centre for Policy Alternatives.

Levant, Alex. 2005. "Canadian Labour Congress Convention 2005." *New Socialist* 53 (September–October). <http://newsocialist.org/newsite/index.php?id=479>.

McBride, Stephen, and John Shields. 1997. *Dismantling a Nation: The Transition to Corporate Rule in Canada*. 2nd ed. Halifax: Fernwood.

McNally, David. 2000. "Globalization, Trade Pacts, and Migrant Workers: Rethinking the Politics of Working-Class Resistance." In Mike Burke, Colin Mooers, and John Shields (eds.), *Restructuring and Resistance: Canadian Public Policy in an Age of Global Capitalism*. Halifax: Fernwood. 262–75.

McNally, David. 2002. *Another World is Possible: Globalization and Anti-Capitalism*. Winnipeg: Arbeiter Ring.

Moody, Kim. 1997. *Workers in a Lean World: Unions in the International Economy*. London and New York: Verso.

Murray, Gregor. 2002. "Unions in Canada: Strategic Renewal, Strategic Conundrums." In Peter Fairbrother and Gerard Griffin (eds.), *Changing Prospects for Trade Unionism: Comparisons Between Six Countries*. London and New York: Continuum. 93–136.

Ollman, Bertell. 2000. "What is Political Science? What Should it Be?" *New Political Science* 22(4): 553–62.

Palmer, Bryan D. 1987. *Solidarity: The Rise and Fall of an Opposition in British Columbia*. Vancouver: New Star.

Palmer, Bryan D. 1992. *Working-Class Experience: Rethinking the History of Canadian Labour, 1800–1991*. Toronto: McClelland and Stewart.

Panitch, Leo, and Donald Swartz. 2003. *From Consent to Coercion: The Assault on Trade Union Freedoms*. 3rd ed. Aurora: Garamond.

Rapaport, David. 1999. *Beyond Service: The 1996 OPSEU Strike Against the Harris Government in Ontario*. Montreal and Kingston: McGill-Queen's University Press.

Reshef, Yonatan, and Sandra Rastin. 2003. *Unions in the Time of Revolution: Government Restructuring in Alberta and Ontario*. Toronto: University of Toronto Press.

Rinehart, James. 2005. *The Tyranny of Work: Alienation and the Labour Process*. 5th ed. Toronto: Nelson.

Roberts, Marcus. 1996. *Analytical Marxism: A Critique*. London: Verso.

Roemer, John (Ed.). 1986. *Analytical Marxism*. Cambridge: Cambridge University Press.

Saad-Filho, Alfred, and Deborah Johnston. 2005. "Introduction." In Alfred Saad-Filho and Deborah Johnston (eds.), *Neoliberalism: A Critical Reader*. London and Ann Arbor: Pluto. 1–6.

Swimmer, Gene (Ed.). 2001. *Public-Sector Labour Relations in an Era of Restraint and Restructuring*. Don Mills: Oxford University Press.

Wilmot, Sheila. 2005. *Taking Responsibility, Taking Direction: White Anti-Racism in Canada*. Winnipeg: Arbeiter Ring.

THREE

Organized Labour in Canadian Politics: Hugging the Middle or Pushing the Margins?

Charlotte Yates

The 2006 winter federal election underscored the increasingly contradictory relationship of organized labour to Canadian politics. Its tone was set early when, in December 2005, Buzz Hargrove, leader of the CAW, sent shock waves through the Canadian media, labour supporters, and analysts with the announcement that his union was recommending to its members that they vote Liberal, except in ridings it designated as winnable by the NDP. Of even greater symbolic significance was Hargrove's presentation of a CAW jacket to Liberal Leader Paul Martin and photos of a hug between the two men. Even though the CAW had recommended strategic voting in the previous election, and had a long history of uneasy relations with the NDP, these events suggested a shift in CAW partisan politics and revealed the depth of ambiguity in labour politics in Canada more generally.

Although many unions continued their long-standing policy of support for the NDP during the 2005–06 election campaign, it would be a mistake to see the CAW's recommendation for strategic voting as an outlier political strategy among Canadian unions. Many, most notably those in the construction industry, have a history of support for the Liberal Party. Moreover, Canadian election studies have long revealed a paradox in union/working-class voting patterns and electoral behaviour. Unions that have affiliated with the NDP increase the likelihood that their members will vote NDP, yet nonetheless, members of affiliated unions continue to show greater support for the Liberal party than for the NDP (Archer and Whitehorn, 1993). It is also common knowledge that when in power, NDP governments have been unable and sometimes unwilling to deliver on many of the pledges they made to their supporters. Recently, union political activism has been undermined by the lack of a unifying alternative vision for the future of political and economic life that wrestles with the problems of growing economic inequality and diversity among the working class.

Yet, as labour veers towards centrist politics with no alternative vision of the future, there is also growing evidence of workplace militancy and the politicization of strikes by unions. In 2004, over 40,000 hospital and long-term care facility health care workers in British Columbia, most of whom were women of colour and members of the Hospital Employees' Union (HEU), went on strike to protest government cutbacks; they mobilized thousands of other workers in a one-day strike. A year later, 38,000 teachers in the same province engaged in a two-week illegal strike to demand improved wages as well as a series of improvements to the public education system. Led by Jinny Sims, an immigrant from India and a teacher, this union withstood fines and threats of imprisonment whilst mobilizing tens of thousands of other workers in support actions (Sims, 2006). Then in the summer of 2005, a strike at Tyson meatpacking plant in Brooks, Alberta—where 60 per cent of the workforce were immigrants, a large number of them Sudanese—saw racial tensions rise. While immigrants walked the picket line to demand basic human rights, the provincial government refused to uphold basic labour standards and some in the community disparaged striking immigrants, half hoping that the plant would close and that immigrants would be forced to move out of this largely white, rural Alberta community. Finally, in the fall of 2005 CBC producers, radio, and television celebrities walked off the job to protest contracting out; they mobilized nascent nationalism among Canadians in support of national public broadcasting. Evidence of such militancy, as well as the issues over which workers are striking, point to a politicization of the everyday worklife of workers as well as a shift within the labour movement in which workers and unions are at the forefront of working-class politics.

These events speak to the complexity of understanding labour's engagement with politics in the present period. But they also speak to a shift in militancy among unionized workers and the potential growing divisions within the working class. This chapter seeks to shed light on these developments, providing readers with an explanation for recent shifts in organized labour's intervention in Canadian politics as well as growing schisms within the labour movement.

The chapter makes two arguments. Under pressure of neoliberalism, operating in a climate hostile to unions, the divide between both private and public sector unions and the new and old working class has widened. Older industrial unions increasingly revert to economistic tendencies as they fight to protect existing membership gains from encroachment by capital. These once staunch defenders of socialist or social democratic alternatives find themselves engaged in a non-ideological politics of pragmatism. Conversely, public sector unions find their workplace activism increasingly politicized. Strikes and collective bargaining force public sector unions up against the state's neoliberal agenda of retrenchment of the public sphere and restoration of market forces in the allocation of resources. Politicized workplace activism by public sector unions becomes intermingled with a democratic equality politics that speaks to memberships that are overwhelmingly women aware of the dangers of dismantling of the welfare state for women as clients, workers, and mothers. Unions also find themselves pulled between the defensive politics of older, long-standing union members, most of whom are men, and a more radical, mobilized politics of equality-seeking groups, involving more racialized minorities and women. I argue that these shifts explain the changing nature of labour's engagement in politics. A second line of argument looks at the ways in which the lack of articulated alternatives to capitalism feed into labour's non-ideological politics and its incapacity to build on growing workplace militancy to produce a new, more democratic radical politics. The inability of the labour movement to wrestle with these political shortcomings endangers its long-term viability and capacity for revitalization through the representation of emerging workforces.

To explore these dimensions of the politics of labour, I begin with a brief discussion of why unions have traditionally been seen as the "natural" ally of socialist or social democratic politics. Within this section I offer a definition of politics that is broad enough to encompass a range of activities, including but not focused exclusively on party politics. This is followed by a brief history of organized labour's involvement in politics in Canada. These early sections set the stage for the core of the chapter, which is laid out in three sections. The first describes the political challenges facing labour and its responses to the neoliberal climate and discourse of politics. The next discusses the growing diversity of the Canadian labour force and under what conditions a politics of diversity has been embraced by certain sections of the labour movement. Finally, I turn to the implications of a lack of alternative political vision for labour politics and the dangers of non-ideological politics for the long-term viability of the labour movement.

Labour and Politics: An Historical Overview

Since the late nineteenth century, working people have organized their own political parties to redress the inequities and indignities of work and life in a capitalist economy. In reaction to their exclusion from the bourgeois politics of property ownership and privilege that dominated nineteenth-century political parties, workers formed socialist, communist, and social democratic parties to gain representation in and influence the political process. These political parties distinguished themselves with their mass membership base, their critique of exploitation under capitalism and oppression by the state, and their advocacy of the transformation of the capitalist system, whether through reformist electoral politics or violent overthrow of existing governments. In many advanced industrialized economies, especially in Europe where union membership was high and central coordination of union political activism was well developed, socialist and social democratic parties wielded considerable power, often times dominating the post-World War II state and political landscape.

Yet, if the working class was seen by many political economists as at the vanguard of transformation, if not abolition, of capitalism, unions as well as socialist and social democratic political parties occupy a more contradictory position. As representatives of workers, unions often find themselves at the forefront of struggles for systemic and structural change as they seek redress to issues as wide-ranging as poverty and dangerous working conditions to lack of access to higher education. The postwar Keynesian welfare state throughout the Western world was built in part in response to these pressures by the organized working class. Yet, unions are also tied to the perpetuation of capitalism and the labour-management relationship. They represent the interests of working people whose livelihood depends upon capital investment and profits. These constraints curb the enthusiasm of organized labour for radical solutions to political economic problems.

Similar structural limits operate on working-class political parties. Social democratic parties support reform of capitalist economic structures and associated social and political practices, yet are constrained by their place in capitalist economies. Adam Prezeworski (1986) argues that the primacy of private ownership of productive assets and the ongoing dependence of nation-states upon private investment constrains the willingness and capacity of social democratic governments to pursue policies that are adverse to the interests of capitalists. Under conditions of globalization, these constraints on social democratic or socialist political parties are even greater, as international institutions place pressure on governments to open their borders and conform to dominant policy practices (Teeple, 2000: 122–27).

In Canada, class politics has always been overshadowed by the politics of regionalism, language, and nationhood (Brodie and Jenson, 1988). The ideological and political foundations for socialist politics were therefore disarticulated, the result of which was a distinctively Canadian form of labour politics. Weaker organizationally than their European counterparts and shaped by the regional political economy that divided Canada, left-wing politics in Canada was fragmented, and unions learned early to forge alliances with other social groups in order to wield political power. After a brief period of syndicalist politics around World War I, it was the Depression of the 1930s that laid the conditions for a more sustained socialist politics among Canadian workers and their allies. The Communist Party played a critical role in organizing workers into unions throughout Canada in the 1930s and 1940s; it also played a decisive role in political debate within the labour movement until the Cold War.

The only lasting left-wing political alternative formed out of this period was the CCF, which was formed in 1932 out of an alliance of farmer groups, unions, and progressive academics. Initially espousing a socialist agenda, the CCF quickly moderated its political stance and advocated a blend of populist, farmer cooperative politics with social democratic state intervention in the economy to achieve redistribution of political and economic power. The party experienced a surge of success during World War II. In 1943, it became the official opposition in Ontario and in 1944 formed the government of Saskatchewan, with Tommy Douglas as premier. The CCF remained in power in Saskatchewan from 1944 until 1964, introducing the first public medicare program in Canada and being the first government to accord public sector workers the right to organize into unions and strike. But the Cold War took its toll. The 1958 federal election, when the CCF elected only eight MPs, marked a turning point for the party. This coincided with a period of reorganization of the Canadian labour movement which in 1956 forged an alliance between two competing national federations of labour to create the Canadian Labour Congress (CLC) in 1956. This merger in part reflected a political shift within unions and a greater willingness among unions to follow the British and European traditions of affiliation with a political party. In 1958, the CCF and the newly formed CLC initiated a three-year period of negotiation, at the end of which was the formation of the NDP in 1961 (Avakumovic, 1978; Horowitz, 1968). Unions were given a privileged position within party affairs, through special affiliation procedures, representation on party bodies, and eventually informal guarantees of a position on the party executive.

During this same period, many unions, especially the growing industrial unions, established political action committees in recognition of the new-found importance attached to ongoing political engagement by unions, particularly to partisan activities. The NDP won power from 1969–77 in Manitoba, resumed power in Saskatchewan in 1971 until 1982, and won the 1972 election in British Columbia. Through the 1960s and 1970s, the NDP advocated expansion of the welfare state, the use of public ownership to pursue Canada's national economic interests, and the use of the tax system to redistribute wealth from the rich to the poor.

Organized labour, in particular large industrial unions such as the USWA, the meatpackers, and the UAW–Canada,[1] had greatly increased their partisan influence with the creation of the NDP. Yet, the history of union-party relations continued to be fraught with tension. The NDP saw itself as an alliance of labour, farmers, and progressively minded liberals and resisted granting unions too much control over party decision-making. For their part, many in the labour movement felt that their financial and organizational support for the NDP, especially during election times when unions would donate staff time and office resources as well as cash, should grant them even greater leverage over party decisions and policy. This tension first came to a head in the late 1960s when a left-wing group within the NDP, called the Waffle, urged the NDP to adopt a more radical socialist position that emphasized democracy and greater national control over the Canadian economy. Included in the broad sweep of the Waffle's nationalist criticisms was domination of the Canadian labour movement by American-based international unions, which had a record of weak internal union democracy for their Canadian components. In taking aim at international industrial unions, the Waffle also took on the NDP's most stalwart union supporters. At the same time, Waffle criticisms resonated with the newly emerging public sector unions that saw in the international unions a lack of democracy and an unwillingness to advance the cause of national control over the economy. In the end, the NDP threw the Waffle out of the party in 1972 and, in so doing, confirmed their commitment to their allies in the labour movement (Brodie and Jenson, 1988; Hackett, 1980). This was merely the first of many internal battles between the party and its union constituency as the NDP tried to maintain its relative autonomy from the unions while the unions sought to increase their political leverage.

Although much scholarly attention has been paid to the elaboration of union-CCF/NDP relations, little attention has been paid to union relations with the Liberal Party. Electoral studies have repeatedly shown that union members, while more likely to vote NDP than non-union workers, are most likely to vote Liberal in federal elections. Within the labour movement, industrial unions, especially the USWA, tended to foster the closest relationship with the NDP, whereas construction and public sector unions were more ambivalent in their political alliances. The Liberal Party's support among workers was built when national Liberal governments constructed the welfare state: Mackenzie King introduced unemployment insurance; Lester Pearson introduced the Canada Pension Plan as well as national medicare; and Pierre Trudeau embraced multiculturalism and human rights, policies with some appeal to new immigrants, many of whom were workers. Notwithstanding the fact that many of these policies were first articulated by the NDP, and strongly supported by organized labour, the repeated translation of these ideas into policy by Liberal governments built this party long-standing support among working people. Liberal representatives in ridings where unions were especially powerful, such as Paul Martin Sr. in Windsor, built close relations with organized labour, often championing their rights and ensuring a flow of government monies to boost local economies. The almost uninterrupted tenure of the Liberal Party as government of Canada in the postwar years cemented these ties. The Liberal Party also has been able to attract a disproportionate level of electoral support from youth and immigrants, particularly such ethnic groups as the Italian community. As distinct immigrant groups also tend to be clustered in certain types of employment, these alliances with the Liberal Party often also find expression in union-Liberal party ties.

Although union-party alliances differ in several of the provinces, the most distinctive pattern has emerged in Quebec where unions became ardent supporters of nationalist politics, and in particular the PQ. Workplaces were fertile ground for nationalist politics in the postwar period as American and Canadian multinational firms denied Québécois workers the right to speak French in the workplace, paid them substandard wages, and prevented promotions of Québécois workers. Years of repression of union activities by the national and Quebec state fed workers' support for more radical politics. It was therefore not surprising that many unions were key players in the formation of the PQ in 1968 and that workers and their unions were instrumental in securing the party's victory in 1976. The introduction of radical new labour laws, including anti-scab legislation, combined with legislative protection of the right to use French in the workplace, consolidated labour's support for the PQ. Despite the strains that emerged between nationalist and social democratic goals, a considerable number of unions and workers in Quebec see nationalism and separatism as a crucial first step towards other political economic improvements in that province (McRoberts, 1988).

Yet, unlike unions in Europe for which partisan activity became the primary union political strategy, the failure of worker-friendly parties to win elections outside of a few western provinces and Quebec meant that labour could not possibly put all its political eggs in one basket. From the early days of "cap-in-hand" representations by unions to elected national and provincial elected representatives, unions have engaged in lobbying for policies favourable to workers and their families. Anticipated benefits from lobbying caused many unions to keep an arm's length from the NDP and cultivate closer relationships with individuals within the governing party, namely, the Liberals.

Organized labour's lobbying strategies thus developed hand-in-hand with the consolidation of the Liberal Party's hold over national politics in the postwar period. Labour federations at both the national and provincial levels, such as the CLC, were especially prominent in lobbying activities, mandated as they were by constituent unions to advance labour's interests in the political arena between elections. Individual unions would periodically engage in direct lobbying over a policy or bill that had particular effects on its membership, such as the UAW's role in the Autopact, a trade agreement between Canada and the US that freed movement of automotive parts and vehicles across the Canada-US border in exchange for certain guarantees of investment in Canada and Canadian vehicle content. Yet, it was the CLC that held regular annual meetings with the prime minister and senior cabinet ministers to lay out labour's political demands. Organized labour's political pressure was critical for securing such national social policies as unemployment insurance, public pensions, medicare, and universalistic social welfare benefits (Yates, 1990). Through the postwar period, the CLC and a handful of larger unions made representations to royal commissions and provincial task forces, and the CLC nominated representatives to a number of government advisory boards and commissions, such as the Unemployment Insurance Advisory Committee. Overall, labour's lobbying efforts secured organized labour "a junior insider role in the policy process" (Jackson and Baldwin, 2005: 3).

These patterns of labour's engagement in politics remained relatively stable and somewhat successful until the mid 1970s. The politics of organized labour tended to be dominated by Anglo-Saxon male industrial unionists who advanced moderate political agendas in fear of alienating governments of the day. By the 1970s, however, the labour movement like the rest of society became subject to pushes from below and outside for the embrace of a more radical politics. The women's movement demanded access to some of the better, exclusively male jobs (Women into Stelco), taking on union rules and practices that protected these jobs for men (Corman *et al.*, 1993; Briskin and McDermott, 1993); the civil rights movement similarly found its mark in the labour movement as Mexican farm workers under Cesar Chavez and African Americans demanded basic human and union rights as well as access to good union jobs. In this way, organized labour began to be pushed to the left by its own rank and file as well as broader social developments.

Labour was also pushed by the changing actions of government, beginning in the mid 1970s. Amid growing concerns about rising inflation and declining productivity, the federal Liberal government imposed wage and price controls in 1975, blaming rising wages for the upward spiral of inflation. Wage controls kept wages below the rate of inflation, thus forcing workers to bear the brunt of government attempts to rebalance the economy (Maslove and Swimmer, 1980). Organized labour fought back. The CLC and a number of individual unions cut off all meetings with government, therefore signaling that lobbying could only fail in such a hostile climate to labour. Unions mobilized tens of thousands of workers in marches on Parliament Hill to protest wage controls, while a number of unions went on strike to resist the imposition of wage controls through collective bargaining (Yates, 1993: 177–81).

Overall, then, the 1970s saw a significant increase in the militancy of organized labour's political strategies, with a return to the use of the strike and workplace action for political purposes. This strategic shift carried into provincial politics but with much different results. By the late 1970s, unions in Ontario had begun to extend their organizational reach into a new set of workplaces in which a growing number of women worked. What they were not prepared for was the tremendous employer hostility to unionization found in these workplaces. Perhaps as surprising to the union movement as employer hostility was the militancy of women workers and their willingness to engage in strike action to defend their claims. Strikes at Fleck Manufacturing and Radio Shack, and a little later at Eaton's department store, challenged union views of women as docile, in need of protection, and reluctant union members. Under growing pressure, the Ontario provincial government introduced legislative improvements that included protection of automatic dues check-off, restrictions on strike-breaking activities by employers, and improved health and safety legislation (Walters, 1983). The 1970s was also a decade of heightened labour militancy in Quebec, which culminated in the election of the PQ in 1976.

Militancy in the 1970s gave way to crisis and retrenchment in the 1980s (Jenson and Mahon, 1993). In early 1981, Canada entered into a deep recession with double digit unemployment, inflation, and interest rates. As factories closed and working-class families lost their houses, wages, and benefits, union rules governing work and employment relations were blamed for contributing to Canada's high costs of production, declining competitiveness, and high rates of unemployment. Governments of all stripes exhorted Canadians to tighten their belts in a collective effort to share the pain of restraint needed to turn around the economic crisis. The federal and provincial governments introduced restraint packages that limited or rolled back wage increases for public servants and unilaterally imposed collective agreements. Governments also embarked on a dramatic restructuring process aimed at reducing costs, seen in program closures, contracting out, and privatization (Panitch and Swartz, 2003). These government actions fed the overall climate of crisis to which private employers responded with demands for concessions from unions and workers and heightened resistance to unionization.

Perhaps what would prove the most significant policy response to the growing economic crisis and subsequent globalization of the economy was the federal Liberal government's appointment in 1982 of Donald MacDonald to head the Royal Commission on the Economic Union and Development Prospects for Canada (otherwise known as the MacDonald Commission) which was charged with devising a new plan for Canada's economic development. Before the Commission could deliver its report, the federal Liberal government was replaced in 1984 by a majority Progressive Conservative government under the leadership of Brian Mulroney. Committed to opening up the economy to market forces, reducing the role of government, and balancing the budget, Mulroney's government marked the shift federally to neoliberal policy. The report issued by the MacDonald Commission buttressed the government's goals for economic development, as it recommended that the only way forward for Canada was the negotiation of free trade with the US. The federal government moved quickly to negotiate such a deal, and in 1988 the federal election was fought primarily over whether Canadians supported free trade or not (Cameron and Watkins, 1993). The re-election of the Progressive Conservative federal government was seen as an endorsement of free trade, and so began more than a decade of neoliberal policy re-orientation in Canada.

The 1980s marked an important turning point in the politics of labour in Canada. The recession of 1981–83 sharpened the conflict between labour and management and highlighted the lengths to which governments would go to appease corporate power at the expense of individual Canadian consumers and workers. Although by the mid 1980s the economy had recovered in terms of rates of growth, high rates of unemployment persisted, real wages fell throughout the 1980s, and economic restructuring by companies and governments continued unabated (Burke and Shields, 2000). The late 1970s return by unions to militancy persisted. In 1981, the Canadian labour movement led a mass protest of 100,000 workers and citizens to Parliament Hill to protest high interest rates. Public sector union strikes to protest the end to free collective bargaining in the public sector were met by heavy fines and in some cases union leader imprisonment. In response to the announcement of several factory closures beginning in 1980, Canadian members of the UAW occupied factories and engaged in sit-downs to demand better severance, advance notice of plant closures, and government action to protect workers against the ravages of high unemployment and widespread recession (Yates, 1993: 200–01). In British Columbia in 1983, the Social Credit government introduced 26 bills that attacked the rights of unions and stripped away all but the bare essentials of such institutions as the Human Rights Commission. A coalition of unions, social movements, and citizen groups responded by organizing Operation Solidarity with the goal of using a general strike to force the government to retract these bills. Widespread demonstrations and strikes seemed to promise a new day of worker-citizen coalition and power. But the end to the story of Operation Solidarity pointed to tensions everywhere within the labour movement and in its alliances with other progressive social movements. On the verge of a general strike in 1983, key labour leaders negotiated a settlement, winning the withdrawal of some of the worst changes to labour law but leaving unchanged many of the attacks on human rights and social welfare. Labour had sold out its allies (Palmer, 1987).

Events in British Columbia and elsewhere also pointed to growing divisions between private and public sector unions. Governments across the country restricted free collective bargaining for their public sector employees, imposed wage restraints, and meted out heavy punishments, ranging from jail terms to heavy fines, for those public sector unions and labour leaders that defied these restrictions (Panitch and Swartz, 2003). Governments, supported by policy think tanks such as the C.D. Howe Institute, rationalized these restrictions as necessary given the need to roll back the public sector, which acted as a drag on economic recovery and competitiveness. Public sector workers were painted as privileged, and often lazy, due to their lack of exposure to the vicissitudes of competitive market forces and their greater job security than workers in the private sector. Public sector unions decried these attacks on the rights of labour and as harbingers of government retrenchment of the state's commitment to social welfare and economic regulation. But many private sector unions sympathized with arguments about the privileged status of public sector workers; they felt that public sector unions should accept government-imposed restrictions as part of the collective pain of economic recovery. They saw no alternative but to cooperate with management in concessionary bargaining, hoping that this would secure their jobs and hold on to some of what they had negotiated over the years (Gindin and Stanford, 2003).

Overlaying the growing tensions between public and private sector unions, and between concessionary bargaining and militant opposition to neoliberal restructuring, were strains between national and international unions. American unions were in a highly defensive position in the 1980s, faced as they were with plummeting national union density rates (proportion of the workforce who are members of a union), vicious anti-unionism from the Reagan Republican government, and a lack of labour leadership. Many Canadian workers, represented by both national and international unions, bristled at the influence of American policy on Canadian unions through the international unions. Moreover, in the early 1980s many Canadian workers and unions articulated a Canadian-made version of the economic future in which the state would continue to play a role in health and social welfare and in the economy through active labour market and industrial policy. These policy and ideological differences manifested themselves between as well as within unions. The most decisive breach over strategic differences developed between the Canadian and American sections of the UAW. Since 1980, auto workers faced mounting pressure for concessions as North American automakers fought to survive competition from off-shore producers, in particular the Japanese. Concessions included wage give-backs, loss of cost-of-living allowances, cutbacks in benefits including days off, changes to work rules, and the breakdown of company-wide bargaining in favour of local bargaining. The effects of these concessions were quickly felt in conflicts between workers, disillusionment with a union that would not protect its members, and competition between different local branches of the union as companies pitted one local against another in their bid to drive down wages, benefits, and restrictive work rules. Under the leadership of Bob White, Canadian auto workers decided to fight back against concessionary bargaining, a fight that pitted them against automotive companies as well as their own international union. After months of tense negotiations and American union attempts to pressure Canadian workers into accepting concessions, Bob White and his supporters "wrapped themselves in the Canadian flag" and fought back successfully against concessions, while simultaneously advocating a new industrial policy for the auto industry. The immediate outcome of these struggles was the split in 1984 of the Canadian branch of the UAW from its American parent union to form a new national Canadian Auto Workers Union (CAW). The CAW quickly became the darling of the media, a potent symbol of worker militancy and national determination, and a magnet for disgruntled workers throughout the Canadian labour movement (Yates, 1993).

It was in this context of growing militancy and a determination to fight back against what unions dubbed "the corporate agenda" of neoliberal restructuring that unions opposed the free trade agreement. And it was the federal election fought over this issue that opened up the cracks in the relationship between the NDP and organized labour (Whitehorn, 1993: ch. 8). As the free trade debate heated up between 1986 and 1988, a new coalition of labour and social activists, nationalists, and environmentalists, entitled the Pro-Canada Network, was formed to put forward an alternative industrial policy in which governments would continue to play important roles in regulating the economy and protecting Canadians. Bob White was one of several labour leaders who allied themselves with this group, seeing coalitions with social movements as critical to labour's politics. During the federal election, two dynamics strained relations between the NDP and parts of organized labour. First, the NDP was outflanked by the Liberal Party, which presented itself as the true opponent of free trade. Secondly, political parties often took the back seat in public debates over free trade, with Bob White, leader of the CAW, often usurping the role of the NDP as the spokesperson for opponents to free trade. To many, the NDP's failure to focus their campaign on free trade was evidence that it was no longer capable of articulating the alternatives to neoliberalism demanded by workers and their unions. The victory of the Progressive Conservatives and the free trade deal marked a significant shift in Canadian politics in favour of neoliberalism, the primacy of the market, and greater vulnerability to the influence of American policies. Canadian governments were more restricted than ever in their capacity to shape the economy.

By the end of the 1980s, labour politics looked considerably different than it had in much of the postwar period. The Canadian labour movement was increasingly internally divided along public-private and national-international lines as well as over whether militancy or cooperation with management should be the primary strategic response to restructuring. Many governments across Canada went on the attack against unions and froze them out of the policy process. While the early 1980s saw many among organized labour continue their militant strategies in the face of corporate and government attacks, by the end of the decade strike rates were down in Canada, many unions were engaged in partnership arrangements with employers, and unions had given up hope that an alternative to free trade and continued restructuring of the welfare state and labour-management relations was possible. These tensions and difficulties were only compounded when Canada entered into another deep recession from 1990 to 1993 during which unemployment skyrocketed, working poverty grew, and a pervasive sense of risk and uncertainty settled into the Canadian psyche. This brings us to the discussion of contemporary labour and politics.

Political-Economic Challenges to the Labour Movement: The 1990s and Beyond

The 1990s revealed a different type of economy, both in Canada and abroad. Begun in deep recession, and followed by more than a decade of unprecedented levels of growth, this decade marked the triumph of capitalism, symbolically represented by the tearing down of the Berlin Wall in 1990. This was a different capitalism than the one that had dominated Canada in the postwar period. Growth meant unprecedented prosperity for some and worsening poverty and insecurity for thousands of others. High unemployment persisted at the same time as unprecedented levels of growth in the national economy (Burke and Shields, 2000). Child poverty became headline news as Canada suffered the reputation of being one of the countries with the worst child poverty rates, with approximately one in five children living in poverty. Neoliberal discourse and policy became dominant, which meant continued priority to tax breaks for the wealthy and deficit cutting through reduced social and welfare benefits. Progressive Conservative governments laid the blame for many of Canada's woes on individuals and a decaying moral fibre (Little, 1998).

Among unions and in workplaces, continued change and restructuring were driven by threats of global capital mobility and exhortations that the Canadian economy needed to become more competitive and boost its productivity. As

North American employers became increasingly hostile to unions, governments introduced regressive labour laws that restricted unionization and
weakened regulations that protected the minimum wages and working conditions of all working people. Real wages continued to decline for large groups
of working people, in particular young workers and racialized minorities
(Jackson, 2005: 105, 107). Employers preferred to schedule long hours and
rely on overtime rather than hire new workers, thus increasing the polarization between those with good, well-paying jobs and those on the margins of
the labour market. Employers further contributed to polarization within the
workforce by negotiating two-tier agreements with unions, whereby newly
hired workers would be paid lower wages and reduced benefits. More recently, unionized employers have identified pensions as the source of lack of
competitiveness as the proportion of retirees drawing a pension versus those
working and contributing to the pension plan has shifted, opening the door
to unfunded pension liabilities and employer demands for pension cutbacks.
Overall, the number of good jobs has continued to decline since the 1990s as
unionized employers, whether private or public, shed jobs and responsibility
for workers either through technological innovation or through outsourcing
and privatization (Jackson, 2001; Vosko, 2005).

These changes to the employment relation and labour market have created
a core and periphery labour force, with some reaping enormous rewards from
growth and thousands of others constantly changing jobs in the search for
secure employment that pays a living wage and offers predictable hours and
decent working conditions (Vosko, 2005; Yates and Leach, 2006). Moreover,
the rewards of labour market activity are unequally distributed across groups,
with women, young workers, racialized minorities—whether Canadian-born
or not—and Aboriginal Canadians bearing the brunt of economic restructuring (Jackson, 2005). Unions are therefore presented with enormous challenges
that threaten to deepen the internal union divides between public and private
sector unions, women and men, and those employed in the private service sector versus those in heavy industry. As a growing number of unions represent
both the best and the worst paid, unions are confronted with the strategic
dilemma of how to defend the privileges of long-standing members while
advancing the cause of more vulnerable members. In the next two sections,
I explore how these tensions have created a crisis in labour politics in the last
decade.

The Growing Divide in the Labour Movement

As a consequence of economic restructuring and volatility, unions in Canada
have experienced a slow but steady attrition in membership, with union

density dropping from 37.6 per cent in 1981 to 30.6 per cent in 2004 (Statistics Canada, 2004). Traditionally, union membership strength was concentrated in manufacturing, resource extraction (fishing, forestry, and mining), and the public sector. Most analysts agree that recent membership decline is related to shifts in employment away from these areas in which unionization rates were high and the failure of unions to build a membership base in sectors when employment has grown, such as amusement and recreation establishments and personnel services. Employment in government services declined in real terms over the same period, associated with widespread contracting out and privatization. In many instances work is being shifted from unionized to non-unionized establishments. The result is declining union presence and reduced bargaining leverage in industries that once set the standard for wages and benefits.

Some of the most powerful unions in Canada that had a decisive influence on labour politics, such as the USWA and CAW, were confronted with declining memberships as industries either shut down or became more efficient, able to produce more with significantly fewer workers. The USWA experienced perhaps the most dramatic drop in membership; between 1980 and 1983 it lost 55,000 members in Canada, more than 25 per cent of its membership (Yates, 2003: 223). In response, unions across Canada placed a high strategic priority throughout the 1990s on organizing the unorganized, although this commitment has waned since 2000. Although breakthroughs in retail and restaurant chains such as Wal-mart or McDonald's have been missing, unions have been quite successful in organizing workers employed in home care, auxiliary hospital services, university support staff, security guards, and casinos. Recent union membership growth has tended to be disproportionately among women, those with relatively high levels of education, and workers over 35 years of age (Yates, 2000).

For unions, organizing the unorganized has meant growing diversity in their own ranks, as well as growing conflict between unions as they compete with one another for new members. Internal membership diversity has challenged union strategic capacity as unions struggle to reconcile the demands of aging, often male members who expect the union to protect their benefits versus new members who are more likely to be women and/or racialized minorities. These differences resonate in the political arena with union members often deeply divided over what issues and which political party to support. Analysis suggests that the aging men who have done well through their unions want to protect their privileged position, therefore often supporting more conservative governments that promise tax breaks and resist expanding the equity based agenda. Reports of auto workers in Oshawa voting Progressive Conservative in the 1990s are indicative of this shift (Wilson, 1999). Election studies indicate a strong valence in voting between men and women over social welfare issues, with women more likely to support an expanded welfare state. More recently this has taken the form of support for a government child care program. Arguably one of the reasons for the CAW's advocacy for strategic voting in the 2006 election lay in its strong support for an expanded not-for-profit child care system that was on the verge of successful completion when the Liberal minority government was brought down.

This discussion leads to three conclusions. First, unions find their members polarized around different issues as their membership becomes more diverse. This makes it much more difficult for them to articulate a common collective political strategy and in particular to mobilize successfully around a single political party. Second, without clear cut differences between the Liberals and NDP on many issues, and faced with the threat of elections of conservative governments that are much more hostile to unions, unions have often ended up reconciling their internal differences with an issue-based approach to politics, which allows them to straddle the partisan divide between the Liberals and NDP. Third, union political strategies have been considerably shaped by the extent to which their memberships have grown to include more women and racialized minorities. In those unions in which diversity has greatly increased, such as the National Union of Provincial Government Employees, USWA, and CAW, political strategies have tended to highlight human rights and social issues. Those that have changed less, such as the Labourers International Union or many in the construction trades, have ended up engaged in defensive politics that buttress the place of men in the labour market.

While growing internal diversity has driven changes to union politics, so too has the heightened competition between unions. While organizing the unorganized breathes new life into the labour movement through expanded membership, it has also pitted unions against one another as they often fight to organize the same group of workers. Such union competition has spread into other areas of union life, including political and collective bargaining strategies. The weakness of the CLC has exacerbated these internal fragmentary tendencies. The end result is a declining capacity of the labour movement to coordinate concerted political campaigns around common political goals.

But greater union diversity and a greater emphasis on organizing the unorganized has also had positive changes on union politics. As more women and racialized minorities become union members, there has been a noticeable shift in union political issues with a greater recognition given to issues of work/life balance and human rights in the workplace. And these workers often bring with them a tradition of militancy, such as was evidenced in the Brooks, Alberta strike. Unions have wrestled with how to appeal to young workers, along with a commitment since the 1980s to leadership representation from women, gays and lesbians, and visible minorities. In this way, union politics has expanded beyond political parties and the formal political arena to include recognition of the politics of everyday worklife and identities. This enhances the likely political collaboration between unions and social movements and, therefore, may open up new possibilities for labour politics in Canada.

Is Socialism Dead?

Since the nineteenth century, socialism (or some variation thereof) has been advocated in working-class politics as the imagined alternative to the exploitation and powerlessness of capitalism. Since the 1980s, many analysts on the political left have predicted a new phase of capitalism in which both the working class as the vanguard of radical political change and socialism were dead. André Gorz's "Farewell to the Working Class" (1982) anticipated this shift in politics. Writing in the early 1980s, Gorz could not have expected the rapidity with which globalization would contribute to the smashing down of the Berlin Wall, the collapse of the Eastern Bloc, and the seeming triumph of capitalism worldwide. This last section examines the implications of the lack of alternatives to neoliberal capitalism for labour politics in Canada (Gindin and Stanford, 2003), including a critical examination of labour-NDP political relations.

One of the most significant elements in the decline of the postwar left, including social democratic politics, came with the declining legitimacy of Keynesian economic policy ideas. Keynesians argued in favour of demand management through state fiscal and social policy as a means for stabilizing national economies. This provided the theoretical framework needed for the construction of the welfare state. The welfare state coincided with demands for expanded democracy, the effects of which included increased representation inside the state to include organized labour and other organized social groupings and a role for the state in promoting equity in society and the economy. With the elections of Ronald Reagan and Margaret Thatcher in 1980 and 1979 respectively, along with economic changes across the globe associated with heightened international competition and economic integration across borders, Keynesian economy policy came under attack. Although this was delayed in Canada, by the 1990s neoliberalism had become dominant, and the role for the state in guaranteeing greater equality, democratic representation, and economic redistribution was undermined. The state's primary role became one of facilitating the market and enhancing national competitiveness.

The consolidation of neoliberalism eroded both the foundations for social democratic policy and political support for state intervention in the economy. Left-wing parties, whether social democratic or old-line communist, lost credibility and, in many instances, political power. The NDP seemed to avoid some of these problems: in 1990, it formed the Ontario government under Bob Rae, followed in 1991 with election to government in British Columbia and Saskatchewan. The Saskatchewan NDP was able to consolidate its hold on power, quietly combining some old-style social democratic policies with neoliberal initiatives. The experience with the NDP in Ontario was a debacle, however, resulting in a breach of labour-party relations (Carroll and Ratner, 2005). As David Camfield notes in Chapter 2, the NDP in Ontario imposed wage and other restraints on public sector unions and succeeded in deepening the divide between public and private sector unions. The only private sector union to support public sector union resistance to the provincial government's restraint measures was the CAW, an alliance that some saw as also deepening the divide between national and international unions. Arguing that there was no alternative to wage restraint and government-facilitated economic com-petitiveness, NDP governments began to look very much like their Liberal opponents, thereby contributing to the decline in alternative visions for left-wing politics in Canada.

The resulting loss in credibility for the party was seen in the 1993 federal election when the federal NDP lost official party status with its drop to nine elected representatives. This was followed in 1995 by a resounding defeat in Ontario by the Harris Progressive Conservatives, who immediately carried the neoliberal policy agenda to new heights with dramatic cutbacks to the welfare state, deregulation of the labour market, and active government support for private enterprise. Although the NDP under Jack Layton has restored some of its political support, winning 29 seats in the 2006 federal election, these new political fortunes have been built by distancing the party from organized labour and shying away from any critique of capitalism. When the NDP threw Buzz Hargrove out of the party for advocating strategic voting by CAW members, this action reflected the changing nature of NDP-union relations and the grow-ing ambivalence about which political party best serves the interests of working people and their families.

If the 1990s was a decade of centrist party politics for labour, it was also a decade of mounting protest for many in the labour movement. The Days of Action in Ontario peaked in Toronto in 1996 when more than 200,000 people marched through the city to protest government cutbacks by the Harris government. This was followed in 1997 by a two-week illegal work stoppage by public school teachers protesting cutbacks to school funding and increased class sizes (Camfield, 2000). Other signs of labour militancy were seen in the participation of many unions in the protests against the WTO, first in Seattle in 1999 and then again in Quebec City in 2001. However, the cracks and tensions within the labour movement over political strategy continued to emerge beneath these shows of mass protest and solidarity. Although tens of thousands of union members marched in Days of Action across Ontario, unions were divided between those who saw this as a build-up to forcing the hand of the Progressive Conservative government to reverse many policies and those who saw labour's only avenue for changing government policy as lying in ballot box support for the NDP. This latter group ultimately prevailed, and protests were halted, leaving many social activists estranged from the labour movement. A similar fate was in store for the New Politics Initiative, a group of left-wing academics, unionists, and social activists, who attempted unsuccessfully in 2001 to pressure the NDP to form a new more radical left-wing party. Finally, the events of 9/11 put a chill on the regrouping of left and labour politics, especially protests against the WTO, as these became reframed as attacks on Western democracy and feeding into the hands of terrorists.

The lack of vision of an alternative and better future, combined with the internal divisions and competition that riddle the Canadian labour movement, has reduced the possibility of future concerted labour political activism. Consequently, many individual unions are pursuing their own political goals using their own means, often resorting to a politics of pragmatism. Unions do what they have to do to protect their own members. Yet this politics of pragmatism can only work in the short term as it tends to leave a growing number of workers exposed to the risk and misfortunes of the market. Moreover, without an ideological and moral compass, the politics of pragmatism can lead unions to some perverse, often conservative, political positions that erode their long-term viability.

However, there are signs of a new labour politics with a vision of a different future. As public sector unions take on the state through workplace politics, and as new immigrants, young workers, women, racialized minorities, Aboriginal Canadians, and gays and lesbians demand more both from their employers and governments, there is a piecing together of an alternative society guided by commitments to greater equality, democracy, and a celebration of diversity and work/life balance. These new members are realizing the potential of unions as organizations of liberation from the tyranny of work. Signs of support for this alternative within the labour movement were evident in the leadership contest at the 2005 CLC national convention. Incumbent leader Ken Georgetti faced an electoral challenge by a black social union activist, Carol Wall. Even though Georgetti had the active support of all major unions, except the postal workers, and had the weight of past leadership experience in his favour, Wall garnered 37 per cent support from convention delegates. Wall argued "I believe that the single-minded focus on back room lobbying has been to our detriment. Lobbying government is important but we need to mobilize our members if we want to be a force for change in society" (cited in Cain, 2005). She suggested leadership in the fight to unionize Wal-mart workers, confronting labour's problems with internal competition, building new coalitions with community partners and social activists, and building a labour movement that is more inclusive and representative of the increasingly diverse workforce.

The old socialist and social democratic left offered a blueprint for labour politics in the postwar years that had a decisive effect on political economies around the world. This vision of politics has been eclipsed, and many of the underlying organizational relationships that underpinned unions' involvement in politics are being undone. The most recent conflicts between the NDP and the CAW signify this break in labour politics.

What this means for the future is unclear. But what is clear for organized labour is that unions cannot afford to "hug the middle," pursuing a non-ideological politics of pragmatism. We only need to look at the state of the American labour movement with its long-standing commitment to business unionism to get a window into such a future. Such politics of pragmatism reduces labour politics to particularistic issues and single union actions, a politics that fails not only to harness the collective power of working people but also to address the growing diversity and difficulties experienced by workers across Canada.

Note

1. The UAW–Canada was a branch of the American-dominated international union until 1984. In this year, Canadian autoworkers split from their American parent over bargaining strategy in response to company demands for concessions. Led by Bob White, the Canadian Autoworkers Union (CAW) was formed.

References and Further Reading

Archer, Keith, and Alan Whitehorn. 1993. *Canadian Trade Unions and the New Democratic Party*. Working Paper. Kingston: Queen's University School of Industrial Relations.

Avakumovic, Ivan. 1978. *Socialism in Canada: A Study of the CCF-NDP in Federal and Provincial Politics*. Toronto: McClelland and Stewart.

Briskin, Linda, and Patricia McDermott. 1993. *Women Challenging Unions: Feminism, Democracy, and Militancy*. Toronto: University of Toronto Press.

Brodie, Janine, and Jane Jenson. 1988. *Crisis, Challenge, and Change: Party and Class in Canada Revisited*. Ottawa: Carleton University Press.

Burke, Mike, and John Shields. 2000. "Tracking Inequality in the New Canadian Labour Market." In Mike Burke, Colin Mooers, and John Shields (eds.), *Restructuring and Resistance: Canadian Public Policy in an Age of Global Capitalism*. Halifax: Fernwood. 98–123.

Cain, Sean. 2005. "Mobilizing Members to be a Force for Change." Interview with Carol Wall. *Rabble News*. June 14. <http://www.rabble.ca/rabble_interview.shtml?x=39926>.

Cameron, Duncan, and Mel Watkins. 1993. *Canada under Free Trade*. Toronto: Lorimer.

Camfield, David. 2000. "Assessing Resistance in Harris's Ontario, 1995–1999." In Mike Burke, Colin Mooers, and John Shields (eds.), *Restructuring and Resistance: Canadian Public Policy in an Age of Global Capitalism*. Halifax: Fernwood. 306–17.

Carroll, William, and R.S. Ratner (Eds.). 2005. *Challenges and Perils: Social Democracy in Neoliberal Times*. Halifax: Fernwood.

Corman, June, Meg Luxton, D.W. Livingstone, and Wally Secombe. 1993. *Recasting Steel Labour: The Stelco Story*. Halifax: Fernwood.

Gindin, Sam, and Jim Stanford. 2003. "Canadian Labour and the Political Economy of Transformation." In Wallace Clement and Leah Vosko (eds.), *Changing Canada: Political Economy as Transformation*. Montreal and Kingston: McGill-Queen's University Press. 422–42.

Gorz, André. 1992. *Farewell to the Working Class: An Essay on Post-industrial Socialism*. London: Pluto Press.

Hackett, R. 1980. "Pie in the Sky: A History of the Ontario Waffle." *Canadian Dimension*, special ed. (October–November).

Horowitz, Gad. 1968. *Canadian Labour in Politics*. Toronto: University of Toronto Press.

Jackson, Andrew. 2005. *Work and Labour in Canada: Critical Issues*. Toronto: Canadian Scholars' Press.

Jackson, Andrew, and Bob Baldwin. 2005. *Policy Analysis by the Labour Movement in a Hostile Environment*. Working Paper 41. Kingston: Queen's University School of Policy Studies.

Jackson, Andrew, and David Robinson with Bob Baldwin and Cindy Wiggins. 2000. *Falling Behind: The State of Working Canada 2000*. Ottawa: Canadian Centre for Policy Alternatives.

Jenson, Jane, and Rianne Mahon. 1993. *The Challenge of Restructuring: North American Labor Movements Respond*. Philadelphia: Temple University Press.

Little, Margaret H. 1998. *No Car, No Radio, No Liquor Permit: The Moral Regulation of Single Mothers in Ontario, 1920–1997*. Toronto: Oxford University Press.

Maslove, Allan, and Gene Swimmer. 1980. *Wage Controls in Canada, 1975–78*. Ottawa: Institute for Research on Public Policy.

McRoberts, Kenneth. 1988. *Quebec: Social Change and Political Crisis*. Toronto: McClelland and Stewart.

Palmer, Bryan. 1987. *Solidarity: The Rise and Fall of an Opposition in British Columbia*. Vancouver: New Star Books.

Panitch, Leo, and Donald Swartz. 2003. *From Consent to Coercion: The Assault on Trade Union Freedoms*. 3rd ed. Toronto: Garamond.

Prezeworksi, Adam. 1986. *Capitalism and Social Democracy*. New York: Cambridge University Press.

Sims, Jinny. 2006. "Women in BC Talk Success." *Asian Pacific Post.* <http://www.asianpacificpost.com/portal2/ff808081099d6ba201099ea838590036_Jinny_Sims.do.html>.

Statistics Canada. 2004. *Perspectives on Labour and Income* (Autumn): 58–65.

Teeple, Gary. 2000. *Globalization and the Decline of Social Reform.* 2nd ed. Aurora: Garamond.

Vosko, Leah (Ed.). 2005. *Precarious Employment: Understanding Labour Market Insecurity in Canada.* Kingston and Montreal: McGill-Queen's University Press.

Walters, Vivienne. 1983. "Occupational Health and Safety Legislation in Ontario: An Analysis of its Origins and Content." *Canadian Review of Sociology and Anthropology* 20 (November): 413–34.

Whitehorn, Alan. 1993. *Canadian Socialism: Essays on the CCF-NDP.* Don Mills: Oxford University Press.

Wilson, Kevin. 1999. "Me and My Tiny Poll: Straw Vote shows Windsor Auto Workers Have No Truck with Tories." *Now* [Toronto]. 20–26 May. <http://www.nowtoronto.com/issues/18/38/News/featureid.html>.

Yates, Charlotte. 1990. "Labour and Lobbying: A Political Economy Approach." In W. Coleman and G. Skogstad (eds.), *Policy Communities and Public Policy in Canada.* Toronto: Copp and Pitman. 266–90.

Yates, Charlotte. 1993. *From Plant to Politics: The Autoworkers Union in Postwar Canada.* Philadelphia: Temple University Press.

Yates, Charlotte. 2000. "Staying the Decline in Union Membership: Union Organizing in Ontario, 1985–1999." *Relations Industrielles/Industrial Relations* 4(55): 640–74.

Yates, Charlotte. 2003. "The Revival of Industrial Unions in Canada." In Peter Fairbrother and Charlotte Yates (eds.), *Trade Unions in Renewal: A Comparative Study.* London: Continuum Books. 221–43.

Yates, Charlotte, and Belinda Leach. 2006. "Why Good Jobs lead to Social Exclusion." *Economic and Industrial Democracy* 27(3): 343–71.

FOUR

Boardrooms and Barricades: Anti-Poverty Organizing in Canada[1]

Jonathan Greene

Between March and May 2003, Canadians were witness to a unique judicial event. Three leading members of the Ontario Coalition Against Poverty (OCAP) were on trial for their alleged actions during a demonstration at Queen's Park, the provincial legislature in Toronto. Two of the members, Stefan Pilipa and Gaetan Heroux, were charged with "participating in a riot" and, if convicted, faced maximum prison sentences of two years each. The third member, John Clarke, was charged with the more serious offences of "counselling to participate in a riot" and "counselling to assault police" and, if convicted, faced a maximum prison sentence of five years. On the day of the demonstration—subsequently dubbed the "Queen's Park Riot"—OCAP had mobilized around 1,500 people to demonstrate at Queen's Park. Nominally a demonstration to demand political action on the growing crisis of homelessness, the more immediate request was to allow a delegation of six homeless people to address the legislature directly. Having been rebuffed by the government, the demonstrators took a more militant stance; the police responded with action to clear the park. In the resulting mêlée, dozens of demonstrators, police, and horses were injured. Over the coming weeks the police laid minor charges against 45 protesters. More significant were the criminal charges laid against the three OCAP leaders (Kraus, 2003). The ensuing trial resulted in a mistrial: the jury was unable to determine what constituted a "riot" and therefore was unable to find the defendants guilty. The Crown dropped the charges against Pilipa and Heroux. After electing to hold Clarke for another trial, the court stayed the charges because he was not brought to trial in a reasonable amount of time, thereby violating his rights under the *Charter of Rights and Freedoms*. The Crown chose not to appeal, putting an end to the eight-month saga.

For many members of the activist, academic, and legal communities, the significance of the trial was that it marked a further criminalization of dissent in the country, a topic that has received a growing amount of attention in recent years. Yet, perhaps more significant was the fact that the trial was based on the activities of protesters demonstrating against poverty. The "riot" and its aftermath marked the peak of a movement among poor people and their supporters that had emerged in the province in the years after 1995 but that had its roots in a period of reform beginning much earlier. A group of citizens often considered quiescent and lacking mobilizing capacity had successfully staged one of the most militant demonstrations in contemporary Canadian history. It is this contemporary movement of poor people and their supporters that this chapter will examine.[2]

Describing and analyzing the anti-poverty movement in Canada, especially within the confines of a single chapter, is a daunting task. Not only is there a problem of scope but also of scale. In terms of scope, scholars studying the anti-poverty movement must define its parameters. Does the anti-poverty movement include groups agitating on behalf of, and in conjunction with, disabled people? Does it include pensioners and women's rights organizations? At its broadest level, the answer must be "yes." In their book on the national "poverty lobby" in Britain, Whiteley and Winyard defined the lobby broadly as "those national voluntary organizations which regularly or sporadically attempt to influence the income maintenance policies of government in favour of the poor" (1987: 16). The approach adopted in this chapter is both more specific and more extensive than that of Whiteley and Winyard. It is more specific insofar as the discussion is limited to those social movement organizations that have as one of their *central* organizing interests the amelioration of poverty. It is more extensive insofar as the analysis is not limited to the "poverty lobby" or those organizations that advocate on behalf of poor people through formal institutional channels. It also includes activist groups—those organizations that may engage in advocacy but that also mobilize people, including poor people, for collective extra-institutional political action. The approach taken in this chapter draws upon the insights of both breakdown and political process theories of social movements and emphasizes the role of social strain, political opportunities, mobilizing resources, and cultural frames in the development of insurgency.

The second problem is one of scale. Although the most important legislation regarding poverty—both directly and indirectly—has emanated from federal and provincial governments, most anti-poverty organizing takes place at the local level (see, for example, Wagner, 1993; Rosenthal, 1994: Chs. 3 and 4; Wright, 1997; Cress and Snow, 2000; Roth, 2000; Gilbert, 2001). Poor people experience their poverty locally and therefore respond locally. "It is the daily experience of people that shapes their grievances, establishes the measure of their demands, and points out the targets of their anger" (Piven and Cloward, 1979: 20–21). In contrast to pluralist theory, which emphasizes the open nature of democratic institutions to competing interests, Canadian politics has historically been biased towards the interests of those with economic power. This has been the case for at least two reasons. First, poor people have generally lacked the resources—both of a tangible and intangible nature—to develop large national and provincial groups that have been able to effectively lobby government on their behalf. Second, as Canadian political economists have argued, the nature of liberal capitalism structurally and ideologically privileges the interests of economic elites over other interests in society (Panitch, 1995). As a result, poor people and their supporters have often found it necessary to organize outside of the traditional institutions of political power both to alter people's perceptions of poor people and to win concessions from the state. Analytically, it is therefore necessary to look at anti-poverty activism and advocacy at all three levels of governance using a political economy and social movement framework. The first half of this chapter examines anti-poverty advocacy at the national level. The second half provides an overview of contemporary anti-poverty mobilization in Toronto. It is in Toronto, and Ontario more generally, that some of the most dynamic mobilization has taken place in the past decade.

The Development of Canada's Welfare Policy Landscape

The contours of contemporary Canadian policies targeted towards poor people were consolidated in the decades following World War II. The culmination of expanded federal involvement in the assistance field was the establishment of the Canada Assistance Plan (CAP) in 1966, based on a proposal first put forward by the Canadian Welfare Council (CWC) (Dyck, 1976). Under the CAP, the federal government agreed to pay half of the direct costs of social assistance and associated services, creating an incentive for the provinces to increase spending, and established for the first time national standards of eligibility. Provincial and, where applicable, municipal governments maintained control over the levels and administration of assistance and associated services. The result of the CAP was to expand both the number and types of recipients eligible for assistance and the associated services provided. A second major postwar program targeted at poor people was the creation of public, non-profit, and cooperative housing schemes commencing in the 1950s under the *National Housing Act*. These programs resulted in a dramatic increase in the rental stock available for low-income families, especially in Ontario, British Columbia, and Quebec, where provincial governments were most active.

It was during this period that the first serious poor people's social movement organizations and national advocacy groups emerged as a direct response to the "rediscovery of poverty" in the country. Hitherto excluded from institutional influence over poverty policy and administration, local welfare rights groups proliferated between 1966 and 1971, demanding improved assistance benefits and services, humane treatment from welfare administrators, and better representation on agency boards (Felt, 1978; Buchbinder, 1979; Little, 2003). Many welfare recipients were organized with the support—the mobilizing resources—of young activists employed in the federal government agency, the Company of Young Canadians, or through funds provided by the federal government (Walker, 1971: 9). In 1970 the federal government restructured the advisory body, the National Council of Welfare (NCW), to be a more representative advocate for poor people within government, in part by ensuring its membership included poor people. The NCW also laid the groundwork for a national poor people's conference in 1971, which resulted in the establishment of the National Anti-Poverty Organization (NAPO).[3] Since its inception, NAPO's board has been comprised of representatives of local poor people's organizations from all regions of the country. The CWC also entered a period of adjustment in recognition of new political realities (Haddow, 1993: 87). It changed its name to the Canadian Council on Social Development (CCSD), operational unity was strengthened, and the governing structure was altered and reduced in size (Splane, 1996: 39–41).

Despite the vibrancy and modernization of the anti-poverty movement in the late 1960s, anti-poverty activism and influence during this period was short-lived. Both Liberal cabinet and caucus members, especially those with close connections to civic leaders in Toronto, began to voice concerns about the "disquieting effect that low income groups were having on urban government, especially in the Toronto area" (Walker, 1971: 68). In response, the federal government withdrew funding from local anti-poverty groups. Lacking indigenous organizational resources, most local groups dissolved or became politically marginalized (Daly, 1970; Loney, 1977; Felt, 1978). National and provincial advocacy groups had an equally difficult time being heard (Splane, 1996: 145). The CCSD would never develop a close connection to poor people, being more inclined to cultivate relationships with professional community groups. The NCW was similarly unproductive as both an advocate for poor people and influential policy innovator. By contrast, NAPO had a direct and positive relationship with poor people, but it was also ineffective as a policy advocate because it lacked both a strong presence in Ottawa and the strategic capacity to make detailed commentaries on evolving policy debate (Haddow, 1993: 179–83). NAPO was so weak that it almost collapsed in the early 1980s.

*The Shifting Terrain of National Poverty
Politics in the 1980s and 1990s*

By the middle of the 1970s, the political, economic, and social context was slowly shifting away from concerns about poverty and welfare state expansion to managing the effects of a shifting global economic environment, and specifically Canada's unsatisfactory economic performance, growing deficit and debt, and supposed uncontrollable program spending. When the Progressive Conservative Party was elected in 1984, welfare state reform became a critical agenda item. Most of the important national social programs, including social assistance and housing schemes, were affected (Moscovitch, 1990; Rice and Prince, 1993; McBride, 1992; Campbell, 1992; NCW, 1987, 1992). Within a context of neoliberal institutional, economic, and social reform, the major national anti-poverty advocacy groups were forced to spend much of their time defending past gains, although the manner in which to do this was the subject of some debate within the poverty community.

Both the CCSD and NAPO engaged with the government on a variety of social issues and were received rather well within government circles. Greater effort was also made to coordinate the work of various national advocacy groups concerned with social policy. The CCSD, confronted with financial difficulties, expanded its publishing program and extended its work beyond research and advocacy, adding a service and information function to its repertoire and winning the right to administer the federal government's new Court Challenges Program. NAPO became a more professionalized advocacy organization with a much stronger and more consistent presence in Ottawa, while at the same time maintaining close contacts with its network of anti-poverty groups at the local and provincial levels. The NCW, no longer inclusive of poor people, used its resources (as it does today) to produce important research on poverty-related issues.[4] Nevertheless, despite these organizational achievements, national anti-poverty groups were not powerful institutional actors and were ineffective at halting the Progressive Conservatives' reform agenda.

In 1993, a revitalized Liberal Party under the leadership of Jean Chrétien swept the federal Progressive Conservative government from office. Initially, the election of the new government aroused a sense of optimism within social policy circles. The Liberal Party election platform had called for a balanced approach to economic and social issues, and soon after taking office in 1994 the Liberals established a Social Security Review under the leadership of Lloyd Axworthy, the new minister for Human Resources Development Canada (HRDC). The proposals put forward for discussion later in the year held out the prospect for a radical restructuring of existing programs but in a direction that, if implemented, would undermine future federal involvement in social policy.

Through the next two years the Social Security Review dominated social activism at the national level. All of the major national advocacy groups focused their attention on lobbying the government against the existing proposals and in favour of more progressive alternatives, especially the maintenance of national standards. NAPO received funding from HRDC to consult low-income people about the Review and followed this up with an information outreach campaign, a meeting with Lloyd Axworthy, and a presentation to the Human Resources Committee (Spendlove, 2005). At the local level, this committee was met with protests in cities around the country (Monsebraaten, 1994: A29). Most vociferous of all the critics were post-secondary students, who believed that the proposals concerning funding for post-secondary education would greatly affect accessibility. Eventually, frustrated at the pace of the process and bent on making expenditure reductions, Finance Minister Paul Martin pre-empted the outcome of the Review and announced dramatic program changes in the 1995 federal budget (Greenspon and Wilson-Smith, 1996).

The alterations realized as a result of the 1995 budget changed the face of national poverty policy. The most dramatic policy shift was the elimination of both the CAP and Established Programs Financing and their replacement by the Canada Health and Social Transfer (CHST). Not only did the implementation of the CHST result in a reduction of transfers totalling $7 billion dollars over two years for post-secondary education, health, and social assistance and social services, it also eliminated most of the national standards imposed on the provinces with regard to social assistance. This opened the door for provinces to create more restrictive and onerous eligibility requirements, opportunities taken advantage of by many provincial governments.

National advocacy groups initially responded to the 1995 federal budget by publishing critical responses delineating the potentially deleterious effects of the changes (NCW, 1995; CCSD, 1995). In conjunction with the Pro-Canada Network, NAPO also organized a week-long series of demonstrations against the CHST (NAPO, 1996a). Two months later, on the day the CHST came into force, protests again took place in over 50 cities (NAPO, 1996b). Recognizing the futility of the struggle, however, the CCSD altered its strategy and, on behalf of HRDC, convened a series of roundtable discussions with the objective of developing proposals to "minimize the pitfalls" of the new arrangement. Based on these discussions, the CCSD recommended that the federal government act to ensure that cash transfers would not be phased out and to utilize the cash transfers as a mechanism to enforce national standards for social assistance and social services (CCSD, 1996). The CCSD has continued to promote these ideas. All of these initiatives had little effect. Most groups, therefore, turned their attention to other areas of concern.

The dissemination of independent research became the central function of the CCSD. Having lost all its core government funding in 1992–93, it became dependent on project grants for most of its financing, a transition the organization adapted to rather well under the leadership of David Ross in the second half of the decade. After Ross left the CCSD, "knowledge brokering"— facilitating discussions between officials in Social Development Canada, stakeholder groups, and social experts—has taken on primary importance and become a critical means of attracting financial support from the government (Ross, 2005). Meanwhile, the CCSD has tried to retain some relevance in national social policy circles. The 1990s, however, continued to be trying times for all social policy advocates as decision-making processes continued to shift to the Department of Finance. The only area where the CCSD, and other national social policy advocates, have had any impact on national policy has been on child poverty, an arena that has attracted support from a cross-section of society, including key members of the government.

NAPO shifted its attention to the perceived problem of "poor bashing" and became active assisting provincial and local advocacy and legal groups fighting the implementation of municipal anti-panhandling by-laws in Winnipeg and Vancouver. Threatened by the prospect of having these laws challenged in the courts, the City of Winnipeg repealed its by-law and the municipal government in Vancouver altered its policy in a manner more acceptable to anti-poverty groups. NAPO also began to take its concerns about poverty in Canada to the international level, most notably appearing before the United Nations Committee on Economic, Social, and Cultural Rights (UNCESCR) on three occasions during the 1990s (CCPI *et al.*, 1995; NAPO, 1998). UNCESCR's responses were critical, citing concerns over persistent poverty, hunger, housing, homelessness, and the weak protection provided for social rights (UNCESCR, 1993, 1998). Despite this flurry of activity, NAPO had no success influencing national poverty policy in the 1990s and, as the turn-of-the-century approached, entered a free-fall. Internal squabbling, weak and divided leadership, deteriorating provincial and local networks, and financial problems all took their toll on the organization. NAPO became practically invisible as a national voice for poor people in the first years of the twenty-first century (*NAPO News*; Spendlove, 2005; Howlett, 2005a).

In 2003, with funding from Social Development Canada, NAPO hired a strategic consulting firm to assist the organization in the process of restructuring. Under the direction of its new executive director, Dennis Howlett, NAPO has begun to re-establish itself, based on a strategy consisting of four inter-related components: reconnecting with existing local and provincial anti-poverty groups and networks—the grassroots; increasing its profile in the media; re-establishing a presence on Parliament Hill as an influential, non-partisan, policy advisor; and becoming active in political campaigns with like-minded social policy groups, both inside and outside the poverty community directly. In large measure, NAPO has determined its policy priorities strategically, based on an assessment of where potential exists for successful political action and further enhancement of networks. It has been focusing most of its energy on three initiatives: (1) a national campaign to increase the minimum wage to $10.00 an hour, indexed to inflation; (2) a national campaign against child poverty; and (3) the fight against homelessness, as a member of the Canadian Coalition Against Homelessness (Howlett, 2005a, 2005b).

It is probably in the area of housing and homelessness where the most articulate national movement has developed. It is also an area where, after years of neglect, anti-poverty activists have achieved some notable victories. These victories, however, must be considered as much, if not more so, a result of the efforts of local anti-poverty groups operating across multiple scales of governance, as they have been the work of nationally located housing and homeless coalitions. In a context in which little opportunity has existed for effective advocacy at the national level, the most visible and sustained anti-poverty mobilization has taken place at the local level through the emergence of anti-poverty social movement organizations. Organizing activity has been especially prevalent in Quebec, Ontario, and British Columbia. The rest of this chapter will examine the anti-poverty movement that developed in Toronto in the 1980s and 1990s.

Anti-Poverty Organizing in Toronto

A year after the Progressive Conservatives came to office federally in 1984, a Liberal government was elected in Ontario. Forced to rely on the support of the New Democratic Party (NDP) in their first two years in office, the Liberal government embarked on a massive public review of social assistance in July 1986. Once in place, the Social Assistance Review Committee (SARC) heard from people in 14 cities and received over 1,500 submissions, an historically unprecedented response (Wharf, 1992: 72–77). The SARC released its report in 1988 and recommended massive increases in social assistance. Already by this time local anti-poverty groups and unemployed workers' unions, many established by welfare recipients directly, had emerged during the recession of the early 1980s as the numbers of people unemployed and forced on to social assistance spiked (Clarke, 1992: 216–18). Even as the economy improved after 1983, the numbers of people on social assistance did not recede and, for the first time in contemporary history, homelessness became a visible problem in large urban centres. Both of these issues, but especially the housing crisis, attracted political and media attention and provided a political opportunity for collective mobilization (Clarke, 1992: 216–18; Layton, 2000: 3–5; Klassen and Buchanan, 2005: 4–8; Greene, 2006: 76–85). It was the initiation of SARC, however, that provided the most significant political opportunity for a more coordinated effort across the province to take shape, especially after the Liberal government hesitated to act on its progressive recommendations. Eventually, in the wake of a mass province-wide protest in 1989 bringing together poor and unemployed people, anti-poverty advocates and supporters, trade unionists, and elected officials, the government responded with an increase in welfare rates of 9 per cent (Clarke, 1992: 216–18).

The following year, the NDP came to power for the first time in the province's history. Notwithstanding its early support for welfare reform, by 1992 the NDP had begun a process of welfare retrenchment that attracted criticism from anti-poverty advocates and activists (Lightman, 1997; Scott, 1996; Little, 1998: 160–63; Sheldrick, 1998). Having successfully established a coordinated response during the SARC reform process, anti-poverty groups in the province formalized their alliance by creating OCAP, initially bringing together anti-poverty groups from 27 communities in the province (Clarke, 2000). Very quickly, however, the coalition effort weakened, and OCAP's organizational base became largely restricted to Toronto under the leadership of John Clarke, a former unemployed worker and long-time anti-poverty activist. After 1992, as it became apparent that the NDP was implementing regressive measures, OCAP's tactics became more visibly militant. OCAP was also able to attract financial and moral support, most notably from the labour movement, which was crucial in assisting it to develop a sustained organizational presence. Recessionary budget-cutting measures at the local level also brought a new coalition of groups together in Toronto in an effort to halt dramatic program cuts, especially those targeted at poor people. This local effort, like the SARC process before it, provided the impetus for the establishment of a more formal organizational presence in the form of the Metro Network for Social Justice, which continued its work through the decade, focusing chiefly on influencing the Metro budget process through institutional channels (Conway, 2004: 78–88, 143). For the most part, though, anti-poverty activism remained in its infancy. Neoliberalism had not entirely become entrenched either locally or provincially, and institutional channels of influence had not yet been entirely closed.

The election of a new Progressive Conservative government in Ontario in May 1995 severely altered the context for anti-poverty organizing in Ontario. Almost immediately upon taking office, Premier Mike Harris began to implement the party's neoliberal reform agenda. Few groups were left unscathed. Poor people were particularly hard hit. Social assistance rates were cut by 21.6 per cent, a welfare fraud hotline was instituted, the "Spouse in the House" rule was reinstated, workfare was implemented, rent control was virtually eliminated, the development of new social housing was halted, and the budget for social agencies was slashed 7.5 per cent over two years (NCW, 1997; Little, 1998; Ibbitson, 1997: Ch. 6; Peck, 2001: 236–60). The dramatic effects became clear quite quickly. Within six months of taking office, government figures showed that 100,000 people had left the welfare rolls; by May 2001, this number had increased to 584,255 (Workfare Watch, 2001). A strengthened economy and falling unemployment were part of the reason. But research also showed that tightened eligibility requirements made it much more difficult for people to become, and remain, eligible for assistance (NCW, 1997; Little and Morrison, 1999; Workfare Watch, 2001). Food-bank use also increased (CAFB, 1998, 2004). Perhaps most significantly, homelessness became increasingly visible on the streets of Ontario cities. It also became more dangerous. Within the span of one month in early 1996, three homeless men froze to death on the streets of Toronto, an "incident" that would continue to recur with increasing frequency (Freed, 1996: A10; Welsh, 1996: A1; Rankin, 1996: A1; Layton, 2000). In the face of these social problems, the government proved unwilling to recognize the political legitimacy of its critics, effectively silencing institutional advocates who feared the loss of government funding for services.

All these developments set in motion a series of mass protests by teachers, public sector workers, trade unionists, students, and anti-poverty activists, among others. OCAP captured the opportunity provided by the enhanced desperation of poor people and the new cycle of activism to organize poor people and their supporters for independent political action against the provincial government. In doing so, OCAP continued to mobilize at the local level in efforts to defend poor and homeless people against the processes of neoliberal urbanism at work in Toronto, especially the regulatory and legislative measures implemented to clear the streets of panhandlers and squeegee merchants, whose presence was considered a threat to the city's competitiveness (*Safe Streets Act*, 1999; Kipfer and Keil, 2002; Hermer and Mosher, 2002). More intensive gentrifying processes also took place, pitting homeowners, residents' and business associations, and supportive city councillors against poor and homeless people, service providers, and anti-poverty groups (notably OCAP). The result of these regulatory and policy shifts was to exacerbate the already existing problems of poverty, homelessness, and inequality, providing an opportunity for OCAP to attract broader support and involvement—both tangible and intangible resources—for its mobilizing actions from poor people, activists, and conscious constituents (Greene, 2006: Ch. 2).

OCAP's repertoire of collective action has consisted of two strategic elements. First, through its program of "direct action casework," it has worked with poor people directly to help them resolve legal and bureaucratic problems (Groves, 2003). Using a flexible, yet fairly standardized strategy of tactical escalation—ranging from a phone call to mass invasions of benefit offices—OCAP has won more than 90 per cent of its welfare cases. Casework has expanded to encompass an array of issues, including receipt of wages and compensation, housing and eviction, hostel conditions and availability, and tickets given out to panhandlers. One area where OCAP has been particularly active is immigration, which became a crucial part of the casework repertoire in 1997 (Scott, 2000). With a success rate of close to 70 per cent, OCAP's methods have proven much more effective than traditional forms of advocacy (Clarke and Podur, 2004). Strategically, casework has served the dual purposes of addressing the immediate needs of poor people in an inclusive and empowering manner and has provided a basis for movement growth.

The second element of the OCAP repertoire has been to mobilize poor people and their supporters in actions that have challenged broader political, economic, and social policies and practices. In response to repressive government policies, humiliating remarks by government ministers, and discriminatory local practices, OCAP has organized mass marches to Queen's Park and wealthy neighbourhoods, demonstrated against businesses considered complicit with government policies, and taken its demands directly to people's homes. This latter tactic drew the ire of many of their supporters and financial backers, eventually leading OCAP to terminate this activity (Kastner, 1997; Brown, 1999; Watson, 2000). It has been with regard to homelessness, though, that some of the most sustained and exciting movement activity has emerged in the city. Once again, OCAP has been a principal mobilizing force in bringing together poor and homeless people and their supporters to defend squatters' and hostel users' rights, demanding affordable housing, fighting gentrification, opposing the closure of emergency hostels, and defending the use of public space. On more than one occasion, OCAP and its supporters have taken over city council meetings to force the city to keep open emergency hostels or to fight proposed by-laws outlawing second suites and rooming houses. They have also taken over buildings with the intention of forcing the various governments to open more emergency shelters and to build more affordable housing (OCAP, 2001). 1999 was an especially noteworthy year, as OCAP was able to mount three mass actions: two large and vociferous demonstrations on Parliament Hill and an outdoor squat—"Safe Park"—in a downtown park in Toronto lasting four days (OCAP, 1999; Garrett and OCAP, 2001; Greene, 2006: 129–37). OCAP's capacity to successfully carry out these actions gave it the confidence to organize a large, province-wide demonstration at the Ontario legislature the following summer with the objective of having a delegation of homeless people address the members of the legislature directly. This demonstration subsequently became dubbed the "Queen's Park Riot."

One reason for OCAP's mobilizing success is that it has provided a more militant alternative to other forms of political organizing taking place in the province. OCAP has also been able to draw upon support—tangible and intangible—from various organizations and communities in the province, including existing and newly established organizations concerned specifically with the homeless problem in Toronto. One of the more significant of these anti-poverty groups has been the Toronto Disaster Relief Committee (TDRC).

The TDRC was established in 1998. Its origins date back to the 1980s, but its immediate impetus came from the events of January and February 1996 when three homeless men froze to death on the streets of Toronto. In the wake of these deaths a coroner's inquest was convened to study the problem and make recommendations on the homeless problem. A new coalition—Toronto Coalition Against Homelessness (TCAH)—came together to advocate on behalf of homeless people at the inquest (Bragg, 1996: A24). After the inquest, the TCAH lobbied the provincial government to implement the coroner's recommendations but without success. It was at this time that Cathy Crowe, a street nurse and member of the TCAH, developed the idea that homelessness was a "national disaster" (Crowe, 2000). With institutional channels closed at both the local and provincial levels of governance, Crowe and her colleagues recognized that it would be necessary to adopt the political approach of a professional social movement organization. Thus the TDRC was born, with seed money from the labour movement and other supporters.

The founding members of the steering committee brought together individuals from a cross-section of society, including business, academia, and social services; noticeably absent were homeless people. Unlike OCAP, TDRC was not founded with the objective of organizing poor people for political action but rather to act as a political advocate for homeless people (German, 2000). Nevertheless, the steering committee has expanded to include homeless or formerly homeless individuals, and homeless and/or formerly homeless individuals have at times taken part in TDRC's political actions. TDRC's principal demand has been for all levels of government to increase the amount of money they spend on housing by 1 per cent of their total annual budget—the "one per cent solution." More immediately, though, TDRC's objectives have been to force the city to provide adequate and secure temporary shelter for homeless people and to alter people's perceptions about homelessness to create a groundswell of support for the cause. In this latter regard, the concept of homelessness as a "national disaster" has proven a useful mobilizing frame.

The campaign to have homelessness declared a "national disaster" was officially launched on 8 October 1998, and the mayors of the 10 biggest cities, including Toronto, quickly adopted the resolution. The TDRC has adopted a flexible tactical approach, combining sporadic demonstrative action with more traditional forms of political mobilization, and has sought to lobby government and attract attention through media events—including tours of homeless shelters—press releases, and reports on the homeless crisis. Drawing upon its members' experiences working with homeless people, their contacts in various agencies and hostels, and expert advice, the TDRC has been an important source of information about homelessness in the city.

As the two pre-eminent anti-poverty groups in Toronto, and arguably in the province as a whole, OCAP and TDRC have at times worked closely together. However, OCAP's relationship with less militant groups in the province has proven quite hostile at times, largely because of OCAP's strict adherence to direct action, a strategy that in part led the Canadian Auto Workers (CAW) to withdraw its funding in 2001. The result has been that both organizations have sought to build their own networks and, in doing so, have been central in broadening the movement beyond the borders of Toronto.

Almost from the moment Harris was elected, OCAP took the initiative to make greater linkages with anti-poverty groups outside Toronto. Since 1995, groups have been established in communities across the province, including Kingston, Kitchener-Waterloo, Peterborough, Sudbury, Ottawa, Belleville, Guelph, Northumberland, and Port Dover. Most of these groups have adopted a similar tactical repertoire to that of OCAP, and many have established a strong local presence fighting gentrification, police harassment, and homelessness (Freeman and Lamble, 2004; Lamble, 2005; TAG, 2005). In addition to these local efforts, these groups have also come together to form a provincial network under the banner of the Ontario Common Front, initially to campaign to defeat the Harris government and, more recently, to campaign for an increase in social assistance rates in the province.

The TDRC has also sought to take part in joint efforts with other organizations not only around homelessness but also in support of poor people more generally. Its central objective—the "one per cent solution"—has been, by its very nature, a multi-level policy goal. One important ally has been Homes not Bombs, a non-violent pacifist group led by Reverend Brian Burch. Perhaps the most notable achievement in this regard was the formation of the National Housing and Homelessness Network (NHHN) in March 1999 by Michael Shapcott, a long-time housing activist and founding member and research coordinator for the TDRC (NHHN, 2004). Strategically, the NHHN has sought both to publicize the issue of housing—and specifically promote the "one per cent solution"—through the dissemination of annual report cards on housing and homelessness in Canada and lobbying provincial and federal ministers to commit their governments to take remedial and positive action on the housing and homeless front. Following the example of the NHHN, housing advocacy groups from 14 communities in Ontario came together in 2002 to form a new partnership, the Housing and Homeless Network of Ontario.

In spite of the strategic variability and ideological differences between the social movement organizations in Ontario, the movement has had some clearly defined and shared substantive goals. Its overriding objective has been for governments to establish a program for addressing homelessness and poverty both in the short and long term. In the short term, the movement has had some important victories. Using its strategy of direct action casework, OCAP has been very effective as an advocate for poor individuals and families. These victories have helped put food on people's tables and roofs over people's heads and ensured that refugees have been able to remain in Canada. Moreover, in pursuing casework, OCAP has disrupted the seamless operation of the government's regulatory and bureaucratic machinery and, in doing so, has questioned the legitimacy of existing rules and regulations. OCAP has also been effective in defeating a by-law to outlaw rooming houses and, in at least one instance, forced the municipality to open emergency shelter spaces. For its part, the TDRC has forced the municipal government to make arrangements for more emergency shelter space and has been instrumental in the development of new local policies concerning homelessness, including the establishment of both cold and warm weather advisories and "cooling" centres in the city. In 2003, the TDRC also took the lead in working with the residents of "Tent City"—a mass squat on polluted waterfront land—to negotiate with the city for a program of rent supplements to assist the residents to move into formal accommodation.

Although more difficult to substantiate, it does seem evident that both the TDRC and OCAP have had some impact on the longer term development of strategies to solve the homeless problem. Both have been instrumental in publicizing homelessness as a crisis, brought greater visibility to the issues, and mobilized conscious constituents in Toronto and elsewhere to become vocal participants in the debate. Perhaps most significantly, OCAP and TDRC have played a leading role in the diffusion of activism in local communities across the country, and have been central actors in the development of a provincial and national movement against homelessness. This movement has forced governments to implement policy initiatives aimed at addressing the problem of homelessness in the longer term. Working with allies both in Ontario and elsewhere in the country, TDRC and OCAP have been instrumental in obliging the federal government to respond, first with the appointment of a minister responsible for homelessness in 1999, and then with a series of initiatives to address the housing crisis, including the establishment of bilateral federal-provincial agreements for the development of new affordable housing. To be sure, homelessness still exists, the "one per cent solution" has yet to be accepted, welfare rates remain miserly, and the depth of poverty has increased and spread to a growing number of neighbourhoods in Toronto. However, the movement has achieved some positive results, especially if measured against the state of the crisis in the late 1990s. Much work, nevertheless, remains to be done.

Conclusion

The last two decades have been trying times for poor people in Canada. Not only have national programs established following World War II to address poverty been restructured or eliminated, but the national standards governing these programs have been eroded, and with them an important basis for the maintenance of a national sense of community and citizenship. In short, the national social rights afforded to poor people have been retrenched.

In response to the shifting political climate, anti-poverty groups at the national level have been critical of federal and provincial initiatives. Indeed, almost from the moment of their establishment, national anti-poverty advocacy organizations have been on the defensive. For the most part, they have been entirely ineffective at halting federal retrenchment initiatives. On the one hand, the federal policy-making process has increasingly been centralized within the Department of Finance since the 1980s. Moreover, even within those ministries that are charged specifically with responsibility for social policy, the nature of the federal civil service has been altered in such a manner that these departments no longer house employees that have any particular interest in social policy. As a result, the informal linkages forged between national advocates and civil servants have been, at least in part, severed (Ross, 2005). This has fundamentally altered the nature of federal social policy-making and the relationship between advocacy groups and the government. Less a matter of deliberating over the best methods to deliver income assistance programs, social policy has largely become defined as a tax matter.

These issues raise at least two important questions about the possibilities for anti-poverty organizing at a national level. First, is it possible to develop truly national anti-poverty organizations that are able to legitimately represent poor people directly? A number of scholars have suggested that the development of a national anti-poverty movement is very difficult, if not impossible (Miliband, 1974; Bauman, 1998; Cloward and Piven, 1999). Even when national organizations are established, does the reliance on federal government monies inherently limit the critical capacity, and therefore effectiveness, of these organizations? Second, are national anti-poverty advocacy and interest groups—and perhaps national social movement organizations more generally—only successful when favourable political opportunities present themselves? Or can well organized groups affect the political process even in unfavourable environments? What tactics might be most useful to achieve the sought-after goals? National anti-poverty groups in Canada have primarily adopted an institutionalized approach. Would a more dynamic and confrontational approach sometimes be more effective?

At the same time as national advocacy groups in Canada have proven weak and ineffective, anti-poverty organizing at the local level has blossomed, at least in some cities and provinces. This chapter has briefly described the movement that developed in Toronto beginning in the middle of the 1980s. Although it has not proven entirely effective, it has clearly been the case that anti-poverty mobilization has expanded and become a visible political force within the community. It has also achieved some notable gains for poor people and been an instrumental force in the development of a province-wide movement against poverty and homelessness. Movements in other cities and provinces, notably Quebec and British Columbia, have also emerged in the past decade. The movement in Quebec has been especially effective, working with the provincial government to produce legislation aimed at combating poverty and social exclusion in December 2002 (Noël, 2002; Ninacs *et al.*, 2003; Dufour, 2004). These developments at the local and provincial levels also raise a number of questions.

First, are there specific moments when anti-poverty activism is more likely to emerge in a local environment? What are the conditions and factors that promote activism among a population that is widely considered quiescent and lacking in organizational capacity? Second, what are the most effective tactics for local anti-poverty groups to utilize? Does the movement benefit from an ensemble of organizations using a variety of tactics, which may produce a "radical flank" effect, or would the movement be better served by organizations coming together to pursue their objectives as a coherent whole? Finally, given the paucity of resources available to poor people, is it necessary for anti-poverty groups to cultivate ties with sympathetic allies such as the labour movement? What effects do these ties have on the forms in which mobilization might take? All these questions require answers. One of the biggest roadblocks to answering these questions, however, has been that interest in studying anti-poverty organizing in Canada has been weak. In a context of global neoliberal hegemony, welfare state retrenchment, and increased deprivation, it is an area of social movement research that begs further study.

Notes

1. I would like to thank Abigail Sone for reading a draft of the paper.

2. A conceptual distinction must be made between "poor people's movements" and "anti-poverty movements." "Poor people's movements" denotes movements that involve poor people directly in some capacity. "Anti-poverty movements," by contrast, may or may not include poor people directly. In this paper the concept of "anti-poverty" activism is used most often, but it should be noted that some of the groups that will be discussed, such as OCAP, do include poor people directly.

3. Much of the information on NAPO comes from various issues of *NAPO News* and a personal interview with Rosemary Spendlove, Resource Coordinator and long-time staff-person at NAPO.

4. Since the 1980s NCW appointments have been entirely at the discretion of the governing party. Almost all appointments have been to "middle-class" individuals.

References and Further Reading

Bauman, Zygmunt. 1998. *Work, Consumerism, and the New Poor*. Buckingham: Open University Press.

Bragg, Rebecca. 1996. "Helpers for Homeless Seek Role at Inquest." *Toronto Star*, 19 June.

Brown, Desmond. 1999. "Are You His Enemy?" *National Post*, 21 August.

Buchbinder, Howard. 1979. "The Just Society Movement." In Brian Wharf (ed.), *Community Work in Canada*. Toronto: McClelland and Stewart. 129–52.

Campbell, Robert M. 1992. "Jobs.... Jo.... J... The Conservatives and the Unemployed." In Frances Abele (ed.), *How Ottawa Spends 1992–93: The Politics of Competitiveness*. Ottawa: Carleton University Press. 23–55.

CAFB (Canadian Association of Food Banks). 1998. *Hunger Count 1998*. Ottawa: CAFB.

CAFB. 2004. *Hunger Count 2004*. Ottawa: CAFB.

CCPI (Charter Committee on Poverty Issues), NAPO (National Anti-Poverty Organization), and NAC (National Action Committee on the Status of Women). 1995. "Presentation to the Committee on Economic, Social, Cultural Rights by Non-Governmental Organizations from Canada." 1 May. Ottawa: CCPI.

CCSD (Canadian Council on Social Development). 1995. *Social Policy Beyond the Budget*. Ottawa: CCSD.

CCSD. 1996. *Position Statement: Maintaining a National Social Safety Net: Recommendations on the Canada Health and Social Transfer*. Ottawa: CCSD, 5 March.

Clarke, John. 1992. "Ontario's Social Movements—The Struggle Intensifies." In Colin Leys and Marguerite Mendell (eds.), *Culture and Social Change: Social Movements in Québec and Ontario*. Montreal: Black Rose Books. 213–24.

Clarke, John. 2000. Personal Interview. February.

Clarke, John. 2002. "A Short History of the Ontario Coalition Against Poverty." *OCAP 2002 Calendar*. Toronto: OCAP. <http://www.ocap.ca>.

Clarke, John and Justin Podur. 2004. "When the Class Line is Drawn, Which Side Will You Be On?" Znet, May 3. Online at <http://www.zdnet.org/content/showarticle.cfm?ItemID=5456>.

Cloward, Richard A., and Frances Fox Piven. 1999. "Disruptive Dissensus: People and Power in an Industrial Age." In Jack Rothman (ed.), *Reflections on Community Organization: Enduring Themes and Critical Issues*. Ithaca: F.E. Peacock Publishers. 165–93.

Conway, Janet. 2004. *Identity, Place, Knowledge: Social Movements Contesting Globalization*. Halifax: Fernwood.

Cress, Daniel M., and David A. Snow. 2000. "The Outcomes of Homeless Mobilization: The Influence of Organization, Disruption, Political Mediation, and Framing." *American Journal of Sociology* 105(4): 1063–1104.

Crowe, Cathy. 2000. Personal Interview. February.

Daly, Margaret. 1970. *The Revolution Game: The Short, Unhappy Life of the Company of Young Canadians*. Toronto: New Press.

Dufour, Pascale. 2004. "The Inequality of Political Representation in Quebec and the Adoption of Bill 112: The Exception that Confirms the Rule?" Paper Presented at the Annual Meeting of the Canadian Political Science Association. Winnipeg, 2–5 June.

Dyck, Rand. 1976. "The Canada Assistance Plan: The Ultimate in Cooperative Federalism." *Canadian Public Administration* 19(4): 587–602.

Felt, Lawrence. 1978. "Militant Poor People and the Canadian State." In Daniel Glenday, Huibert Guindon, and Allan Turowetz (eds.), *Modernization and the Canadian State*. Toronto: Macmillan. 417–41.

Freed, Dale Anne. 1996. "Homeless Man Freezes to Death in Bus Shelter." *Toronto Star*, 6 January.

Freeman, Lisa, and Sarah Lamble. 2004. "Squatting and the City." *Canadian Dimension* 38(6): 44–46, 60.

Garrett, Rebecca, and OCAP (Ontario Coalition Against Poverty) (video). 2001. *Safe Park*. Toronto: OCAP.

German, Beric. 2000. Personal Interview. March.

Gilbert, Melissa R. 2001. "From the 'Walk for Adequate Welfare' to the 'March for Our Lives': Welfare Rights Organizing in the 1980s and 1990s." *Urban Geography* 22(5): 440–56.

Greene, Jonathan. 2005. "'Whatever It Takes': Poor People's Organizing, OCAP, and Social Struggle." *Studies in Political Economy* 75: 5–28.

Greene, Jonathan. 2006. "Visibility, Urgency, and Protest: Anti-Poverty Activism in Neoliberal Times." Ph.D. dissertation. Queen's University.

Greenspon, Edward, and Anthony Wilson-Smith. 1996. *Double Vision: The Inside Story of the Liberals in Power*. Toronto: Doubleday.

Groves, Tim. 2003. *Direct Action Casework Manual*. Toronto: OCAP.

Haddow, Rodney. 1990. "The Poverty Policy Community in Canada's Liberal Welfare State." In William D. Coleman and Grace Skogstad (eds.), *Policy Communities and Public Policy in Canada: A Structural Approach*. Mississauga: Copp Clark Pitman. 212–37.

Haddow, Rodney. 1993. *Poverty Reform in Canada 1958–1978: State and Class Influences on Policy Making*. Montreal and Kingston: McGill-Queen's University Press.

Hermer, Joe, and Janet Mosher (Eds.). 2002. *Disorderly People: Law and the Politics of Exclusion in Ontario*. Halifax: Fernwood.

Heroux, Gaetan. 2000. Personal Interview. February.

Howlett, Dennis. 2005a. Personal Interview. 19 May.

Howlett, Dennis. 2005b. "The Call for a Living Wage—Cross Canada Campaigns." *Canadian Dimension* 39(3): 25–28.

Ibbitson, John. 1997. *Promised Land: Inside the Mike Harris Revolution*. Scarborough: Prentice-Hall.

Kastner, Susan. 1997. "Taking Fight to the Streets." *Toronto Star*, 13 September.

Kipfer, Stefan, and Roger Keil. 2002. "Toronto Inc? Planning the Competitive City in the New Toronto." *Antipode* 34(2): 227–64.

Klassen, Thomas R., and Dan Buchanan. 2005. "Ideology, Policy, and Economy: Lessons From the Liberal, New Democratic, and Conservative Reforms of Ontario's Welfare Program, 1985–2000." 21 November. <http://www.glendon.yorku.ca/english/faculty/researchcentres/api/documents/KlassenBuchanan.pdf>.

Kraus, Krystalline. 2003. "Activism on Trial." *Rabble News*, 14 January. <http://www.rabble.ca/everyones_a_critic_shtml17x=18173>.

Lamble, Sarah. 2005. Personal Interview, May.

Layton, Jack. 2000. *Homelessness: The Making and Unmaking of a Crisis*. Toronto: Penguin.

Lightman, Ernie. 1997. "It's Not a Walk in the Park: Workfare in Ontario." In Eric Shragge (ed.), *Workfare: Ideology for New Underclass*. Toronto: Garamond. 85–107.

Little, Margaret. 1998. *'No Car, No Radio, No Liquor Permit': The Moral Regulation of Single Mothers in Ontario, 1920–1997*. Toronto: Oxford University Press.

Little, Margaret Hillyard. 2007. "Militant Mothers Fight Poverty: The Just Society Movement, 1968–1971," *Labour/Le Travail* 59 (Spring): 179–97.

Little, Margaret, and Ian Morrison. 1999. "'The Pecker Detectors are Back': Regulation of the Family Form in Ontario Welfare Policy." *Journal of Canadian Studies* 34(2): 110–36.

Loney, Martin. 1977. "A Political Economy of Citizen Participation." In Leo Panitch (ed.), *The Canadian State: Political Economy and Political Power*. Toronto: University of Toronto Press. 446–72.

McBride, Stephen. 1992. *Not Working: State, Unemployment, and Neoconservatism*. Toronto: University of Toronto Press.

Miliband, Ralph. 1974. "Politics and Poverty." In Dorothy Wedderburn (ed.), *Poverty, Inequality and Class Structure*. Cambridge: Cambridge University Press. 186–96.

Monsebraaten, Laurie. 1994. "Quiet Arguments Bolster Quest for Reform." *Toronto Star*, 8 December.

Moscovitch, Allan. 1990. "'Slowing the Steamroller': The Federal Conservatives, the Social Sector and Child Benefits Reform." In Katherine A. Graham (ed.),

How Ottawa Spends 1990–91: Tracking the Second Agenda. Ottawa: Carleton University Press. 171–218.

NAPO (National Anti-Poverty Organization). *NAPO News* (various years).

NAPO. 1996a. *Anti-Poverty News,* 51.

NAPO. 1996b. *Anti-Poverty News,* 52.

NAPO. 1998. "The 50th Anniversary of the UN Declaration: A Human Rights Meltdown in Canada." 16 November.

NCW (National Council of Welfare). 1987. *The Tangled Safety Net.* Ottawa: Minister of Supply and Services Canada.

NCW. 1992. *Welfare Reform.* Ottawa: Minister of Supply and Services Canada.

NCW. 1995. *The 1995 Budget and Block Funding.* Ottawa: Minister of Supply and Services Canada, Spring.

NCW. 1997. *Another Look at Welfare Reform.* Ottawa: Minister of Public Works and Government Services Canada.

NHHN (National Housing and Homelessness Network). 2004. *Submission to Federal-Provincial-Territorial Housing Ministers' Meeting,* 30 November.

Ninacs, William, with Anne-Marie Béliveau and Francine Gareau. 2003. *Le Collectif pour un Québec sans pauvreté: Étude du cas.* Ottawa: Caledon Institute of Social Policy.

Noël, Alain. 2002. "A Law Against Poverty: Quebec's New Approach to Combating Poverty and Social Exclusion." <http://www.pauvrete.qc.ca>.

OCAP (Ontario Coalition Against Poverty) (video). 1999. *Homeless on the Hill.* Toronto: Satan Macnuggit Popular Arts.

OCAP (video). 2001. *OCAP Strikes Back.* Toronto: OCAP and Satan Macnuggit Popular Arts.

Panitch, Leo V. 1995. "Elites, Classes, and Power in Canada." In Michael Whittington and Glen Williams (eds.), *Canadian Politics in the 1990s.* 4th ed. Scarborough: Nelson Canada. 152–75.

Peck, Jamie. 2001. *Workfare States.* New York: The Guilford Press.

Piven, Frances Fox, and Richard A. Cloward. 1979. *Poor People's Movements: Why They Succeed, How They Fail.* New York: Vintage.

Porter, Ann. 2003. *Gendered States: Women, Unemployment Insurance, and the Political Economy of the Welfare State in Canada, 1945–1997.* Toronto: University of Toronto Press.

Rankin, Jim. 1996. "Another Homeless Man Dies from Cold." *Toronto Star,* 3 February.

Rice, James J., and Michael J. Prince. 1993. "Lowering the Safety Net and Weakening the Bonds of Nationhood: Social Policy in the Mulroney Years." In Susan D. Phillips (ed.), *How Ottawa Spends 1993–94: A More Democratic Canada...?* Ottawa: Carleton University Press. 381–416.

Rosenthal, Rob. 1994. *Homeless in Paradise: A Map of the Terrain.* Philadelphia: Temple University Press.

Roth, Roland. 2000. "New Social Movements, Poor People's Movements and the Struggle for Social Citizenship." In Pierre Hamel, Henri Lustiger-Thaler, and Margit Mayer (eds.), *Urban Movements in a Globalizing World.* London and New York: Routledge. 25–44.

Ross, David. 2005. Personal Interview (Phone). November.

Safe Streets Act, 1999, S.O. 1999, c.8.

Scott, Katherine. 1996. "The Dilemma of Liberal Citizenship: Women and Social Assistance Reform in the 1990s." *Studies in Political Economy* 50: 7–36.

Scott, MacDonald. 2000. Personal Interview. April.

Sheldrick, Byron. 1998. "Welfare Reform Under Ontario's NDP: Social Democracy and Social Group Representation." *Studies in Political Economy* 55: 37–63.

Spendlove, Rosemary. 2005. Personal Interview. May.

Splane, Richard. 1996. *75 Years of Community Service to Canada: Canadian Council on Social Development*. Ottawa: CCSD.

TAG (Tenant Action Group). 2005. Focus Group, May.

UNCESCR (United Nations Committee on Economic, Social, and Cultural Rights). 1993. "Concluding Observations of the Committee on Economic, Social and Cultural Rights: Canada." 10 June.

UNCESCR. 1998. "Concluding Observations of the Committee on Economic, Social and Cultural Rights: Canada." 4 December.

Wagner, David. 1993. *Checkerboard Square: Culture and Resistance in a Homeless Community*. Boulder: Westview Press.

Walker, David Charles. 1971. "The Poor People's Conference: A Study of the Relationship Between the Federal Government and Low Income Interest Groups in Canada." M.A. Thesis, Queen's University.

Watson, Steve. 2000. Personal Interview. March.

Welsh, Moira. 1996. "Death on Our Streets: Patrol Finds Body of Homeless Man under Gardiner." *Toronto Star*, 2 February.

Wharf, Brian. 1992. *Communities and Social Policies in Canada*. Toronto: McClelland and Stewart.

Whiteley, Paul F., and Stephen J. Winyard. 1987. *Pressure for the Poor: The Poverty Lobby and Policy Making*. London: Methuen.

Workfare Watch. 2001. "After the Boom." *Workfare Bulletin*, No. 3.

Wright, Talmadge. 1997. *Out of Place: Homeless Mobilizations, Subcities, and Contested Landscapes*. Albany: State University of New York Press.

PART TWO
Ethnicity, Gender, and Religion

FIVE

Ethnocultural Political Mobilization, Multiculturalism, and Human Rights in Canada

Audrey Kobayashi

Ethnocultural political mobilization became a significant feature of Canadian political life with the adoption of multiculturalism as both a public policy and a discourse on national identity during the latter decades of the twentieth century. There are isolated historical moments when ethnocultural or racialized groups have taken a stand against oppression, but these were relatively rare—and ineffectual—until the 1970s, when changes occurred both in official state policy and at the grassroots to propel such groups to fight for human rights.

Our national discourse over multiculturalism is based on these fundamental ideological questions: who is, and who has the right to be, Canadian; and how can those rights be achieved and protected in a plural society? I argue here that whereas the movement for full and equal citizenship has been the basis for ethnocultural mobilization, the terms of the discourse are overwhelmingly influenced by the structural conditions set by public policy, from the anglo-conformist conditions of the late nineteenth century to the neoliberal framework of the early twenty-first century. Whereas the *Charter of Rights and Freedoms* (the Charter) and other legal or constitutional devices have provided a very important enabling framework, the achievement of political rights also requires a high level of political openness and a will to action from government, the public in general, and ethnocultural groups themselves.

Since World War II, the concept of human rights has become a part of discourses over the fundamental characteristics of Canada, and Canadians as a whole now see themselves as representing the best of liberal democratic ideas of inclusion. The ability of ethnocultural and racialized minority groups to achieve full citizenship and to overcome human rights injustices, however, has been limited. Where achievements have occurred, as in the case of the Japanese-Canadian redress settlement described below, it is in that space created by both public policy and political will and given energy by the actions of the community itself. Within that space, four main factors—political will, coalition-building, community support, and public opinion—can create the most effective structures of "political opportunity" (as Miriam Smith has called them in the Introduction of this volume) for social movements. But such confluences are rare and unlikely to occur in the current neoliberal climate.

As Laura Pulido (2006) and others writing on social movements in the US have shown recently, social activism is very much a product of its times, and in my discussion here I try to show that the neoliberalism of the past decade has had a dampening effect, much as the human rights fluorescence of the previous decade resulted in openings. In what follows I discuss three examples of social activism in context: the Japanese-Canadian redress movement; Canadian participation in the World Conference on Racism, Racial Discrimination, Xenophobia, and Related Intolerance (WCAR); and the national lobby group, the Canadian Ethnocultural Council. Before going on to a discussion of some of the ways in which the political opportunity structure has opened up, and closed down, for ethnocultural and racialized minority groups in Canada, I discuss the background to Canada's particular form of multiculturalism.

Getting to the Table: A Brief History

Although the concept of Canadian citizenship has been based on pluralism and built upon immigration since colonial times, most of the immigrants who made up what was to be known as the Canadian "mosaic"[1] were not originally invited to partake at the table of citizenship, and many were deliberately shunned. The stories of those thousands of citizens who became the "others" in the mosaic are of struggling to make a place for themselves and their families in the face of exclusion, discrimination, and economic marginalization. The struggle has been to become full citizens not only in law but in the dominant political imaginary.

Black Canadians of African, Caribbean, and American origin were shunned and spatially marginalized from the time of the Loyalist movement (1780s) to the Underground Railway (mid-nineteenth century) and gained only a very tenuous presence, often as slaves or indentured servants (Winks, 1997; Mensah, 2002; Cooper, 2006). Asian immigrants were imported in large numbers as cheap and expendable labour for the railways, mines, and forest industries of western Canada from the time of Confederation until the first decade of the twentieth century (Li, 1998; Kobayashi and Ayukawa, 2002). Settlers from eastern and southern European countries were largely discouraged, shunted into the lowest-paid jobs (e.g., Italian immigrants in the construction industry;

see Zucchi, 1988), or used to support the agricultural settlement of the Prairies (Knowles, 1992).

From a public policy perspective, these are stories of government action both to preserve the dominance of British and French heritage and to use immigration policy instrumentally to serve a growing need for oppressed workers based on what Bonacich (1972) more than three decades ago called a "split labour market." Canadian history, like that of other settler societies, is based on a recursive relationship between the economic marginalization and social stigmatization of ethnocultural and racialized minorities and the ideological justification of the founding "nations" as dominant. While Others were imported as cheap labour, therefore, settlers of first French, then British origin were encouraged as the vanguard of colonial presence. Upon British ascendancy, Lord Durham envisioned immigration as a means of establishing the dominance of the British as an "effective barrier against the recurrence of many of the existing evils" (quoted in Knowles, 1992: 41; see Craig, 1963: 172)—who, of course, included the French Canadians. Federal and provincial governments went to extraordinary measures during the latter years of the twentieth century to keep Canada a "white man's country" (Ferguson, 1975; Ward, 1978), while still controlling the tap on cheap, particularly Asian labour. The *Chinese Immigration Act* (1885), which imposed a "head tax" on new immigrants after their labour had been expended in building the national railroad, represents perhaps the most cynical of such measures.

Instrumentalism peaked during the Laurier administration (1896–1911) when Clifford Sifton, as Minister of the Interior, embarked upon his ambitious scheme to populate the prairie provinces with Eastern Europeans, whom he described as a "stalwart peasant in a sheepskin coat ... with a stout wife and a half dozen children" (quoted in Knowles, 1992: 64, *passim*). Sifton engaged in secret negotiations with European governments to promote movement to Canada and augmented a plan to disperse them on agricultural land across vast swathes of the prairies. His successor, Frank Oliver, oversaw revisions to the *Immigration Act* that clearly set out the definition of "undesirable" Canadians (Knowles, 1992: 75–86). When Sifton returned to the portfolio during the 1920s, he responded to pressure from business for more immigrant labour by overseeing a startling agreement that turned the immigrant recruitment over to the two national railways, opening the door to greater diversity in the highly selective selection process (Knowles, 1992: 107–08).

Thus Sifton and others who controlled public policy actually set the conditions for ethnocultural mobilization decades later, albeit in a deeply ironic manner. It seems they had no intention of creating "equal" status for groups other than the dominant groups; on the contrary, their vision was deeply racist. Nonetheless, their actions, based on a deliberative attempt to diversify the Canadian population on the basis of putative racial characteristics linked to the capacity for labour resulted in the creation of a significant number of minority ethnocultural groups, particularly in the farming regions of the prairie provinces, the very heartland from which ethnocultural political mobilization was to emerge decades later. I shall return to this point below.

Were we to speak of ethnocultural mobilization during those early years, however, it would be most accurate to describe it as mobilization of *white* Canadians of Western European origins organizing in an attempt to keep Canada white. The "Vancouver Riot" of 1907, while it was a spontaneous event sparked by public speeches, skirmishes over a thrown rock, and fuelled by alcohol (Ward, 1978: 53–76), was also the result of organized demands from ethnoculturally defined (white) trade unionists to curb immigration levels. The subsequent Royal Commission Report—part of a string of similar documents—contains the vision of fledgling politician W.L. Mackenzie King for the restriction and regulation of the non-white population (Canada, 1908). To cite another example, several decades later, the Christie Pits anti-Semitic riot in Toronto, also spontaneous, occurred in a context of organized political mobilization to support one particular ethnocultural vision, that of Nazism (Levitt and Shaffir, 1985). To call these events the result of social movements may be overstating the case, but there is no question that they represented the active arm of ideologically formed social groups.

During the 1940s, in the most comprehensive program yet of racial exclusion, the Canadian government, now led by the same Mackenzie King, responded to organized public and political pressure after Canada's entry into the Pacific War (December 1941) with the uprooting, dispossession, and internment of Japanese Canadians (Adachi, 1976; Sunahara, 1981).

These events—and many others—were not completely without organized response. Following the Vancouver riots in October 1907, for example, Asian workers traumatized the city by going on strike and depriving wealthy white citizens of both laundry services and domestic labour. As early as 1938, the Japanese-Canadian community organized to send a delegation to Ottawa to lobby for the franchise, which was denied to most non-whites until passage of the *Citizenship Act* in 1947[2] (Goto and Shimizu, 1981). The Canadian Jewish Congress, formed in 1919 in the aftermath of World War I, began a serious human rights lobby in 1934, both to address anti-Semitism in Canada and to call attention to the escalating persecution of Jews in Europe. The Congress would grow to become a formidable political voice in the years following World War II (Canadian Jewish Congress, n.d.).

Such early attempts at organizing for ethnocultural rights, however, were on the whole reactive, fragmentary, and unsustained. It took the widespread adoption by Canadians of the concept of human rights in the wake of World

War II, and the promulgation by the UN of the International Declaration of Human Rights, to usher in a way of recognizing minority groups that would also lead over the next several decades to the rise of multiculturalism.

Canada's "Third Force"

A number of events in Canada during the 1960s, beginning with the passage of the *Human Rights Act* in 1960, set the context for the rise of ethnocultural political mobilization that became one of the defining features of social movements and public debate during the 1970s and 1980s. Immigration policy was entirely revamped, resulting in an increase in both the numbers and the diversity of immigrants (Knowles, 2000). The student movement and, more specifically, the American civil rights movement sparked discussion over human rights issues. The arrival of war resisters from the US, then embroiled in the Vietnam War, prompted considerations of Canada's role in international peace and justice. These events occurred amidst ongoing and often acrimonious debate over the relationship between the province of Quebec and the rest of Canada.

In 1963, Prime Minister Lester B. Pearson established the Royal Commission on Bilingualism and Biculturalism, which submitted a preliminary report in 1965 followed by three volumes comprising the main report in 1967. In 1969, the commission tabled a fourth volume entitled *The Cultural Contribution of the Other Ethnic Groups*, which resulted from discussions that took place across Canada during its investigations.

More important than the findings of the commission, however, is the fact that this era represented a period of unprecedented development of ethnocultural political awareness. In 1964, Paul Yuzyk, born in Saskatchewan in 1913 to Ukrainian immigrants, became the first individual of non-British, non-French background to be appointed to the Senate. He is credited with having introduced the term "multiculturalism" in his inaugural speech, in which he claimed that "Canada has become multicultural in fact" (Yuzyk, n.d.). Yuzyk went on to identify what he termed a "third force" in Canadian political life. Thus began his indefatigable Senate career as a champion of ethnocultural rights.

Pearson's successor, Pierre Elliott Trudeau, received the fourth volume of the commission and responded with a multiculturalism policy, introduced in Parliament on 8 October 1971 with the comment that "although there are two official languages, there is no official culture, nor does any ethnic group take precedence over any other" (Canada, 1971).[3] In the more than three decades since, the policy has undergone several reinventions, according to shifting political ideologies (Kobayashi, 1993; Abu-Laban and Gabriel, 2002: ch. 4; Fleras and Elliott, 2003: ch. 10), an issue that I take up again in the next section.

Mobilizing Ethnocultural Activists

Ethnocultural political mobilization took form in Canada as both a push for and a response to the introduction of multiculturalism. During the first decade of official multiculturalism, government documents show a decided sense of ethnicity as an add-on, a touch of flavour enriching, but not fundamentally changing, a society in which the concept of biculturalism (overlain with anglocentrism) remained both dominant and normative. A strong partnership developed nonetheless between the federal government and multiculturalism stakeholders, although that partnership was contained and channelled through the Multiculturalism Secretariat.

To the extent that we can speak of a multicultural "movement," it occurred during the lead-up to the repatriation of the Constitution, when grassroots community groups came together to influence public policy on multiculturalism and human rights. Up until that time, multiculturalism had not been taken very seriously by the federal government that created it since the government was deeply concerned with appeasing francophones who might view multiculturalism as a threat to their historical status (Burnet, 1976: 206). Its public statements played upon the growing and colourful idea that Canada was a "mosaic" in contrast to the American "melting pot."[4] But while the government promoted its program in simplistic terms as supporting so-called "red boots" multiculturalism—food and festivals—it also provided the resources for minority groups to begin to organize. The largesse intended by Prime Minister Trudeau to "assist all Canadian cultural groups ... to continue to develop a capacity to grow and contribute to Canada" (Canada, 1971) supported a growing social movement.

The Canadian Ethnocultural Council (CEC) was formed in 1980 as a national umbrella organization for groups representing varied communities and has the following mission statement printed on the masthead of its newsletter, *Ethno Canada*:

> ... to secure equality of opportunity, rights and dignity for ethnocultural communities in Canada. The CEC membership works by sharing information so as to develop a consensus on issues of concern to its membership and by advocating for changes on behalf of ethnic and visible minority groups.

Elsewhere, I have described the process through which the CEC became a significant lobby organization that influenced a range of public policy and legislative changes that took place during the heady days of the 1980s (Kobayashi, 2000). It was a very active organization with a significant educational role that not only empowered national ethnocultural groups to further their human rights concerns but also reached out to "mainstream" society in an attempt to push that agenda.

As Canadians became more and more aware of the implications of the Charter, proposed by the Trudeau government in 1980 (Kobayashi, 2000), group after group (many but not all organized under the auspices of the CEC) appeared in the hearing held by the Special Joint Committee of the Senate and House of Commons. These groups emphasized three issues in particular: the entrenchment of multiculturalism, the preservation of non-official heritage languages, and support for ethnoculturally based religious education.

The result was only a partial victory. In the final version of the Charter, passed in 1982, freedom from discrimination is specified under section 15 and gender equality is guaranteed under section 28, while "the multicultural heritage of Canadians" is recognized in an elusive interpretive clause in section 27. This point is important for two reasons. First, both clauses (section 28 on gender and section 27 on multiculturalism) were fought for strongly on the part of their relative constituents, especially because of the fact that section 15 on equality rights can be overridden by federal or provincial governments using the notwithstanding clause while sections 27 and 28 are not subject to the override. However, while section 28 clearly requires gender equality under the law, section 27 is a loose interpretative clause. The fact that one struggle resulted in a guarantee while the other did not speaks significantly of the effectiveness of the enthocultural lobby vis-à-vis the feminist lobby at the time: the latter was able to secure effective legal guarantees of gender equality while the former was unable to secure the same level of protection. Secondly, whereas section 15 guarantees *individual* freedom from discrimination, including discrimination based on race, ethnicity, religion, and national origin—all of which protect individuals who are members of minority ethnocultural groups—multiculturalism is a much more comprehensive notion, which would permit the adoption of policies and practices that address problems such as structural and systematic discrimination and racism in addition to the treatment of the individual under the law.

It was not long after the adoption of the Charter before legal experts began to confirm what had been obvious to the many groups that had appeared before the committee: the legal basis for upholding the rights of ethnocultural groups was very ambiguous (Hudson, 1987). Furthermore, it had become clear that such rights were considerably down the list of political priorities for rights claims. Ethnocultural group organizers were told by politicians that their "issues" took a back seat to questions of the status of Quebec, land claims, and gender equity, creating the sense on all sides of a hierarchy of citizenship claims (Stasiulis and Abu-Laban, 1991; Stasiulis, 1994, 1997; Kobayashi, 2000).

In retrospect, the paradox of the multicultural rights movement of the 1980s was that its very success was its eventual undoing. The government opened the door through its multiculturalism policy, providing not only the resources but the forum in which to push for concerns that were quite different from those envisioned under the Trudeau administration. The multicultural movement stretched the concept of "culture" beyond the traditional definition of folkways to one that encompassed full citizenship; it was not the right to *culture* that was most important, it was the right to equality in every sense. Equality entails not only the right to express one's own cultural identity but the right to full participation in all aspects of Canadian society, whether that means freedom from discrimination because of one's religion or equal access to employment opportunities. Once the naïve notion of folkways had been transcended, there was no turning back.

The 1980s represented a window of openness—indeed, something close to partnership—between parts of the federal government and ethnocultural communities. That openness allowed ethnocultural groups to strengthen a commitment to achieving equality rights and overcoming racism. There is probably no better example than the creation of another special committee, this time on the Participation of Visible Minorities in Canadian Society. Its *Report*, released in 1984 (Canada, 1984), is based on evidence from more than 400 groups and individuals who argued passionately that, given the inadequacies of the Charter, there was a need for a broad range of public policy initiatives across a number of areas, including social integration, employment, immigration, the justice system, media, and education. The 80 specific recommendations that result read as one of the most significant human rights documents ever written. And they envision human rights not simply as something that inheres in the freedom of the individual but, rather, as something fostered in an open and inclusive society. Furthermore, for perhaps the first time in Canadian history, this was a report compiled by a group of public servants drawn from racialized communities, who were able to bring both their functionary and their activist roles to bear on the question of racism (see Canada, 1984: iv–v).

The next few years saw the implementation, both directly and indirectly, of some of the measures called for in the *Report* in a range of legislative acts (employment equity, multiculturalism, broadcasting, immigration), in a proliferation of cases before the Canadian Human Rights Commission, and in a range of Charter cases before the Supreme Court (Kallen, 2003: ch. 9).[5] The Department of Multiculturalism became a full department for the first time in 1988 (although this status was short-lived as it was again downgraded to secretariat status after the Liberal government was elected in 1993). Organizations such as the CEC flourished under a reasonably high level of funding, community support, and both public and official recognition (Kobayashi, 2000).

The signing of the Japanese-Canadian redress settlement in 1988 represents very well the culmination of this decade of multicultural fluorescence.

The Japanese-Canadian Redress Settlement: A Case Study

The Japanese-Canadian redress settlement is one of very few high points of successful ethnocultural anti-racist activism in Canadian history. The story is told elsewhere (Kobayashi, 1992; Miki and Kobayashi, 1991; Miki, 2005). Here, I am only concerned with the process of mobilizing activists to achieve the settlement. My analysis rests primarily on my observations as a member of the negotiating committee that represented the National Association of Japanese Canadians (NAJC).

Activism for full citizenship rights for racialized minorities had few precedents prior to World War II. For Japanese Canadians, as mentioned above, there had been limited activism for full citizenship on the part of a small group of second-generation individuals (*Nisei*) in the 1930s. Their concern to achieve the franchise, however, would pale in the context of the uprooting, dispossession, and denial of human rights and physical freedom that would occur from 1942 to 1949. The story of human rights activism begins during the latter part of this period, when up to 10,000 Japanese Canadians were slated for "repatriation"—which was actually deportation or exile, since many of them were born in Canada. During the wartime uprooting, there emerged in Toronto a small group of activists from mainstream (white) organizations, mainly churches, calling themselves the Cooperative Committee for Japanese Canadians (CCJC). It advocated against the human rights abuses towards Japanese Canadians and, in particular, was instrumental in lobbying to stop the deportations, albeit after more than 4,000 had been sent to Japan in 1946.

The actions of the CCJC are ironic in two respects. First, they occurred at a time when Canada and other Allied nations were congratulating themselves for having won a just war in the name of human rights. Secondly it took a group of white activists, not the Japanese-Canadian community or its own spokespersons, to achieve some political effect. As Ross Lambertson (2005: 141) notes, "Only a 'white'-dominated organization like the CCJC, with links to the Canadian establishment and support from a number of well-known respectable and largely middle-class citizens ... could have exerted much pressure on Ottawa."

The attempts on the part of Japanese Canadians to organize at that time have been studied in some detail. Peter Nunoda (1991), while recognizing the reality that a racialized minority, especially one as socially reviled as the Japanese Canadians had been in the 1940s, could not (and indeed did not) achieve justice on their own behalf, also suggests that what the CCJC achieved was not necessarily what Japanese Canadians wanted. For, while the CCJC recognized the injustice of deportation, it also supported the concept of dispersal to eastern Canada rather than return to the communities and property that Japanese Canadians had held prior to 1942. This was an assimilationist perspective. The CCJC fixed on the justifiable concern over what many saw as the totalitarian power of government to deport its own citizens under the *National Emergency Transitional Powers Act* (see MacLennan, 2003: 37–38), but that concern in itself was not directed to overcoming racism.

Nunoda also chronicles in some detail the conflicts within a community divided over how hard to push for rights, that division a product of the experiences of racism that had left many community members afraid of further reprisals. He ties the reluctance to organize for rights to complicity on the part of a group of Nisei that came to dominate the community with the CCJC and their relatively conservative strategy. Roy Miki (2005: 128) goes beyond Nunoda's complicity argument, suggesting that, "The young Nisei who found themselves at the centre of a social and political cyclone were so bound up in the trauma of a displaced collective ... that their own language quickly reached the limits of its grasp."

World War II, and the period of febrile human rights activism that marked its aftermath, may have created political opportunities for the mainstream to organize for a new vision of Canada, but those opportunities would be some time coming for Japanese Canadians and other racialized minorities. For years afterward, mobilization from within the community was limited. The close-knit communities on the Pacific Coast, particularly in Vancouver, had been physically dispersed. The physical dismantling also involved the destruction of most community infrastructure, although some of the churches re-established themselves during the 1950s. But there were no initiatives to continue the fight for redress; indeed, those who tried to do so were deemed to be troublemakers. People were concerned with starting new lives, fulfilling new hopes, and maintaining a positive image in the eyes of both public and government officials.

The redress movement began to take hold during the 1970s, at a time when the international student movement, the civil rights movement in the US, and the rise of multiculturalism in Canada had created an escalated human rights discourse and a climate of social change. Japanese Canadians came together in 1977 to celebrate the centennial of the arrival of the first immigrant from Japan to Canada, and this occasion sparked discussion of a new push to obtain redress. The young people, mostly university students, who initiated those discussions were branded as "radicals" by many in the community, for whom the thought of raising sensitive issues still brought forth painful memories. But the movement gained momentum, and the next decade saw a concerted effort, intensified from about 1986, to obtain a settlement.

Four elements are key to the settlement that was finally reached in September 1988. First, there was political will on the part of the federal government, which crafted redress as part of an emerging social justice agenda that was also politically popular. At a rally on Parliament Hill in April, the newly appointed Minister of Multiculturalism, Gerry Weiner (the first full minister in that portfolio), gave a speech that opened the way to negotiations that would see an agreement reached in the month of August, followed by a public announcement on 22 September. During the final negotiation, which occurred in secret over several days, it became clear that key members of the government, including the prime minister, supported the process fully. When the settlement was announced in the House of Commons, it was greeted with unqualified support from all parties as expressed in a standing ovation by the entire House and emotional speeches from the opposition leaders.

Part of this political will may have come from the fact that the US had implemented a redress agreement with Japanese Americans a month before. That settlement had certainly sparked considerable discussion in Canada, including calls in the media for the Canadian government to follow suit. But it would be far too simplistic to say that the settlement was simply a matter of following the Americans. From the government perspective, there were several other factors. For one, it also came shortly after the retirement of parliamentary veteran and Minister of Veterans Affairs, George Hees, who had been a strong opponent of a settlement and used every opportunity to link redress discussion with the plight of Canadian soldiers who had been captured by the Japanese at Hong Kong: a completely different issue, of course, involving a different national government, but one that nonetheless brought out reactionary views. For another, this was a key time in the build-up towards both a national election (October 1988) and what two years later would become a crisis of national unity (the Meech Lake Accord). Lucien Bouchard was still Secretary of State in 1988; indeed, it was he who, in person, initiated the redress negotiations with the NAJC prior to turning it over to Minister of Multiculturalism Weiner. This period, in which Bouchard and Prime Minister Mulroney were seen to be working together for unity and for a broader understanding of human rights, was perhaps the highest point of "red Tory"-ism in Canadian history. During the stormy second Mulroney term that followed, however, marked by an economic recession as well as the failure of the Meech Lake Accord and Bouchard's break with the government to form the Bloc Québécois, the political opportunity for an achievement such as the Japanese-Canadian redress settlement would not have occurred.

Second, mobilization at the community level had been sufficient that the vast majority of Japanese Canadians, originally reticent because of the fear of backlash, were now supportive of the negotiations. Broad community support was necessary in order to quell arguments from a succession of ministers who preceded Weiner that the NAJC could not represent all Japanese Canadians. That support was hard-won by community organizers who called meetings, staged fundraising and educational events, and encouraged people to talk about an issue that had been repressed for decades. The community discourse was part of a process of healing that had to occur before people could muster the will to fight for justice.

There is no more exhilarating feeling than the sense of common cause that occurs in the midst of a movement for social justice that is gaining ground. We can see a similar phenomenon on film in the pulsing crowds of South Africans prior to the downfall of apartheid or in the quiet, stubborn elation beneath the stoic crowds assembled to support the Polish Solidarity movement (both events that were developing at the same time as the redress settlement), expressions of collective optimism that belie the pain and suffering from which they emerged. To be part of the redress movement, frankly, was exciting. We felt so strong in our resolve. The sense of urgency was both compelling and contagious, especially with regard to the aged first generation (*Issei*) for whom a few months might make the difference of seeing a settlement in their lifetimes. And nothing mobilizes a community so much as the collective conviction that their cause is right and just and winnable. And so, at the same time that the political conditions for redress advanced on Parliament Hill, the community readied itself for a victory and, sensing a victory, those who may have been reticent in the past were eager to be part of this shared experience.

It is unlikely, nonetheless, that Japanese Canadians would have been so strong in their resolve were it not for a third factor: the swelling support of human rights groups, religious groups, labour unions, and other ethnocultural organizations who came together to make our battle theirs. A major difference between the late 1980s and the late 1940s is that Japanese Canadians were no longer bystanders for their own cause but leaders for a cause that was seen not only as providing justice for Japanese Canadians but as setting a precedent for other oppressed groups. There was widespread recognition among those groups (if not on the part of the government) that our common cause was against a history of racialization.

When the NAJC staged a rally on Parliament Hill in April 1988, representatives of other groups came out in force and spoke eloquently and passionately. The sound of Japanese-Canadian taiko drums and Aboriginal drums reverberating together through the halls of Parliament in a call for justice was symbolic of mutual support. So were the thousands of yellow postcards from Canadian citizens of many backgrounds signed and delivered to the minister's office. Key to the participation of a broad spectrum of human rights activists was not only their commitment to overcoming injustice but also their assertion that this settlement provided a model for addressing other injustices, including the Chinese head tax and treatment of Aboriginal children in residential schools.

Finally, the approbation of the Canadian public in general brought together the perspectives of government and community. Popular opinion had swung drastically since the 1940s so that ordinary Japanese Canadians found that what had been a hidden and shameful topic could now be talked about in public. Their fellow citizens commonly expressed outrage at the injustices of the 1940s and were willing to support the redress movement vocally. The government clearly had a sense that the settlement would be a popular political move. It was seen as a good thing to do, especially in the lead-up to the federal election of October 1988.

Such moments as that in which the Japanese-Canadian redress settlement was negotiated occur rarely. Without taking away from the very high level of dedication to human rights that fuelled this initiative from the grassroots, I do not believe that it would have been successful had not the political conditions at the time been so accommodating. Political will, grassroots mobilization, coalition-building, and popular opinion came together at a time that, in retrospect, represented the high point of public policies designed to give minority ethnocultural groups a voice in national politics. Those who negotiated the settlement did so with a sense of optimism, therefore, because they saw it as the first of what could be several settlements to right wrongs of the past. But that course has not developed. Over the decade and a half following the redress settlement, there has occurred instead a significant shift in public policy towards a neoliberal agenda against which mobilization of ethnocultural groups has become more and more difficult.

Negotiating the Neoliberal Present

While the neoliberal trajectory in which the Canadian state has been caught up has certainly gained strength for several decades, for ethnocultural organizations lobbying for human rights, the point of transition came during the second administration of the Progressive Conservative Party under Prime Minister Brian Mulroney (1988–93) and accelerated after the return in 1993 of the Liberal Party under Prime Minister Jean Chrétien. As Miriam Smith (2005) argues cogently, the neoliberal era has seen a fundamental restructuring of the relationship between the state and advocacy groups that has involved a general move from a collaborative relationship during the post-Charter era to an "accountability" relationship that was firmly in place by the end of the 1990s when the federal government formalized this shift with the adoption of the Volunteer Sector Initiative (Phillips and Graham, 2000; Brock, 2002). Abu-Laban and Gabriel (2002: 110–17) point out that even as commitment to the concepts of multiculturalism and anti-racism deepened during the 1980s, the Mulroney government was moving to a neoliberal model with a focus on ethnocultural entrepreneurialism, symbolized by a "Multiculturalism Means Business" conference held in Toronto in 1986.

Abu-Laban and Gabriel believe that the neoliberal shift has intensified over the past decade. On the one hand, "selling diversity," as they put it, gives Canada a marketing edge in a global environment where multiculturalism can be packaged as a Canadian asset. On the other, there is a growing sense that "the state should not play a role in the area of culture—[which is] a 'private' matter to be dealt with in the home and family" (2002: 111). The "privacy" of culture is not, of course, a new concept. When Trudeau first introduced multiculturalism decades ago, he made it very clear that, for him, multiculturalism was about the freedom to make *individual* identity choices. Such a notion encourages the expression of multiculturalism as a set of choices around "ethnic" food and other consumer items. The very different model of multiculturalism as human rights, anti-racism, and civic participation epitomized by the Japanese-Canadian redress settlement was probably not, therefore, what politicians and policy-makers had in mind back in the early 1980s.

What emerged from that decade, claims Howard-Hassmann (2003: 132–33) was the creation of a civil society based on "weak" cultural relativism (see also Donnelly, 1989) and an abiding notion of compassion based on the rights of the individual over those of the group. Howard-Hassmann's study of the opinions of leaders in the City of Hamilton shows that there are limits to the concept of multiculturalism and that those limits are met when people come up against what they see as hard cultural relativism that either sets group rights ahead of those of the individual or that creates an undemocratic ethnocentrism, social exclusion, or "tyranny of multiculturalism" (see Green, 1994: 116). Howard-Hassmann joins Kymlicka (1995, 2001) in endorsing this model of liberal democracy as a basis for balancing the rights of individuals and groups in ways that will advance multiculturalism as an expression of individual rights.

The liberal democratic model of citizenship and multiculturalism, and Kymlicka's vision in particular, has been debated extensively, and I make no attempt to cover it here (for a review, see Sunday, n.d.). Kymlicka has been widely criticized, however, for what Parekh (1997, 2000) and others have identified as a hierarchical notion of citizenship based on a distinction between national and cultural minorities in relation to dominant majorities (see also Young, 1997). The emphasis on the individual is usually seen as a way out of the dilemma of accommodating group rights, but the intractable conflict between liberalism and pluralism remains (see Burtonwood, n.d.).

My much simpler point here, however, concerns the pragmatic results of this tension for ethnocultural and racialized minority groups for whom overcoming racism is not necessarily served by the terms of the debate over multiculturalism. Herein lies one of the paradoxes of the Japanese-Canadian redress settlement. Whereas the settlement represented for activists at the time an opening up of possibilities through which social movements could play a transformative role for both state and civil society, their hopes have not been realized. First, for all that it represented an important achievement of justice, the settlement was still based on individual rights as defined within a liberal democracy. And it was partly that emphasis that made the settlement so popular. Notwithstanding the creation of the Canadian Race Relations Foundation (CRRF) as part of the settlement, the rights of individual citizens always trump attempts to combat racism, especially when overcoming racism involves recognizing the extent to which Canada remains a colonial society based on ethnocultural hierarchies and a broad culture of whiteness.

Second, perhaps because the settlement was more about individual rights than about racism, the strength of that anti-racist message was lost as the neoliberal project gained momentum throughout the 1990s. In the process, minority ethnocultural groups—who had worked so hard to find a place at the table two decades ago and who, it could be argued, were instrumental in rewriting the potential social and political role of minority groups in human rights advocacy—found that it became increasingly easier to sell diversity than to lobby for human rights. The two are not, of course, *intrinsically* opposed, but there are two significant difficulties. First, it is difficult to "sell" multiculturalism as an idyllic made-in-Canada social condition if questions of human rights, especially questions of racism, are raised. There is therefore a strong business incentive for keeping the lid on discussions of racism and other forms of oppression in the interests of marketing diversity. Secondly, ethnocultural groups, like others in the not-for-profit sector, are faced with the dilemma of having to choose between projects that will attract funding— especially those that follow a neoliberal model—and waging a human rights campaign in a climate where resources are increasingly scarce. Two further examples illustrate these two problems.

Canada's Role in the World Conference on Racism, Racial Discrimination, Xenophobia, and Related Intolerance (WCAR)

Canada was one of the more active nations in this international conference, which took place in Durban, South Africa, 28 August to 7 September 2001. The process began a year earlier when the federal government set up a consultation process with racialized minorities and Aboriginal groups. The WCAR Secretariat organized regional meetings across the country designed both to mobilize non-governmental organization (NGO) participation and to hear concerns from grassroots organizations. The preparation/consultation process culminated in a national conference held in Ottawa on 23–24 February.[6] The Canadian contingent that left for South Africa in August consisted of a strong group of NGOs, who met in the days prior to the official government meetings.

The enthusiastic response from community groups might have resulted in another high point in the history of mobilizing for human rights in Canada, almost reminiscent of the events that took place during the 1980s. There was a sense among many of the participants of a partnership between officials and NGOs. The meetings were not, however, without tension. Some objected to the fact that the Secretariat had created a separate national advisory committee for Aboriginal peoples but had "lumped" visible minorities together. Unity threatened to dissolve at the Toronto regional meeting when a group called for a separate advisory committee for those who experience anti-black racism, for whom issues such as slavery reparations were significant. Others were concerned that should the agenda be focused on the contemporary effects of the Atlantic slave trade, then issues such as present-day human trafficking, particularly of people from Asia, would be sidelined. Government officials, and the majority of those who attended the meetings, remained firm in their commitment to a single visible minority advisory committee, however, that would address all the issues on what turned out to be a rather contentious international agenda.

Unlike the US, who pulled out of the meetings as soon as the discussions began to hit areas where that administration had disagreements,[7] Canada stayed the course and played a prominent role in drafting the final declarations of the conference (WCAR Secretariat, n.d.). Internationally, the result was to place—or replace—on the agenda a range of significant issues of racism and xenophobia that have been the basis of oppression and its lingering effects for centuries. The UN and a significant number of international NGOs used the conference to continue to focus attention on injustices worldwide. One of the most significant concrete results was a draft international Resolution on the Rights of Indigenous Peoples (Dialogue Between Nations, n.d.).

As a basis for mobilizing racialized minorities in Canada, however, the WCAR has had few, if any, lasting effects. As my description above shows, the process discouraged coalition-building, especially in an environment where groups had to compete for coveted NGO designations and for government funding. The atmosphere of the regional preparations meetings was more one of getting individual issues on the agenda than of developing a concerted approach to addressing racism in Canada.

Indeed, while there was support for selling Canada as a nation in which racism does not occur, there was very little public support for using the WCAR as an opportunity to address racism. During and immediately after the conference, my monitoring of the media coverage in Canadian news-papers revealed that there was far more coverage of the claim that racism doesn't exist in Canada than anything else, with virtually no attention paid to the issues put forward by "special interest groups" such as ethnocultural minorities. Margaret Wente (2001) dubbed the conference "an exercise in self-flagellation, a make-work project for our antiracism industry." Rex Murphy (2001) referred to it as "Babble from genocide's bystanders." In a more subtle message, Mark MacKinnon (2001), the main *Globe and Mail* correspondent at the conference, ended his description of the Canadian delegation with the com-ment, "And they're doing so with taxpayers' money. One government source said that a large chunk of the $2-million the federal government has spent on preparing for the conference was used to help the 60 NGOs take part in the civil-society anti-racism talks this week and the UN forum that begins today." And some time later, Christie Blatchford (2001), one of the most conservative of Canadian journalists, argued that, "It is only the federal Liberals, and those whose reputations (and occasionally livelihoods) are inextricably tied to the operating assumption that racism is a pervasive reality in this country, who continually see this bogeyman beneath the Canadian bed."

These comments are, of course, text-book examples of what anti-racist scholars term the "new racism": vociferous denial, spoken by powerful white voices, that racism exists, with shades of (in this case not-so-subtle) innuendo that to bring up the topic of racism, therefore, is to give insult, to waste tax-payers' money, or to somehow gain advantage. It is a discourse of denial and discreditation (see Henry and Tator, 2006: 19–22). Of course, the voices cited above are not the only ones that we might listen to, but it is not unimportant that these are the voices of the *Globe and Mail*, which may not represent all Canadians but is arguably the most public venue for the expression of opinions in this country, and they are the voices of white Canada. In the face of such overwhelming media oppression, the opportunities for the WCAR to become a forum for building coalitions among Canada's racialized groups were limited indeed.[8]

Attention to the conference ended abruptly, however, a few days later on 11 September 2001, with the attacks against the World Trade Center in New York and the Pentagon in Washington, DC. In the following days, among the millions of words and images that were devoted to 9/11, there was consider-able attention paid to the need to guard against racism and intolerance towards minority groups, but whatever opportunity there may have been for groups to join together in light of the events in Durban simply never materialized.

Events had followed too closely upon one another, and the international reaction was too raw to be able to make the obvious links between post-9/11 and the issues raised at the WCAR.

Of course the timing of these events was unfortunate. Attention quickly shifted away from the WCAR with the result that opportunities for further mobilization and public dialogue were no doubt lost. An electronic search today for Canadian activities to follow up and maintain some of the momentum of the conference yields almost nothing. But there are two important ways in which the events in Durban and 9/11 came together. Racial profiling, including that by police departments as well as by a range of national security bodies, quickly became a major item of public discourse and public policy. As well, the discussions at the WCAR laid the basis for advancing discussions of redress and reparations for a number of Canadian groups, including First Nations, Chinese, German, Italian, Sikh, and Ukrainian Canadians, for whom the claims of injustice remain unresolved (CRRF, 2005). All of those issues are ongoing, but aside from the efforts of the CRRF to make a case that they are related, there is little effective coalition-building among the affected groups to overcome human rights abuses. And recent research by Matt James (2006) supports my suggestion that issues that involve redress for racist acts are still relatively poorly understood in Canada.

Contrasting the pre- and post-WCAR world allows an interesting take on the question of how minority group concerns fit into a neoliberal agenda. Prior to the conference, the federal government spent a considerable sum to support a Canadian delegation, whose mandate rested very significantly on the fact that Canada markets itself as a progressive place where multiculturalism makes good business. Notwithstanding the very sincere concern on the part of some politicians and policy-makers to overcome discrimination and inequality, it was nonetheless a giant marketing exercise with almost nothing to follow up the specific concerns of groups who continue to face racism and inequality. After 9/11, considerable efforts were turned to managing a radically transformed security environment in which occurred expressions of intolerance and hatred, including no few incidents of physical violence and vandalism against the property of brown-skinned people. But it has been business as usual on the multiculturalism front.

The Canadian Ethnocultural Council Today

Business as usual for those mobilizing for equality means an increasing struggle both to maintain resources and to address a political and social context in which multiculturalism is viewed as a source of inequality rather than a principle of justice. On 21 March 2006, International Day for the Elimination of

Racism, the *Globe and Mail* ran an on-line poll asking, "Is it time for Canada to abandon its multiculturalism policy and insist that immigrants adopt Canadian cultural values?" The response was "Yes," 19,842 votes (66 per cent), "No," 10,153 votes (34 per cent), for a total of 29,995 votes. While this should not really be considered a poll, let alone either in-depth or unbiased, the sheer number of responses is telling. Even the most controversial issues debated in these daily "polls" seldom receive more than 20,000 votes (*Globe and Mail Insider Edition*, 2006). Either the number of responses indicates a widespread public feeling about multiculturalism, or the anti-multiculturalism movement was especially successful on that day in encouraging its supporters to log on to the newspaper's website, or both.

Be that as it may, that "poll" is but one piece of evidence in a growing number of indications that since 9/11 the public attitude to multiculturalism has "hardened" because it is seen as promoting the difference of brown-skinned immigrant groups from countries considered to have cultural traditions less similar than others to Canadian traditions. A similar and more scientific poll conducted by the Strategic Council in 2005, for example, showed that "Canadians are overwhelmingly in favour of abandoning the 'mosaic' approach to multiculturalism that has long been a defining feature of the nation's identity" (Curry and Jimènez, 2005). This finding concurs with Howard-Hassmann's (2003) finding cited above that the civic leaders in her study accepted and supported multiculturalism, but within limits.[9]

Acknowledging what seems to be a continuing development, the CEC reports that the trend that makes mobilization for equality rights more difficult—trends that I noted in my in-depth fieldwork seven years ago (Kobayashi, 2000)—has continued.[10] The CEC no longer acts as a lobbying organization, both because their efforts to influence federal politicians have been rebuffed and because the resources to bring members to Ottawa no longer exist. Funding from the Department of Canadian Heritage's Multiculturalism program, long the mainstay of ethnocultural activism, has significantly decreased. Those funds available have shifted from sustaining to project-based funds, as they have for the entire third sector (Brock, 2002). The CEC now operates as an "outreach organization," providing information to groups on such things as health care, social services, and immigration. According to Executive Director Anna Chiappa, the sense of partnership with government that had been developing two decades ago has now dissolved, replaced with a message that "grassroots organizations [should] do things for themselves" (Chiappa, 2006).

Some CEC member organizations have had some success in doing things for themselves. The Canadian Armenian Federation opened an office in Ottawa for the specific purpose of encouraging the government to recognize the

Armenian genocide, and they received an acknowledgement by Parliament of the genocide as a "crime against humanity."[11] The Chinese Canadian National Congress has kept up a small but concerted mobilization around the Chinese head tax and *Exclusion Act* between 1885 and 1947 (CCNC, n.d.) and achieved a much-contested settlement in June 2006 (Harper, 2006). The Ukrainian Canadian Congress similarly maintains a struggle for redress for Ukrainian Canadians interned during World War I, linking that issue to present-day support for multiculturalism in Canada and democracy in the Ukraine (Ukrainian Canadian Congress, n.d.). The Canadian Arab Foundation was behind the creation of an Ottawa-based office to lobby for public information on Islam (CAIR-CAN, n.d.).

All of these are fraught issues, with implications that go far beyond Canadian borders and involve complex webs of human rights issues. What characterizes all of them, however, is that they are targeting what they consider to be extreme examples of human rights abuses. The majority of the other national groups (at least those that maintain websites where I can review current issues) are focused on institution-building, and their agendas are driven by specific projects such as needs or capacity-building studies, youth forums, and cultural education projects, the sorts of projects that receive funding in the contemporary non-profit environment.

Ethnocultural Mobilization in a Neoliberal Regime

I do not mean to suggest that capacity-building projects, aimed at strengthening education, national linkages, and ethnocultural identity, are not important or worthwhile. What is troubling about the current situation, however, is the extent to which the national mobilization of human rights activists to support multiculturalism and anti-racism that seemed to be building across Canada two decades ago has been largely abandoned. The struggle to define multiculturalism as a program of equality rights and anti-racism, rather than (only) as a program to maintain cultural communities, has largely given way to the latter. And as the general perception of multiculturalism as something intended for a minority, especially new immigrants, has flourished, public opinion has inexorably begun to turn away from the concept. The majority of Canadians still support the idea of a cultural mosaic, but they believe strongly in an overriding "Canadian" culture, and that culture is a matter of private identity, not public policy. The sentiment is increasingly that multiculturalism has "gone too far," that there are limits to difference, and that ethnocultural groups should take care of themselves. Most of all, we have been unsuccessful in the attempt to make multiculturalism fundamentally about anti-racism. The failure of the activities both surrounding the WCAR and of the CEC point to the diminishing capacity for ethnocultural and racialized groups to muster either the will or the resources to extend the concept of multiculturalism as human rights to those who face the consequences of racism today, including African-origin groups enduring increasing relative poverty, Asians subject to human smuggling, and those of Islamic and Arab origin who experience racial profiling.

Researchers who have studied the course of multiculturalism and the role of ethnocultural groups in promoting human rights have remarked over and over that the course of the 1970s and the 1980s saw a movement from multicultural-ism as song, dance, and food festivals, to human rights advocacy (e.g., Day, 2000; Abu-Laban and Gabriel, 2002; Fleras, 2002; Biles, Tolley, and Ibrahim, 2005). Over the past decade we have come full circle. However, that does not mean that we have returned to the quaint festivals that marked ethnocultural groups' activities before the Charter era politicized them. Multiculturalism as a cultural commodity today is hip, not quaint.

Multiculturalism, and even putative racial equality, are increasingly commodities sold to "draw a link between diversity and business prosperity, international trade links, and Canada's global competitiveness" (Abu-Laban and Gabriel, 2002: 124). Ethnocultural groups must market themselves if they are to survive as institutions, and there is little room on the business agenda for human rights activism, much less for the kind of cross-cultural activism through which coalitions and social movements might be forged. Multiculturalism has become cosmopolitanism, more aptly epitomized by the diversity of ethnic restaurants in Canada's largest cities than by increasing access to human rights on the part of those most marginalized. Having found their place at the table, ironically, ethnocultural groups have more scope for eating than talking.

Notes

1. The metaphor of the mosaic is widely used in public policy, by social scientists, and in public discourse to describe Canadian demographic pluralism and to distinguish it from the American "melting pot." The notion comes from John Murray Gibbon's publication, *Canadian Mosaic: The Making of a Northern Nation* (1938), which, ironically, is based on a set of racialized categories of human difference and that leaves all non-white groups out of the picture. John Porter (1965) later coined the phrase "vertical mosaic" to address the issue of social class and power differences, although Porter, too, pays little attention to the process of racialization.

2. The 1947 *Citizenship Act* gave the franchise to all Canadians, except Japanese Canadians, who gained the right to vote in 1949, and status Indians (as defined under the *Indian Act*), who obtained it in 1960.

3. Popular critics of multiculturalism argue that Trudeau was less concerned with the status of minority ethnocultural groups than with using the policy to contrast Canada with the US and to weaken the notion of two founding groups by repositioning French and English Canada within a pluralist framework. See, for example, Coleman, 2006: 51.

4. See, for example, *The Canadian Family Tree* (Canada, 1967), a romantic depiction of Canada as a nation based on immigration where everyone gets along, with no issues of class or status, a remarkable piece of what even three decades ago Kostash (1977) called "whitewashing" (for a fuller discussion see Kobayashi, 1993: 214).

5. This period also saw the creation of the Court Challenges Program, established in 1978 to help individuals bring forward test cases that would clarify the Charter. In September 2006, the Harper government cancelled the program, citing as problematic the concept of government expending funds to challenge itself. This action perhaps more than any other signals an end to the reciprocal relationship between state and civil society that the period of multiculturalism building in the 1980s epitomized.

6. I attended both the regional meeting held in Toronto and the national meeting held in Ottawa as a participant. My comments are based in part on my notes from these meetings.

7. The two most contentious issues were slavery reparations and Israeli xenophobia against Palestinians, both issues on which the US took a minority opinion.

8. Of course, the agenda for the WCAR was much more complicated, devolving to a series of acrimonious debates over the issues of slavery reparations and—even more acrimonious—Arab-Israeli relations. These issues are not, however, the focus of my discussion here.

9. These indications notwithstanding, a comprehensive poll undertaken by Environics in 2001–02 showed that about 80 per cent of Canadians support the concept of multiculturalism (Jedwab, 2002). But those who tout the strength of Canadian support for multiculturalism often fail to acknowledge that supporting the concept and putting limits to the concept are two different things.

10. Interview with Anna Chiappa, Executive Director, Canadian Ethnocultural Council, 10 May 2006.

11. *Bill M-380* passed by a vote of 153–68 on 22 April 2004. Members of the Liberal cabinet, however, were instructed to vote against the bill, because of its implications for Canada-Turkish relations.

References and Further Reading

Abu-Laban, Yasmeen, and Christina Gabriel. 2002. *Selling Diversity: Immigration, Multiculturalism, Employment Equity, and Globalization.* Peterborough: Broadview.

Adachi, Ken. 1976. *A History of the Japanese Canadians: The Enemy that Never Was.* Toronto: McClelland and Stewart.

Biles, John, Erin Tolley, and Humera Ibrahim. 2005. "Does Canada Have a Multicultural Future?" *Canadian Diversity* 41: 23–28.

Blatchford, Christine. 2001. "$2.4 Million to Preach to the Converted." *National Post*, 20 October: A17

Bonacich, Edna. 1972. "A Theory of Ethnic Antagonism: The Split Labor Market." *American Sociological Review* 47: 547–59.

Brock, Kathy (Ed.). 2002. *Improving Connections Between Governments and Nonprofit and Voluntary Organizations: Public Policy and the Third Sector.* Montreal and Kingston: School of Policy Studies and McGill-Queen's University Press.

Burnet, Jean. 1975. "Multiculturalism, Immigration, and Racism: A Comment on the Canadian Immigration and Population Study." *Canadian Ethnic Studies* 8(1): 35–39.

Burnet, Jean. 1976. "Ethnicity: Canadian Experience and Policy." *Sociological Focus* 9(2): 199–207.

Burtonwood, Neil. N.d. "Reconciling Liberalism and Pluralism? On Mark Olssen's 'Revisioning' of Citizenship Education." Unpublished paper, Institute of Education, University of London. <http://www.ioe.ac.uk/pesgb/x/Burtonwood.pdf>.

CAIR-CAN (Council on American Islamic Relations of Canada). N.d. <http://www.caircan.ca/aboutus.php>.

Canada. 1908. *Report of W.L. Mackenzie King, C.M.G., Commissioner Appointed to Enquire into the Methods by Which Oriental Labourers have been Induced to Come to Canada:* Ottawa: King's Printer.

Canada. 1967. *The Canadian Family Tree.* Secretary of State, Citizenship Branch. Ottawa: Queen's Printer.

Canada. 1971. *House of Commons Debates.* 8 October.

Canada. 1984. *Equality Now! Report of the Special Committee on Participation of Visible Minorities in Canadian Society.* Bob Daudlin, Chair. Ottawa: Queen's Printer.

Canadian Ethnocultural Council. N.d. "CEC Activity Report." <http://www.ethnocultural.ca/activities.html>.

Canadian Jewish Congress. N.d. "A Historical Overview of the Early Years of Canadian Jewish Congress." <http://www.cjc.ca/template.php?Language=EN&action=history>.

CCNC (Chinese Canadian National Council). N.d. "The Chinese Head Tax and Exclusion Act." <http://www.ccnc.ca/redress/history.html >.

Chiappa, Anna. 2006. Personal interview. May 10.

Coleman, Ronald. 2006. *Just Watch Me: Trudeau's Tragic Legacy.* Victoria: Trafford.

Cooper, Afua. 2006. *The Hanging of Angelique: Canada, Slavery, and the Burning of Montreal.* Toronto: HarperCollins.

Craig, Gerald M. (Ed.). 1963. *Lord Durham's Report.* Carleton Library No. 1. Toronto: McClelland and Stewart.

CRRF (Canadian Race Relations Foundation). 2002. *From Racism to Redress: The Japanese Canadian Experience.* <http://www.crr.ca/en/Publications/ePubHome.htm>.

CRRF. 2005. *A Background Paper on the CRRF's Policy on Redress and Reparations.* <http://www.crr.ca/Load.do?section=28&subSection=46&type=2>.

Curry, Bill, and Marina Jimènez. 2005. "Many Believe European Newcomers Make More Positive Contribution, Poll Shows." *Globe and Mail*, 8 August: A6.

Day, Richard. 2000. *Multiculturalism and the History of Canadian Diversity.* Toronto: University of Toronto Press.

Dialogue Between Nations. N.d. <http://www.dialoguebetweennations.com/dbnetwork/english/selfdetermination.htm>.

Donnelly, Jack. 1989. *Universal Human Rights in Theory and Practice.* Ithaca: Cornell University Press.

Ferguson, Ted. 1975. *A White Man's Country: An Exercise in Canadian Prejudice.* New York and Toronto: Doubleday.

Fleras, Augie. 2002. "Multiculturalism as Critical Discourse: Contesting Modernity." *Canadian Issues/Thèmes canadiens* (Spring).

Fleras, Augie, and Jean Leonard Elliott. 2003. *Unequal Relations : An Introduction to Race and Ethnic Dynamics in Canada.* 4th ed. Toronto: Prentice Hall.

Gibbon, John Murray. 1938. *Canadian Mosaic: The Making of a Northern Nation.* Toronto: McClelland and Stewart.

Globe and Mail Insider Edition. 2006. "Is It Time for Canada to Abandon its Multiculturalism Policy and Insist That Immigrants Adopt Canadian Cultural Values?" <http://www.theglobeandmail.com/servlet/Page/document/v5/content/poll/pollResultHub>.

Goto, Edy, and Ron Shimizu. 1981. "On the N.A.J.C. Presentation to the Special Joint Committee on the Constitution: An Entrenched and Inviolate Charter of Rights." In Victor Ujimoto and Gordon Hirabayashi (eds.), *Asian Canadians: Regional Perspectives, Selection from the Proceedings, Asian Canadian Symposium V.* Montreal: Canadian Asian Studies Association. 380–90.

Green, Leslie. 1994. "Internal Minorities and Their Rights." In Judith Baker (ed.), *Group Rights.* Toronto: University of Toronto Press. 101–17.

Harper, Stephen. 2006. "Address by the Prime Minister on the Chinese Head Tax Redress." <http://www.pm.gc.ca/eng/media.asp?category=2&id=1220>.

Henry, Frances, and Carol Tator. 2006. *The Colour of Democracy: Racism in Canadian Society.* 3rd ed. Toronto: Thomson Nelson.

Howard-Hassmann, Rhoda. 2003. *Compassionate Canadians: Civic Leaders Discuss Human Rights.* Toronto: University of Toronto Press.

Hudson, Michael. 1987. *Multiculturalism and the Charter: A Legal Perspective.* Toronto: Carswell.

James, Matt. 2006. "Do Campaigns for Historical Redress Erode the Canadian Welfare State?" In Keith Banting and Will Kymlicka (eds.), *Multiculturalism and the Welfare State: Recognition and Redistribution in Contemporary Democracies.* Oxford: Oxford University Press. 222–46.

Jedwab, Jack. 2002. "Thirty Years of Multiculturalism in Canada, 1971–2001." <http://www.acs-aec.ca/Polls/Poll2.pdf>.

Kallen, Evelyn. 2003. *Ethnicity and Human Rights in Canada.* 3rd ed. Toronto: Oxford University Press.

Kobayashi, Audrey. 1992. "The Japanese-Canadian Redress Settlement and its Implications for 'Race Relations.'" *Canadian Ethnic Studies* 24(1): 1–19.

Kobayashi, Audrey. 1993. "Multiculturalism: Representing a Canadian Institution." In James Duncan and David Ley (eds.), *Place/Culture/Representation*. London: Routledge. 205–31.

Kobayashi, Audrey. 2000. "Advocacy from the Margins: The Role of Minority Ethnocultural Associations in Affecting Public Policy in Canada." In Keith Banting (ed.), *The Nonprofit Sector in Canada: Roles and Relationships*. Montreal and Kingston: School of Policy Studies and McGill-Queen's University Press. 229–66.

Kobayashi, Audrey, and Midge Ayukawa. 2002. "A Brief History of Japanese Canadians." In Akemi Kikumura Yano (ed.), *Encyclopedia of Japanese Descendants in the Americas: An Illustrated History of the Nikkei*. Walnut Creek: Altamira. 150–61.

Knowles, Valerie. 1992. *Strangers at Our Gates: Canadian Immigration and Immigration Policy, 1540–1990*. Toronto: Dundurn Press.

Knowles, Valerie. 2000. *Forging Our Legacy: Canadian Citizenship and Immigration, 1900–1977*. Ottawa: Citizenship and Immigration Canada.

Kostash, M. 1977. *All of Baba's Children*. Edmonton: Hurtig.

Kymlicka, Will. 1995. *Multicultural Citizenship: A Liberal Theory of Minority Rights*. Oxford: Oxford and Clarendon Press.

Kymlicka, Will. 2001. *Politics in the Vernacular: Nationalism, Multiculturalism, and Citizenship*. Oxford: Oxford University Press.

Lambertson, Ross. 2005. *Repression and Resistance: Canadian Human Rights Activists 1930–1960*. Toronto: University of Toronto Press.

Levitt, Cyril, and William Shaffir. 1985. "The Christie Pits Riot: A Case Study in the Dynamics of Ethnic Violence—Toronto, August 16, 1933." *Canadian Jewish History Society Journal* 9(1): 2–30.

Li, Peter. 1998. *The Chinese in Canada*. 2nd ed. Toronto: Oxford University Press.

Li, Peter. 1999. *Race and Ethnic Relations in Canada*. 2nd ed. Toronto: Oxford University Press.

MacKinnon, Mark. 2001. "Canadian Delegates Blast Homeland: Intolerance Exists, Say Activists Sponsored by Ottawa, But Few Turn Up to Listen." *Globe and Mail*, 31 August. <http://www.theglobeandmail.com/servlet/story/LAC.20010831.UCANAM/PPVStory/?DENIED=1>.

MacLennan, Christopher. 2003. *Toward the Charter: Canadians and the Demand for a National Bill of Rights, 1929–1960*. Montreal and Kingston: McGill-Queen's University Press.

Mensah, Joseph. 2002. *Black Canadians: History, Experiences, Social Conditions*. Halifax: Fernwood.

Miki, Roy. 2005. *Redress: Inside the Japanese Canadian Call for Justice*. Vancouver: Raincoast Books.

Miki, Roy, and Cassandra Kobayashi. 1991. *Justice in Our Time: The Japanese Canadian Redress Settlement*. Vancouver and Winnipeg: Talonbooks and National Association of Japanese Canadians.

Murphy, Rex. 2001. "Babble from Genocide's Bystanders." *Globe and Mail*, 1 September. <http://www.theglobeandmail.com/servlet/story/LAC.20010901. COREX/PPVStory/?DENIED=1>.

Nunoda, Peter Takaji. 1991. "A Community in Transition and Conflict: The Japanese Canadians, 1935–1951." Ph.D. dissertation, University of Manitoba.

Parekh, Bhikhu. 1997. "Dilemmas of a Multicultural Theory of Citizenship." *Constellations* 4(1): 54–62.

Parekh, Bhikhu. 2000. *Rethinking Multiculturalism: Cultural Diversity and Political Theory.* London: Macmillan.

Phillips, Susan D., and Katherine A. Graham. 2000. "Hand-in-Hand: When Accountability Meets Collaboration in the Voluntary Sector." In Keith Banting (ed.), *The Nonprofit Sector in Canada: Roles and Relationships.* Montreal and Kingston: School of Policy Studies and McGill-Queen's University Press. 149–90.

Porter, John. 1965. *The Vertical Mosaic: An Analysis of Social Class and Power in Canada.* Toronto: University of Toronto Press.

Pulido, Laura. 2006. *Black, Brown, Yellow, and Left: Radical Activism in Los Angeles.* Berkeley: University of California Press.

Smith, Miriam. 2005. *A Civil Society? Collective Actors in Canadian Political Life.* Peterborough: Broadview.

Stasiulis, D.K. 1994. "'Deep Diversity': Race and Ethnicity in Canadian Politics." In Michael S. Whittington and Glen Williams (eds.), *Canadian Politics in the 1990s.* Toronto: Nelson. 181–217.

Stasiulis, D.K. 1997. "Participation by Immigrants, Ethnocultural/Visible Minorities in the Canadian Political Process." Paper prepared for Heritage Canada, presented at the Research Domain Seminar on "Immigrants and Civic Participation: Contemporary Policy and Research Issues." Montreal, 23 November.

Stasiulis, D.K., and Y. Abu-Laban. 1991. "The House the Parties Built: (Re)constructing Ethnic Representation in Canadian Politics." In Kathy Megyery (ed.), *Ethno-cultural Groups and Visible Minorities in Canadian Politics: The Question of Access.* Vol. 7 of the Research Series, Royal Commission on Electoral Reform and Party Financing. Toronto: Dundurn Press.

Sunahara, Ann Gomer. 1981. *The Politics of Racism: The Uprooting of Japanese Canadians During the Second World War.* Toronto: Lorimer.

Sunday, Julie. N.d. "Minority Rights." *Globalization and Autonomy Online Compendium.* Ottawa: SSHRC-MCRI. <http://www.globalautonomy.ca/global1/glossary_entry.jsp?id=CO.0030>.

Ukrainian Canadian Congress. N.d. "Issues." <http://www.ucc.ca/issues.htm>.

Ward, Peter W. 1978. *White Canada Forever: Popular Attitudes and Public Policy Toward Orientals in British Columbia.* Montreal and Kingston: McGill-Queen's University Press.

WCAR Secretariat, Government of Canada. N.d. <http://www.pch.gc.ca/multi/wcar/intro_e.cfm>.

Wente, Margaret. 2001. "A Burning Cross to Bear." *Globe and Mail* 1 September. <http://www.theglobeandmail.com/servlet/story/LAC.20010901. COWENT01/PPVStory/?DENIED=1>.

Winks, Robin W. 1997. *The Blacks in Canada: A History.* Ottawa: Carleton University Press.

Young, Iris Marion. 1997. "Polity and Group Difference: A Polity of Presence?" In R.E. Goodin and P. Pettit (eds.), *Contemporary Political Philosophy.* Oxford: Blackwell.

Yuzyk, Paul. N.d. <http://www.yuzyk.com/biog-e.shtml>.

Zucchi, John E. 1988. *Italians in Toronto: Development of a National Identity, 1875–1935.* Montreal and Kingston: McGill-Queen's University Press.

SIX

The Women's Movement in Flux: Feminism and Framing, Passion, and Politics[1]

Alexandra Dobrowolsky

The women's movement embraces multiple ideas, identities, and strategies. It articulates diverse views about feminism such as liberal, socialist, and radical as well as anti-racist, lesbian, disability, and post-structuralist. These different visions are not only intellectually rooted but are often emotionally charged and experientially felt, validated, and vindicated. This stems from the fact that the women's movement is made up of a range of actors, organizations, and coalitions. The women involved have fluid, multiple, and intersecting identities in terms of race, ethnicity, class, sexual orientation, ability, age, and so on. Women's organizations take different shapes "ranging from informal women's collectives, to women's studies programs in universities, to more structured professional organizations" (Gelb and Hart, 1999: 177). Moreover, they have varied network structures, networking within the women's movement (intra-movement; see Phillips, 1991) and forming alliances with other social movements (inter-movement networking; see Dobrowolsky, 2000) and sometimes other representational forms (e.g., political parties, the state). Such networks can be consciously crafted "and embedded in society and institutions" (Tarrow, 1994: 184) or can be "dispersed, fragmented and submerged" emerging only "sporadically in response to specific issues" (Melucci, 2000: 94).

This sweep of ideas and identities, along with such organizational complexity, shape various forms of activism. The women's movement can model itself on a pressure group or even a political party. It can also take the form of a service provider offering practical assistance directly to women (Michaud, 1997: 201). Alternatively, it can eschew institutionalization and hierarchies, push countercultural buttons, and resort to dramatic disruptions and even violent protests. It pioneered the idea that "the personal is political," drawing attention to the fact that if politics is truly about power relations, then political struggles can occur beyond formal political arenas in workplaces, community groups, homes, and families, as well as in personal interactions. All this gives rise to highly contested views and contentious choices that are made about whether to work outside conventional structures, or to engage with them (Adamson *et al.*, 1988; Bashevkin, 1993; Briskin and Eliasson, 1999; Whitaker, 1999), or to do both, which is typically the case (Macpherson, 1994). In Canada, the women's movement is also diversified in terms of nation (e.g., Canadian nationalism versus Quebec and Aboriginal nationhood), region and province (e.g., as the West differs from Atlantic Canada) (Rankin, 1996), and even in terms of urban versus rural locales (e.g., the agrarian feminist movement in Canada) (Carbert, 1995; Wiebe, 1995).

In spite of the heterogeneity of the women's movement and its forms of organizing, in different periods it has sought to achieve degrees of consensus and coordinate efforts to press for change. In Canada, certain perceived injustices served to focus the movement: suffrage as the defining feature of the so-called "first wave" of the women's movement and abortion and violence against women in the "second" and "third waves." This chapter highlights the complex strategies, identities, and ideas of Canada's women's movements. Whereas identities and ideas clearly affect strategies (see Dobrowolsky, 1998, 2000, 2002a; Dobrowolsky and Hart, 2003), here the main focus will be on strategies. More specifically, women's movements' strategic interventions— and interruptions—are analyzed by selectively drawing from and building on the "framing" approach (Snow and Benford, 1988, 1992; Benford and Snow, 2000). The aim is to show how the women's movement has demonstrated the capacity to engage across multiple levels and how it may act to shape the broader "universe of political discourse" in Canada (Jenson, 1989).

The first part of the chapter showcases the women's movement by providing a sampling of the forms its mobilization has taken. In the second section, I review social movement theories and provide a critical look at the framing approach. By providing different examples of the Canadian women's movements' work, I show how coordinating social movement action across multiple levels can lead to challenges to existing political meanings and practices. In the third section, I draw on a feminist-inspired framing analysis to evaluate the oft-proclaimed demise of the women's movement. A more nuanced account is given through an examination of certain pan-Canadian women's groups whose "collective-action frames" tended to be more *pro-active* in the 1960s, 1970s, and early 1980s but grew more *reactive* from the late-1980s to the present. This, in turn, has had a detrimental impact on the women's movement's passions and politics. Explanations for such changes will be provided in the final part of the chapter.

Women's Movements: Passion and Politics

Because it has always been concerned with ideological and cultural as well as legislative change, and given that it operates on many fronts, the women's movement engages in a passionate politics of the deepest and broadest kind. This can entail small "p" politics that takes different shapes. Political statements have been woven through quilts and promoted through performance pieces. Guerrilla grrrl graffiti has elicited emotive responses as when third-wave feminists spray "FEED ME" across billboards featuring stick-like female fashion models. The group Equality Eve encouraged Canadian women's constitutional activism around kitchen tables by printing women's equality rights concerns on placemats (see Dobrowolsky, 2000). These are examples of using wit and ingenuity to spark changes in individual consciousness and spur broader collective action. These activities and other direct action tactics are often associated with mobilizing ideas and action from "without" and are considered typical of the grassroots women's movement.

While the women's movement has undoubtedly provided a challenge from without, in civil society, in everyday speech and acts, and in the so-called "private" sphere, it has also mobilized from "within," contesting various public, and mostly male-dominated institutions (Katzenstein and Mueller, 1987; Whitaker, 1999) making it somewhat distinctive from other social movements. For example, as Mary Katzenstein observes, "Most feminists of the second wave live their lives inside institutions—inside universities, churches, professions, unions, hospitals, social service agencies, schools, police forces, military corps, athletic teams. They have learned that the linkages connecting those on the inside to those on the outside are multi-layered" (1998: 41).

In fact, the women's movement has been intent on infiltrating and influencing large "P" politics or traditional political forms. Examples include more professional organizations, such as Canada's Committee for 94, which sought to increase women's numbers in the House of Commons by 1994 (Young, 2000); Equal Voice (www.equalvoice.ca), which promotes women in politics; and the American organization Emily's List, which works to raise funds to ease women's entry into formal politics (Gelb and Hart, 1999: 153). Some organizations, such as the British Women's Labour Network, are directly tied to conventional political institutions like political parties, but they may also work outside them, as does Britain's long-standing but recently reinvigorated Fawcett Society (established 1866). These organizations study, scheme, and support various actions—from training workshops and fundraising to sustaining educational and media outreach—aimed at boosting women's traditional political participation and keeping a wide range of women's issues in the public eye.

Whereas some accounts distinguish these more conventional or "institutionalized" women's movement organizations (Adamson *et al.*, 1988) from grassroots efforts, or categorize them as reformist versus radical groups, such distinctions are problematic (Ryan, 1992). Radical activism can take place inside institutions (Katzenstein, 1998). Moreover, reformist organizations can radicalize, just as grassroots groups can institutionalize. Similarly, inside/outside orientations can change over time and space. In Canada, the National Action Committee on the Status of Women (NAC) was once considered a more reformist institutional group, but it certainly displayed a different face and focus in the 1990s as compared to the 1970s. In its early years, NAC was headed by white, middle-class women and reflected the priorities of an interest group trying to cajole the state to take action on women's concerns. By the 1980s and 1990s, however, NAC's executive diversified, and the organization increasingly adopted confrontational social movement tactics that fundamentally challenged the state's core policies from free trade to constitutionalism (Bashevkin, 1989; Vickers, Rankin, and Appelle, 1993; MacDonald, 1995).

Since the women's movement tackles different fronts and takes on different forms, it necessarily draws upon a wide and diversified strategic repertoire. Among other measures, protest, direct action tactics, coalition-building, campaigning, public education, training, media work, service provision, litigation, and lobbying have been deployed. Certain actions may be manifestly obvious, but others may be imperceptible. Visible activities can include the work of forming women's caucuses in political parties or on university campuses, establishing women's centres or feminist publishing houses, striking task forces, creating collectives, and organizing marches and demonstrations. Raising public awareness about sexism among other intertwined forms of oppression, inventing and spreading new discourses, and inspiring individual consciousness, as well as forging alliances and cultivating different communities' support, are not as easily observable. Gains at this level are especially difficult to assess. However, even discursive innovations—such terms coined by the women's movement as gender, sexual harassment, date or marital rape, maternity/paternity leave, and pay or employment equity—have not only changed "social discourse" (Fraser, 1992) but politico-legal practices as well.

Women's concerted mobilization at both provincial and federal levels was necessary to ensure that many (most, but not all) women could vote by 1918. Even so, 11 years later, five prominent women had to resort to launching a notorious legal battle just to achieve the simple acknowledgement that women in this country were indeed "persons" and thus could be appointed to the Senate. This fight went to what was then Canada's highest court, the Judicial Committee of the Privy Council in Britain. Over five decades later, in the 1970s, the Aboriginal women's movement along with non-Aboriginal women's groups resorted to sit-ins, marches, and legal battles, not only in Canadian courts but as far as the UN's Human Rights Committee, to ensure that equality before the law applied to Aboriginal women.

In other places as well, acquiring political and legal rights for women involved more than lobbying and legal challenges. The tactics used to get women the vote in the US and Britain could be quite dramatic. American militant suffragettes declared: "We ... believe in standing on street corners and fighting our way to recognition forcing the men to think about us....We glory that we are theatrical" (Dubois, 1990: 189). In Britain, suffragettes not only "stormed the House of Commons, heckled cabinet ministers, broke windows and went to prison" but also, while in jail, resorted to hunger strikes and endured force feeding, all just to secure the female franchise (Rowbotham, 1997: 11). At the same time, while the women's movement has undoubtedly mobilized from "without," it has also been compelled to bring about change from "within" male bastions like states. For instance, "status-of-women" machinery was constructed by the Department of Labor in the US in the 1920s and in the Women's Bureau established in Canada's Labour Department in 1950 (Rankin and Vickers, 2001: 7). Femocrat (feminist bureaucrats) efforts intensified especially in the 1970s and early 1980s in Australia and Canada and in the late 1990s in Britain (Eisenstein, 1996; Findlay, 1987; Thomson, 2001; Chappell, 2002). There were also attempts at forging inside-outside connections with the establishment of bodies like the Canadian Advisory Council on the Status of Women (CACSW, established 1973; see Burt, 1998). At times, this kind of mobilization has had to take "unobtrusive" forms (Katzenstein, 1990). At others, it was quite disruptive, as Katzenstein recounts in relation to women's forays into patriarchal institutions like the Catholic church and the American military (Katzenstein, 1998).

Women's movements have been bold and confrontational, but they have also mobilized in less combative ways, using silence and non-violent means, playing on psyches, and counting on personal transformations to build support. They have challenged conventional and unconventional political spaces in very noticeable as well as less conspicuous manners by keeping gender at the forefront and often accommodating other identities as well. In sum, the women's movement has used *multilevel political coordination* to act as a *signifying agent*. In so doing, it has helped to transform the terms of what it means to be political, as well as the terrain of political struggle.

Social Movement Theory and the Women's Movement

Given its complexity, the women's movement poses analytical challenges. In general, there have been three schools of thought in the study of social movements: (1) resource mobilization; (2) the political process model; and (3) new social movement theory (Smith, 2005: 38–39). The first two approaches largely stem from the work of American social movement scholars who conceive of movements propelled by rational actors preoccupied with strategically mobilizing resources and/or traditional political forms that, in turn, play a large role in influencing social movement behaviour. The third approach, the new social movement school, is associated with European theorists who have been more concerned with the role of broader socio-economic structures, along with ideology and identity, in determining the course of collective action.

Each approach contains strengths and weaknesses. However, all have difficulty grappling with the fact that social movements negotiate both strategy and identity; that politics must be understood broadly in ways that encompass traditional political forms as well as a wider universe of political discourse; and that while social movements are certainly affected by politics, they can also affect politics themselves. As we have seen, these are precisely the issues at stake when examining women's movements.

The framing approach attempts to bridge the divide between American and European scholarship on social movements by factoring in formal political considerations along with issues, such as identity, that have not, until recently, been at the forefront of American social movement studies (see Polletta and Jasper, 2001). What is more, framing includes a "sense of a dynamic evolving process" (Benford and Snow, 2000: 614), as well as an appreciation of agency, which have been lacking in both political process and European structuralist models. Framing is based on collective action frames: "action-oriented sets of beliefs and meanings that inspire and legitimate the activities and campaigns of a social movement organization" (Benford and Snow, 2000: 614). In others words, framing underscores the fact that social movement strategies involve meaning construction. This approach is useful when it comes to evaluating the scope of the women's movement because it considers not only conventional mobilization patterns but also the politics of ideas and signification.

Still, there are gaps in the framing approach, particularly when it comes to grappling with the nature and impact of discursive processes. Framing tends to lose sight of powerful, structural determinants and has been criticized by some feminist scholars for essentially "cooling" the analysis of social movements. That is, framing is ultimately more at home in the American camp in that it often relies on "cool" calculations and "cold" cognitive analyses (Masson, 1997: 64; Ferree and Merrill, 2000: 457). These tendencies mean that less quantifiable variables such as emotion have not, until recently, been prominent features (Taylor, 1995; Aminzade and McAdam, 2001; Tarrow, 2001: 8). The framing approach may, in effect if not intent, be gendered as it succumbs to a reason versus emotion dichotomy that corresponds to male/female social constructions in which men are considered rational and dispassionate and women irrational and emotional (Ferree and Merrill, 2000: 457). In contrast, feminist scholarship has not only exposed "the rationalist assumptions that disconnect reason and emotions" but also points to "the emotional dimension of rationality" (Aminzade and McAdam, 2001: 23).

The balance of this chapter will attempt to fill in the gaps of the framing approach by highlighting important discursive interventions on the part of the women's movement, drawing on the work of feminist scholars whose work often preceded the framing analysis (Jenson, 1985, 1989). It will also keep "up the heat" by not losing sight of the passionate, emotional, and provocative side of women's movement organizing and how it feeds and fans its strategizing fires. At the same time, however, it will remain heedful of some of the excesses of new social movement theorists who contend that collective action is mostly cultural and that traditional political actors and institutions are waning in importance (Melucci, 1996). The women's movement aptly illustrates that both passion and politics (in the broadest sense) are significant. In fact, they are intertwined as women's movement organizing has attempted to transform politics in bedrooms and kitchens, on the streets as well as throughout various institutions at home and abroad.

At the same time, while structures, dominant ideologies, institutional discourses, and traditional political practices matter—and they can certainly influence women's movement's organizational forms and affect strategic choices—nevertheless, the women's movement does not necessarily grow out of structural arrangements, conventional political institutions, or ideologies (the view taken in Vickers, Rankin, and Appelle, 1993). Rather, the claim being made here is that the women's movement has been, in and of itself, a *signifying agent* particularly when it engages in *multilevel political coordination*. When this occurs, the women's movement produces alternative words and deeds, challenging, and in some cases changing, institutions, ideas, and identities. As we shall see, this also can create a backlash; and so, repercussions and remedies also require exploration.

From Pro-active to Reactive Frames

Today, the general perception is that the women's movement is, if not dead, in chronic decline (Rebick, 2005: 254). However, framing analysis helps us to understand these changes in a more nuanced way. From the 1960s to the present, the Canadian women's movement, broadly speaking, has shifted the nature of its strategizing, with an overall change in orientation from *pro-active* to more *reactive* "collective action frames." Pro-active frames challenge ideas, identities, and institutions on a range of fronts, epitomizing multilevel political coordination. Here the blurring of small and big "P" politics is most apparent: the women's movement truly acts as a *signifying agent* promoting new discourses and actions through its work on the ground and in society, working to challenge and change various informal and formal political structures and spaces. In contrast, *reactive* frames draw on strategies that are less diversified. Compelled to respond to socio-economic and political developments, the women's movement is unable to achieve the same degree of political and cultural recognition and responsiveness. Consequently, its efforts at signification, re-signification, and transformation are slowed and/or stymied.

Very briefly, the second wave of the women's movement in Canada grew and diversified from the 1960s onward. Until the mid 1980s, the movement seized and helped to open various "windows of reform" (Helfferich and Kolb, 2001: 145) at a time when the political climate was warmer. Inside/outside political interactions proliferated and helped to push and prod the state to take action. The women's movement not only prompted the construction of state machinery but also made strategic alliances with women on the inside (Findlay, 1987; O'Neil, 1993; Geller-Schwartz, 1995). Institutions like the Status of Women Canada (1971) and the Secretary of State's Women's Program were established, the latter providing pivotal funding to women's organizations (Chappell, 2002: 87). The state's financial support of the women's movement grew, and while the state did not necessarily create new organizations in and of itself, it certainly facilitated movement expansion. For example, the state allocated resources to support the projects of women's organizations large and small and set up initiatives like the Court Challenges Program, which could assist women's litigation strategies and equality struggles, bolstering the efforts of groups like the Women's Legal Education and Action Fund (LEAF, established 1985).

In the 1970s and early 1980s, the tail end of the welfare state meant there were funds available to support organizational activity, and launch new structures and programs. This was legitimized by prevailing notions of a socially just, fair, and equitable society. The women's movement not only seized but also tried to shape these opportunities by, for instance, formulating new sexual equality provisions for the new *Charter of Rights and Freedoms* in the hope that they would prompt the move beyond formal to more substantive equality.

Women mobilized in the streets, in collectives, and in various types of organizations, but they also tried to influence policy on issues than ran the gamut from pensions to constitutionalism. Increasingly, however, the growing and more diversified women's movement required nuanced, and often more complicated, thought and action. Feminist fundamentals were unpacked and deconstructed. They not only had to accommodate liberal, socialist, and radical feminist ideas but anti-racist, critical disability, post-modernist, and

post-structuralist feminism, causing some feminists to tie "themselves in theoretical knots" (Rebick and Roach, 1996: 189). At the same time, while raging
debates about, for example, the need for a multi-racial women's movement
were difficult and often highly emotionally charged, building such a movement proved even harder and more impassioned.

This growing sophistication and hybridization took place as the socio-economic, political, and cultural environment grew less congenial (Brodie, 1995;
Bashevkin, 1998, 2002) and the nature and meanings of citizenship began to
change (Jenson and Phillips, 1996; Broadbent, 2001; Dobrowolsky and Jenson,
2004). The women's movement had helped to promote discourses having to
do with equality and social citizenship, but these no longer resonated. First
came the move from the Keynesian welfare state to a neoliberal one, whose
focus on downsizing, downloading, deregulation, and a more individualistic,
market-oriented culture disproportionately and negatively affected women
(Bashevkin, 2002; Cossman and Fudge, 2002; Dobrowolsky, 2004). The discourse of equality of opportunity eclipsed social justice concerns and served
to undermine a collectivist women's movement more occupied with equality
of condition and equality of end result (Jenson, 2000, 2001).

By this point, the women's movement's multilevel political coordination
had clearly had an impact. It had left its mark on both the formal and informal
political terrain, influencing discourses and practices not only at the level of
the state but also with respect to people's identities, thinking, and ways of
acting. Symbolically, not only had there been many women's "firsts" on political and legal fronts—from the first female Supreme Court justice (Bertha
Wilson) to the first female prime minister (Kim Campbell)—but there had
been other, more destabilizing political benchmarks. Women had put issues
like employment and pay equity, abortion, and pornography on the policy
agenda. What is more, societal transformations had taken place through the
instigation of the women's movement. For instance, more women than ever,
including women with small children, were working outside the home, and
there had truly been a sexual revolution. To be sure, women still worked for
less pay than men; women were typically employed in "pink collar ghettos";
and women's sexuality was still not unconstrained by both social mores and
political circumstances. Nevertheless, it was widely recognized that the wom-
en's movement had effected change. This, in turn, contributed to a backlash
against the movement and feminism in Canada and elsewhere, which took on
various political and cultural forms (Faludi, 1992; Bashevkin, 1998, 2002).

In the conventional political realm, given neoliberal priorities, Canadian
state funding was dramatically cut. Moreover, the federal government stepped
up its campaign of de-legitimization, as the women's movement and other
social movements were continually portrayed as irksome "special interests"

(Dobrowolsky, 1998). Increasingly, by the 1990s, when it came to national political parties and public policy, women fell off the radar screen (Young, 2000). Even state feminism contracted, as in 1995, when the CACSW and the Women's Program were collapsed into the Status of Women Canada (Jenson and Phillips, 1996; Burt, 1998; Dobrowolsky, 2004), which, in turn, was progressively downsized and marginalized.

At the same time, during this period, the women's movement had to change its identity and strategies. It could no longer work on the assumption that all women were concerned about the same things. It had to both diversify and specialize. Its mostly white, middle-class leadership was challenged; increasingly, equality concerns had to include concerns of difference, not just between men and women, but between women as well. This had an impact on how the women's movement organized. It found it increasingly difficult to speak with one voice and had to work more concertedly and carefully at its intra-movement (in the women's movement) networking. Inter-movement (between various social movements) networking and coalition-building grew, also out of necessity. However, divisions over issues of race, ethnicity, sexual orientation, ability, and even nationalism could freeze movement activism. For example, when some women's organizations in the rest of Canada opposed the Meech Lake Accord, many Québécois feminist organizations were outraged as this constitutional deal was meant to bring Quebec back into the constitutional family (Roberts, 1988). Then, when it came to the next constitutional round, the Charlottetown Accord of the early 1990s, which not only tried to accommodate two nations (Quebec and rest of Canada) but Three Nations (adding First Nations), some national women's organizations refrained from taking a public stand on the multi-layered identities and issues involved (Dobrowolsky, 2000, 2003).

While the women's movement is no stranger to being dismissed or marginalized, caricatured, and even ridiculed, the intensity and pervasiveness of such critiques grew. Moreover, counter-movements such as REAL (Real, Equal, and Active for Life) Women emerged in the 1980s to rail against women's movement gains, promote anti-feminist policies, and challenge funding provided to it by the Secretary of State Women's Program (Levan, 1996: 331; MacIvor, 1996: 145–46). High profile feminist organizations like NAC and LEAF were specifically targeted in both the academic and popular press. The representativeness of an umbrella group like NAC was questioned. For example, in the early 1990s some women produced buttons that read "NAC does not speak for me," given NAC's highly visible role as part of the "No" forces in the constitutional battles around the Charlottetown Accord.

As a result of this political and cultural backlash, and given discursive shifts, the women's movement, in general, as Sylvia Bashevkin (1998) recounts, was on "the defensive." Pauline Rankin and Jill Vickers also note that its relationship with the state grew "increasingly disengaged and conflictual" (2001: 2). In fact, the women's movement appeared to retreat from the national political scene, focusing more on organizing at both the local and global level. It had little alternative but to concentrate on providing services for women on the ground, given the fallout from state streamlining and privatization, but this had to be done with dwindling resources. Coalition work grew out of necessity as women worked with other beleaguered cash-strapped social movements. Given growing disillusionment with politics on the national scene, networking at the transnational level intensified. This was especially evident around and after the UN 1995 Fourth World Conference on Women held in Beijing, China (Rankin and Vickers, 2001: 53).

As the 1990s progressed, and into the new millennium, the state started to take a new tack, no longer castigating special interests but increasingly promoting partnerships. By this point, however, it seems that the women's movement was not the preferred partner (Dobrowolsky and Jenson, 2004; Dobrowolsky, 2004), and discourses had shifted to such a degree that women's movement claims appeared anachronistic. At best, gendered identity became "coded as just one of many identities that make up the Canadian cultural mosaic, rather than a fundamental structuring principle informing the daily lives of Canadians" (Brodie, forthcoming).

Explaining the Changing Frames

Like other movements, the women's movement needs to identify targets that cause injustice, propose solutions, and motivate people to action (Benford and Snow, 2000: 616–17). And so, as Benford and Snow outline, a movement's collective action frames need to resonate (2000: 619). In the case of the women's movement, this resonance might have been affected by its own successes at multilevel political coordination and signification, as it adopted new discourses and changed political realms. On one hand, this caused the backlash recounted above, but on the other, for new generations of women, it might appear as if the women's movement had won the war when in many cases the battle has not even been decided. This came at a time when women's movement resources (financial, physical, and emotional) were depleted. Long-time feminist activists were burnt-out and worn out. New blood was needed, and yet the women's movement (with some exceptions) did not seem to be able to capture young women's imagination and inspire action as it used to. In short, this has contributed to the diminution of the women's movement's passions and politics.

Consider just one example of how this plays out. Because in all its waves, the women's movement has promoted equality, now society in general, and many young people in particular, assume equality exists between men and women. Recall that the women's movement not only ensured that women were considered "persons" but helped to entrench formal equality guarantees for women in the Charter in 1982 and fend off perceived incursions to these rights in the Meech Lake and Charlottetown Accord dramas (1987, 1992). These formal victories do not necessarily translate into substantive ones. Still, the assumption is that women have achieved equality, and thus it is difficult to stir young women's hearts or to spread awareness about how much more needs to be done so that substantive equality becomes a reality.

As traditional political opportunities closed, the women's movement was compelled to redirect its focus from conventional political forums to the legal realm (Cossman and Fudge, 2002). Since Charter equality guarantees came into force in 1985, high profile court cases again would seem on the surface to point to women's movement successes. For example, the Supreme Court invalidated the state's restrictive abortion laws in the 1988 Morgentaler decision (*R. v. Morgentaler*). This was considered to be a women's movement coup. However, 15 years later, one could suggest that such feminist gains have become losses: with no abortion law on the statute book, services are patchy and inconsistent, with huge accessibility gaps across provinces and between urban versus rural areas (Haussman, 2000). Moreover, the women's movement high profile "win" spurred violent anti-choice mobilization, which turned abortion clinics (where stalking and even firebombing took place) and doctors who performed abortions into targets, sometimes culminating in murder. Access is eroded even further as health practitioners question whether it is worth risking their lives to provide abortion services. Yet, the perception is that the abortion issue has been resolved, and so what is the women's movement still going on about?

Many feminists are dubious about the equality focus altogether. Some have wanted to prioritize differences between women and men, from as far back as the first wave of the women's movement. In the second and third waves, equality has been further problematized as differences between women were highlighted. This has an impact on what Benford and Snow (2000) describe as frame consistency; that is, social movements require a measure of consistency in the messages they propagate. And yet, the women's movement, in particular, has had to grapple with such seemingly contradictory demands as equality, difference, and diversity (Harrison, 2003; Squires, 2003).

This challenge heightened as the women's movement dealt with the fallout of its false universalism in the 1960s and 1970s. As Jacinthe Michaud explains, "the building of solidarity and consensus among several women's organizations set in motion a variety of ideological tendencies aimed at creating a convergence of interest or at least reaching solidarity at the level of organization forms" (1997: 201). While the women's movement tried to broaden its appeal in an effort to create a "universal sisterhood," it downplayed the multi-faceted nature of the movement and the identities involved. Thus, Aboriginal women, women of colour, immigrant women, lesbians, women with disabilities, and others contested these portrayals (Lachappelle, 1982; Driedger, 1996; Agnew, 1996; Stone, 1997). Again, diverse women pointed out that the picture being painted was one that highlighted the figures and emphases of a largely white, middle-class, able-bodied, and often straight leadership. Therefore, more and sometimes competing issues were added to the women's movement agenda. This certainly helped make the women's movement more inclusive, but it meant that consensus became harder to reach, and it made framing less consistent. As Arun Mukherjee observed, this was when "plurality and difference" split "feminism" into "feminisms" and resulted in a "crisis of legitimation" (1992: 165–66).

The issue of violence against women is instructive. For instance, women's movement efforts to deal with rape were not as clear-cut when Aboriginal women and women of colour problematized what was at stake for them. Women of colour criticized strategies that called for more police intervention given their more contentious relations with police due to the intersecting dynamics of gender, race, and class. As Vijay Agnew explained, "It is unlikely that an abused black woman in Ontario would have much confidence in the police force, whose racism has so often been publicly examined and criticized" (1996: 202). To be clear, these were important interventions that showed how crucial it was for the women's movement to be more sensitive to diversity and divergent experiences. However, this also necessitated the disruption of frame consistency.

Finally, Benford and Snow (2000) point to the importance of the credibility of the frame articulators. To be sure, women's movement leaders across the waves have been vilified. The caustic and even cruel cartoons drawn of women suffragettes in the first wave provide one highly visible example (e.g., these often featured unattractive female caricatures and the slogan "Women who've never been kissed"). However, in the 1980s and 1990s as women made advances (albeit, one step forward and two steps back) the leaders were also fundamentally challenged. Given the "general atmosphere of mistrust and a well-organized backlash against feminism" (Levan, 1996: 350), women's movement icons of the 1960s and 1970s were often portrayed as misguided, even mentally imbalanced, whereas feminists who retracted their commitments were championed.

Women's movement leaders were blamed for the struggles of women's groups in a more challenging socio-economic and political context. Credibility was also (highly inappropriately) affected by the fact that many of the new leaders of women's organizations were no longer typically privileged white women. Here both racism and sexism clearly came into play. Consider the following headline in the *Globe and Mail*: "NAC has fallen into a 'skin trap,' critic says." After Judy Rebick's tenure as president of NAC ended, for the first time a series of women of colour went on to lead the organization: Sunera Thobani (1993–96), Joan Grant Cummings (1996–2000), Kudooka Terri Brown (2000–01), Denise Andrea Campbell (2001–02), and, most recently, Dolly Williams (2006). In a case of very bad timing, their leadership coincided with the period when NAC faced its most significant financial crises, as the state would no longer provide operational but only project funding. These leaders did not necessarily contribute to NAC's organizational decline, and yet the media spread misinformation in describing how women of colour had taken over the organization and had alienated NAC's foundational white, middle-class female support base. Negative framing by the media, combined with lack of federal support, helped to bring the organization to its current weakened state.

In sum, both women's movement passion and politics have suffered of late, and the situation, at present, is not improving. Stephen Harper's Conservative government decided against adopting an improved federal pay equity law and, what is worse, sanguinely declared that inequality between women and men was no longer a problem.

In fact, the federal government proceeded to delete the goal of equality from the mandate of the Women's Program and, in the fall of 2006, initiated ruinous cuts to the Status of Women ($5 million in budget "streamlining"). This required the closing of most of its regional and provincial program offices (by 31 March 2007). It also suggested that the Status of Women Canada would soon follow in the footsteps of the defunct CACSW. What is more, not only women's research but women's advocacy was targeted. Along with significantly compromising research funded by the Status of Women, the Harper administration shut down the federal government's Gender-Based Analysis Unit, and it prohibited the use of federal funds to engage in advocacy at any level of government. Other equality-seeking routes were also cut off when funding to the Court Challenges Program was effectively eliminated. In so doing, the Harper government swiftly swept away the last vestiges of the status of women machinery in this country and did its best to wipe out any other avenues for equality seeking by the women's movement. As a result, the women's movement's multilevel action coordination and its capability to be a signifying agent have been seriously and negatively affected.

However, the foregoing is by no means a freeze frame. Given the mutability and perseverance of the movement outlined above, it does not represent a static, inevitable process. Potential exists to reframe the women's movement.

Framing: The Women's Movement Reframed

Just as feminism is always in the process of being reborn, so is the women's movement. For instance, the Harper government's outrageous acts spurred various local actions. In Halifax, "A Call to Equality in Governance" was organized where diverse women's groups—from university women's groups and provincial sexual assault centres to the Canadian Research Institute for the Advancement of Women and the Atlantic Centre of Excellence for Women's Health, as well as the Nova Scotia government, General Employees Union, and the CLC—gathered to decry the federal government's actions.

Clearly, the politics was there, but so too was the passion on the part of women, young and old, as the "Raging Grannies" sang their songs of protest and new groups made their debut, such as "The Radical Feminists"—radical cheerleaders, young twenty-something women, who cheered, sang, and performed street theatre, thereby vividly vocalizing their outrage. Alongside the Raging Grannies and The Radical Feminists, another newly formed group, "The Women Are Angry" mobilized, the latter making national headlines by launching a website (www.womenareangry.com) and organizing a postcard campaign to oppose the Harper government.

And so, while we continue to experience socio-economic and political flux, we may also be able to discern certain changes occurring, or tensions and contradictions that can be plumbed, to once again begin to pry open windows of reform. Otherwise, the marginalization of women becomes an inevitable, unmovable process.

Dominique Masson argues, for example, that "localized versions of restructuring coexist that have different implications in terms of the perspectives they open, preserve or foreclose for the pursuit of feminist politics" (1999–2000: 50). She shows how women's movement service organizations in Quebec were conceived of as "partners" in welfare by the state and thus stemmed the tide and challenged the restructuring that seemed to marginalize feminist activism in the rest of Canada. This experience provides food for thought as the Canadian state increasingly relies on "partnerships" of various kinds (see Brock, 2001, 2002). Instead of simply demonizing "special interests," the state is now more apt to enlist the voluntary sector to help carry out its "Third Way" strategies (Bashevkin, 2002; Dobrowolsky, 2004; Dobrowolsky and Jenson, 2004; Dobrowolsky and Saint-Martin, 2005). While such partnering relationships are not without their risks, they may constitute potential openings for the women's movement to increase leverage lost in the 1990s. The women's movement has been a political signifier and can again adopt this role, but it needs to revive its multilevel political coordination in the context of new local, national, and transnational configurations.

In other words, the women's movement must renegotiate national as well as local and global spaces with a combination of strategies that are more pro-active rather than reactive. It needs to draw on destabilizing tactics that involve both the grassroots as well as conventional political forms. This means reforging alliances between outsiders and insiders. This also requires both personal and cultural change. And as Ryan suggests "mobilization of people is not enough; social movements must also mobilize sustaining ideas" (1992: 156), and these ideas need to have an impact on many political and societal levels.

To do this, there has to be work done on challenging prevalent assumptions about frame consistency and legitimacy. This does not mean reverting to a focus on universal ideals and single identities but, rather, harnessing fluid, multiple reflexive feminist solidarities (Desai, 2002: 33) and reviving multi-level political coordination. The Bread and Roses march in Quebec provides an example: women organized at the grassroots level and put pressure on politicians with clear, direct demands. They marched through local towns and villages raising awareness but also forged transnational networks. What began as *la marche des femmes à travers le Québec* in 1995, when the *Fédération des femmes du Québec* worked with 20 different women's organizations across the province to focus on poverty and violence against women (Rebick and Roach, 1996: 183) transmuted into the pan-Canadian Bread and Roses March of 1996, which mobilized over 100,000 women in more than 100 communities across the county ("La marche," 1999: 4). This then developed into the World March of 2000. Women networked; built inter- and intra-movement alliances; and consolidated local, national, and global networks.

More than any other social movement, then, the women's movement has helped to blur the distinctions between small "p" and big "P" politics, between the institutional and non-institutional. It has brought new issues to the fore, devised new discourses, and engaged in multilevel political coordination to elicit both societal and political action whereby countless, diverse women "transformed themselves from passive observers of the world into active agents of change" (Rebick, 2005: xiv). In sum, the women's movement can be characterized as a dynamic, evolving process, that is at once passionate and political, and therefore has had a multi-dimensional impact. It is truly a signifying agent, albeit one marked by changes over space and time.

Note

1. My sincere thanks to Mathieu Lapointe and Steve Lelievre for their research assistance and to Marc Doucet for his comments on an earlier draft of this chapter.

References and Further Reading

Adamson, Nancy, Linda Briskin, and Margaret McPhail. 1988. *Feminist Organizing for Change: The Contemporary Women's Movement in Canada*. Toronto: Oxford University Press.

Agnew, Vijay. 1996. *Resisting Discrimination: Women From Asia, Africa, and the Caribbean and the Women's Movement in Canada*. Toronto: University of Toronto Press.

Aminzade, Ronald, and Doug McAdam. 2001. "Emotions and Contentious Politics." In Ronald Aminzade *et al.* (eds.), *Silence and Voice in the Study of Contentious Politics*. Cambridge: Cambridge University Press. 14–50.

Bashevkin, Sylvia. 1989. "Free Trade and Canadian Feminism: The Case of the National Action Committee on the Status of Women." *Canadian Public Policy* 15(4): 363–75.

Bashevkin, Sylvia. 1993. *Toeing the Lines: Women and Party Politics in English Canada*. 2nd ed. Toronto: Oxford University Press.

Bashevkin, Sylvia. 1998. *Women on the Defensive: Living Through Conservative Times*. Toronto: University of Toronto Press.

Bashevkin, Sylvia. 2002. *Welfare Hot Buttons: Women, Work, and Social Policy Reform*. Toronto: University of Toronto Press.

Benford, Robert D., and David Snow. 2000. "Framing Process and Social Movements: An Overview and Assessment." *Annual Review of Sociology* 26: 611–39.

Briskin, Linda, and Mona Eliasson. 1999. *Women's Organizing and Public Policy in Canada and Sweden*. Montreal and Kingston: McGill-Queen's University Press.

Broadbent, Edward (Ed.). 2001. *Democratic Equality: What Went Wrong?* Toronto: University of Toronto Press.

Brock, Kathy. 2001. "State, Society, and the Third Sector: Changing to Meet New Challenges." *Journal of Canadian Studies* 35(4): 203–20.

Brock, Kathy. 2002. *Improving Connections Between Governments and Nonprofit and Voluntary Organizations: Public Policy and the Third Sector*. Montreal and Kingston: McGill-Queen's University Press.

Brodie, Janine. 1995. *Politics on the Margins: Restructuring and the Canadian Women's Movement*. Halifax: Fernwood.

Brodie, Janine. Forthcoming. "Putting Gender Back In: Women and Social Policy Reform in Canada." In Yasmeen Abu-Laban (ed.), *Gendering the Nation-State: Canadian and Comparative Perspectives*. Vancouver: University of British Columbia Press.

Burt, Sandra. 1998. "The Canadian Advisory Council on the Status of Women: Possibilities and Limitations." In Manon Tremblay and Caroline Andrew (eds.), *Women and Political Representation in Canada*. Ottawa: University of Ottawa Press. 115–44.

Carbert, Louise. 1995. *Agrarian Feminism: The Politics of Ontario Farm Women*. Toronto: University of Toronto Press.

Chappell, Louise. 2002. "The 'Femocrat' Strategy: Expanding the Repertoire of Feminist Activists." In Karen Ross (ed.), *Women, Politics and Change*. Oxford: Oxford University Press. 84–98.

Cossman, Brenda, and Judy Fudge. 2002. *Privatization, Law, and the Challenge to Feminism*. Toronto: University of Toronto Press.

Desai, Manisha. 2002. "Transnational Solidarity: Women's Agency, Structural Adjustment, and Globalization." In Nancy A. Naples and Manisha Desai (eds.), *Women's Activism and Globalization: Linking Local Struggles and Transnational Politics*. New York: Routledge. 15–33.

Dobrowolsky, Alexandra. 1998. "'Of Special Interest': Interest, Identity, and Feminist Constitutional Activism in Canada." *Canadian Journal of Political Science* 31(4): 707–42.

Dobrowolsky, Alexandra. 2000. *The Politics of Pragmatism: Women, Representation, and Constitutional Activism in Canada*. Toronto: Oxford University Press.

Dobrowolsky, Alexandra. 2002. "Crossing Boundaries: Exploring and Mapping Women's Constitutional Interventions in England, Scotland, and Northern Ireland." *Social Politics* 9(2): 291–340.

Dobrowolsky, Alexandra. 2003. "Shifting States: Women's Constitutional Organizing Across Time and Space." In Lee Ann Banaszak, Karen Beckwith, and Dieter Rucht (eds.), *Women's Movements Facing the Reconfigured State*. Cambridge: Cambridge University Press. 114–40.

Dobrowolsky, Alexandra. 2004. "The Chrétien Legacy and Women: Changing Policy Priorities With Little Cause for Celebration." *Review of Constitutional Studies* 9(1/2): 171–98.

Dobrowolsky, Alexandra, and Vivien Hart. 2003. *Women Making Constitutions: New Politics and Comparative Perspectives*. Houndmills: Palgrave.

Dobrowolsky, Alexandra, and Jane Jenson. 2004. "Shifting Representations of Citizenship: Canadian Politics of 'Women' and 'Children.'" *Social Politics* 11(2): 154–80.

Dobrowolsky, Alexandra, and Denis Saint-Martin. 2005. "Agency, Actors, and Change in a Child-Focused Future: Path Dependency Problematized." *Journal of Commonwealth and Comparative Politics* 4(1): 1–33.

Driedger, Diane. 1996. "Emerging from the Shadows: Women with Disabilities Organize." In Diane Driedger, Irene Feika and Eileen Giron Batres (eds.), *Across Borders: Women with Disabilities Working Together*. Charlottetown: Gynergy Books.

Dubois, Ellen Carol. 1990. "Working Women, Class Relations, and Suffrage Militancy: Harriot Stanton Blatch and the New York Woman Suffrage Movement." In Ellen Carol DuBois and Vicki L. Ruiz (eds.), *Unequal Sisters: A Multi-cultural Reader in US Women's History*. New York: Routledge. 176–94.

Eisenstein, Hester. 1996. *Inside Agitators: Australian Femocrats and the Australian State*. Sydney: Allen and Unwin.

Faludi, Susan. 1992. *Backlash: The Undeclared War Against American Women*. New York: Anchor Books.

Ferree, Myra Marx, and David A. Merrill. 2000. "Hot Movements, Cold Cognition: Thinking about Social Movements in Gendered Frames." *Contemporary Sociology* 29(3): 454–62.

Findlay, Sue. 1987. "Facing the State: The Politics of the Women's Movement Reconsidered." In Heather Jon Maroney and Meg Luxton (eds.), *Feminism and Political Economy*. Toronto: Methuen. 31–50.

Fraser, Nancy. 1992. "The Uses and Abuses of French Discourse Theories for Feminist Politics." In Nancy Fraser and Sandra Lee Bartky (eds.), *Revaluing French Feminism: Critical Essays on Difference, Agency, and Culture*. Bloomington: Indiana University Press. 177–94.

Gelb, Joyce, and Vivien Hart. 1999. "Feminist Politics in a Hostile Environment." In Marco Giugni, Doug McAdam and Charles Tilly (eds.), *How Social Movements Matter*. Minneapolis: University of Minnesota Press. 149–81.

Geller-Schwartz, Linda. 1995. "An Array of Agencies: Feminism and State Institutions in Canada." In Dorothy McBride Stetson and Amy G. Mazur (eds.), *Comparative State Feminism*. Thousand Oaks: Sage.

Harrison, Cynthia. 2003. "'Heightened Scrutiny': A Judicial Route to Constitutional Equality for US Women." In Alexandra Dobrowolsky and Vivien Hart (eds.), *Women Making Constitutions: New Politics and Comparative Perspectives*. Houndmills: Palgrave. 155–72.

Haussman, Melissa. 2000. "What Does Gender Have to Do with Abortion Law? Canadian Women's Movement-Parliament Interactions on Reform Attempts, 1969–1991." *International Journal of Canadian Studies* 21 (Spring): 127–54.

Helfferich, Barbara, and Felix Kolb. 2001. "Multilevel Action Coordination in European Contentious Politics." In Doug Imig and Sidney Tarrow (eds.), *Contentious Europeans: Protest and Politics in an Emerging Polity*. New York: Rowman and Littlefield. 143–61.

Jenson, Jane. 1985. "Struggling for Identity: The Women's Movement and the State." *West European Politics* 8(4): 5–18.

Jenson, Jane. 1989. "Paradigms and Political Discourse: Protective Legislation in France and the United States." *Canadian Journal of Political Science* 22(2): 235–58.

Jenson, Jane. 2000. "Canada's Shifting Citizenship Regime. Investing in Children." In T.C. Salmon and Michael Keating (eds.), *The Dynamics of Decentralization*. Montreal and Kingston: McGill-Queen's University Press. 107–23.

Jenson, Jane. 2001. "Rethinking Equality and Equity: Canadian Children and the Social Union." In Edward Broadbent (ed.), *Democratic Equality: What Went Wrong?* Toronto: University of Toronto Press. 111–29.

Jenson, Jane, and Susan D. Phillips. 1996. "Regime Shift: New Citizenship Practices in Canada." *International Journal of Canadian Studies* 14 (Fall): 111–35.

Katzenstein, Mary Fainsod. 1990. "Feminism Within American Institutions: Unobtrusive Mobilization in the 1980's." *Signs* 16(11): 27–52.

Katzenstein, Mary Fainsod. 1998. *Faithful and Fearless: Moving Feminist Protest Inside the Church and Military*. Princeton: Princeton University Press.

Katzenstein, Mary Fainsod, and Carol McClurg Mueller. 1987. *The Women's Movements of the United States and Western Europe: Consciousness, Political Opportunity, and Public Policy*. Philadelphia: Temple University Press.

"La marche mondiale des femmes 2000." 1999. *A L'action! Bulletin trimestriel du Comité canadien d'Action sur le statut de la femme* (CCA) 9: 1, 4.

Lachappelle, Caroline. 1982. "Native Women and the Women's Movement." In Maureen Fitzgerald, Connie Guberman and Margie Wolfe (eds.), *Still Ain't Satisfied! Canadian Feminism Today*. Toronto: Women's Press.

MacDonald, Martha. 1995. "Economic Restructuring and Gender in Canada: Feminist Policy Initiatives." *World Development* 23(11): 2005–17.

MacIvor, Heather. 1996. *Women and Politics in Canada*. Peterborough: Broadview.

Macpherson, Kay. 1994. *When in Doubt Do Both: The Times of My Life*. Toronto: University of Toronto Press.

Masson, Dominique. 1997. "Language, Power, and Politics: Revisiting the Symbolic Challenges of Movements." In William K. Carroll (ed.), *Organizing Dissent: Contemporary Social Movements in Theory and Practice*. 2nd ed. Toronto: Garamond. 57–75.

Masson, Dominique. 1999–2000. "Constituting 'Post-Welfare State' Welfare Arrangements: The Role of Women's Movement Service Groups in Quebec." *Resources for Feminist Research* 27(3/4): 49–69.

Melucci, Alberto. 1996. *Changing Codes: Collective Action in the Information Age*. Cambridge: Cambridge University Press.

Melucci, Alberto. 2000. "Social Movements in Complex Societies: A European Perspective." *Arena* 15: 81–99.

Michaud, Jacinthe. 1997. "On Counterhegemonic Formation in the Women's Movement and the Difficult Integration of Collective Identities." In William K. Carroll (ed.), *Organizing Dissent: Contemporary Social Movements in Theory and Practice*. 2nd ed. Toronto: Garamond. 197–212.

Mukherjee, Arun. 1992. "A House Divided: Women of Colour and American Feminist Theory." In Constance Backhouse and David H. Flaherty (eds.), *Challenging Times: The Women's Movement in Canada and the United States*. Montreal and Kingston: McGill-Queen's University Press. 165–74.

O'Neil, Maureen. 1993. "Citizenship and Social Change: Canadian Women's Struggle for Equality." In William Kaplan (ed.), *Belonging: The Meaning and Future of Canadian Citizenship*. Montreal and Kingston: McGill-Queen's University Press. 314–32.

Phillips, Susan D. 1991. "Meaning and Structure in Social Movements: Mapping the Network of National Canadian Women's Organizations." *Canadian Journal of Political Science* 24(4): 755–82.

Polletta, Francesca, and James M. Jasper. 2001. "Collective Identity and Social Movements." *Annual Review of Sociology* 27: 283–305.

Rankin, Pauline. 1996. "Experience, Opportunity, and the Politics of Place: A Comparative Analysis of Provincial and Territorial Women's Movements in Canada." Ph.D. thesis. Ottawa: Carleton University Department of Political Science.

Rankin, Pauline, and Jill Vickers. 2001. "Women's Movements and State Feminism: Integrating Diversity into Public Policy." Study for the Status of Women Canada (May). Ottawa.

Rebick, Judy. 2005. *Ten Thousand Roses: The Making of a Feminist Revolution.* Toronto: Penguin.

Rebick, Judy, and Kiké Roach. 1996. *Politically Speaking.* Vancouver: Douglas and McIntyre.

Roberts, Barbara. 1988. "Smooth Sailing or Storm Warnings? Canadian and Quebec Women's Groups on the Meech Lake Accord." A report prepared for the Canadian Research Institute for the Advancement of Women. Ottawa: CRIAW.

Rowbotham, Sheila. 1997. *A Century of Women: The History of Women in Britain and the United States.* London: Viking.

Ryan, Barbara. 1992. *Feminism and The Women's Movement: Dynamics of Change in Social Movement Ideology and Activism.* New York: Routledge.

Smith, Miriam. 2005. *A Civil Society? Collective Actors in Canadian Political Life.* Peterborough: Broadview.

Snow, David, and Robert D. Benford. 1988. "Ideology, Frame Resonance, and Participant Mobilization." *International Social Movement Research* 1: 197–218.

Snow, David, and Robert D. Benford. 1992. "Master Frames and Cycles of Protest." In Aldon D. Morris and Carol McClerg Mueller (eds.), *Frontiers in Social Movement Theory.* New Haven: Yale University Press. 133–55.

Squires, Judith. 2003. "Reviewing the UK Equality Agenda in the Context of Constitutional Change." In Alexandra Dobrowolsky and Vivien Hart (eds.), *Women Making Constitutions: New Politics and Comparative Perspectives.* Houndmills: Palgrave. 200–15.

Stone, Sharon Dale. 1997. "From Stereotypes to Visible Diversity: Lesbian Political Organizing." In William K. Carroll (ed.), *Organizing Dissent: Contemporary Social Movements in Theory and Practice.* 2nd ed. Toronto: Garamond. 171–96.

Tarrow, Sidney. 1994. *Power in Movement: Social Movements, Collective Action, and Politics.* Cambridge: Cambridge University Press.

Tarrow, Sidney. 2001. "Silence and Voice in the Study of Contentious Politics: Introduction." In Ronald Aminzade *et al.* (eds.), *Silence and Voice in the Study of Contentious Politics.* Cambridge: Cambridge University Press. 1–13.

Taylor, Verta. 1995. "Watching for Vibes: Bringing Emotions into the Study of Feminist Organizations." In Myra Marx Ferree and Patricia Yancey Martin (eds.), *Feminist Organizations: Harvest of the New Women's Movement.* Philadelphia: Temple University Press. 223–33.

Thomson, Michael. 2001. "Femocrats and Babes: Women and Power." *Australian Feminist Studies* 16(35): 193–208.

Vickers, Jill, Pauline Rankin, and Christine Appelle. 1993. *Politics As If Women Mattered: A Political Analysis of the National Action Committee on the Status of Women.* Toronto: University of Toronto Press.

Whitaker, Lois Duke. 1999. *Women in Politics: Outsiders or Insiders?* 3rd ed. New Jersey: Prentice Hall.

Wiebe, Nettie. 1995. "Farm Women: Cultivating Hope and Sowing Change."
    In Sandra Burt and Lorraine Code (eds.), *Changing Methods: Feminists
    Transforming Practice*. Peterborough: Broadview. 137–62.
Young, Lisa. 2000. *Women and Party Politics*. Vancouver: University of British
    Columbia Press.

SEVEN

Identity and Opportunity: The Lesbian and Gay Rights Movement[1]

Miriam Smith

Until the 1960s, lesbians and gay men led their personal lives in the shadows of Canadian society. Same-sex relationships were stigmatized and considered to be shameful and indicative of moral deviance or mental illness. The police routinely raided lesbian and gay gathering places such as bars, rounding up the clientele and sending them off to the police station to be charged with "gross indecency" or "buggery." The RCMP's "fruit machine" weeded out lesbians and gay men from government service, especially in the military and diplomatic services where their presence was thought to undermine moral and state security (Kinsman, Buse, and Steedman, 2000). Many lesbians and gay men socialized with each other in private networks, meeting only in each other's homes for fear of discovery; hiding their relationships and sexual lives from their families, co-workers, and communities; and living a veritable double life, in some cases, for all of their lives. Homosexuality was illegal, shameful, and hidden.

The status of lesbians and gay men in Canadian law, society, and politics has changed fundamentally since the 1960s. In 2002–03, courts in Quebec, British Columbia, and Ontario ruled in favour of same-sex marriage, and, as these rulings were followed by courts in other provinces and territories, the Liberal government of Paul Martin legalized same-sex marriage in 2005. Anti-discrimination laws are on the books in all Canadian jurisdictions. Lively gay villages exist in Montreal, Toronto, and Vancouver. Huge Pride festivals in Canadian cities have brought lesbian and gay life out into the open. Courts no longer routinely bar lesbian mothers from custody of their children, and, in most Canadian jurisdictions, same-sex couples have gained the right to adopt (including the right of second-parent adoption) and to enjoy a range of partner benefits. In Quebec and British Columbia, lesbian partners enjoy full filiation rights, meaning that same-sex parents can be listed together on the birth certificate, obviating the need for second-parent adoption. Queer student organizations exist on most Canadian university campuses, and professional associations have recognized lesbian and gay networks in their midst, such as the Sexual Orientation and Gender Identity Conference of the Canadian Bar Association.

Like the women's movement, the environmental movement, and other new social movements of the 1960s and 1970s, the lesbian and gay movement challenges dominant social norms. As Alberto Melucci (1997) has pointed out, social movements do not always primarily dedicate themselves to changing public policies but also to changing the dominant "codes" of society. The lesbian and gay rights movement challenges heteronormative norms or social codes. Heteronormativity means that social organization is structured around the assumption that heterosexual sexual preference and heterosexual coupling is the dominant mode of sexual, intimate, and family organization and that homosexuality is deviant. Even when dominant norms are not openly homophobic or hostile towards homosexuality, lesbian and gay people are outside of the "norm." So, for example, people are usually assumed to be heterosexual unless they state or are shown to be otherwise, an assumption that is an example of "heteronormativity." Some lesbian and gay people label themselves "queer"—traditionally a hostile epithet aimed at them—in part to call attention to the power of "naming" as a means of enforcing social expectations and defining "normalcy." Heteronormativity is not confined to social attitudes, norms, and values but is also enshrined in public policies. Until very recently, same-sex couples were not entitled to benefits provided to heterosexual couples, such as pensions or medical benefits provided by private or public sector employers. Such policies are "heteronormative" because they assume that heterosexual couples are the only form of couple or the only form of couple that is worthy of the social and economic support they provide.

This chapter will present the contemporary history of the lesbian and gay rights movement in terms of its origins in the gay liberation and feminist movements and will survey the major issues that have been raised by lesbian and gay activists in light of the theories of social movements outlined in the Introduction. Theories that highlight the role of the political process in creating obstacles and opportunities for social movement action are particularly relevant to the Canadian lesbian and gay movement, which has successfully exploited the new political opportunities created by the empowerment of the judiciary under the *Charter of Rights and Freedoms*. While resource mobilization approaches stress the internal resources of the movement, the political process model stresses its external opportunities. The lesbian and gay movement has exploited external opportunities, despite the fact that it is not well resourced in terms of formal organizations or large-scale funding. At the same time, new social movement theories call attention to the role of identity in the mobilization of collective actors. While the lesbian and gay movement engages the dynamics of recognition by the state and other societal actors as well as that of redistribution (e.g., through the material stakes in relationship recognition; see Fraser, 1995), the movement calls our attention to the ways in which collective identity is constructed through social and political processes. While same-sex behaviour has existed in many societies, it is only in the Western world since the 1960s that the identities of "gay" and "lesbian" have been formulated as identity options that are culturally available. The lesbian and gay movement could not exist unless lesbians and gays were willing to "come out" and embrace their identity. This "coming out" process constituted a direct and open challenge to heteronormative social codes. Therefore, theories that pay attention to culture and identity as well as to the political process of movement mobilization are the most useful in understanding the dynamics of this movement.

The 1960s: Homophile Organizing and the 1969 Reforms

A number of developments during the 1960s formed the essential backdrop for the emergence of the modern lesbian and gay rights movement as we know it in Canada today. In 1964, a homophile group called the Association for Social Knowledge (ASK) was founded in Vancouver to advocate for the legalization of homosexuality and for greater education and understanding of same-sex relationships. This group was similar to the homophile groups in the US such as the Mattachine Society and the Daughters of Bilitis, which had been founded over the postwar period. The 1960s were dangerous times for lesbians and gay men, making political organizing difficult. These dangers were called to public attention by the case of Everett George Klippert in the Northwest Territories, who was convicted of "gross indecency" after admitting that he had engaged in consensual sex with other men. Klippert was then labelled a dangerous sex offender, meaning that he could be imprisoned indefinitely, and his sex offender status was upheld on appeal to the Supreme Court of Canada in 1967. The Court's decision "raised the chilling prospect that any gay man could be imprisoned for life unless he could prove he was unlikely to recommit a same-sex act" (Warner, 2002: 46).

Partially in response to the public outcry over the Klippert case and to advocacy work by ASK and by the Canadian Bar Association, the federal government in 1967 followed the lead of Britain in tabling a bill to decriminalize homosexual acts between consenting adults 21 years of age or over. This bill, which was passed in 1969, meant that homosexual sex was "legal" in Canada, although the age of consent was higher for homosexual acts than for heterosexual acts. The 1969 reforms also provided for no-fault divorce and established a procedure by which women could obtain legal abortions. Therefore, the decriminalization of homosexuality was part of that package of legal reforms of the late 1960s that were epitomized by the famous quote from Pierre Trudeau "the state has no place in the bedrooms of the nation" (cited in English, 2006: 471). As for Klippert, he was released from prison in 1971, his only crime having been his relationships with other men.

Aside from the 1969 legal changes, the late 1960s and early 1970s also saw other developments that were important for the evolution of the lesbian and gay rights movement in Canada. The effervescent youth movement of this period and the rise of the women's movement were important precursors to the gay liberation movement. The women's movement politicized the questions of gender and sexuality as never before. It challenged traditional gender roles, the patriarchal nuclear family, and the regulation of women's bodies by men and by the state. Many lesbians were active in the women's movement, although the movement itself was not always friendly to lesbian politics. The youth movement of the late 1960s and the arrival of a large number of baby boomers in higher education helped fuel countercultural movements of the new left. Many of the early activists in the gay liberation movement were drawn from university campuses. They led the transition from the homophile organizing of the previous generation, which had focused on the guarded strategies of education, and transformed themselves into gay liberation groups in 1970–71. As we shall see, unlike the early homophile activists of the 1950s and 1960s, gay liberation and lesbian feminist activists directly challenged the idea that homosexuality and lesbianism should be stigmatized or that they were in any way inferior to heterosexuality.

The 1970s: Gay Liberation and Lesbian Feminism

The 1969 Stonewall riots in New York City marked the beginning of a new phase of radical gay politics in the US that almost immediately had repercussions in Canada. The police raid on a New York bar was similar to many other police raids on such establishments in both the US and in Canadian cities such as Montreal and Toronto. The difference in 1969 was that a group of lesbians, transsexuals,[2] transvestites, and gay men at the Stonewall bar fought back against the police, defending their right to a public space—the bar—free from state repression (Duberman, 1993). By 1970 gay liberation groups, such as the Gay Liberation Front, had sprung up in New York.

An important aspect of the gay liberation movement was the way in which it was organized. While the homophile movement had been dominated by small groups of professionals who held educational evenings, the gay liberation movement held kiss-ins (or "zaps"), and demonstrations. The more radical tactics were borrowed from strategies of the other countercultural movements of the 1960s. Further, the gay liberation movement was not centred in formal organizations but in a plethora of relatively small groups, which operated according to new left principles of democratic and participatory decision-making rather than by conventional majoritarian decision-making. Its resources were located much more in informal organizing networks rather than in large-scale social movement organizations.

With regard to its interpretation of homosexuality and its demands on society and the state, gay liberation went much further than the homophile movement. Early gay liberationists claimed that everyone was inherently bisexual and aimed to free everyone from the rigid categories of gender and sexual preference (Altman, 1993 [1971]). At the same time, however, the gay liberation movement early on encountered a tension between the idea that categories of gender and sexuality should be erased and the need to construct lesbian and gay identities as a necessary prerequisite to the building of the movement. If everyone was inherently bisexual and "polymorphously perverse" (in the Freudian term used by early gay liberationists), then what was the distinctive basis for a gay liberation movement? Like other social movements, the gay liberation movement eventually sought to build a collective identity. Boundaries were drawn around the idea of "gay" as innate sexual orientation. The claim that people were born lesbian or gay was used to advance the cause of human rights. After all, it would be unfair to discriminate against people based on an innate characteristic they could neither change nor control (Epstein, 1987: 13–20). Therefore, in terms of the networked methods of organization of the movement, the emphasis on the personal as political, and the importance of culture and identity in the process of political identity, the lesbian and gay movement conformed to the model of new social movements and, with respect to these characteristics, was similar to and inspired by the second-wave feminisms of the 1960s and 1970s.

The gay liberation movement took off in major Canadian cities over the course of the 1970s. Groups such as Toronto Gay Action, Gay Alliance Toward Equality in Toronto and Vancouver, the *Association des gai(e)s du Québec* in Montreal, the Coalition for Gay Rights in Ontario, and the Canadian Lesbian and Gay Rights Coalition worked on a common human rights agenda. Their demands were articulated in the document presented to Parliament by the protesters at the first gay liberation demonstration on Parliament Hill in August 1971. These included:

- removing "gross indecency" and "buggery" from the Criminal Code (and as a basis for declaration of dangerous offender status);

- equalizing penalties for sexual assault between heterosexual and homosexual acts;
- providing the same age of legal consent for heterosexual and homosexual sex;
- amending the *Immigration Act* to enable lesbians and gay men to immigrate to Canada;
- providing that lesbians and gay men may not be discriminated against in employment or promotion in public service;
- removing sodomy and homosexuality as grounds for divorce or for denial of child custody;
- permitting lesbians and gay men to serve in the Canadian Forces without discrimination;
- forcing the RCMP to publicly report on its witch hunt against lesbians and gay men in government service;
- providing equal status for homosexuals with respect to legal marriage, pensions, and income tax; and
- amending the *Canadian Human Rights Act* to include sexual orientation as a prohibited ground of discrimination (Waite and DeNovo, 1971).

Gay liberation groups throughout the 1970s used different strategies in pursuing this agenda, including demonstrating, lobbying, and litigating. Except in Quebec, where sexual orientation was included in the province's human rights legislation in 1977, these efforts at public policy change were not successful (for examples, see Higgins, 2000; Korinek, 2003).

Like other social movements, gay liberation was deeply structured by gendered relations between women and men. Many women felt that the movement's emphasis on sexuality and discrimination was not as relevant for lesbians as it was for gay men. They argued that, as women, they occupied a different position in society than men. Discrimination based on sex was probably more important for many lesbians than discrimination based on sexual orientation, even assuming that these could be meaningfully separated. A plethora of women's issues—such as male violence, gender inequality in the labour market, and child care—were also important issues. Similarly, sexual freedom was not prioritized by many lesbians, who viewed gay male activities such as public sex, bathhouses, and bars as activities that were not particularly worthy of political energies (Ross, 1995).

While some women participated in the gay liberation movement, others participated in the women's movement or in the autonomous lesbian movement. The women's movement was not particularly friendly to lesbian issues during the 1970s and early 1980s; many lesbians worked mainly on "women's" rather than "lesbian" issues over this period. The autonomous lesbian movement focused on building social and political space to define the distinctive political interests of lesbians as separate from gay men or from straight women. Aside from the creation of social space and the building of collective identity, the autonomous lesbian movement spawned a range of groups such as the Lesbian Organization of Toronto and Lesbians against the Right in Vancouver (Ross, 1995). One of the most important groups to emerge from lesbian politics of this decade in Canada were lesbian mothers' groups, which took up the important political and legal issue of securing child custody for lesbian parents (Stone, 1991).

Yet, over the course of the 1970s, the subcultures of lesbian and gay life grew substantially in Canada's major cities. Whether at Church/Wellesley in Toronto, the famous gay village of Montreal, or the West End of Vancouver, lesbian and gay male life was increasingly lived out in the open. The cultures of queer life spawned social institutions ranging from Pride Day to the women's chorus. Community institutions such as the 519 Community Centre in Toronto and queer media such as *RG*, *Fugues*, and (later) *Être* in Montreal or *The Body Politic* and, later, the *Xtra* chain in Ottawa, Toronto, and Vancouver, all permitted the construction of a collective culture and identity for Canadian gay men and, to a lesser extent, lesbians.

The 1980s: AIDS and the Charter

The AIDS epidemic had important effects on the evolution of lesbian and gay politics in Canada as elsewhere. The epidemic resulted in the deaths of many of the pioneers of the gay communities of Canada's major cities, while, at the same time, it reinforced the rise of the new right by associating gay male sexuality with the spread of disease. The idea of open sexual expression became problematic as some argued that traditional gay spaces such as washrooms, parks, bars, and bathhouses should be regulated in the interests of public health. Others argued that what was needed was education about safe sex. Either way, the stigma of HIV/AIDS was very strong during the 1980s, and the liberatory potential of sex and sexual expression that had been so important in the gay liberation movement was undermined. The rise of the Moral Majority in the US, the election of the Progressive Conservative government of Brian Mulroney in 1984, and the establishment of the right-wing populist Reform Party in 1987, all indicated that the 1960s and 1970s had not been a one-way street to sexual openness and liberation but that traditional social conservative values, especially those associated with evangelical Protestantism, were still an important political force. The forces of moral regulation brought a new vulnerability to the lesbian and gay communities, which expressed itself in part in new forms of politics (Herman, 1994).

AIDS organizing shifted the balance in lesbian and gay organizing away from the human rights campaigns of the 1970s and toward political action centred on ending the epidemic. This does not mean that human rights issues went away. On the contrary, AIDS drew attention to the legal inequality of gay men, especially with regard to relationship recognition. When a gay man fell ill or died, his partner was often left with no legal rights and could be shut out by his partner's family of origin. A particularly important issue was that of medical decision-making. Same-sex partners were often prevented from participating in medical and health decisions.

The effects of AIDS were also felt in political organizing. The perceived lack of attention to HIV/AIDS in the medical community and the direction of resources for research and treatments sparked the revival of some of the earlier tactics of gay liberation as well as new forms of direct action. ACT UP (AIDS Coalition to Unleash Power), the radical American AIDS group, pioneered the use of direct action tactics to focus public action and attention on the AIDS crisis. With the slogan "Silence=Death," ACT UP used civil disobedience such as demonstrations and "die-ins" (a variation of a "sit-in") and directly targeted pharmaceutical corporations as well as the US Food and Drug Administration, which was responsible for certifying new drugs in the US (Sommella, 1997). In Canada, groups such as AIDS Action Now! in Toronto played an important role in putting AIDS on the agenda of the federal government (Rayside and Lindquist, 1992: 37–70). Further, over the course of the late 1980s, a number of groups were established to deal with the specific needs of racialized people with HIV/AIDS. Toronto's Black Coalition for AIDS Prevention and Vancouver's Black AIDS Network were formed to provide services and education in black communities. Gay Asians Toronto established the Gay Asians AIDS project, and similar organizations were established in the early 1990s by other groups (Warner, 2002: 325–26).

The radicalization and decentring of social movement politics over this period can also be seen in the rise of groups such as Lesbian Avengers and Queer Nation. These focused on direct action tactics to counter bashing and homophobic attacks on lesbians and gays in urban areas, as well as other issues (Visser, 1990: 1). The ideology and tactics of Queer Nation formed a striking contrast to the mainstream political organizations. Instead of simply demanding that lesbians and gays be treated in the same way as straights through claims to equal rights, Queer Nation asserted a distinctive queer political identity while at the same time questioning the binary opposition of queer and straight. Instead of presenting briefs to government, Queer Nation engaged in direct action such as kiss-ins and street patrols. It represented a return to gay liberation ideology, especially in its assertion of a broader vision of social transformation. The tactic of kiss-in or "zap," for example, had been used in the early days of gay liberation in New York, Toronto, and elsewhere. While Queer Nation groups themselves were short-lived as political organizations in Canadian cities, they raised the flag on important issues that would animate lesbian and gay politics in the 1990s and after; in particular, groups such as Queer Nation and Lesbian Avengers called attention to the fact that lesbian and gay life constituted a distinctive culture or set of cultures of its own.

These forms of social movement politics highlighted the ways in which the movement over this period was not represented in a single movement or movement organization. Rather, lesbians and gay men organized in different locations, in AIDS organizing, in the women's movement, and in other locations. Often, as well, the targets of social movement activism were not only governments but also corporations, scientists, pharmaceutical companies, and the media. AIDS organizations such as ACT UP and urban groups such as Queer Nation and Lesbian Avengers often drew upon the radical template of the gay liberation and feminist movements, especially in their commitment to direct action (see Shepard and Hayduk, 2001). During this period, the resources of the movement were built up in AIDS organizations, yet much of the politics of the movement still occurred in decentred and decentralized social movement networks.

While the AIDS crisis and the radical politics of Queer Nation were emerging in the 1980s and early 1990s, another important development occurred that would shape lesbian and gay politics in Canada over the coming decades: the entrenchment of the *Charter of Rights and Freedoms* in the Canadian constitution. The Charter was proposed as part of Pierre Trudeau's "people's package" of constitutional reforms in 1980. It was intended to reinforce a sense of Canadian identity and to defuse regionalism and Quebec nationalism by reinforcing a sense of pan-Canadian political identity. The Charter became the object of a substantial political mobilization by First Nations, the disabled people's movement, the women's movement, and ethnocultural groups who were partially successful in shaping its equality rights guarantees in the debate over its enactment in 1980–81 (as discussed in Chapter 5, 6 and 12). The lesbian and gay rights movement did not play a major role in these developments in part because it lacked a viable pan-Canadian organization at the moment of the Charter debates. In addition, the human rights agenda of the gay liberation groups of the 1970s had exhausted itself. As the pursuit of legislative and policy change had not been successful over the course of that decade, the fragmented gay rights groups were not very interested in the Charter, did not have the political and financial resources to mount a substantial mobilization, and were preoccupied with the first onset of the AIDS crisis. However, the issue was raised by MP Svend Robinson, who was unsuccessful in his efforts to have sexual orientation included in the proposed Charter. Despite this exclusion, it was understood that the open-ended wording of the equality rights section of the Charter (section 15) left the door open to the addition of sexual orientation in the future. The Liberal government was well aware that sexual orientation might be added to the Charter by the courts because of the wording of the clause (Smith, 1999).

Over the course of the mid-1980s and into the 1990s, political mobilizing in the lesbian and gay rights movement slowly began to focus on the political opening provided to the movement by the Charter. This realization was slow to take hold. In cities such as Toronto, Montreal, and Vancouver, this was the major period for AIDS activism. In Quebec, attention was not as focused on the Charter because of the impact of the Quebec nationalist movement, which perceived it as part of the politically illegitimate constitutional patriation of 1982. Lawyers were among the first to realize the potential impact of the Charter: lesbian and gay lawyers and law students began to organize both within law schools and bar associations, and lesbian and gay legal issues began to obtain coverage in law journals and legal scholarship (Duplé, 1984; Girard, 1986; Herman, 1989; Cossman, 1994). Moreover, lesbian and gay movement organizing at the pan-Canadian level was spurred in part by the political opportunity provided by the Charter. Therefore, rather than resources making the movement, as resource mobilization theory would contend, in this case it was the existence of political opportunities that galvanized resources and organization. The parliamentary sub-committee on section 15 equality rights, held in 1985, was a major fulcrum for legal and political debate. The equality rights hearings drew a large number of submissions from lesbian and gay groups and resulted in the creation in 1986 of Egale, a lesbian and gay rights group that would work on human rights issues at the federal level.

The 1990s: The Charter and Beyond

Over the course of the 1990s, lesbian and gay organizing occurred in many different institutions and organizations of Canadian society and across a broad range of issues ranging from the use of queer-positive reading materials in the education system to the issue of same-sex marriage. We will now explore these diverse forms of organizing in terms of the issues they raised, including discrimination in housing and employment, relationship recognition, sexual freedom, and policies and practices on lesbian and gay issues in the public education system. During this period, substantial social change took place in Canadian society, partly as a result of the movement's politicization of lesbian and gay identities. As we will see, the Charter provided an important opening for lesbian and gay litigation. In keeping with the political process model, the movement was able to take advantage of this opportunity and to secure public policy change through the courts in areas ranging from discrimination in employment to same-sex marriage. The movement was able to achieve this despite the fact that its main organization in federal politics—Egale—was poorly resourced.[3]

One of the major areas of public policy change has been that of freedom from discrimination based on sexual orientation in areas such as employment and housing. With regard to government policies, this was the main goal of gay liberation groups of the 1970s, although in most cases this type of discrimination is covered by provincial and federal human rights legislation. The Charter itself does not directly regulate relationships between private citizens (such as the relationship between landlord and tenant), although it indirectly shapes human rights legislation at both federal and provincial levels. Human rights campaigns in the provinces focused on amending provincial human rights legislation to include sexual orientation as a prohibited ground of discrimination, while at the federal level lobbying and litigation focused on the addition or "reading in" of section 15 to include sexual orientation and the amendment of the federal human rights act along the same lines. Citizen-to-citizen discrimination is governed by a patchwork of provincial and federal human rights legislation, including the Charter itself, which governs state-to-citizen relationships. A major campaign to change the Ontario Human Rights Code in the 1970s failed, even in the wake of such high-profile employment discrimination cases as that of John Damien, a racing steward who was fired from his job with the Ontario Racing Commission for being gay (Warner, 2002: 145–52). In British Columbia, the Social Credit government gutted human rights protections in the province, and one case of discrimination—the *Vancouver Sun*'s refusal to publish an ad from a gay rights group—was defeated in the Supreme Court of Canada (*Gay Alliance Toward Equality v. Vancouver Sun*; see also Black, 1979). In other provinces, lesbian and gay communities of this period were too fragile to mount major campaigns for human rights changes.

In the 1980s, a sustained campaign in Ontario by groups such as the Coalition for Lesbian and Gay Rights in Ontario and by the Right to Privacy Committee finally led to the amendment of Ontario's Human Rights Code to include sexual orientation in 1986 (Rayside, 1988), while, at the federal level, a Charter challenge by litigants Haig and Birch resulted in the de facto addition of sexual orientation to the federal human rights code in 1992. However, even then, the Liberal government of Jean Chrétien prevaricated on the formal amendment of the federal *Human Rights Act* to include sexual orientation by 1996. The Alberta government only included sexual orientation in its human rights legislation when forced to do so by the Supreme Court decision in *Vriend* in 1998. Most provinces had amended their human rights legislation to include a formal ban on sexual orientation discrimination in provincial/ territorial jurisdiction by the early 1990s (Smith, 2005b).

The recognition of same-sex relationship and parenting rights is another important area of social movement mobilization. The question of recognizing same-sex relationships for the purpose of employment benefits became an issue almost as soon as the Charter came into effect. One of the first cases on relationship recognition was brought by Brian Mossop, a federal government employee and long-time gay liberation activist, in 1985; although Mossop did not directly invoke Charter rights in his claim for bereavement leave to attend the funeral of his partner's father, the final decision against Mossop in the Federal Court of Canada invited the recasting of the claim on Charter grounds. Meanwhile, the *Veysey* case had established the right of same-sex partners to spousal rights in prisons, a case in which the Federal Court of Canada recognized that sexual orientation was analogous to the other grounds of discrimination named in section 15. Finally, in the 1995 *Egan* case on same-sex spousal benefits under the Old Age Security program, the Supreme Court of Canada ruled that sexual orientation was included in section 15. However, the court ruled that the "reasonable limits" clause of the Charter provided grounds on which to deny benefits to same-sex couples. The Court's decision to subject the equality rights guarantees of section 15 to the general limitation clause in section 1 to deny government benefits to same-sex couples was taken as a threat to equality rights in general by other stakeholder groups, and, following the *Egan* ruling, a number of groups, including ethnocultural groups and women's groups, mobilized to work against this interpretation of section 15 across equality rights cases (Go and Fisher, 1998). In the late 1990s, two important cases were decided, one on the right of same-sex couples to access spousal benefits in employer pensions under federal tax rules (*Rosenberg*) and the other on the constitutionality of Ontario's *Family Law Act*, which denied spousal support to same-sex partners upon the break-up of their relationship (*M v. H*). In the latter case, the most important ruling on same-sex spousal rights to date, one of the former partners, "M," pursued "H" for support upon the break-up of their relationship, arguing that the family law of Ontario discriminated against same-sex couples in preventing former same-sex couples from making claims of spousal support. In ruling that Ontario's family law discriminated against same-sex couples and violated their equality rights under the Charter, the Supreme Court of Canada moved away from the logic of the *Egan* case and indicated that it would not accept anything less than full equality under the law for same-sex couples and, in so doing, set the stage for the next step, which was the move to same-sex marriage.

Therefore, litigation and lobbying in response to litigation have constituted important political strategies for the movement. In this context, once again, we can see the impact of the structure of political opportunity in social movement politics. The movement was not particularly well resourced during this period and did not have the means of bringing political pressure to bear on the Liberal government, except through the courts. It is highly unlikely that the Liberal government would have recognized lesbian and gay rights if it had not been for these court decisions. In the mid-1990s, Parliament voted on several occasions against spousal recognition for same-sex couples, and it was only in response to the Supreme Court decision in *M v. H* (which recognized the constitutional necessity of equality in spousal support laws) that the federal government passed the *Modernization of Benefits and Obligations Act* of 2000, which extended most benefits (except immigration rights) to same-sex couples in federal jurisdiction, short of marriage (Smith, 2005b). Similarly, the move from relationship recognition in common law (or *union de fait*) relationships to the recognition of same-sex marriage was also sparked by a series of court decisions in the early 2000s and not by the pressure brought to bear by the movement on the Liberal government.

Same-sex marriage litigation took place across Canada. In 1998, a Quebec gay couple brought a legal challenge to the heterosexual definition of marriage in Quebec's civil law. In 2000, the first of what would eventually be two sets of couples began their litigation on same-sex marriage in British Columbia. In 2001, four couples were married in Metropolitan Community Church in Toronto after the publication of banns, in a challenge to Ontario's laws governing marriage. Evangelical Christians and their supporters have been forceful opponents of such measures, arguing that recognizing same-sex benefits will undermine the traditional family or that such recognition will "condone" a "lifestyle" that leads to AIDS and other diseases (Canada, 2000). A wide range of religious organizations and lesbian and gay organizations spoke to the courts through the litigation in British Columbia, Quebec, Ontario, and other provinces which led to the key set of court decisions in 2002–03. The first decision, in British Columbia, rejected the same-sex couples' claims for the right to access to legal marriage. The judge argued that marriage had always been heterosexual and that the Charter did not require marriage equality for same-sex couples. However, this decision was appealed to the provincial Court of Appeal, which ruled that barring same-sex couples from same-sex marriage was unconstitutional but that the legislature should have the right to devise a solution. At the same time, in Quebec, a long battle for parenting and partnership rights, led by a wide range of social movement organizations including the labour movement, resulted in the recognition of parenting rights and the creation of a new civil union regime in Quebec, one that included same-sex partners (Nicol, 2005). Nova Scotia passed domestic partnership legislation in 2001. For a time, therefore, it looked as though civil unions might emerge as the dominant policy in this area. However, this was brought to an end by the Court of Appeal decision in Ontario in 2003 in the case of *Halpern v. Canada*, in which the Ontario Court of Appeal not only agreed with the British Columbia court that same-sex marriage was constitutional but ruled that marriage licences had to be issued immediately. Quebec followed with a decision in favour of same-sex marriage in 2004. Rather than appealing these decisions, the Chrétien government developed legislation to legalize same-sex civil marriage and then referred the question of its constitutionality to the Supreme Court. The Court (*Reference* 2004) indicated that the government's same-sex marriage was constitutional and that it did not infringe on religious freedom. Under the Liberal government of Paul Martin, the same-sex marriage legislation became law in June 2005. Although the Conservative government elected in January 2006 opposes same-sex marriage, it did not roll back the measure, despite holding a vote on the possibility of doing so in December 2006.

A number of voices within the lesbian and gay communities questioned the extent to which same-sex marriage was a worthwhile expenditure of movement resources. Some opposed relationship recognition as a co-optation of the original goals of the gay liberation movement—sexual freedom—and as marking the conservatization of the movement (Hannon, 1999: 3), while others were critical of relationship recognition because they shared the feminist critique of family as a patriarchal institution. Others argued that relationship recognition might radicalize and transform the traditional family or mark the full recognition of lesbians and gay men as citizens (on this debate, see Herman, 1989; Cossman, 1994; Boyd and Young, 2003). Despite the debates that have occurred in lesbian and gay communities over same-sex marriage, in general lesbian and gay rights-seeking organizations are caught up in a political dynamic that demands the articulation of a clear-cut, almost "ethnic" identity in order to make their rights claims legible to the Canadian public, the media, the courts, the governing caucus, and policy-makers (Smith, 2005a, 2005b; see also Epstein, 1987). In this dynamic, it was very difficult for the movement(s)—especially as decentred networks of activism and community—to counter the dynamic generated by the course of litigation. In this sense, then, opportunities not only shaped the success of the movement but also its priorities, claims, and demands.

The settling of the debates over discrimination, relationship recognition, and parenting and same-sex marriage has had a profound effect on lesbian and gay organizing at the federal level. Many of the other policy issues for lesbian and gay communities are local, provincial, or urban, which creates challenges for the maintenance of stable pan-Canadian organizations (Grundy and Smith, 2005). Political mobilization to reduce homophobia in schools and to ensure that health research and health care delivery reflect the health needs of lesbian and gay citizens is another important area of political activism. A number of other political issues concern the regulation of sexual behaviour and pornography through the criminal law. In these areas, there are important differences in the lesbian and gay movement, especially between gay men and some lesbians over the ways in which the state should regulate sexual freedom and sexual expression. There is increasing recognition of the importance of transgender legal and political issues within lesbian and gay communities, especially with respect to the recognition of gender identity as a prohibited ground of discrimination and with respect to the availability of sexual reassignment surgery in the provinces (which are responsible for this policy as the administrators of the medicare system). For these reasons, lesbian and gay organizing faces challenges in maintaining the relatively high level of success that was achieved in the 1990s and early 2000s.

The lesbian and gay movement has been active in the area of sexual freedom, a central characteristic of the gay liberation movement. For some, sexual freedom is the main goal of the movement and a key dimension of lesbian and, especially, gay political identity (Cossman *et al.*, 1997). Issues in this area include censorship of lesbian and gay bookstores, pornography, criminalization of anal sex, police attempts to regulate public sex, and age of consent laws. Sexual freedom is an issue that has the potential to openly challenge the line between "good sex" and "bad sex," and between sexual order and sexual chaos, in Gayle Rubin's terms (Rubin, 1984). While relationship recognition has the potential to (in part) fit lesbian and gay couples into an acceptable "family" model (precisely the point of the feminist and gay liberationist critiques of "family" in the lesbian and gay communities), the political issues surrounding sexuality and sexual expression such as pornography threaten this cozy picture of middle-class and monogamously coupled respectability by pushing at the line between "good" and "bad."

A series of legal cases on the issue of censorship and pornography results from the Little Sisters Book and Art Emporium in Vancouver. This lesbian and gay bookstore has been battling Canada Customs since 1986 over the seizure and censorship of lesbian and gay materials shipped from the US. Lesbian and gay erotica is often deemed to be pornography by customs officials and is help up at the border. Even literary novels published in the US by well-known Canadian novelists, such as Jane Rule, have been stopped at the border (Fuller and Blackley, 1995). Little Sisters is not the only bookstore to have faced this kind of ongoing and systematic harassment by the state: Glad Day in Toronto, After Stonewall in Ottawa, and Androgyne in Montreal have all faced similar problems. State regulation of lesbian and gay sexual expression also continues to be at issue in police behaviour with regard to the lesbian and gay communities in Canada's major cities. In 2000, undercover police in Toronto raided the lesbian bathhouse, the Pussy Palace, and, reminiscent of the bath raids of the

1970s and 1980s, made a number of arrests in a seeming attempt to shut down the space (Gallant, 2001).

Another important arena of contestation by the lesbian and gay rights movement is the area of education and social policy. The legal advances of the movement at the level of public policy cannot obscure the fact that, at the local level, life is still very difficult for lesbian and gay people. There are still tremendous social sanctions and dangers in coming out, especially in Canada's smaller communities. Queer youth face bullying and harassment in school, and the stresses caused by facing such harassment are surely one of the factors behind the higher suicide rate for queer teens than for straight youth (Bagley and Tremblay, 1997). In some parts of Canada, notably Toronto, Vancouver, and the lower mainland of British Columbia, lesbian and gay activists have attempted to put the issue of heteronormativity on the educational agenda through the adoption of school board policies on homophobia and through the introduction of gay- and lesbian-positive reading materials in the schools. A sustained and concerted effort by activists in the Toronto boards of education (merged into the Toronto District School Board) over the course of the 1990s resulted in the adoption of equity policies on sexual orientation and gender identity, although there are still important problems with the implementation of these policies, especially because of budget cuts (Frances, 2000). In the lower mainland of British Columbia, the British Columbia Teachers' Federation has played a leading role in implementing anti-homophobia and anti-racism policies. Further, the province's lesbian and gay educators group, Gay and Lesbian Educators of British Columbia, has worked to create a social and support space for teachers and school administrators. From this effort came the campaign led by James Chamberlain and Murray Warren to introduce gay- and lesbian-positive reading materials into the elementary school grades in the Port Coquitlam and Surrey school districts. Chamberlain and Warren sought to use books that depicted families with same-sex parents for young children. This sparked a backlash from the evangelical movement, which had undertaken a concerted campaign to control school boards in the "bible belt" of the province. The Surrey School Board banned the gay- and lesbian-positive books from the elementary school classroom and was immediately challenged by parents, teachers (including Chamberlain and Warren), and others who undertook a successful Charter challenge to this censorship of reading materials.

The conflict between lesbian and gay equality rights and religious rights was also at issue in the case of Marc Hall, the gay Oshawa teen who claimed the right to take his boyfriend to the prom in a Catholic school (Kennedy, 2001). These challenges were not directed by social movement organizations such as Egale but were brought by individuals who decided to pursue a legal avenue in the face of what they believed to be discrimination or who were connected with lesbian and gay activism through their trade union (such as the British Columbia Teachers' Federation) or local lesbian and gay groups. The myriad networks of lesbian and gay activism span unions, the education system, and the workplace (Hunt, 1999). Strategically, litigation has been an effective political strategy for lesbian and gay activists in the late 1990s and beyond, and litigation, by its very nature, bubbles up when individuals choose to undertake a legal fight and cannot be directed by social movement organizations.

Finally, new forms of local and pan-Canadian organizing have arisen recently in the area of lesbian and gay health policy. The Canadian Rainbow Health Coalition, founded in Saskatoon, has been paralleled by local organizations across Canada, which centre on the health needs of lesbian and gay people with regard to issues including sexual health, breast cancer, domestic violence, mental health, sex reassignment surgery, and other health needs of trans people (Rainbow Health Coalition, 2006). In most major cities, queer youth projects have sprung up, in some cases funded by local government and public health agencies; these provide health and social services for queer youth, as well as facilitating organizing and community-building by them. To date, efforts to politicize social and economic policy to highlight the situation and needs of lesbian and gay youth communities have not succeeded. For example, they are at greater risk of homelessness than straight youth. Yet, social services for youth and the homeless do not clearly recognize how sexuality is intertwined with other bases of social and economic inequality (Grundy and Smith, 2005).

Conclusions: Lesbian and Gay Politics and Social Movement Theories

Social movement theories from sociology and political science provide a useful perspective on some aspects of lesbian and gay social movement challenges in Canadian politics. As discussed in the Introduction, resource mobilization theory stresses the idea that movements arise when they are able to obtain economic and political resources, the political process model stresses that movements must have political opportunities in order to achieve success, and new social movement theory stresses the cultural dimension of movement challenges which lead to the formation of collective identity (Della Porta and Diani, 1999).

All three of these dimensions may be seen at work in the evolution of lesbian and gay organizing described here. Without a common sense of political identity and without a mass exit of lesbian and gay people from the closet, the modern lesbian and gay rights movement in Canadian would not exist. The first step in the formation of the movement was the process of establishing a collective identity. In the early years of gay liberation, the very act of holding a gay dance posed a radical challenge to the dominance and raw economic, social, and political power of heteronormativity. By allowing lesbian and gay people to come together, if only for the purpose of recreation, such events helped to build and reinforce lesbian and gay cultures, which, in turn, formed the basis of social movement networks. Formal organizations such as Egale are the tip of the iceberg of these broader networks of organizing. New social movement theories highlight the creation of new social and political identities which underpin collective action. Similarly, they highlight post-materialism and historical specificity in the context of the politics of the 1960s and after, at least in the context of developed countries such as Canada. The women's movement, the gay liberation movement, and the lesbian feminist movements were the product of this period of youth revolt and, initially at least, drew on the template of 1960s organizing.

Resources have played less of a role in the politics of the lesbian and gay movement in Canada. The movement is not well resourced at the pan-Canadian level, and even at the height of the same-sex marriage debate in the early 2000s, the movement's organizational resources consisted of two small lobbying groups with meagre budgets. While the movement enjoys some material support from allies in the labour movement, lesbian and gay organizations in the US are much better resourced than organizations in Canada. Nonetheless, despite these far greater resources, the US is far behind Canada in its recognition of the legal equality of lesbian and gay citizens or the recognition of same-sex relationships and parenting rights (see Cahill, 2004). Therefore, the success of the gay and lesbian movement cannot be attributed to resources alone.

The political process model offers a more convincing account of the recent history of the lesbian and gay rights movement. In particular, the political and legal opportunities afforded by the Charter have provided an opening for lesbian and gay organizations and individual litigants to use the courts to force public policy changes on reluctant governments. These Charter challenges have also disrupted the normative status of straight life by calling media and public attention to issues ranging from censorship and discrimination to the right of one young man to take another young man to the prom. In the lesbian and gay rights case, the material consequences of changes to public policy such as the right of same-sex couples to pension, medical, and dental benefits are intertwined with the symbolic and cultural challenge to the traditional norms of Canadian (and other) societies. The Charter has proven to be a potent and effective weapon for lesbian and gay litigation and organizing and has forced governments to act where, otherwise, they were clearly unwilling to touch the "gay rights" hot button. The result has been a dramatic period of change in

Canadian politics and one of the few successful stories of progressive social movements in the neoliberal era.

Notes

1. This research was financed in part by grants from the Social Sciences and Research Council of Canada, and this support is gratefully acknowledged. I would like to thank Michael Orsini for helpful comments on this paper.

2. This article does not treat the politics of transgender ("trans") and transsexual issues in any detail. Sexual orientation and gender identity are not the same thing. Many people who identify as "trans" do not identify as "lesbian" or "gay," and, indeed, transgender and transsexual people may be straight in their sexual orientation. The terms sexual orientation and gender identity are often used together to denote this distinction. For accounts of trans politics and law, see Namaste (2000) and findlay (2003).

3. Information on Egale's resources comes from a number of sources. For example, in several interviews with former executive director of Egale, John Fisher (in 1995 and 2001), he indicated to me that the Egale budget was very small—under $500,000. Egale's 2006 President Gemma Schlamp-Hickey estimated the budget at $350,000 in 2006, just before the Harper government held a free vote on rolling back same-sex marriage (see Barsotti, 2006).

Cases Cited

Correctional Service of Canada v. Veysey [1990], 109 N.R. 300
Egan & Nesbitt v. Canada 124 D.L.R. (4th) 609 SCC
Gay Alliance Toward Equality v. Vancouver Sun [1979] 2 S.C.R. 435
Halpern v. Canada [2003] O.A.C. 405
Klippert v. the Queen [1967] S.C.R. 822
M v. H [1999] S.C.J. No. 23
Canada (A.G.) v. Mossop [1993] 1 S.C.R. 554
Reference re Same-Sex Marriage [2004] SCC 79
Rosenberg v. Canada (Attorney General) [1998] 38 O.R. (3d) 577
Vriend v. Alberta [1998] 1 S.C.R. 493

References and Further Reading

Adam, Barry D. 1995. *The Rise of a Gay and Lesbian Movement*. Rev. ed. New York: Twayne Publishers.

Altman, Dennis. 1993 [1971]. *Homosexual Oppression and Liberation*. New York: New York University Press.

Bagley, C., and P. Tremblay. 1997. "Suicidal Behaviors in Homosexual and Bisexual Males." *Crisis, The International Journal of Suicide and Crisis Studies* 18(1): 24–34.

Barsotti, Natasha. 2006. "More Resignations Rock Egale." *Xtra West* [Vancouver], 6 December. <http://www.xtra.ca/public/viewstory.aspx?AFF_TYPE =1&STORY_ID=2416&PUB_TEMPLATE_ID=2>.

Black, W.W. 1979. "Gay Alliance Toward Equality v. Vancouver Sun." *Osgoode Hall Law Journal* 17: 649–75.

Body Politic [Toronto]. 1976 (August) and various issues 1971–87.

Boyd, Susan B., and Claire F.L. Young. 2003. "From Same-sex to No Sex? Trends Towards Recognition of (Same-sex) Relationships in Canada." *Seattle Journal for Social Justice* 3: 757–93.

British Columbia Civil Liberties Association. 1998. "B.C. CLA Intervenes in Surrey Book Ban Case." 29 June. Vancouver: Press Release.

Cahill, Sean. 2004. *Same-Sex Marriage in the United States: A Focus on the Facts.* Lanham: Lexington Books.

Canada. 2000. *Minutes of Proceedings and Evidence.* Ottawa: House of Commons, Standing Committee on Justice and Human Rights (16 March): 1606.

Cossman, Brenda. 1994. "Family Inside/Out." *University of Toronto Law Journal* 44: 1–39.

Cossman, Brenda, Shannon Bell, Lise Gotell, and Becki Ross. 1997. *Bad Attitude/s on Trial: Pornography, Feminism, and the "Butler" Decision.* Toronto: University of Toronto Press.

Della Porta, Donatella, and Mario Diani. 1999. *Social Movements: An Introduction.* Oxford: Blackwell.

Demczuk, Irène, and Frank Remiggi. 1998. *Sortir de l'ombre : Histoires des communautés lesbienne et gaie de Montréal.* Montréal: VLB Éditeur.

Duberman, Martin. 1993. *Stonewall.* New York: Dutton.

Duplé, Nicole. 1984. "Homosexualité et droits à l'égalité dans les Chartes canadienne et québécoise." *Les cahiers de droit* 25: 1–32.

English, John. 2006. *Citizen of the World: The Life of Pierre Elliott Trudeau, Vol. 1 1919–1969.* Toronto: Knopf.

Epstein, Steven. 1987. "Gay Politics, Ethnic Identity: The Limits of Social Constructionism." *Socialist Review* 17: 9–54.

findlay, barbara. 2003. "Real Women: *Kimberly Nixon v. Vancouver Rape Relief.*" *University of British Columbia Law Review* 36: 58.

Frances, Margot. 2000. "Chalkboard Promises." *Xtra* (7 September).

Fraser, Nancy. 1995. "From Redistribution to Recognition? Dilemmas of Justice in a 'Post-Socialist' Age." *New Left Review* 212: 68–93.

Fuller, Janine, and Stuart Blackley. 1995. *Restricted Entry: Censorship on Trial.* Vancouver: Press Gang.

Gallant, Paul. 2001. "Who Should Be Ashamed?" *Xtra* (November): 1.

Girard, Philip. 1986. "Sexual Orientation as a Human Rights Issue in Canada, 1969–1985." *Dalhousie Law Journal* 10(2): 267–81.

Go, Avvy, and John Fisher. 1998. *Working Together Across our Differences: A Discussion Paper on Coalition-building, Participatory Litigation, and Strategic Litigation.* Ottawa: Court Challenges Program.

Grundy, John, and Miriam Smith. 2005. "The Politics of Multiscalar Citizenship: The Case of Lesbian and Gay Organizing in Canada." *Citizenship Studies* 9(4): 389–404.

Grundy, John, and Miriam Smith. 2007. "Activist Knowledges in Queer Politics." *Economy and Society* 36:2 (May): 295–318.

Hannon, Philip. 1999. "Sexual Outlaws or Respectable In-laws?" *Capital Xtra* (3 June).

Herman, Didi. 1989. "Are We Family? Lesbian Rights and Women's Liberation." *Osgoode Hall Law Journal* 28(4): 789–815.

Herman, Didi. 1994. *Rights of Passage: Struggles for Lesbian and Gay Legal Equality.* Toronto: University of Toronto Press.

Higgins, Ross. 2000. *De la clandestinité à l'affirmation.* Montreal: Comeau/ Nadeau.

Hunt, Gerald. 1999. "No Longer Outsiders: Labor's Response to Sexual Diversity in Canada." In Gerald Hunt (ed.), *Laboring for Rights: Unions and Sexual Diversity Across Nations.* Philadelphia: Temple University Press.

Kennedy, Sarah. 2001. "Gay Teen Goes to the Prom." *Globe and Mail,* 10 May: A1.

Kinsman, Gary. 1996. *The Regulation of Desire: Homo and Heterosexualities.* 2nd ed. Montreal: Black Rose.

Kinsman, Gary, Dieter K. Buse, and Mercedes Steedman (Eds.). 2000. *Whose National Security? Canadian State Surveillance and the Creation of Enemies.* Toronto: Between the Lines.

Korinek, Valerie J. 2003. "'The Most Openly Gay Person for at Least a Thousand Miles': Doug Wilson and the Politicization of a Province, 1975–1983." *Canadian Historical Review* 84(4): 517–50.

Melucci, Alberto. 1997. *Challenging Codes: Collective Action in the Information Age.* Cambridge: Cambridge University Press.

Namaste, Vivian K. 2000. *Invisible Lives: The Erasure of Transsexual and Transgendered People.* Chicago: University of Chicago Press.

Nicol, Nancy. 2005. *Politics of the Heart/La politique du coeur.* Film. Toronto.

Pinello, Daniel R. 2006. *America's Struggle for Same-Sex Marriage.* Cambridge: Cambridge University Press.

Rainbow Health Coalition. 2006. *About Us.* <http://www.rainbowhealth network.ca/about>.

Rayside, David. 1988. "Gay Rights and Family Values: The Passage of Bill 7 in Ontario." *Studies in Political Economy* 26: 109–47.

Rayside, David, and Evert Lindquist. 1992. "AIDS Activism and the State in Canada." *Studies in Political Economy* 39: 37–76.

Ross, Becki. 1995. *The House That Jill Built: A Lesbian Nation in Formation.* Toronto: University of Toronto Press.

Rubin, Gayle. 1984. "Thinking Sex: Notes for a Radical Theory of the Politics of Sexuality." In C.S. Vance (ed.), *Pleasure and Danger: Exploring Female Sexuality.* Boston: Routledge and Kegan Paul.

Shepard, Benjamin, and Ronald Hayduk (Eds.). 2001. *From ACT UP To The WTO: Urban Protest and Community Building in the Era of Globalization.* London: Verso.

Smith, Miriam. 1999. *Lesbian and Gay Rights in Canada: Social Movements and Equality-Seeking, 1971–1995.* Toronto: University of Toronto Press.

Smith, Miriam. 2005a. "Resisting and Reinforcing Neoliberalism: Lesbian and Gay Organizing at the Federal and Local Levels in Canada." *Policy & Politics* 33(1): 75–93.

Smith, Miriam. 2005b. "Social Movements and Judicial Empowerment: Courts, Public Policy, and Lesbian and Gay Organizing in Canada." *Politics & Society* 33(2): 327–53.

Smith, Miriam. 2007. "Framing Same-Sex Marriage in Canada and the United States: *Goodridge, Halpern,* and the National Boundaries of Political Discourse." *Social and Legal Studies* 16(1): 5–26.

Sommella, Laraine. 1997. "This Is about People Dying: The Tactics of Early ACT UP and Lesbian Avengers in New York City." In G.B. Ingram, A.-M. Bouthillette, and Y. Retter (eds.), *Queers in Space: Communities, Public Places, Sites of Resistance*. Seattle: Bay Press.

Stone, Sharon Dale. 1991. "Lesbian Mothers Organize." In S.D. Stone (ed.), *Lesbians in Canada*. Toronto: Between the Lines.

Visser, Andy. 1990. "Queer Notions." *Xtra* (14 September): 1.

Waite, Brian, and Cheri DeNovo. 1971. *We Demand*. Toronto: August 28th Gay Day Committee.

Warner, Tom. 2002. *Never Going Back: A History of Queer Activism in Canada*. Toronto: University of Toronto Press.

EIGHT

Populist and Conservative Christian Evangelical Movements: A Comparison of Canada and the United States[1]

Trevor W. Harrison

Recent decades have witnessed the resurgence throughout much of the Western world and elsewhere of political movements claiming to represent "the people" in opposition to threats arising from powerful "others." Side by side with the rebirth of "populism" in North America, especially in the US, has been a resurgence of conservative Christian, mainly Protestant, evangelicalism. This chapter is in two parts. The first briefly explores the wider phenomenon of "populism." The second details some conceptual links between populist and Christian evangelical movements and then goes on to examine evangelical movements in Canada and the US. Ultimately, it is argued the greater strength of the conservative Christian evangelical movement in the US results from a number of societal and organizational factors, including the greater fusion of religion and nationalism in that country or what is often referred to as "civil religion."

Populism: Definition

While the term "populism" is sometimes used to describe a personal leadership style, it is analytically more useful if we consider some of the key elements held in common by populist movements (Sinclair, 1979; Conway, 1978; Harrison, 1995). First, populist movements and parties appeal to a mass audience, specifically a group defined as "the people." Second, this appeal is made urgent by the perception of a crisis threatening "the people." Third, the source of this threat is an identifiable group (a "power bloc"), sometimes geographically but often socio-culturally "external" to "the people," including various elites. In short, populism is defined as a mass political movement, mobilized around

[203]

symbols and traditions congruent with the popular culture, which expresses a group's sense of threat arising from powerful outside elements and directed at their perceived "peoplehood."

The term's use is relatively recent. It originated in Russia in the turbulent 1870s (Di Tella, 2001) following the emancipation of the serfs at a time when many in the country were attempting to find a third way between capitalist modernization and Marxist socialism. By the mid-twentieth century, the term was often used in Latin and South America in connection with the twin concepts of corporatism and clientelism (see Rea *et al.*, 1992), populism being viewed as a political mechanism for nationalist mobilization. In between these two uses, populism first gained currency in North America in 1892 when American journalists adopted the term to describe supporters of the People's Party (mainly farmers and small business people) founded that year.

In Canada, the term is most familiarly associated with the various farmers' parties that arose in several provinces, but especially the Canadian West, in the early twentieth century, inspired by similar movements across the border. As in the US, Canadian farmers (already beset by an unpredictable climate and grasshoppers) often found themselves victims of the monopoly practices of bankers, grain companies, and railways. The result was the emergence of "farmers' parties" in several provinces in the years immediately follow-ing World War I and, during the federal election of 1921, the sudden rise to prominence of the newly founded Progressive Party, which took 65 seats, second only to the victorious Liberals (Morton, 1978). In the context of the Great Depression of the 1930s, other populist parties were formed, notably the socialist CCF in Saskatchewan (Lipset, 1968) and the Social Credit party in Alberta (Macpherson, 1953; Finkel, 1989; Bell, 1993).

After World War II, it seemed to some that populism as a mode of political mobilization was in retreat in both Canada and the US with the shrinking of its agrarian base and the institutionalization of the party system. It appeared to survive only in particular locales, such as the American south and in rural Quebec (see Pinard, 1971), in both cases drawing upon suppressed nationalism and a sense of defeat. In retrospect, however, it is clear the spirit of populism remained ready to be awakened. The sources of this later awakening are many, but disenchantment with the party system and with "big government" (in general) was a major contributor. In consequence, both left and right varieties of the populist expression began arising again in the US and Canada in the early 1980s. In Canada, the vehicle for this resurgence was the Reform Party, a brief history of which is instructive.

In 1987, Preston Manning, son of former Alberta Social Credit Premier Ernest Manning (Harrison, 1995; Flanagan, 1995), founded the Reform Party. The party resurrected several themes common to past western Canadian populist parties, such as demands for a more direct say in political matters (as opposed to representative democracy) and a belief in the "common sense of the common people" (in opposition to "elite" control). Within only a few years, the party became Canada's Official Opposition in the House of Commons. It soon stalled, however, and some supporters began complaining that it had become too "top-down" (see Harrison, 1995), losing its grassroots, populist appeal. Three years after the 1997 Canadian federal election, and in time for the 2000 election, the party transformed itself into the Canadian Alliance Party and chose a new leader, Stockwell Day, in a bid to break out of its western political base. But the new party quickly disintegrated—a not uncommon trait of populist parties (see Harrison, 2002: 192–94)—resulting in its merger in early 2004 with the Progressive Conservative Party to form the "new" Conservative Party of Canada. The Conservative Party subsequently dropped many of the populist-inspired ideas carried over from Reform-Alliance, such as those suggesting the widespread use of referendums and initiatives to decide policy.[2] Nonetheless, the Reform Party played a major role in Canadian political history, breaking up the traditional two-party system, giving a greater voice to the regions, and bringing to the fore numerous concerns, such as the need for balanced budgets and concern for debt repayment, later acted upon by the governing party.

It is important to note that populism has no specific ideological content. Appeals to populism do not do away with the need to address questions such as the nature of society, the role of government, or the kind of economy preferred. Attempting to answer such questions, populist parties historically have often varied a great deal.

Types of Populism

Canovan (1981: 8) distinguishes two broad types of populism, based on American case studies. Agrarian populism is defined as "a particular kind of socioeconomic base (peasants or farmers), liable to arise in particular socioeconomic circumstances (especially modernization of one sort or another), and perhaps sharing a particular socioeconomic program." By contrast, political populism is defined as a "particular kind of political phenomenon where the tensions between the elite and the grass roots loom large."

By contrast, Richards's (1981) typology, based on Canadian experiences, situates populist movements along a traditional right-left continuum. Specifically, Richards argues that, historically, left populist movements in Canada have tended (1) towards class (farm-labour) alliances; (2) to present a general critique of corporate capitalism; (3) to demand a greater role for the government and state in countering the power of the corporate sector; and

(4) to spring from rural cooperative organizations. By contrast, right populist movements have tended (1) to mobilize along regional rather than class lines; (2) to restrict their critique to the power of banks, the money supply, and credit; (3) to view big government as the primary enemy; and (4) to downplay participatory democracy in favour of plebiscites.

Laycock's (1990) typology expands upon Richards's work and lists four categories of populism common to western Canada. Social democratic populism (e.g., the Saskatchewan CCF) opposed capitalism in general and emphasized national ownership and control of key industries. Radical democratic populism (e.g., the Ginger group within Alberta's United Farmers) opposed the party system, sometimes arguing in favour of group government. Plebiscitarian populism (e.g., Alberta Social Credit) favoured (in particular) "direct democracy" mechanisms, such as plebiscites, initiatives, and referendums to give voice to the people. Finally, crypto-Liberal populism (e.g., Manitoba in the 1940s) emphasized individual, market-based solutions to problems to offset "elite" control.

More recently, Harrison (2000) has introduced a temporal aspect to populist typologies, examining differences in populism in Alberta old and new. Table 8.1 attempts a provisional mapping of the core elements of populist movements in Canada during the past hundred years, borrowing from, and elaborating upon, the work of Richards (1981) and Harrison (2000).

It is one thing to classify movements. If different types of populist movements exist, how might these differences be explained? What factors underlie the rise of populist movements?

Explanations of Populism

There are six prominent explanations of populist movements. Keep in mind that while each emphasizes a particular explanation, none is necessarily exclusive of the others.

Economic explanations (both of the neo-Marxian and more liberal approach of scholars such as Harold Innis) typically argue populist movements arise out of the cyclical problems and uncertainties of hinterland or regional economies tied, in the larger sense, to the world capitalist economy. The structure of unequal exchanges between the hinterland and a more prosperous centre is viewed as the catalyst for local anger directed at the power of outside economic interests, such as bankers, financiers, and industrialists. One implication of economic explanations is that populist unrest is more likely to occur in volatile than in stable economies. The creation of the CCF in 1933 in Saskatchewan and the coming to power of Social Credit in Alberta in 1935, in the midst of the Great Depression, are events supportive of this theory.

Table 8.1: A Comparison of Left-Wing vs. Right-Wing
Populist Movements, Past and Present, in Canada

	Characteristic	Left	Right
Old	"The People"	workers	small scale producers
	"The Power Bloc"	capitalists	bankers/big interests
	Organizational basis	co-operatives, community groups	plebiscites/strong leaders
New	"The People"	citizens	consumers
	"The Power Bloc"	corporations	special interests/ government
	Organizational basis	NGOs, unions	corporate think tanks and media

Source: Adapted with modifications from Richards (1981) and Harrison (2000).

Political explanations also contend that populist movements are most likely to arise in hinterland regions. While recognizing that economic issues play an important role in populist discontent, political explanations nonetheless emphasize the role of powerlessness and alienation, and the subsequent capacity of local elements to mobilize this discontent. In this sense, economic disparity is viewed as merely a consequence of structural-institutional inequities in the political realm. Political explanations are hinged upon the impact of people in regions who feel left out of political decision-making.

Class explanations take their cue initially from Marx and Engels's (1977 [1848]) theory of class conflict as first outlined in *The Communist Manifesto* and later elaborated on by Lenin (1960, 1970) in his writings on the Narodniks in pre-revolution Russia. In particular, populist movements are explained as products of a particular class—the petite bourgeoisie—facing destruction at the hands of larger capitalists, yet reactionary and nostalgic in defending the ideal of capitalism itself. These explanations point to the impact of economic and political changes upon specific classes. The clearest application of this theory to a Canadian situation is Macpherson's (1953) study of the rise of Social Credit in Alberta, though he also combines it with a political/hinterland explanation (see also Bell, 1993).

Cultural explanations argue that populist movements stem from a disturbance of cultural or symbolic order of the "the people" (see Hofstadter, 1955, 1964). Accordingly, populist movements might be predicted to arise during periods of rapid demographic and economic change. Likewise, cultural threats to deeply held values and beliefs might result in populist movements (e.g., as in the rise of evangelical populist movements, examined below).

Resource mobilization theory explains populist movements as arising not out of discontent—discontent is always present in every society—but rather from organizational factors (see Zald and McCarthy, 1987). That is, the emergence of a populist alternative is a product of a leadership's capacity to mobilize such resources as people, money, and materials. To give one example, Rev. William Aberhart's weekly religious radio broadcasts in the 1920s and 1930s provided a means later of not only disseminating Social Credit's political platform but also of obtaining funding and of mobilizing supporters (Finkel, 1989).

Hegemonic crisis explanations adopt the ideas of Italian political theorist Antonio Gramsci (1988) to argue that populist movements emerge in the context of "organic crises"—all-inclusive political, economic, and social crises—that (at least temporarily) disrupt the ability of the dominant class to shape the world view of subordinate classes (Harrison, 1995). In the midst of such crises, existing political alliances become unravelled, "freeing" some previously incorporated or suppressed elements. Under specific socio-historical circumstances, these elements may then coalesce in a populist (counter-hegemonic) movement.

None of these explanations are necessarily exclusive of each other; each provides a possible answer to why populist movements arise. The next section of this chapter provides a comparative case study of a particular variety of populism, movements often mobilized specifically around a religious sense of mission.

Christian Evangelical Movements in the US and Canada: A Comparison

What is a conservative Christian evangelical?[3] Following Hadden and Shupe (1988: 79–82) and Marsden (1991: 4–6), I use the term here to refer to refer to persons belonging to a trans-denominational grouping of conservative Protestants whose belief system revolves around the following essential elements:

- a belief in the inerrancy and final authority of the Bible, including acceptance of a creationist explanation for the origins of the universe, earth, and humanity;
- a belief in the historical reality of Christ's crucifixion, atonement, and resurrection and the message of salvation;
- a belief in a Holy mandate to promote the redeeming message of Christ to all the peoples of the world; and
- a belief in the spiritually transformed life (i.e., the capacity to be "born again").

Christian evangelicalism, in general, was a powerful force in both British North America and the US following the American Revolution. Citing Hatch (1989), Carroll (2005) argues that Protestant evangelicals (notably Methodists and Baptists), especially in the American south, adopted elements of the revolution—opposition to hierarchy, acceptance of emotional impulses, the concept of personal salvation, and belief in creating a better world—into religious precepts. Likewise, Rawlyk (1996: 10) argues that Radical Evangelicalism "set the religious tone" in the Maritimes and Upper Canada into the early nineteenth century. The War of 1812 blunted evangelicalism's rise in Canada, however. Its embrace of "American" (republican) ideas was headed off by the rise in English-speaking Canada of British Toryism, advanced by the growing middle class and the Anglican Church, while, in French-speaking Quebec, the Catholic Church reigned supreme. Similarly, defeat of the south in the American Civil War (1861–65) drove evangelicalism underground or, rather, to the outskirts of mainstream American thought as determined by the victorious north and the more established churches of that region.

Despite these setbacks, Protestant evangelicalism (in particular) continued to grow on both sides of the border during the remainder of the century. "Especially during the Victorian era, broadly evangelical Protestants ... were *the* establishment" (Smith, 1998: 2) in the US. Likewise, in the early days of the twentieth century, most Protestants in the US—and a goodly number in Canada—thought themselves evangelical Christians (Hadden and Shupe, 1988: 79). In both countries, however, there existed two versions of Protestant evangelicalism (see Smith, 1998; Allen, 2005; also, Reimer, 2003: 28). The "right" version was primarily concerned with personal salvation and the hereafter. By contrast, the "left" version—reflected in the Social Gospel movements of the 1880s and after—was concerned with social salvation and the here and now.

As traditional, rural society gave way to industrial and urban society, with its many social changes, many Christian evangelicals came to support the populist movements that dotted the political landscape on both sides of the border in the late nineteenth and early twentieth centuries (see Smith, 1998: 2–6; Allen, 2005). Prominent among American populist religious figures were William Jennings Bryan, a well-known evangelical preacher, today remembered mainly as the prosecutor in the 1925 Scopes Monkey trial,[4] who contested the presidential election for the People's Party in 1896 and 1900. Others in that country included Father Coughlin and, on his opposite ideological wing, the Rev. Martin Luther King. In Canada, the list included the Rev. William Aberhart (founder of Social Credit in Alberta and that province's premier 1935–43) and his successor, Rev. Ernest Manning (premier, 1943–68), whose movements/parties appeared on the right of the political spectrum. On the left, coming directly out of the Social Gospel tradition (see Allen, 2005), the list included the Rev. J.S. Woodsworth (first leader of the CCF) and the Rev. Tommy Douglas (CCF premier of Saskatchewan and later NDP federal leader).

Besides a sense of mission based upon a perceived biblical injunction to work for society's salvation, there are several analytic links between the concept of populism and evangelicalism. First, it should be noted that the notion of "a people" is often religiously constituted, for example, the notion of a religious group as a "chosen" people. Second, evangelical movements and religious movements, like populist movements, often arise at moments of crisis when "the people" are threatened. Indeed, the history of both populist and evangelical movements shows they have often risen simultaneously amidst circumstances of perceived economic, political, and cultural threat, and with a "mission" to deal with the threat.

Third, like populist movements, evangelical followers are often suspicious of elites. As a result, just as populists often eschew the intermediating influence of intellectuals/experts or institutions in favour of a direct relationship with a leader, so also evangelicals often seek a personal relationship with God unmediated by a formal church establishment. In turn, this relationship is often channelled through individual leaders viewed as "charismatic."

Though today often applied indiscriminately to telegenic political leaders, the term "charisma" was coined originally by sociologist Max Weber to refer to individuals perceived as having a "gift of grace" (Gerth and Mills, 1946: 52), of being filled with "the spirit." Weber argued that charismatic authority arises during periods of crisis, when traditional leaderships and authority structures have been "de-legitimated." Charismatic leaders are viewed (at least by their followers) as divinely gifted with extraordinary insights that allow them to show the people "the way" out of the current crisis. For instance, Rev. William Aberhart was a populist/evangelical leader viewed as charismatic.

Like populism, the role and strength of religion generally was often viewed after World War II as in decline, especially in those parts of the world experiencing "modernization," but also including North America. Recent years, however, have seen a resurgence of religious faith throughout much of the world—Christian, Islamic, and otherwise. In Western countries, this resurgence is particularly obvious among the Christian fundamentalists and evangelicals. In Latin America, for example, the Catholic Church has found itself competing with evangelical and charismatic Christian movements for followers, especially among the poor. Nowhere, however, has the resurgence of evangelical religion been more apparent, or exerted greater social and political consequences, than in the US.

Conservative Christian Evangelicals
in the US in Recent Years

No American president in recent memory has declared so strongly his Christian values or used religious imagery so openly as George W. Bush. A reformed alcoholic and born-again Christian, Bush came to office in 2000 on a platform supportive of "family values" and promising to bring in "faith-based" initiatives that (along with tax cuts) would downsize "big government." In the immediate aftermath of 9/11, he initially proclaimed he would lead a crusade against terrorism—until warned by some that the word "crusade" was viewed poorly in the Moslem world.[5] But his language since continues to emphasize a religious world view, one in which people of Christian faith are engaged in a conflict with "evildoers."[6] Indeed, there have been repeated allegations that Bush claims divine inspiration for his actions, including the invasions of Afghanistan and Iraq (Landau, 2005).

George Bush's rise to the presidency is a testament to the growing power of conservative Christian evangelicals in the US since the 1960s. Full appreciation of this accomplishment can only be gained if one considers that, at that time, the US was widely viewed as a "liberal" democracy gradually converging on social and political matters with other Western industrialized countries (Kerr *et al.*, 1964). By contrast, the US today appears to be taking a course markedly different from Canada and Europe on both foreign and domestic issues. The Christian evangelical movement has played a significant role in transforming the US into a conservative and deeply Christian nation (see Micklethwait and Wooldridge, 2004). How has this come about?

As we have seen, Christian—especially Protestant—evangelical beliefs have deep roots in American soil, especially in the southern states, but these roots atrophied throughout the early twentieth century in the context of what is often referred to as the Fundamentalist-Modernist struggle (Smith, 1998; Reimer, 2003). The US's already wide array of Protestant denominations splintered, the fundamentalist wing pursuing a separatist strategy in regards to the "profane" world. While Christian evangelicals sustained their fight (and their faith) against "Godless Communism," the other great champion of modernization—liberalism—remained largely impervious to the assaults of such far right evangelical leaders as the Rev. Carl McIntyre.

Things began to change in the 1960s, however. Social and political unrest, including the assassinations of John F. Kennedy, Martin Luther King, and Robert F. Kennedy, combined with a declining economy and military defeat in Vietnam, highlighted a period of intensified conflict over the country's identity and role in the world. The period also coincided with intense social changes, for example, sexual liberation, the emergence of new family forms, and the rise of feminism. Out of these events arose the New Left, a loose amalgam of students, intellectuals, feminists, civil rights advocates, and environmentalists. In turn, the New Left created its own counter-movement, the New Right, an umbrella movement that included among its adherents many Christian evangelicals (Harrison, 1995).

Before this time, many conservative Christian evangelicals had remained apolitical. But concerns that the US was on a path to economic, political, and *moral* ruin stimulated disparate elements of the community to action. A key moment was the founding in 1979 of the Moral Majority coalition by the Rev. Jerry Falwell and Paul Weyrich, who was also founder of the right-wing Heritage Foundation (Micklethwait and Wooldridge, 2004: 16–17). The New Right brought together traditional conservatives and neo-conservatives, right-wing populists and evangelicals who—despite differences—held in common especially strong beliefs in free enterprise capitalism, the value of individualism, and a need to shrink government that, since Franklin D. Roosevelt, they believed had become too big. Each of these broad beliefs, in turn, was given specific interpretation and embellishment by conservative Christian evangelicals. Hill and Owen (1982: 17) describe the issues that mobilized the New Religious Political Right (NRPR) at that time:

1. an opposition to governmental support for and general social tolerance of abortion;
2. a determination to restore the right of public schools to hold concerted moments of prayer on a voluntary basis;
3. a lament over the weakened military position of the US against the Soviet Union and a pledge to make this nation's military defence strongest;
4. hostility to pornography—actually, to any and all flagrant exhibitions of sex; and
5. a commitment to defeat the Equal Rights Amendment and all forces that threaten to undermine the traditional roles of women in society.

With the exception of the specific threat of the Soviet Union, now past, conservative Christian evangelicals in the US are impelled by the same things today: strong families (nuclear, father-headed, and heterosexual), Christian values, and a powerful nation (see Diamond, 1998).

Conservative Christian evangelicals gained what they believed to be their first victory in 1980, electing Ronald Reagan as president. Their hopes were often dashed in practice, however. Though a hawk on international matters, and a staunch supporter of free enterprise, Reagan proved a disappointment to many conservative Christian evangelicals in his efforts to turn back the tide of secular humanism, and its liberal supporters (Hill and Owen, 1982: 17).

Undaunted in their efforts to save the US, conservative Christian evangelicals led by the Rev. Jerry Falwell (head of the Christian Coalition) in 1988 made a bid for the presidency. Though defeated, Falwell's run sent a warning shot across the Republican deck; henceforth, conservative Christian evangelicals gained a major foothold within that party (Diamond, 1998), a foothold that the movement expanded over the next decade through its organizational efforts.

George W. Bush's election as US president in 2000 and again in 2004 resulted from several factors, not the least of which was continued anxiety following 9/11 and his ability to "connect" with "middle America" on such matters as crime and taxes. But at least some of Bush's success can also be attributed to the significant support he received from conservative Christian evangelicals in both elections, for, as noted above, his populist rhetoric is also swaddled in religious imagery and the promise of rewards to that constituency. As one commentator described the result, the US election of 2004 was fought between two nations, "Worldly America and Godly America" (Schama, 2004)—and Godly America won.

Ultimately, G.W. Bush may disappoint conservative Christian evangelicals, as did his father and Reagan before him. Yet, at least rhetorically and often through direct policy, he has proven a staunch supporter of the movement. Almost immediately upon taking office, for example, he invited faith communities to take over government social functions, something that appealed to the broad political right's agenda of shrinking the welfare state. He also cut off funding to agencies, such as Planned Parenthood, which provided information on procuring an abortion, and otherwise supported the Right to Life Movement through such actions as opposing stem cell research. And he publicly endorsed the notion of "intelligent design," giving hope to those who want Creationism taught in public schools on an equal footing with the theory of evolution.

The Conservative Christian Evangelical Movement in Canada

As we have seen, there is a long and deep history of evangelical influence upon politics in Canada. As in the US, this influence has reasserted itself since the early 1980s, particularly on the political right. As is often well-remembered, the Reform Party of Canada, a party led by Preston Manning (an avowed Christian evangelical), was founded in the fall of 1987 (see above). Less remembered is that the Christian Heritage Party (CHP) was founded at the same time. In the federal election held a year later, both of these new religiously inspired parties received a degree of popular electoral support, the CHP primarily in Ontario and the Reform Party in the West, mainly Alberta (Harrison, 1995).[7] Thereafter, the more broadly based Reform Party continued to gain in popularity and influence but ultimately fell short of gaining actual governing power. Thus, in early 2000, Reform disbanded in favour of becoming the Canadian Reform Conservative Alliance Party. Stockwell Day, the Alliance Party's new leader was a prominent—if controversial—former Alberta politician and, like Manning, a devout and even more outspoken evangelical Christian (see quotes in Harrison, 2002). The election of 2000 saw the Alliance Party garner roughly one-quarter of votes cast to gain 66 parliamentary seats and become (like Reform) the Official Opposition.

Many evangelical Christians were outspoken in their support of both the Reform and Alliance parties. Arguably, however, this support came at a price to their future success. In the early days of Reform, Preston Manning's own religious background and the strident positions sometimes taken by party supporters on matters of family, abortion, and gay rights raised concerns among many voters. Day's leadership raised even more concerns, as his public comments suggested to many voters that he would favour using the powers of the state to enforce policies based on his religious beliefs.

As noted above, the Alliance Party disintegrated as a functioning political vehicle shortly after the 2000 election. In 2004, the new Conservative Party was created out of an amalgamation of the Alliance and old Progressive Conservative parties. The new party, similar in many ways to the Republican Party in the US, brought together free enterprisers, libertarians, western reformers, and social conservatives, including many Christian evangelicals. Yet, in contrast to the American experience, the concerns and policies of conservative Christian evangelicals in Canada remain largely outside the mainstream. Why is this the case?

Why is the Conservative Christian Evangelical Movement Stronger in the US than in Canada?

While the conservative Christian evangelical movement in Canada has had some success in having issues important to it discussed, it clearly has not had the success of its American counterpart. Why the difference? First, there are important institutional religious differences between the two countries. Table 8.2 shows that the percentage of Catholics within the Canadian population is much larger than in the US (43.6 per cent vs. 24.5 per cent). In part, this is because of Quebec—Quebec is roughly 80 per cent Catholic. But even if Quebec is excluded from the analysis, the percentage of Catholics remains almost 10 per cent higher in Canada than in the US. And while many practicing Catholics are favourable to some concerns expressed by Christian evangelicals

Table 8.2: Comparison of Religious Affiliation, Canada and the US 2001 (in 000)

	Canada		US	
	Total	%	Total	%
Catholic	12,936	43.6	50,873	24.5
Other Christian	9,915	33.4	108,633	52.2
Other/None	6,788	22.9	48,474	23.3
Total	29,639	100.0	207,980	100

Source: Statistics Canada (2005) and the US Census Bureau (2003).

(e.g., gay rights, abortion), their support for the entire conservative platform is considerably more tenuous.

Even this demographic comparison does not tell the entire story, however. As van Die (2001: 7) notes, the US historically has experienced far greater denominationalism. Whereas two large established "state churches"—the Catholic and Anglican—were historically dominant in Canada, and further consolidation occurred in the 1920s with the founding of the United Church, the US has a far greater smorgasbord of Protestant faiths (Reimer, 2003: 26). It is this plethora of smaller, non-bureaucratically organized faiths—many of them Christian evangelical—that have seen the largest growth in recent years. Altogether, between 25 to 35 per cent of Americans are Christian evangelicals compared with about 1 in 10 of Canadians (Reimer, 2003: 5; Resnick, 2005: 85). In fact, 42 per cent of Americans (including President George W. Bush) describe themselves as Born-Again Christians (Freedland, 2004a: 6).

Yet, even this does not entirely tell the story, for the fact is that, historically, evangelicalism in Canada was more often of the left variety while its counterpart in the US was of the right (see above). Until the emergence of the Reform Party in the 1980s, the influence of the Social Gospel in shaping Canada was far more pronounced than the right evangelical influence that expressed itself through the Social Credit Party and that was confined mainly to Alberta. In short, there are important denominational differences between the two countries, including the form of evangelicalism that has predominated in the past.

Second, surveys also reveal important value and ideological differences between Canadians and Americans at large (Adams, 2003; Grabb and Curtis, 2005). While most people on both sides of the border attend church (at least occasionally) and continue to hold religious beliefs, religion plays a more significant role in the lives of Americans than Canadians—or, for that matter, many other peoples. In a study by the Pew Research Center (2002), 59 per cent of Americans said religion played a very important role in their lives. By contrast, only 30 per cent of Canadians said the same, even less in most Western European countries. In fact, American responses to the question were closer to those found in developing countries.

Interpretation of this data comes with a caveat, however. As a subsequent Pew Research Center Report (2004) points out, there is a significant regional effect. That is, religious beliefs in the US are strongest in the American south—the historic area of the evangelical right (see also Hunter, 1983: 52). When compared with Canada, the values of people living in states along the northern border are only marginally more "religious" or "conservative"—a finding broadly supported by Adams (2003) and Grabb and Curtis (2005). In short, religious differences between regions of North America may disguise themselves as national differences between the two countries (Reimer, 2003).

That said, it is also true that a sizeable number of both Canadians and Americans—46 per cent vs. 56 per cent in a 1996 poll—support Christian values playing a role in politics (Lyon, 2000: 6). What seems different, however, is that Canadians are far less likely to believe that such values should translate into support, or provide justification, for the state's intrusion into individual rights. A recent poll by the Dominion Institute and Innovative Research Group, for example, found that even those Canadians who believed "gay sex is immoral" and that "a woman's place is in the home" were generally unwilling to support having their views enforced by law (reported in Cowan, 2005: A12).

These value differences in turn appear to translate into ideological and political support. Roughly 34 per cent of Americans identify with the Christian right compared with only 18 per cent of Canadians. Even in the heyday of the Reform Party, more evangelicals voted Liberal than for Preston Manning's populist alternative (Lyon, 2000: 6–7; also, Reimer, 2003: 130). As Reimer (2003: 28) notes, there is not the same "alignment" of evangelicalism and conservatism in Canada as in the US.

A third explanation for differences in evangelical support is rooted in historical experience. It is not entirely correct that the framers of the American Constitution sought unambiguously to separate Church and State. It is true, however, that the American state did not historically welcome religious institutions into the service of the state in the same way as occurred in Canada (Lipset, 1990: 16), where (for example) the Catholic and Anglican churches, as well as the smaller Methodist and Presbyterian churches, operated residential schools for the assimilation of Aboriginal children. One consequence of this, in the long term, was that these mainstream churches became "tainted" by their involvement in state policies; indeed, they are still facing legal actions. By contrast, the relative isolation of religious organizations in the US from formal political power has protected them (until now) from the stigma of policies gone wrong; in this sense, evangelical churches in the US—like populist parties—hold the position of outsiders able to denounce the Godless "establishment" for failing to create the New Jerusalem.

A fourth explanation for differences in the degree of political leverage exercised by conservative Christian evangelicals in the two countries can be drawn from resource mobilization theory. Simply put, the American movement consists of a wide swath of organizations, prominent religious leaders and political organizers (e.g., Ralph Reed), and a large membership. The National Association of Evangelicals alone consists of 45,000 churches and 30 million adherents (Sharlet, 2005: 42). Though relying upon "modest donations from hundreds of thousands of people" (Diamond, 1998: 12), it is also well funded. Finally, the conservative Christian evangelical movement in the US obtains considerable publicity through various media, including several television programs and radio broadcasts throughout that country and heard also in Canada, as well as magazines and newsletters. One practical result of these assets is that the American movement is able "to get out the vote" during election time: 80 per cent of whom chose George W. Bush in 2004 (Freedland, 2004b: 5). As bemoaned by supporters (see Gunter, 2005), conservative Christian evangelicals in Canada do not have comparable resources in terms of organization, leadership, money, or media exposure.

Finally, in the very broadest political sense, the US is not like Canada or, frankly, any other Western industrialized (post-industrialized) country. The US is an "exceptional" country, though not in the self-congratulatory and excusatory way some American politicians have used the term. O'Brien (1994: 151) has said, "The United States is the heart and soul of the Enlightenment tradition." Like all large generalities, this statement is not entirely wrong, but it is also overstated. Between the US's east and west coasts—the heartland of liberalism and cosmopolitanism, not to mention the ideals of individual freedom, equality, and justice—there exists another US. It is the country that Hofstadter (1955, 1964) years ago noted is given to anti-intellectualism, paranoia, and irrationalism. While such a depiction is unduly harsh, nonetheless, it is this locale where American populism and much of the conservative Christian evangelical movement meet.

Yet, there is at least one Enlightenment belief that resonates even in these quarters: the idea that the US is the last, best hope of humankind, that it has a mission to civilize the world, and—in the eyes of many conservative Christian evangelicals—even to save it. No other Western country, including Canada, is motivated by such a political and religious imperative, wedded to national purpose; no other current country possesses a similar "civil religion."

Civil Religion: Evangelical Politics and the Nation-State

> I went down on my knees and prayed to Almighty God for light
> and guidance more than one night. And one night late it came
> to me: 1) That we could not give them [the Philippines] back to
> Spain—that would be cowardly and dishonorable; 2) that we
> could not turn them over to France and Germany—our com-
> mercial rivals in the Orient—that would be bad business and dis-
> creditable; 3) that we could not leave them to themselves—they
> were unfit for self-government—and they would soon have
> anarchy and misrule over there worse than Spain's was; and 4)
> that there was nothing left for us to do but to take them all, and
> to educate the Filipinos, and uplift and civilize and Christianize
> them, and by God's grace do the very best we could by them,
> as our fellow-men for whom Christ also died. And then I went
> to bed, and went to sleep, and slept soundly, and the next morn-
> ing I sent for the ... war department map-maker, and told him to
> put the Philippines on the map of the United States ... (quoted by
> Landau, 2005: 16)

Thus spoke President William McKinley, explaining in 1899 how he made
his decision to incorporate the Philippines into the then nascent American
empire. It provides a perfect example of what Bellah (1967) has termed "civil
religion." The term describes the nature of belief in societies that mix religious
and patriotic symbols and often invoke divine support for state actions and
policies. It is a particularly useful term for examining differences in the nature
of power held by Christian evangelicals in the US and Canada.

This is not to say that Canada in the past has not displayed similar elements
of civil religion. Lyon (2000: 8) notes that,

> For well over a century religion and politics in Canada were
> deeply intertwined. In anglophone Canada nationality itself
> was interpreted using evangelical referents, and political life
> was shot through with religious colouring. An alliance between
> Protestantism and British civilization was expressed in the hope
> of some that Canada would be God's Dominion.

However, the decline of Toryism and the British Empire, combined with the
onset of a "weak" Canadian nationalism—weak in part because it had to also
consider the complexities of Quebec's place within the national mythology—

worked against the development of civil religion in Canada (see Reimer, 2003: 26). To be blunt, no imperial ambitions equals no civil religion.

As in Canada, the relationship of politics and religion in the US is old, complex, and often contradictory. For example, the Declaration of Independence invokes God; by contrast, the Constitution does not mention God at all. Side by side with their often stated desire to separate Church and State (for fear of what religious wars had done in Europe), American founders also made clear through their speeches their belief that God had "chosen" their new country for a unique historical role. This latter belief, already well established in the early nineteenth century, subsequently underpinned the twin notions of Manifest Destiny and the Monroe Doctrine that later justified American expansion and intervention in the affairs of other countries in the hemisphere and that still resonate (e.g., the Bush Doctrine of pre-emptive intervention).

Later that century, the American novelist Herman Melville wrote eulogistically of a Messianic populism, "We Americans are the peculiar chosen people—the Israel of our time. We bear the ark of the liberties of the world." President Woodrow Wilson spoke of the US being led by the hand of God and of Americans being "the mortal instruments of His will" (both quotes from Resnick, 2005: 65).

In the nuclear afterglow of Hiroshima and Nagasaki in 1945, numerous American politicians and religious leaders were outspoken in contending that the US had been given the bomb by God, a kind of divine sword with which to defeat communism (Ungar, 1991). In the years afterwards, the US increasingly defined itself as engaged in a quasi-religious battle: thus, President Ronald Reagan's reference to the Soviet Union as the "Evil Empire"; likewise, President George W. Bush's more recent use of the phrase, "the Axis of Evil." A similar claim of "special status" runs through the comments of then Secretary of State Madeleine Albright who, in 1998, referred to the US as the "only indispensable nation" (Johnson, 2000: 217).

American political culture is marked by a fusion of religious beliefs with nationalism, militarism, and consumer capitalism. Imperial expansion goes hand in hand with proselytizing missionhood (Reimer, 2003: 123–24). Taken together, this complex of beliefs results in a well into which the conservative Christian evangelical movement in that country can dip. Rudy Giuliani, mayor of New York, captured this element of American political culture in a speech in December 2001 following the terrorist attacks on that city:

> All that matters is that you embrace America and understand its
> ideals and what it's all about. Abraham Lincoln used to say that
> the test of your Americanism was ... how much you believed in

America. Because we're like a religion really. A secular religion.
(Quoted in Monbiot, 2003: 13)

And so it is. There is no similar idea of Canada held by Canadians at large upon
which conservative Christian evangelicals can build their political movement.

Conclusion

In a curious way, this paper has come full circle. It began by defining populism as a movement defending the "people" against powerful interests; it ends by explaining the increasing power of the conservative Christian evangelical movement in the US as resulting from its incorporation into and defence of the American nation-state. Yet, this should not surprise us. Populist movements, no less than other political efforts, must work within a given historical time and space, using the cultural symbols and images at hand.

While the rise of the conservative evangelical movement in the US poorly fits strict economic and class explanations, it is congruent with cultural explanations that emphasize value conflict in particular. The case study also reinforces, as argued by resource mobilization theorists, the importance of organizational resources (including leadership) in the success of political movements and, from a political perspective, the importance of the political-institutional context in which differential resources are put to use. Finally, the case of evangelical movements illuminates the importance of historically constructed identifications among movement followers.

What is the political future of conservative Christian evangelicalism? As noted, the strength of the movement in the US, as opposed to Canada, stems in part from the fact that, historically, organized religion was not directly involved in political affairs. One possible consequence, therefore, of the conservative Christian evangelical movement taking a seat so close to the American power centre is that it may find itself held responsible for policies that fail. It is also possible that the conservative Christian evangelical movement may face a political backlash from those concerned about a blurring of Church and State or the movement's growing power.

However, we should also keep in mind that, like populism, Christian evangelicalism (in general) is not wedded to any particular political program. Could the current strength of conservative evangelicalism be merely a passing phase, to be replaced by a more socially progressive, left alternative? Only time will tell.

Notes

1. The author wishes to thank Dr. William Ramp and Dr. Reginald Bibby for their helpful comments on an earlier draft of this paper.

2. Referendums and initiatives are similar, the major difference being that referendums are brought about by governments, while initiatives are launched by citizens.

3. There are a number of competing terms describing politically active Christians. The most common competitor to evangelicalism is fundamentalism. Technically, fundamentalism arose in the late nineteenth century as a revolt against modernism, including secularism. Unlike evangelicals, who wanted to change the world and convert non-believers, fundamentalists were then more interested in separating from the world. The lines have become more blurred since, but most scholars view fundamentalism as a subset of evangelicalism that includes Pentecostals, charismatics, and even neo-charismatics (Hadden and Shupe, 1988: 79). Marsden (1991: 1) says of fundamentalists that they are "not just religious conservatives, they are conservatives who are willing to take a stand and fight."

4. The State of Tennessee tried a teacher, John Scopes, for violating a state law prohibiting the teaching in any state-funded educational establishment of "any theory that denies the story of the Divine Creation of man as taught in the Bible, and to teach instead that man has descended from a lower order of animals." The trial pitted Bryan against the prominent defence attorney, Clarence Darrow. After a trial lasting eight days, Scopes was found guilty and ordered to pay a US$100 fine. The Tennessee Supreme Court later overturned the conviction based on a legal technicality (Larson, 1997).

5. The Crusades were a series of military campaigns launched in the name of Christendom between the eleventh and thirteenth centuries in attempts to recapture Jerusalem and the Holy Land from the Moslems.

6. David Frum, a former speechwriter for President George W. Bush, has stated that the term "evildoers," used by the president right after 9/11 to describe the enemy, is taken from one of the president's favourite psalms, Psalm 27 ("When evildoers came upon me to devour my flesh") (Stolberg, 2006).

7. The Reform Party received 275,767 votes (2.09 per cent of all votes cast); the CHP received 102,533 votes (.78 per cent of all votes cast) (see Harrison, 1995).

References and Further Reading

Adams, Michael. 2003. *Fire and Ice: The Myth of Value Convergence in Canada and the United States*. Toronto: Penguin Canada.

Allen, Richard A. 2005. "Social Gospel." *The Canadian Encyclopedia*. <http://www.thecanadianencyclopedia.com>.

Bell, Edward. 1993. *Social Classes and Social Credit in Alberta*. Montreal and Kingston: McGill-Queen's University Press.

Bellah, Robert N. 1967. "Civil Religion in America." *Daedalus* 96: 1–18.

Canovan, Margaret. 1981. *Populism*. New York: Harcourt Brace Jovanovich.

Carroll, Michael P. 2005. "Who Owns Democracy? Explaining the Long-running Debate over Canadian/American Value Differences." *Canadian Review of Sociology and Anthropology* 42(3): 267–82.

Conway, John. 1978. "Populism in the United States, Russia, and Canada: Explaining the Roots of Canada's Third Parties." *Canadian Journal of Political Science* 11(1): 99–124.

Cowan, James. 2005. "Morality Legislation Opposed." *National Post*, 26 September: A12.

Diamond, Sara. 1998. *Not By Politics Alone: The Enduring Influence of the Christian Right*. New York: The Guilford Press.

Di Tella, Torcuato S. 2001. "Populism." In Seymour Martin Lipset (ed.), *Political Philosophy: Theories, Thinkers, Concepts*. Washington: C.Q. Press.

Finkel, Alvin. 1989. *The Social Credit Phenomenon in Alberta*. Toronto: University of Toronto Press.

Flanagan, Tom. 1995. *Waiting for the Wave: The Reform Party and Preston Manning*. Toronto: Stoddart.

Freedland, Jonathan. 2004a. "Faith Against Reason." *Guardian Weekly*, 29 October–4 November: 6.

Freedland, Jonathan. 2004b. "Democrats Need Rebirth." *Guardian Weekly*, 12–18 November: 5.

Gerth, Hans H., and C. Wright Mills (Eds.). 1946. *From Max Weber: Essays in Sociology*. New York: Oxford University Press.

Grabb, Edward, and James Curtis. 2005. *Regions Apart: The Four Societies of Canada and the United States*. Oxford: Oxford University Press.

Gramsci, Antonio. 1988. *An Antonio Gramsci Reader: Selected Writings, 1916–1935*. Ed. D. Forgacs. New York: Schocken Books.

Gunter, Lorne. 2005. "Fighting Canada's Secularist Tide." *National Post*, 26 September: A12.

Hadden, Jeffrey K., and Anson Shupe. 1988. *Televangelism: Power and Politics on God's Frontier*. New York: Henry Holt and Company.

Harrison, Trevor. 1995. *Of Passionate Intensity: Right-Wing Populism and the Reform Party of Canada*. Toronto: University of Toronto Press.

Harrison, Trevor. 2000. "The Changing Face of Prairie Politics: Populism in Alberta." In T.A. Radenbaugh and P. Douaud (eds.), *Changing Prairie Landscapes*. Regina: Canadian Plains Research Centre, University of Regina Press: 95–108.

Harrison, Trevor. 2002. *Requiem for a Lightweight: Stockwell Day and Image Politics*. Montreal: Black Rose.

Hatch, N.O. 1989. *The Democratization of American Christianity*. New Haven: Yale University Press.

Hill, Samuel S., and Dennis E. Owen. 1982. *The New Religious Political Right in America*. Nashville: Abingdon.

Hofstadter, Richard. 1955. *The Age of Reform: From Bryan to F.D.R*. New York: Alfred A. Knopf.

Hofstadter, Richard. 1964. *The Paranoid Style in American Politics and Other Essays*. New York: Alfred A. Knopf.

Hunter, James Davison. 1983. *American Evangelicalism: Conservative Religion and the Quandary of Modernity*. New Brunswick: Rutgers University Press.

Johnson, Chalmers. 2000. *Blowback: The Costs and Consequences of American Empire*. New York: Henry Holt and Company.

Kerr, Clark, J.T. Dunlop, Frederick Harbison, and C.A. Myers. 1964. *Industrialism and Industrial Man*. London: Oxford University Press.

Landau, Saul. 2005. "Conversations with God about Invading Other Countries." *Canadian Dimension* (January–February): 16–17.

Larson, Edward J. 1997. *Summer for the Gods: The Scopes Trial and America's Continuing Debate Over Science and Religion*. Cambridge, MA: Harvard University Press.

Laycock, David. 1990. *Populism and Democratic Thought in the Canadian Prairies, 1910 to 1945*. Toronto: University of Toronto Press.

Lenin, Vladimir. 1960. "The Economic Content of Narodism and the Criticism of it in Mr. Struve's Book." In *Collected Works*. Moscow: Foreign Languages Publishing House.

Lenin, Vladimir. 1970. "The Heritage We Renounce." In *Selected Works*. Moscow: Progress Publishers.

Lipset, Seymour Martin. 1968. *Agrarian Socialism: The Cooperative Commonwealth Federation in Saskatchewan*. Garden City, NY: Doubleday.

Lipset, Seymour Martin. 1990. *Continental Divide: The Values and Institutions of the United States and Canada*. New York: Routledge.

Lyon, David. 2000. "Introduction." In D. Lyon and M. van Die (eds.), *Rethinking Church, State, and Modernity: Canada Between Europe and America*. Toronto: University of Toronto Press.

Macpherson, C.B. 1953. *Democracy in Alberta: Social Credit and the Party System*. Toronto: University of Toronto Press.

Marsden, George M. 1991. *Understanding Fundamentalism and Evangelicalism*. Grand Rapids: George Eerdmans Publishing.

Marshall, David. 2001. "Premier E.C. Manning, *Back to the Bible Hour*, and Fundamentalism in Canada." In Marguerite van Die (ed.), *Religion and Public Life in Canada: Historical and Comparative Perspectives*. Toronto: University of Toronto Press.

Marx, Karl, and Friedrich Engels. 1977 [1848]. "The Communist Manifesto." In D. McLellan (ed.), *Karl Marx: Selected Writings*. Oxford: Oxford University Press.

Mickelthwait, John, and Adrian Wooldridge. 2004. *The Right Nation: Conservative Power in America*. Toronto: Penguin.

Monbiot, George. 2003. "America is a Religion." *Guardian Weekly*, 7–18 August: 13.

Morton, William L. 1978. *The Progressive Party in Canada*. Toronto: University of Toronto Press.

O'Brien, Conor C. 1994. *On the Eve of the Millennium*. Toronto: Anansi.

Pew Research Center for the People and the Press. 2002. "Among Wealthy Nations ... U.S. Stands Alone in its Embrace of Religion." Press Release, 9 December.

Pew Research Center for the People and the Press. 2004. "Americans and Canadians: The North American Not-so-odd Couple." Press Release, 14 January.

Pinard, Maurice. 1971. *The Rise of a Third Party: A Study in Crisis Politics.* Montreal and Kingston: McGill-Queen's University Press.

Rawlyk, George A. 1996. *Is Jesus Your Personal Saviour? In Search of Canadian Evangelicalism in the 1990s.* Montreal and Kingston: McGill-Queen's University Press.

Rea, Julian Castro, Graciela Ducatenzeiler, and Philippe Faucher. 1992. "Back to Populism: Latin America's Alternative to Democracy." In A.R.M. Ritter, M.A. Cameron, and D.H. Pollock (eds.), *Latin America to the Year 2000.* New York: Praeger.

Reimer, Sam. 2003. *Evangelicals and the Continental Divide.* Montreal and Kingston: McGill-Queen's University Press.

Resnick, Philip. 2005. *The European Roots of Canadian Identity.* Peterborough: Broadview.

Richards, John. 1981. "Populism: A Qualified Defence." *Studies in Political Economy* 5: 5–27.

Schama, Simon. 2004. "Onward Christian Soldiers." *Guardian Weekly*, 12–18 November: 19–20.

Sharlet, Jeff. 2005. "Inside the Nation's Most Powerful Megachurch." *Harper's Magazine* (May): 41–54.

Sinclair, Peter. 1979. "Class Structure and Populist Protest: The Case of Western Canada." In C. Caldarola (ed.), *Society and Politics in Alberta: Research Papers.* Toronto: Methuen.

Smith, Christian. 1998. *American Evangelicalism: Embattled and Thriving.* Chicago: University of Chicago Press.

Statistics Canada. 2005. "Population by Religion, by Provinces and Territories." *2001 Census.* Data modified 15 January 2005. Ottawa: Statistics Canada. <http://www40.statcan.ca/101/cst01/demo30a.htm>.

Stolberg, Sheryl Gay. 2006. "Islamo-Fascism's Had its Moment." *New York Times*, 24 September.

Ungar, Sheldon. 1991. "Civil Religion and the Arms Race." *Canadian Review of Sociology and Anthropology* 28(4): 503–25.

US Census Bureau. 2003. "Self-Described Religious Identification of Adult Population 1990 and 2001." *123rd Edition of the Statistical Abstract of the United States. The National Data Book.* Washington: US Census Bureau.

van Die, Marguerite. 2001. "Introduction." In M. van Die (ed.), *Religion and Public Life in Canada: Historical and Comparative Perspectives.* Toronto: University of Toronto Press.

Zald, Mayer N., and John D. McCarthy (Eds.). 1987. *Social Movements in an Organizational Society: Collected Essays.* New Brunswick: Transaction Books.

PART THREE
Nations and Nationalism

NINE

Aysaka'paykinit: Contesting the Rope Around the Nations' Neck

Kiera L. Ladner

The politics of contestation among Indigenous peoples in Canada has a history that predates colonialism. Since political and social dissidents seem to exist in every polity, it could be argued that this history goes back thousands of years. The dissidents and the movements they led spawned much transformation and change within their nations and internationally between and among nations. For instance, about 1,000 years ago, in a time characterized by crime, injustice, international war, and political chaos, the Peacemaker and his assistant, Hiawatha, traveled among the Mohawk, Cayuga, Onondaga, Oneida, and Seneca Nations bringing a message of peace, a good mind (sometimes translated as power), and righteousness. This sparked a peaceful revolution within and among the nations that resulted in the creation of a new Haudenosaunee confederacy and a new constitutional order called the Kayanerenkowa, or the Great Law of Peace. This message of peace and the new constitutional order inspired other revolutionaries and influenced the Constitution designed by the American Founding Fathers (Johansen, 1998: 19–39). While not all dissident efforts resulted in such radical change, there are many other pre-colonial examples where people mobilized and succeeded in achieving social and political change or in completely transforming the political and social structures of a nation or grouping of nations.

Acknowledging this historical foundation and continuity, this chapter will explore Indigenous politics of contestation in an historically grounded manner while focusing primarily on the mobilization of First Nations peoples (not Métis or Inuit). It weaves together a narrative of mobilization that focuses on the historical foundations of, and continuity among, a number of seemingly unrelated episodes of contestation. Rather than drawing on social movement theory or providing a comparative analysis of Indigenous movements vis-à-vis other movements, the chapter proceeds descriptively in a manner grounded in Indigenist theory and methodology that use story-telling or narration to create an awareness of the movement and an understanding of the issues, goals, aspirations, and tensions that define it. In so doing, it will draw attention to the idea that the goals and the mechanisms used to articulate and pursue the resolution of the goals, as well as the factions that exist within the movement, are predicated upon considerations of nationhood and (de)colonization. In this way, this chapter contributes to the theoretical literature on social movements. Indigenous movements contest the very foundation of the Canadian state as a colonial construction while most theories of group politics and social movements take the state for granted.

I will begin by examining the Indigenous politics of contestation historically by telling the story of several defining moments. Then I will describe the goals that have defined (and continue to define) the Indigenous politics of contestation, goals that have remained constant since issues of sovereignty, land, and economic rights have yet to be resolved in a mutually agreeable and mutually beneficial manner. Finally, having explored the history of the movement and explained why it exists, I will conclude by offering a more theoretical assessment of its underpinnings and explain how the deep belief in Indigenous nationhood and decolonization has defined the movement and its development.

Framing the Conflict

With colonization, the Indigenous politics of contestation changed from a focus on national and sub-national issues and organizations to activities and movements that were typically external to the nation, between nations, or between individuals or groups and colonial nations. Discontent and episodes of mobilization focused on the primary concerns of each nation, such as territorial intrusions, territory-sharing arrangements, maintaining sacred relationships with a nation's territory (especially occupied territory), religious and spiritual freedom, sovereignty, self-determination, economic independence, economic assistance (such as farming), health care, treaties, trade networks, and international relations (with both Indigenous and colonial nations). The prominence of these issues and of the emerging international politics of contestation in the initial stages of discontent are apparent in many of the "early" struggles between Indigenous peoples and the colonizers. Among these were the 1763–66 rebellion against the British led by Obwandiyag (Pontiac) and involving a considerable number of nations including Odawa, Potawatomis, Huron, Shawnees, Delaware, Wendat, Kickapoo, and Anishnaabe (Ojibwa); the 1869–70 and 1885 Métis resistance movements led by Louis Riel; and the mobilization between 1870 and 1885 of the Nehiyaw (Plains Cree) led by Mistahimaskwa (Big Bear). Though it should not be construed as being representative of these early struggles, the story of Mistahimaskwa's resistance does serve as a template for these events.

On 15 July 1870, the Government of Canada assumed sovereignty over the North West Territories, or so it was (and is) claimed. This assertion and the preceding purchase of the territory from the Hudson's Bay Company (HBC) were not met with enthusiasm by the Nehiyaw. According to them (and to their neighbouring nations) this was their territory, and the Queen had no claim to it, no right to rule it, and no right to assert any authority over them. This discontent was coupled with a growing array of issues and problems resulting from colonization—American incursions into Nehiyaw territory, a declining buffalo population, the growing influence of whiskey traders, the catastrophic effects of disease and death—and led the Nehiyaw to lobby the Queen and her government for a treaty and a means for addressing their grievances. Employing the assistance of traders, policemen, missionaries, and government employees, Nehiyaw leaders such as Weekuskokisayin (Sweet Grass) effectively lobbied the Canadian government (Taylor, 1985: 2). Though he and other chiefs argued that their land was not for sale and that no one had the right or the ability to sell it (Christie, 1871), they were willing to share it and some of its resources with (a few) settlers and to build a "brotherly" relationship with the Queen and her people. Further, Weekuskokisayin argued that a treaty was needed because:

> Our Land is getting ruined of fur bearing animals, hitherto our sole support, and we are now poor and want help—we want you to pity us. We want cattle, tools, agriculture implements, and assistance in everything when we come to settle—our country is no longer able to support us.
>
> Make provisions for us against years of starvation. We have had a great starvation this past winter, and smallpox took away many of our people, the old, young and children.
>
> We want you to stop the Americans from coming to trade on our lands, and giving firewater, ammunition and arms to our enemies the Blackfeet.... (Christie, 1871; also see Morris, 1880: 186–71)

Six years after the Nehiyaw began lobbying, the government finally acted. However, they did not do so in good faith. Their negotiators failed to invite many Nehiyaw leaders to the table, especially those who were most vocal in their discontent with the Queen, and, worse, they proved unwilling to negotiate (or even discuss) key issues and problems. As a result, while Treaty Six was said to respond to the demands put forth by such leaders as Weekuskokisayin many dissident leaders and their followers did not sign. Foremost among these was Mistahimaskwa who refused to sign because he refused to "live with a rope around his neck" (*aysaka'paykinit*): he would not give up his freedom, nor the freedom and sovereignty of his nation, to be led around like a domesticated animal in a *skunkun* (reserve or roped off piece of land) (Dempsey, 1984: 241). Following the negotiations of 1876, Mistahimaskwa continued his efforts to engage the Queen's representatives in a discussion about the terms of the treaty, to foster a nation-to-nation relationship, and to attempt to mobilize the Nehiyaw to take a collective stance. With his people starving, and the government promising rations for all signatories to Treaty Six, he finally gave up his fight in 1882.

Nonetheless, Mistahimaskwa continued to advocate a message of unity and sovereignty and a peaceful resolution of problems with Canada. Further, despite the starvation and destitute conditions among the Nehiyaw and neighbouring nations, people continued to mobilize and gather at events such as the Thirst Dance that Mistahimaskwa hosted on Pitikahanapiwiyin's (Poundmaker's) reserve in June 1884. Despite the vision, dedication, and leadership of these two leaders, efforts to mobilize the Nehiyaw in peaceful union and to engage the Crown's representatives in discussion failed. Disillusioned by the lack of results of peaceful resistance, militant leaders such as Imasees (Wild Child) and Kapapamahchakwew (Wandering Spirit) used the opportunities provided by the nearby Métis uprising to take over the leadership of their nation and to pursue a more activist and militant strategy that involved the looting of government and HBC supply warehouses in Frog Lake and engaging in an armed conflict (the Northwest Rebellion) with Canada. This strategy did not secure resolution or action on any Nehiyaw grievances. In the end, though Mistahimaskwa did not participate, he was found guilty of treason and sentenced to three years in prison, his followers lost their reserve, the Nehiyaw lost their battle over the treaty with the government and were forcefully confined to the destitute conditions of reserves, and those who participated in the armed insurrection were either hung or escaped prosecution and found refuge in a garbage dump on the outskirts of Helena, Montana.

The subjugation of the Nehiyaw sent a message to other Indigenous peoples and their leaders throughout Canada—and it still serves witness to what can happen when Indigenous peoples engage in politics of contestation, no matter what the strategy or in which arena. Nonetheless, this did not stop Indigenous people from engaging the state and mobilizing within their communities. This incident, and others, served notice that change would be hard fought. However, it remains a necessary battle in pursuit of a worthy vision of a life as individuals and nations defined not by rope but by self-determination, equality, and a standard of living comparable to those who occupy and claim sovereignty over their territories.

A Battle Rekindled

This battle was rekindled after World War I by a Mohawk veteran, Frederick Loft. As a Pine Tree Chief (special appointee to the Haudenosaunee Confederacy Council defined in the Great Law), Loft was active in the immediate postwar period in lobbying the British Crown over issues of concern to the Confederacy Chiefs and Six Nations reserve. However, Loft had a much larger vision than defending the rights of the Haudenosaunee, particularly its sovereignty and self-determination, as the federal government was attempting to overthrow the traditional government and replace it with their own "puppet government" or *Indian Act* band council. Loft envisioned a national organization that would mobilize and unify Indigenous peoples and that would lobby the federal government to improve living standards on reserve, particularly with respect to education (Smith, 1996: 2). In 1918, he succeeded in establishing the League of Indians of Canada. Originally comprised primarily of band leadership from Ontario and Quebec, the League gradually expanded outward until its collapse in the mid-1930s. Though the collapse is typically attributed to Loft's declining health and involvement in the organization, one cannot forget the role that the federal government played in impeding the development and success of this movement and in ushering in its demise simply by enforcing the *Indian Act* and the existing legislative restrictions on Indian mobilization, organization, and travel: Indians could not legally leave their reserves, gather for "unsanctioned" purposes, raise monies for "unsanctioned" use, or hire lawyers. Further, Loft's success was also confined in part by "Indian politics": nationalism, traditional alliances, treaty sentimentalities, internal and international divisions resulting from colonization, and the multiplicity of traditional Indigenous political traditions (including both political systems and political cultures).

Though short-lived, Loft's initiatives can be credited with the creation of several provincial leagues and the growing sense that international cooperation and pan-Indian activism had great potential as a strategy for achieving real change. These efforts were thwarted by the Department of Indian Affairs and the RCMP, whose mere presence at gatherings of the movement posed the threat of arrests. Not only was it illegal for Indigenous peoples to gather, but their ceremonies—dancing, prayers, and the smoking of a pipe—were also proscribed. Loft's trip to Thunderchild's reserve in Saskatchewan in 1921, saw the threat of federal interference become reality as Nehiyaw leaders were arrested. Though these arrests were for dancing (and not treason, as was the case for Mistahimaskwa), they sent a strong message to the Nehiyaw and their leadership. It was a message which, when combined with the experiences of 1885 and the predominant Nehiyaw nationalist sentiments (pan-Indian animosities), stalled the development of a formal provincial organization (the Federation of Saskatchewan Indian Nations) until the late 1950s.

The Movement Takes Hold

Neither these arrests nor the predominant Indigenous nationalist outlook halted efforts to organize. After a successful gathering in Hobemma (Alberta) in 1922, Loft's vision of international mobilization really took hold among the Nehiyaw in Alberta. Established in 1933, the League of Indians of Alberta was essentially an organization of Nehiyaw from Treaty Six in central Alberta that borrowed its leadership from band councils and organizations such as the "Half-Breed Association of Alberta" (later, the Métis National Association of Alberta) led by Joe Dion, a teacher from Kehiwin and nephew of Mistahimaskwa. In an attempt to expand its constituency to include non-Cree, the League joined with political organizations emerging among the Siiksikaawa (Blackfoot Confederacy) to become the Indian Association of Alberta (IAA). Despite their common interests and the fact that leadership continuously shifted between the Nehiyaw and Kainai (Blood Nation of the Blackfoot Confederacy), the organization has been plagued by national conflict, nationalist sentimentalities, and a lack of unity, as the Nehiyaw and Blackfoot Confederacy are historical enemies.

When windows of opportunities presented themselves, the IAA proved itself to be a "mighty power." It was the IAA, under the leadership of Harold Cardinal, that formally responded to the federal government's 1969 White Paper (see discussion below) by releasing the *Red Paper* (Indian Chiefs of Alberta, 1970) and that was in the forefront of the charge to establish the National Indian Brotherhood (NIB). Similarly, the IAA was very active in the constitutional debates of the early 1980s when the opportunity arose to pressure governments to acknowledge and entrench Aboriginal and treaty rights into the *Constitution Act*, an opportunity to which the IAA and other groups responded by actively lobbying Canadian governments, the UN, the Canadian public, the British Crown, and the British Courts (the Judicial Committee of the Privy Council), among other venues (Sanders, 1992: 151–67).

Like other provincial Indigenous organizations, the IAA was a civil rights movement intent on forcing the federal government to assist the people in achieving equality and a standard of living comparable to Canadian citizens by addressing health care, housing, education, social assistance, and justice issues. Similarly, it also focused on specific matters pertinent to the nations that comprised its membership. These included sovereignty, territory, Aboriginal rights, the nation-to-nation relationship, and self-determination (McFarlane, 1993: 42). Unlike those organizations based on non-treaty nations (such as the Union of British Columbia Indian Chiefs), however, the primary focus of "treaty organizations"—the IAA, the Federation of Saskatchewan Indian Nations (FSIN), and the Union of Nova Scotia Indians—is the implementation of the treaties and the treaty order, for the treaties were to have protected the nations from colonial intrusions and provided for economic and social assistance. It should also be noted that this focus on treaties not only served to separate treaty-based pan-Indian organizations from those focused on obtaining treaties (those without treaties), but also acts as a point of division and clash within organizations comprised of two or more treaty areas as different treaties afforded the signatories different rights and protections—a situation that further exacerbated national tensions within these organizations.

A "National" International Brotherhood

Changes to the *Indian Act* in 1951 lifted the restrictions on political activities, enabling status Indians both to gather for political purposes and to raise money to prove land claims and to hire lawyers. Though there had been several federal-sponsored initiatives to create an organization at the pan-Canadian level, it was not until 1968 that a new movement began to take shape. The NIB was created by uniting provincial organizations under a "federal" umbrella organization for reasons of political expediency and the need for organizational capacity and a knowledgeable leadership. A product of the times, the NIB began to take shape as a movement comprised of at least two distinct factions: (1) an organization of political elites intent on lobbying the government for better living conditions and self-determination; and, (2) an activist network comprised of grassroots activists who were intent on creating change by rebuilding their cultures, languages, communities, and economies. These two groups converged when the federal government released its White Paper on Indian Policy in 1969. Threatened by the government's attempt to unilaterally disband reserves, eliminate their rights (their status as "citizens plus"), the First Nations mobilized and took to the streets and "war rooms" of their national, provincial, and federal political organizations and movements. For once, the movement was unified. Treaty divisions and nationalist sentiments mattered not when everyone's basic rights as Indigenous people and nations were in jeopardy. Finally, the movement saw success as the government shelved the White Paper.

The White Paper was a classical political opportunity, which gave a rallying point to the Indigenous movement, encouraged mobilization, demanded the development of organizational capacities, and provided access to the policy network. With the politicization of households, an increasingly unified movement, an increasingly educated Indigenous public[1]—a public with rising political, social, and economic expectations—and increased organizational capacity (both federally and provincially), the "new" Indigenous rights movement was firmly entrenched into the Canadian political landscape. But this unity did not last long, as it continued to be plagued by national and treaty differences and by the differences created by colonial authorities and colonial legislation (such as the *Indian Act*). The Indigenous rights movement was forced to grapple with the divisive legacies of the treaty period, which failed to include all Indigenous people in a treaty area and thus divided nations and families among treaty or status Indians, non-status Indians, and Métis. The *Indian Act* also divided the Indigenous community (and thus Nations) into status and non-status Indians or between federally recognized Indians and those Indigenous peoples recognized only as "Canadians."[2] All this served to divide the movement and in 1971 led to the creation of another national organization, the Native Council of Canada (NCC), which was to represent the interests of those who had never formally been represented by the NIB—off-reserve non-status Indians and Métis people. The movement then also fractured along gender lines, as non-status women (who had lost status by marrying non-status men) and many Métis women and status women living both on and off reserve felt that their interests were not being fairly represented by the NIB. They forged their own movement in the late 1960s—the Native Women's Association of Canada—and created provincial and national organizations in the early 1970s to fight for women's rights under the *Indian Act* and to improve the social, political, and economic situation of Indigenous women.

Still, the NIB stayed at the helm of the movement and forged ahead with an aggressive rights-based strategy, that was very different from Loft's focus on education and social improvements. Though intent on improving the social and economic conditions of Indigenous peoples, the NIB approached this from a "new" vantage defined by national interests and began to frame a pan-Indian discourse of Aboriginal and treaty rights. To this end, it argued that, although the federal government had a responsibility to provide assistance and to address the catastrophic social and economic conditions on reserves, it had no right to interfere politically, as it was time for First Nations to exercise their rights of self-determination. The philosophy of self-determination was, in the words of George Manuel, "just give us the gas, we'll do the driving" (McFarlane, 1993: 72).

The NIB's philosophy of self-determination and rights served to unify Indigenous peoples and created a true pan-Indian vision and movement involving all Indigenous peoples of all nations, treaty or non-treaty. Nonetheless, it was widely criticized by many treaty nations because they had already had their rights affirmed and a nation-to-nation relationship established in the treaties. Thus, despite greater unity, the movement continued to be plagued by the nationalist and treaty divisions of the past (as will be discussed in the final section of this chapter).

The Dawning of a New Era

Viewing the constitutional discussions as an opportunity to put Aboriginal and treaty rights on the centre stage of the political arena and seeing the possibility of gaining constitutional recognition and protection of Aboriginal and treaty rights, the Aboriginal rights movement and organizations such as the NIB, FSIN, NCC, and IAA jumped at every opportunity to pressure Canadian governments into accepting their vision. They were, by all accounts, "the least expected, and most exotic" (Sanders, 1992: 151) part of the patriation process, for they not only lobbied Canadian governments and parliamentarians, the Governor General, the Vatican, the British Parliament, and the Queen, they sought legal action in the UK (Venne, 1989: 105–06), and held mass demonstrations throughout Canada. Though they were never included as participants in the process (several organizations were provided with observer status when warranted), and while many of the issues that they sought to have addressed (such as treaty implementation and the sovereignty of First Nations) were not brought forward, they succeeded in putting their issues front and centre and in achieving some semblance of constitutional protection of their rights.

Pressured by national governments such as the Mi'kmaw Grand Council, treaty activists, and participating federal and provincial Indigenous organizations (such as the NIB and NCC), Indigenous and treaty rights gained constitutional recognition in 1982. But the process strained the leadership and organizational capacities of the movement. The NIB struggled with its relationship with, and its perceived accountability to, First Nations' leadership (*Indian Act* chiefs) and the demands of treaty nations, which, in 1982, took over and restructured the organization, renaming it the Assembly of First Nations (AFN). Meanwhile, in 1983, the Métis (primarily the western Métis and the descendants of the historical Métis Nation) pulled out of the NCC and created the Métis National Council (MNC), leaving the NCC to represent the issues of off-reserve and non-status Indians and those Métis that did not fall within the mandate of the MNC. While these other groups were enduring a makeover, the Native Women's Association of Canada gained momentum. Following patriation of the Constitution, the major Indigenous organizations gathered with First Ministers on several occasions between 1983 and 1987 to discuss the meaning of "Aboriginal and treaty rights" and issues such as gender equality.

Despite momentous transformations of organizations, leadership, and the grassroots movement, the rights-based orientation was enhanced by the new language of constitutional rights, and the Constitution began to demand increased organizational capacity and to structure Indigenous people's relationship with Canada. Neither the movement nor any of the organizations had ever perceived themselves as interest groups, although they had used every opportunity available to force the government into dealing with their rights-based agenda and engaging in discussions of self-determination. Almost immediately, it appeared as though this struggle to frame the discussion of colonialism, past injustices, and the relationship between themselves and the state had been won with sections 25 and 35 of the *Charter of Rights and Freedoms*,[3] and as the governments of Canada began preparing for a series of First Ministers' Conferences on Aboriginal and Treaty Rights. Though these conferences resulted in several constitutional amendments, and though they succeeded in expanding the capacities of the organizations and keeping an exploratory conversation going on matters of Aboriginal and treaty rights, little was achieved. The conferences ended with no agreed-upon interpretation of the meaning of Aboriginal and treaty rights. Constitutional inclusion had failed to result in any meaningful change in the relationship between Indigenous organizations and the Canadian state. This was made particularly clear by the Meech Lake Accord. Though negotiated shortly after the last First Ministers' Conference on Aboriginal Issues, the Accord not only failed to address the relationship between Indigenous peoples and the state or to address Indigenous issues of concern, but also Indigenous people were excluded from both the negotiations and the agreement itself.

The defiant "No" of MLA Elijah Harper "killed" the Accord on the floor of the Manitoba Legislature. Whether the result of Harper's activist gesture, the 1991 stand-off between Mohawk warriors and the Canadian army over the Oka golf course, or the lobby efforts of groups such as the AFN, this is clear: when the constitutional debate was reopened during the "Canada Round" of constitutional talks (the Charlottetown Accord), Indigenous peoples were invited to the table where they succeeded at dominating much of the debate and securing further recognition of their constitutional rights—including the rights of Métis and the inherent right to self-government. It was an enormous victory, albeit a victory that was short-lived, for while it was an overwhelming victory for organizations such as the MNC, much of the AFN's constituency questioned the deal. In the end, internal differences (such as status), nationalisms, and treaty sentimentalities divided the movement, as most treaty nations denounced the Accord as an affront to treaty rights, and status Indians questioned the soundness of the agreement and the potential for disaster in implementation. But it was not just treaty nations and dissident status Indians who opposed the deal and voted against it in the referendum—the majority of Canadians also opposed the Accord, and it was defeated.

What Now? Finding New Meaning in
the Post-Constitution World

Much of the substance of the Charlottetown Accord found life in non-constitutional agreements and policies such as the federal government's 1995 Inherent Right Policy, which affirmed self-government as a constitutionally recognized Aboriginal right. Nonetheless, the defeat of the Accord represented a catastrophic problem for the Indigenous rights movement and its organizations, for they had been so focused on achieving constitutional change that they had become little more than single-issue organizations with little mandate or capacity for anything else and thus had become fragmented and disengaged. As in the post-constitution period of the 1980s, these organizations underwent a tremendous overhaul in the post-constitution period as they adapted to a new policy environment, created new capacities, and looked for new opportunities to engage the government and new ways to use (and fund) the tremendous infrastructure that had been developed (with government assistance).

Indigenous rights organizations have become increasingly bureaucratized, involved in policy networks, and integrated into the federal government's machinery to such an extent that many commonly "share" staff with federal departments (using secondment agreements) and are involved in all aspects of the policy process, including policy formulation and implementation. For example, in 2001 the Department of Indian Affairs and Northern Development contracted out to the NCC the responsibility for the consultations (the *Communities First: First Nations Governance Initiative*) that preceded and were the basis of the controversial *First Nations Governance Act*, 2002. Meanwhile, the AFN has entered into partnerships, service agreements, and contracting relationships with an assortment of departments including Finance, Health, and Indian Affairs to aid in program administration and to engage in policy discussions (agenda setting, development, and implementation) in areas of taxation, membership registries, and land management. While such arrangements offer creative ways of financing the operations of the organizations and provide great opportunities to engage with governments, to advance their Aboriginal rights agenda, and to improve economic and social conditions, they are not viewed favourably by the grassroots, and they are criticized by much of the leadership.

Amid the constant criticisms of these organizations for "sleeping with the enemy" and "being in bed with the government," the AFN was dealt a further blow when the federal government announced its plans in 2001 to use the NCC to consult with Indigenous peoples and revise the *Indian Act* with its *First Nations Governance Act* initiative. The AFN had been sidestepped and made to appear an ineffective (non)participant in the policy process. Despite attempts to demonstrate otherwise, the AFN was unable to shake this label, as it had proven itself unable to shape the policy initiative prior to consultations or to influence the *First Nations Governance Act* before it was tabled in the House of Commons in 2002. Worse yet, despite framing the issue as a threat similar to the White Paper of 1969, the AFN seemed unable to mobilize the grassroots or to get the government to listen—that is, until it called in its "heavy hitters" (its experts, mainly drawn from past constitutional experts) to address a Joint Ministerial Advisory Committee.

Though it was thus able to "save face," and the legislation died on the government's agenda when Paul Martin became prime minister, the AFN set out to alter its relationship or at least the perception of its relationship with the federal government. To this end, following on the heels of the MNC, the AFN appears to be altering its relationship with, and dependence on, the federal government and withdrawing from many of the contracting partnerships. With change afoot within the organizations, the demise of the *First Nations Governance Act* seems to have ushered in a new era for the national Indigenous organizations and the movements that they (sometimes) represent.

While the AFN has engaged in grassroots consultations about the organization and the future, and all of the national organizations have undergone some sort of organizational renewal, the real change has occurred in the area of their relationship with the federal government. Ushered in by both a change in government when Paul Martin became prime minister in December 2003 as well as by changes within all of the key organizations, this relationship was radically transformed in 2004 with the convening of the Canada-Aboriginal Peoples Round Table process (Canada, 2004). The Round Table was promoted as an opportunity to establish a new relationship between all Indigenous peoples (as represented by all of the main federal organizations) and the federal government (as represented by Prime Minister Paul Martin and his cabinet) and to make actual progress on a new agenda. With its transparent, sectorally defined tables, its frank and open discussions, and real commitment to both process and product by all parties, the Round Table was very successful. While substantive improvements in the areas of health, education, economic opportunities, housing, and negotiations have yet to occur, the real change has been less about substance and more a question of process and relationship. It resulted in a Political Accord on the Recognition and Implementation of First Nations Governments (the Kelowna Accord), the convening of a First Ministers' Meeting with Indigenous leaders from all major organizations on 25 November 2005, tremendous progress in the negotiation of several other agreements, and an implementation strategy addressing a wide range of issues including health care (Canada, 2005). It should be noted that this transformation in the relationship between Indigenous peoples and government and the progressive changes in social policies, as negotiated in the Accord, were short-lived. Negotiated in the final days of Paul Martin's minority Liberal government, the Kelowna Accord was immediately repudiated by Stephen Harper's minority Conservative government. This signals not only the end of the Accord but the end of the new and improved relationship that was developing under Martin's leadership. It has likely also signalled a return to, and a worsening of, the chilly climate that characterized Indigenous politics and Indigenous-state relations in the past.

Seeing Beyond the AFN

The AFN is not the only actor engaged in Indigenous politics or the Indigenous rights movement. There have been other actors within the movement and other domains of mobilization since the onset of colonialism. These actors and domains are not limited to the "other" political organizations discussed in this chapter but involve a plethora of international and national (in the case of the Métis and the Inuit) organizations at the provincial, territorial, and federal levels; band councils and other local governments; treaty organizations and tribal councils; national and sub-national governments and NGOs; and issue-oriented groups, warrior societies, grassroots people and leadership (kitchen table organizers as opposed to participants in band government), and "every-day Joes." Though no extensive or formalized network connects all of these individuals and organizations, they are linked informally through the "moccasin telegraph" and seem to be able to develop more formal spontaneous linkages when opportunities or needs arise.

The reason the movement is, and has always been, so extensive is quite simple: individuals, locally "organized" groups (such as fishers), local governments, and international political organizations typically perceive themselves as being in a constant battle with the government over their rights to live as Indigenous peoples in their homelands; to govern themselves; to exercise those rights and responsibilities accorded to them as nations (such as the right to fish in their territory); and to better their economic, social, and political conditions.

This is especially the case when one considers that a simple everyday activity can be a political act for Indigenous peoples—whether it is perceived as such or not. Take, for instance, the crossing of the Canada-US border. While most Canadians see this as a simple, non-political activity, many Indigenous people engage in political activism when they cross the border. When asked to state their nationality or country of origin, they engage in the nationalist and self-determination struggles that have defined the movement by stating their true nation of origin and refusing to engage in the colonial rhetoric of citizenship (King, 1993). Beyond the issues of citizenship and nation of origin, the border poses further sources of contestation for peoples whose territories it runs through and for those whose treaties suggest that they should have free movement for themselves and their goods across the border. In short, the mere existence of the border has made activists out of Indigenous peoples.

Indigenous peoples engage in politics of contestation every day. Yet, aside from the major organizations (band, tribal, provincial, and federal) it is only when opportunities arise (or are created) that the masses mobilize, "kitchen table" networks are engaged, wider networks are rekindled, and the movement becomes organized. Episodes of mobilization have varied and will continue to vary in orientation, issue, the level of mobilization (elite or popular), and the ability (and desire) to organize and create organizational capacity. This is quite evident when one considers the different ways in which the Nehiyaw attempted to engage the Crown's representatives over the course of some 15 years. It is even more evident when one considers that the Nehiyaw under the leadership of Weekuskokisayin, Mistahimaskwa, and Imasees were all "fighting" the government's Indian policy to achieve pretty much the same things as Harold Cardinal was demanding nearly 100 years later when he contested the federal government's Indian policy: assistance (gas) and sovereignty/self-determination (the ability to drive the car). To take this one step further, though using different methods, these are the same issues that are being contested when Indigenous people passively question matters of citizenship, territoriality, and Canadian sovereignty when passing over the imagined line we call the border.

Only Actors and Arenas Change With Time

Recognizing this diversity, and the inherent flux within Indigenous politics of contestation and the Indigenous rights movement, it is fascinating that, by and large, the goals and the issues have remained constant among the various actors, nations, and organizations involved. Having explored several of the episodes of mobilization that have defined Indigenous politics since the outset of colonization, I will now explore several of the goals that have defined the movement over space and time. Acknowledging that the movement has been divided and many of the goals contested, following this discussion, I will turn our attention to explaining the disjunctures and divisions that have characterized the movement.

One of the primary goals of Indigenous activism, both prior to and following the onset of colonization, has been good governance. This was the vision and the mission of the Peacemaker: to bring peace, order, and good governance to the Haudenosaunee through the creation of a new constitutional order based on the Great Law of Peace. This was the vision and mission of Mistahimaskwa when he addressed of the issue of the rope at the treaty talks, and it was behind his attempt to mobilize the Nehiyaw and engage in peaceful negotiations with the representatives of the Crown and the Canadian government. For Mistahimaskwa, the rope symbolized a future in which Canada would attempt to lead the Nehiyaw around like an animal—an animal that had lost the ability to govern itself. Given that these leaders already had a system of good governance, and given that they saw the treaty as a means of protecting their sovereignty, neither Mistahimaskwa, nor any other Nehiyaw leader agreed to be subject to this rope. But Mistahimaskwa did not trust the government and, given the government's already tarnished record and image, he did not see the treaty as providing ample provisions and protections for his people. As a result, he attempted to mobilize the Nehiyaw and to engage the nation in a peaceful resistance against the government.

Similarly, the vision and mission of good governance has been at the forefront of much contemporary activism. For many, the constitutional battles of the late 1970s through to the early 1990s (including the series of First Ministers' Conferences on Aboriginal Issues) were as much about good governance as self-determination—if not more so. This is quite evident if one looks back at the literature from this period (see, for example, Mercredi and Turpell, 1993), which presented self-government as an opportunity to overthrow the colonial system of oppressive government under the *Indian Act* and to (re)create a system of good governance (see Little Bear *et al.*, 1984). This is even more evident in the position advanced by treaty people and organizations. For them, the right to self-government and their distinctive systems of good governance had been recognized in and protected by their treaties; thus, the constitutional battles offered the opportunity to affirm treaty rights, recognize them as constitutional rights, and engage in discussions of implementation (Henderson, 1996).

Sovereignty and self-determination have also been primary goals of Indigenous activism, both prior to and following the onset of colonization, as is evident in episodes of mobilization such as the treaties, the "last stands" of traditional governments, international activism, claims processes, self-government negotiations, and in the reaction to the *First Nations Governance Act*. The central role of the goals of sovereignty and self-determination is especially evident in the mobilization of the Haudensaunee government—the Council of Chiefs—in the Grand River Territory (Six Nations reserve) during the 1920s. From the outset, Canada's Indian policy had advocated regime change or "replacing" Indigenous political systems and constitutional orders with the *Indian Act* system of band government. Despite such policies and previous attempts to depose the Haudenosaunee government, the Council remained in place. But by the 1920s, it was becoming increasingly clear that the federal government would not stop until it had institutionalized the *Indian Act* and put in place a "puppet" government at Six Nations. In an attempt to gain support for their government and to assert their sovereignty as a nation (and thus, their right of self-determination), the Haudenosaunee government sent delegates such as Loft and Deskahe to discuss these matters with the Canadian government and the British Crown and to demand both representation at, and the support of, the newly established League of Nations (Staats, 1996).

Sovereignty and self-determination continue as a primary foundation of contemporary Indigenous politics and mobilization. This, as we saw above, was most evident in the era of constitutional renewal. Even the reaction to the *First Nations Governance Act* should be viewed in terms of the overall goals of sovereignty and self-determination, since people mobilized against this legislation not to support the status quo but to assert their right to govern themselves (Ladner and Orsini, 2005). This was particularly clear in the reaction of treaty nations; they advanced the position that the government had no right to be designing structures of governance nor asserting jurisdiction over Indigenous peoples, for these matters had already been resolved when the treaties were negotiated.

Economic and resource rights have also been primary goals of Indigenous political mobilization and activism, both historically and currently. One need only look back to the words of Weekuskokisayin quoted earlier in this chapter and to the Nehiyaw's reasons for lobbying for a treaty prior to 1876 to understand that economic and resource issues have been part of Indian politics since colonization (and arguably before). Many nations fought for and attained the protection of their economies and resources in their treaties and, as such, have continued to argue for access and resource rights since this time. Such is the case for the Mi'kmaw nation whose negotiations with the British in 1752 led to the recognition of their rights to their resources throughout their traditional territory as well as their rights to trade resources—the products of resource extraction or harvesting (Wicken, 2000). Disregarding such rights (and thus its own responsibilities under the treaties), the Canadian government has failed to protect the Mi'kmaw economy and has denied the Mi'kmaw access to its resources through such measures as the legislated exclusion of Mi'kmaw from, for instance, the salmon fishery (Ladner, 2005). Nonetheless, the recognition and affirmation of Mi'kmaw rights in the treaties has provided the impetus for Mi'kmaw throughout the homeland to engage in the politics of contestation as individuals, organizations, communities and a nation, by using a variety of mechanisms. For example, in Listuguj, despite the illegality of such ventures, many have continued to engage in the fishery and in so doing have become activists in the struggle to have their economic and resource rights (their treaty rights) recognized. They have faced harassment from Canadian officials, continuous legal battles, and, on two occasions, the "invasion" of their reserve by Quebec and Canadian officials to halt the "illegal fishery." The arrest of Donald Marshall Jr. for "illegally" fishing eels led to the mobilization of the Mi'kmaw Grand Council and their engaging the Canadian state in a legal challenge over their treaty rights pertaining to the protection of their economic rights and resources, particularly their right to trade the product of their economic pursuits. It should also be noted that the courts have also been used as a strategy by nations without treaties as they attempt to assert, and gain recognition of, their rights to use the resources within their territories.

Indigenous peoples have also mobilized around issues such as education, social assistance, housing, and water quality in an effort to attain assistance and improve their standard and quality of life. This vision of a better future has driven treaty lobbyists, those active in the League of Indians of Canada and other political organizations, and community activists. Community leadership and grassroots activists have been mobilized against the state since the establishment of reserves and the forced confinement of Indigenous peoples to small plots of mainly economically useless land and deplorable conditions. Though constantly engaged in the lobbying of government officials, the grassroots have typically used issues such as residential school abuse, the lack of adequate housing and sanitation in communities such as Davis Inlet, and the contamination of water in communities such as Kashechewan as opportunities to define and bring attention to "Canada's Indian problem" and to press governments into action. In terms of political organizations, improving the living conditions, standard of life, and educational opportunities for Indigenous people was at the heart of Loft's struggle to mobilize and lobby the government.

Territorial rights and a people's relationship to the land has also been central to the Indigenous movement. Recognition of territory and territorial rights, have been one of the key issues that Indigenous people have been trying to advance since Europeans first arrived and were welcomed as visitors, intruders, and occupiers in their homelands. This has even been a major concern for the Métis—the national product of colonialism—as is evidenced by the struggles of Riel to define and defend a provincial homeland for the Métis within Canada and the lobby effort by Malcolm Norris and Joe Dion to force the government of Alberta to establish Métis settlements (reserves) in the 1930s. These same struggles continue today for most Indigenous nations. This is particularly the case for those nations without so called "land-cession treaties" (and for those whose treaties were not respected), for their relationship with their territory and rights to use that territory have been ignored by the governments of Canada, and they have never been compensated for their lands. These nations have been contesting the unlawful seizure and occupation of their lands since the beginning, using a variety of mechanisms, which today include lobbying governments to have their rights recognized, land claim negotiations, Aboriginal and Treaty rights court cases, and occupation/protest.

Irrespective of treaty issues, both nations and groups of citizens have contested the taking of territory, the use/development of their territory, and their inability to use/have a relationship with their traditional territories. Such episodes of contestation have often resulted in dramatic standoffs. For instance, during the summer of 1990, in an attempt to halt the development of a golf course on sacred land (a forest and graveyard that were already the subject of a land claim) by the town of Oka, citizens of Kanesatake engaged in a peaceful protest and blockade, a protest that escalated into a 78-day armed siege at Kanesatake and Kahnewake between Mohawk warriors, the Quebec police, and the Canadian army (York and Pindera, 1991). Meanwhile, in 1991, in their attempt to halt the development of the Oldman Dam, a project that would flood parts of their homeland and have devastating effects on the sensitive ecological areas created by the river system, Milton Born With a Tooth and the Lone Fighters Society of the Peigan Nation engaged in an armed standoff with the RCMP over a diversion weir that had been constructed on the reserve. While not marked with the same media coverage nor police presence (since the shooting of Dudley George at Ipperwash in 1995), communities such as the Six Nations of the Grand River Territory (Caledonia) have continued to use standoffs, protests, and blockades to bring attention to their issues, to halt development of their lands, and to enable the use and occupation of their own territories (see Edwards, 2001).

Understanding the Movement: Mechanisms and Fractures

For most movements, mechanisms of redress and venues of mobilization are typically defined by opportunity structures and, to a lesser extent, by the nature of the movement and its goals. As has been demonstrated throughout this chapter, the Indigenous movement and its episodes of mobilization have been influenced, shaped, confined, and defined by the state—just as Tarrow (1998) and other social movement theorists who endorse the political process model suggest. That said, however, Indigenous politics of contestation do not fully fit with Tarrow's theorization of social movements or with the theories of other social movement scholars. Though influenced by the state and opportunity structures, Indigenous movements are fundamentally grounded in and defined by issues of nationhood and (de)colonization—considerations that have been largely overlooked in the social movement literature. Considerations of nationhood and decolonization have defined and confined the movement, its issues, goals, values, and the mechanisms it has used. More importantly, they account for the divisions within and the fractious nature of this movement. These issues will be explored in this final section of the chapter.

By and large, venues and points of mobilization are defined and constrained by the intentions of the actors and by their underlying philosophical orientation of nationhood and (de)colonization. Such considerations contribute to the preference for nation-to-nation relationships and the use of international domains to resolve domestic issues, as was the case when Deskahe approached the League of Nations to force the Canadian government to cease and desist in its efforts to overthrow the Haudenosaunee government. They also contribute to the increasingly predominant view that domestic courts are not an appropriate venue for addressing Indigenous issues. Many Indigenous leaders and academics argue that their issues are not "domestic" issues, that Indigenous nations should not be subject to the courts of another nation, and that the courts should not be used because they have been quite ineffective in advancing the Indigenous agenda, providing for decolonization, and dealing with questions of nationhood (Monture-Angus, 1999: 135–52). Still, as a matter of necessity, and for the potential that they offer in addressing the Indigenous agenda, courts continue to be used, just as they are by other movements. Similarly, while party politics and voter mobilization are common strategies in the politics of contestation, they are seldom used by Indigenous people or organizations seeking to influence public policy or party platforms. Relationships with parties seldom develop because such activities are typically viewed as contrary to both the goals of Indigenous peoples and to the foundations of the movement—Indigenous nationhood. Still, relationships with parties do develop, but this is mainly on an ad hoc basis and usually through special policy forums, such as that which led to the development of the Liberals' *Red Book* in 1993.

The philosophical underpinnings of nationhood and (de)colonization can, by and large, account for the mobilization strategies and opportunity choices of the Indigenous movement. While intentions, opportunity structures, and the nature of an organization also hold explanatory value, one must privilege considerations of nationhood and (de)colonization as they are the foundation of the movement. Not only do they assist in explaining the distinctiveness of this movement and the distinctiveness of its choices and strategies, but they also explain points of disjuncture and division within it.

For the most part, the key disjuncture and divisions in the movement are the result of colonization. At issue are the artificial divisions that were created by colonial administrators, and that define and structure relationships among Indigenous nations and individuals and between Indigenous peoples and the state. These artificial divisions or points of inequality include those between treaty and non-treaty nations, treaty and non-treaty individuals, status and non-status people, First Nations and "other" Indigenous nations such as the Métis (a people with few recognized rights and limited recognition of both nationhood and Aboriginality), and men and women (rights and government policies are often gendered, as is the case of status and matrimonial law and inheritance historically and today). These divisions are points of fraction and contestation within the Indigenous movement that have continuously served to divide rather than unify it. They have done so because they create disparate groups with disparate and often contradictory goals.

While all facets of the Indigenous movement agree on the goals of good governance, sovereignty, and self-determination, their framing of these goals is predicated on and defined by considerations of nationhood and (de) colonization. Treaty nations most often frame these goals in terms of their treaties, as most treaties afforded protection to Indigenous political systems, affirmed the existence (and continuance) of Indigenous constitutional orders, and created a nation-to-nation relationship between Indigenous nations and the Crown. Meanwhile, non-treaty nations see the need to engage Canadian governments in policy discussions and negotiations with the intent of defining and implementing self-determination and good governance while dealing with (ceding) claims of sovereignty and territoriality. Whereas treaty nations see these issues as having been dealt with in the past, non-treaty nations have not yet dealt with them. Therefore, while one feels the need to dust off the treaty and rebuild a relationship between equal and mutually dependent nations, the other sees the need to create public policy and legal (or constitutional) frameworks for the negotiation, development, and implementation of self-government. The distinction between these two groups is huge, and it often results in catastrophic fractures within the Indigenous movement as treaty nations view the goals and activities of non-treaty nations as jeopardizing their agenda and view self-government as diluting, abrogating, and derogating the treaties and their relationship with the Crown. Thus, while the shared goals of good governance, sovereignty, and self-determination serve to unify the movement (as is the case with goals related to improving living standards), they also serve as complex and multifaceted points of internal fracture and contestation that likely impede progress on both fronts.

Final Thoughts: Accounting for the Lack of Movement

In order to understand the Indigenous politics of contestation in Canada, it is important to explore and understand its historical roots. By grounding the understanding of Indigenous contestation in an historical approach and by giving due place to Indigenist methodologies such as narrative and storytelling, it is possible to gain an understanding of the movement, its development, and its goals. The contestation of Indigenous people in contemporary Canada reflects a continuity with the past histories of the relationship between Indigenous nations and settler societies (in the case of the Nehiyaw this was comparatively late). It is important for settler cultures to approach Indigenous contestation from the perspective of Indigenous peoples themselves, seeking to understand Indigenous perspectives and traditions on their own terms, rather than strictly in terms of the dominant Euro-Canadian legal and political categories.

Why has there been so little movement for Indigenous peoples in Canada? Over the past 100 years, the government has made many advances in positively addressing its "Indian problem" and in responding to the demands and aspirations of Indigenous people. Indigenous people have achieved constitutional recognition of their Aboriginal and Treaty rights and great victories in court as they have attempted to have these rights recognized and respected by governments. The *Indian Act* has been revised (to a very limited extent) to afford Indigenous peoples greater political rights and equality rights, and social and economic conditions have improved somewhat.

Yet, Indigenous people are still making the same demands today that were advanced by the Nehiyaw in the 1870s. This is because there has been little effort to address the underlying issues that form the foundation of the discontent—nationhood and (de)colonization. These not only account for the choice of venues or domains of mobilization and the fractures and divisions within the Indigenous rights movement, they also account for the differences and distinctiveness of the Indigenous movement vis-à-vis other social movements and for the staying power of both the movement and its demands. Indigenous peoples are still mobilizing in defence of their nations, seeking to have their rights (political, economic, and territorial) as nations recognized and respected, and establishing a relationship between nations based upon mutual respect and mutual benefit. At the end of the day, the dog with the rope around its neck will still want to deal with the issue of the rope, no matter how many cookies it is thrown.

Notes

1. In 1951, federal policy had changed to allow Indians to go to university without loss of status, and reforms to federal education programs meant that high school graduates were increasing both in number and in quality.

2. Until 1985, status or the legal recognition of an Indian under the *Indian Act* with membership and rights in a community could be lost by women who married non-status (Indian or otherwise) men, while status could be gained by non-status (Indian or otherwise) women marrying status men.

3. The relevant sections of the Charter are these:

> 25. The guarantee in this Charter of certain rights and freedoms shall not be construed so as to abrogate or derogate from any aboriginal, treaty or other rights or freedoms that pertain to the Aboriginal peoples of Canada including:
> 35. (1) The existing aboriginal and treaty rights of aboriginal peoples are hereby recognized and affirmed. (Canada, 1989)

Treaty rights refer to the obligations incurred as a result of the signing of peace, friendship, and land treaties throughout this country between the Crown and Indigenous nations. Meanwhile, Aboriginal rights are best explained by Michael Asch as "encompassing a broad range of economic, social, cultural and political rights ... These rights flow, first of all, from the fact that the aboriginal peoples were in sovereign occupation of Canada at the time of contact, and secondly from the assertion that their legitimacy and continued existence has not been extinguished by the subsequent occupation of Canada by immigrants" (Asch, 1984: 30).

References and Further Reading

Alfred, Taiaiake. 1999. *Peace, Power and Righteousness: An Indigenous Manifesto.* Don Mills: Oxford University Press.

Asch, Michael. 1984. *Home and Native Land: Aboriginal Rights and the Canadian Constitution.* Toronto: Methuen.

Canada. 1989. *The Constitution Acts 1867 to 1982.* Ottawa: Department of Justice Canada.

Canada. 2004. *Strengthening the Relationship Report on the Canada-Aboriginal Peoples Roundtable.* 19 April. <http://www.aboriginalroundtable.ca/rtbl/strenght_rpt_e.pdf>.

Canada. 2005. *A First Nations Implementation Plan.* 28 November. <http://www.ainc-inac.gc.ca/nr/prs/s-d2005/2-02749_e.html>.

Christie, W.J. 1871. To A.G. Archibald, 13 April. *Sessional Papers Canada* 22. Ottawa: Queen's Printer, 1872.

Dempsey, Hugh A. 1984. *Big Bear: The End of Freedom.* Vancouver: Douglas and McIntyre.

Edwards, Peter. 2001. *One Dead Indian: The Premier, the Police, and the Ipperwash Crisis.* Toronto: Stoddart.

Henderson, James (Sákej) Youngblood. 1996. "First Nations Legal Inheritances in Canada: The Mi'kmaq Model." *Manitoba Law Journal* 23 (January).

Indian Chiefs of Alberta. 1970. *Citizens Plus.* Edmonton: Indian Association of Alberta.

Johansen, Bruce E. 1998. *Debating Democracy: Native American Legacy of Freedom.* Santa Fe: Clear Light Publishers.

King, Thomas. 1993. *One Good Story, That One: Stories.* Toronto: Harper Perennial.

Ladner, Kiera L. 2005. "Up the Creek: Fishing for a New Constitutional Order." *Canadian Journal of Political Science* 38(4): 923–53.

Ladner, Kiera L., and Michael Orsini. 2005. "The Persistence of Paradigm Paralysis: The *First Nations Governance Act* as the Continuation of Colonial Policy." In Mike Murphy (ed.), *Canada: State of the Federation*. Kingston: Queen's University, Institute of Intergovernmental Relations.

Little Bear, Leroy, J. Menno Boldt, and Anthony Long (Eds.). 1984. *Pathways to Self-Determination: Canadian Indians and the Canadian State*. Toronto: University of Toronto Press.

McFarlane, Peter. 1993. *Brotherhood to Nationhood: George Manuel and the Making of the Modern Indian Movement*. Toronto: Between the Lines.

Mercredi, Ovide, and Mary Ellen Turpel. 1993. *In the Rapids: Navigating the Future of First Nations*. Toronto: Penguin.

Monture-Angus, Patricia. 1999. *Journeying Forward: Dreaming First Nations' Independence*. Halifax: Fernwood.

Morris, Alexander. 1880. *The Treaties of Canada with the Indians of Manitoba, the Northwest Territories, and Kee-wa-tin*. Toronto: Willing and Williamson.

Sanders, Douglas E. 1992. "The Indian Lobby and the Canadian Constitution, 1978–1982." In Noel Dyck (ed.), *Indigenous Peoples and the Nation State: Fourth World Politics In Canada, Australia and Norway*. St. John's: Memorial University of Newfoundland.

Smith, Donald B. 1996. "Mohawk Civil Servant and North American Indian Political Organizer." *Encyclopedia of North American Indians*. New York: Houghton Mifflin. <http://college.hmco.com/history/readerscomp/naind/html/na_020200_loftfred.htm>.

Staats, Sheila. 1996. "Cayuga-Oneida Political and Religious Leader." *Encyclopedia of North American Indians*. New York: Houghton Mifflin. <http://college.hmco.com/history/readerscomp/naind/html/na_013200_generalalexa.htm>.

Tarrow, Sidney. 1998. *Power in Movement: Social Movements, Collective Action, and Politics*. 2nd ed. Cambridge: Cambridge University Press.

Taylor, John Leonard. 1985. *Treaty Research Reports: Treaty Six (1876)*. Ottawa: Treaties and Historical Research Centre, Indian Affairs Canada.

Venne, Sharron Helen. 1998. *Our Elders Understand our Rights: Evolving International Law Regarding Indigenous Peoples*. Penticton, BC: Theytus Books.

Wicken, William C. 2000. *Mi'kmaq Treaties on Trial*. Toronto: University of Toronto Press.

Yarrow, David. 1987. *The Great Law of Peace: New World Roots of American Democracy*. <http://www.kahonwes.com/iroquois/document1.html>.

York, Geoffrey, and Loreen Pindera. 1991. *People of the Pines: The Warriors and the Legacy of Oka*. Toronto: Little Brown Press.

TEN

Nationalism and Protest: The Sovereignty Movement in Quebec[1]

Pascale Dufour and Christophe Traisnel

> The objective of the *Parti Québécois* is radical. Creating a new country from an existing federation is a thrilling project, but it involves rupture. You have to be rebellious if you want to change your political status in a fundamental way. If a party seeking institutional revolution had no radicals, you would need to question the state of its health. (Lisée, 2005)[2]

The rise of new social movements in Canada in the 1960s saw the upsurge of new forms of nationalism. In English-speaking Canada, youth of the late 1960s and 1970s contested American domination of Canada and argued for an independent Canadian approach in politics and culture. At the same time, in Quebec, the Quiet Revolution saw the birth of new forms of nationalist politics, a development that led to two referendums on sovereignty, the first held by the PQ government of René Lévesque in 1980 and the second held in October 1995 by the PQ government led by Jacques Parizeau. Although these referendums did not result in a victory for the sovereignist side, the political independence of Quebec from Canada remains a valid option for almost 50 per cent of the population (CROP, January 2006). In this chapter, we will focus on the political mobilization of the sovereignty movement in Quebec over the last 40 years.

Nationalism in Quebec or in Canada has very often been treated as an ideology (Couture, Nielsen, and Seymour, 1996; Monière, 1981) rather than as a social movement with its own political dynamics (Coleman, 1984; Fraser, 1984; Keating, 1997; Rumilly, 1975). In this chapter, we build on those who study the processes by which differences of language and culture are transformed into a distinct sense of belonging, which is represented and claimed in the political arena. As Benedict Anderson (1991) explained in his important book on nationalism, the "nation" is an "imagined community." Nationalisms create nations and not the reverse (Gellner, 1989: 86). From this perspective, collective identity and the concept of the "nation" are the product of collective "political work," sometimes led by a specific group that believes in the existence of the nation and wants to carry this vision into the heart of the political game (Thiesse, 1999: 11). From this point of view, political actors such as elites and political parties are the main focus of the analysis of nationalism, as it is their collective "political work" that aims to convince citizens of the existence of a distinct nation. It is particularly appropriate and useful to understand nationalist movements through the lens of the literature on social movements and collective action because these approaches offer concrete tools for understanding the role played by nationalist actors in the political space. Drawing on the social movement literature, we differentiate between actors that take on the task of defining the nation (either the state or social actors) and the repertoire of actions used by these actors.

What, then, is the sovereignty movement? Given the definition that views it as a social movement, it can be defined as organizations and individuals sharing common frames of reference (practices, values, beliefs, and a common identity) and united around the advocacy of a particular political option—Quebec sovereignty, meaning, the political independence of Quebec from the rest of Canada. This definition does not reduce analysis of sovereignty to merely an examination of the Parti Québécois (PQ), but neither does it exclude political parties from the analysis. In other words, unlike some of the other studies of social movements in this volume, this chapter explicitly includes the politics of political parties as a key component of social movement politics, an appropriate approach given that the sovereignty in Quebec has been championed by the PQ since its founding and is now championed by the Bloc Québécois (BQ) at the federal level. Indeed, analysis of the relationships between sovereignist social actors and the PQ in the same social movement is central to understanding the dynamic of the movement as a whole. Some authors, such as Jane Jenson (1995: 107–26, 1998: 235–62, 1999: A9), have already paved the way by analyzing the citizenship regime that applies to Quebec and the role the nationalist movement has played in its construction.

It is important to distinguish between nationalism and sovereignty. Nationalism in Quebec is not solely defined by the sovereignty movement. As Rocher and Lecours (2003) argue, there are two major competing nationalisms in Quebec. The first, the nationalism espoused primarily by the Canadian state (but also by some pan-Canadian social movements), aims to convince Canadians (and Quebeckers) that a Canadian nation exists "from coast to coast." The second challenges the nationalism of the Canadian state by claiming the existence of a distinct Quebec nation and the necessity for sovereignty for Quebec. Between these two positions, the Liberal Party of Quebec advocates a Quebec nationalism that is nonetheless federalist (Ryan, 2002).

In this chapter, we focus on the Quebec sovereignty movement as a social movement, demonstrating how its political actions and political thoughts are central in understanding what has happened and what is happening around the question of sovereignty and the rooted idea of the existence of a Quebec nation. Our first focus is the historical trajectory of the sovereignty movement since the 1960s. We then turn to the structure of the movement and its current dynamics. The sovereignty movement is based on two types of protest (social protest and nationalist protest) which, while originally distinct, quickly found common ground and common cause: taking control of the Quebec state and sharing a vision—an independent Quebec (Traisnel, 2004). The last part of the chapter assesses the concrete achievements of the sovereignty movement and the impact of the movement on Quebec society and politics.

The Historical Trajectory of the Sovereignist Movement in Quebec

The contemporary sovereignty movement originates, in part, in French-Canadian nationalism. This nationalism emphasizes the survival of a French-Canadian culture anchored in traditional religious institutions that resist modernity. It is based on the idea that Canada has two founding peoples: (1) an endangered French-Canadian people who must be defended and (2) an English-Canadian people who are threatening the assimilation of French Canadians. Although these beliefs were gradually abandoned during the 1950s and 1960s, the contemporary sovereignty movement was forged first and foremost in reaction to this doctrine. Distinguished and widely popular intellectual figures, such as Lionel Groulx and André Laurendeau,[3] prepared the ground—though each in a different way—for thinking about Quebec's national question in new ways (Morchain and Wade, 1984; Bourque and Duchastel, 1996). They did not associate nationalism with either withdrawal or survival but, rather, developed an approach to nationalism that was more open to modernity and based on a revitalized Quebec nation. They viewed the government of Quebec as a collective institution—a tool with which French Canadians as a whole could take control of their society. In the context of the postwar wave of decolonization in Africa and Asia (and, especially, the Algerian War), the idea of the liberation of Quebec society from the domination of the colonial power over the colonized people became increasingly popular.[4] At the end of the 1950s, contentious actors inside the student movement and among the Quebec intelligentsia gradually adopted this anti-colonial perspective in their quest for more radical social transformations (Vallières, 1971). These actors developed a critique of Marxism based in part on debates on colonialism. Rather than prioritizing the transition to socialism, as in traditional Marxist analysis, this form of anti-colonial nationalism emphasized that socio-economic justice required national liberation. Indeed, their approach formed part of the highly influential intellectual explosion of the 1950s that constituted a prerequisite to the social and political revolution of the 1960s.

As a result of growing industrialization, Quebec, like most modern Western societies, experienced profound social and economic change in the early twentieth century. The growth of an industrial and agricultural working class, mainly French-Canadian and immigrant, and of an overwhelmingly English-speaking industrial and financial bourgeoisie, only served to widen the gap in prosperity between the two communities (Bourque et Legaré, 1979: 113). Slowly, however, the French-speaking middle class grew stronger, establishing itself not only in literature and the arts but also in economics and politics, thereby gradually opening up Quebec society to the modern world. New publications such as *Cité libre*, founded in 1950, dissociated themselves from traditional conservative views. Quebec society opened up to outside influences and increasingly and unambiguously challenged the established order, especially the Church's influence in society. French-speaking elites became much more receptive to liberal ideas. The death of long-serving Quebec Premier Maurice Duplessis in 1959 and the election of the Liberals led by Jean Lesage ushered in the Quiet Revolution, a period of unprecedented modernization of Quebec institutions and strong government intervention in social policy and economic and cultural development. The Quiet Revolution was not only a social and institutional revolution but a political revolution as well. As the old *Union nationale* party of Maurice Duplessis was fatally weakened, the Liberals were in the ascendant, and a number of sovereignist groups were founded (for the whole period, see Laurendeau, Smart, and Howard, 1991).

By the end of the 1960s, part of the leadership of the Quebec Liberal Party believed that the reforms they had undertaken were on the right track but that they had now fulfilled their role. It was time to slow the pace. For others, including René Lévesque, the opposite was true: the time was right to further transform Quebec through continued reform of government and other institutions. The difference in opinion over the pace of reform soon became divisive, as confirmed by the departure from the Liberal Party of Lévesque and many other advocates of more rapid reform, especially those in the trade union movement.

The growing role of the Quebec state profoundly influenced supporters of French-Canadian nationalism. Faced with the threat of linguistic assimilation—a threat that was preying on many people's minds—the French-

Canadian nationalist camp, which had gradually come under the influence of young militant Quebec nationalists, experienced a split of its own. The division was between those who openly advocated Quebec independence, supported by new movements such as the *Rassemblement pour l'indépendance nationale* (RIN, the National Independence Movement) or the *Ralliement national* (RN, the National Movement), and those who wished instead to keep Quebec within Canada—which, in their view, would guarantee and protect the French fact.

In addition to these splits, there was a rapprochement between Quebec separatists and those who advocated further political and social reform in the province. They rallied to a common objective: to strengthen the Quebec government and use it as a vehicle for social as well as national liberation. A nationalist and social-democratic group gradually formed around the RIN and Lévesque, and it quickly found a remarkable echo in Quebec society. Between 1967 and 1970, Quebec's political landscape changed. The *Mouvement souveraineté-association* (MSA, the Sovereignty-association Movement) had appeared on the political scene, and in 1968 the PQ was born. The latter represented a coalition of the main nationalist organizations (the party merged the RN, the MSA, and the RIN) and a constellation of activists from the militant Left and unions. The majority of nationalist organizations—such as the *Mouvement national des Québécois* (MNQ, the National Movement of Quebeckers), the *Société Saint-Jean-Baptiste* (SSJB), and the *Front du Québec français* (FQF, the Front for a French Quebec)—and labour organizations lent their support to the new political movement that was now taking shape.

The initial period was difficult for the PQ, even though as early as 1970 it was able to muster as many as 90,000 members, and win 24 per cent of the vote. Lévesque tried to unite activists of various political stripes (liberals, militant leftists, and both radical and moderate nationalists) around a common moderate program. In addition, the social and political situation of the period was far from favourable to his agenda. The *Front de libération du Québec* (FLQ, the Front for the Liberation of Quebec), a radical separatist organization, kidnapped a British diplomat (James Cross) and a Quebec minister (Pierre Laporte). In October 1970 the tension was at its peak. Liberal Premier Robert Bourassa asked for help from the federal government to deal with the situation. The Trudeau government invoked the *War Measures Act* and sent in the army. A state of emergency was declared in Quebec, and many sovereignist activists and sympathizers were immediately harassed, arrested, and imprisoned. By the end of the "October Crisis," Laporte had been killed by his kidnappers while Cross was released. Although the PQ had opposed any form of violence from the time of its founding and strongly dissociated itself from FLQ activists, the consequences for the political work of the party

Box 10.1: The Period from the Quiet Revolution to 1975

1957	Founding of the *Alliance laurentienne*.
1960	Founding of the *Rassemblement pour l'indépendance nationale* (RIN).
1966	Founding of the *Ralliement national* (RN).
1967	Creation of the sovereignty-association movement around René Lévesque.
1968	Creation of the Parti Québécois (merging and rallying of the RIN, the MSA, and the RN).
1970	APRIL: The PQ obtains 24 per cent of the vote in the provincial elections and seven seats in the National Assembly.
	OCTOBER: Kidnapping of a minister, Pierre Laporte, and a British diplomat, James Richard Cross; the *War Measures Act* is adopted.
1973	The PQ obtains 33 per cent of the vote in the provincial elections and forms the official opposition.

were disastrous. In March 1971, the PQ saw its membership decline from 90,000 to 30,000, and even sovereignist sympathizers distanced themselves from the party. In 1973, the PQ received 33 per cent of the vote but only six seats in the National Assembly. For the first time, it had become the official opposition and the alternative to the Liberal Party.

Until 1976, the PQ, with help from other sovereignist organizations, sought to reassure its electors by proposing a gradual approach. In other words, an eventual sovereignist victory would not lead to the immediate independence of Quebec. Unions such as the *Fédération des travailleurs du Québec* (FTQ, the Workers' Federation of Quebec) now officially supported the PQ, and the social base of the sovereignty movement gradually broadened. In the 1976 elections, everyone was surprised when the PQ won 41 per cent of the vote and was called upon to form a majority government.

Two years after its victory, the PQ, in keeping with its plan, delineated its preference for Quebec sovereignty within the framework of an association with Canada. The citizens of Quebec were called upon to either support or reject the following statement:

> The Government of Quebec has made public its proposal to negotiate a new agreement with the rest of Canada, based on the equality of nations; this agreement would enable Quebec to acquire the exclusive power to make its laws, levy its taxes and establish relations abroad—in other words, sovereignty—and at the same time to maintain with Canada an economic association including a common currency; any change in political status resulting from these negotiations will be effected with approval

by the people through another referendum; on these terms, do
you give the Government of Quebec the mandate to negotiate
the proposed agreement between Quebec and Canada? (*Le
Devoir*, 1979)

Although a united front of sovereignists had formed around the PQ, the referendum failed to pass, receiving only 40 per cent of the vote. Ultimately, it was Prime Minister Trudeau who emerged victorious from the campaign. He used the victory to repatriate the Canadian Constitution in spite of opposition from the government of Quebec. The upshot was that Quebec seemed more isolated than ever within Confederation. Notwithstanding these significant setbacks, the PQ won the provincial elections of 13 April 1981 (with 49.2 per cent of the vote and 80 members elected to the legislature) following its decision to retain its sovereignist option yet not organize another referendum should they eventually obtain a second mandate.

A few months after the elections, the PQ entered a period of crisis as the party was split between its leader, René Lévesque, who was still in favour of a moderate sovereignist approach, and the majority of riding representatives who sought a more radical project. This conflict intensified when the Progressive Conservative Party, led by Brian Mulroney, came to power in Canada in the fall of 1984. The Mulroney government aimed to settle the constitutional question with Quebec through negotiation rather than confrontation. Lévesque supported the *beau risque* (the "Great Gamble") of renewed federalism, which meant turning away from the sovereignty option. The tension reached a climax when "orthodox" *péquistes* (members of the PQ), who rejected the abandonment of the party's prime focus on sovereignty, came into conflict with "revisionists," who sought to jettison the orthodox option. Some leaders left the party caucus, five government ministers resigned, and 495 delegates left the special convention that had been called to settle this question. The break-up of the PQ was only narrowly avoided by Lévesque's resignation and the organization of a party leadership race that resulted in the victory of Pierre Marc Johnson as leader. A few months later, the PQ lost the elections and became the opposition after eight years in power.

The years it spent in opposition provided sovereignists with an opportunity to take stock and make choices. The PQ established itself as the main focal point for discussing sovereignty in Quebec and the vehicle for attaining this sovereignty. The divisions within the party demonstrated the extent to which the party was capable not only of rallying and of surviving the departure of its founder but also of delineating an everyday government agenda while planning national independence. With Jacques Parizeau at the helm, the PQ gradually started to win back the electorate, opening up multi-faceted opportunities for

Box 10.2: The Parti Québécois in Power (1976–85)

1976   The PQ wins the election with 41 per cent of the vote and forms the
        government.

1979   The VII Convention of the PQ outlines its plan for sovereignty-association
        with Canada.

1980   The referendum on sovereignty-association loses, taking only 40 per cent of
        the vote.

1981   The PQ wins the provincial elections (49.2 per cent of the vote) and remains
        in power.

1982   The Prime Minister of Canada, Pierre Elliot Trudeau, repatriates the
        Canadian Constitution without the agreement of Quebec.

1985   JUNE: René Lévesque resigns; leadership race results in Pierre Marc Johnson
        being elected leader of the PQ.
        DECEMBER: The PQ loses the elections, and the Quebec Liberal Party forms
        the new government.

---

reflection on the leading constitutional, social, economic, and linguistic issues of the day. From 1987 to 1991, the PQ headed up a broad protest movement whose ranks would soon include more than just sovereignists; this movement opposed the Meech Lake Accord, which was negotiated by the Mulroney government with the Liberal government of Quebec, led by Robert Bourassa. The Meech Lake Accord made provision for constitutional change offering full participation for Quebec in Canada's constitutional evolution. The debates that occurred in Quebec on the Accord were considered very disappointing by some Quebec nationalists who preferred renewed federalism to sovereignty and who viewed the content of the Accord as a minimal response to minimal claims. By 1990, a number of ministers and MPs from the governing Progressive Conservative Party, including Lucien Bouchard, departed the government to create the Bloc Québécois (BQ), a sovereignist party at the federal level. Disaffection with the Accord also led to the formation of a new political party in Quebec, the *Action démocratique du Québec* (ADQ, Quebec Democratic Action), which was receptive to the sovereignist option. At this point, the pro-sovereignty vote was ahead in the polls. In the federal elections of 1993, the BQ captured 54 seats in Quebec and became the official opposition in Ottawa. The following year, the PQ won the election and Jacques Parizeau became premier. The time seemed ripe for another referendum bid.

Following virtually on the heels of the election, the PQ started to organize the promised referendum mobilization, and a coalition of political parties, unions, movements, and representatives of various social or professional groups formed a coalition of "Partners for Sovereignty." Coalition members participated in the major public debates that the government organized across

Box 10.3: Build-up to the Second Referendum (1986–95)

1988	Jacques Parizeau is elected leader of the PQ.
1990	Failure of the Lake Meech Accord.
1990	The Bloc Québécois (BQ) is formed at the federal level.
1992	Rejection of the Charlottetown Accord.
1993	The BQ obtains 54 seats in the federal election and forms the official opposition.
1994	Founding of a new party, the *Action démocratique du Québec* (ADQ), in the provincial arena.
	The PQ wins the provincial election.
1995	Referendum campaign and creation of a coalition, Partners for Sovereignty (unions, intellectuals, students, community groups).
	The second referendum is held; with only 49.7 per cent of the vote, the sovereignist side loses.

the province on the question of the political future of Quebec. This time, the referendum question was framed as follows:

> Do you agree that Quebec should become sovereign, after having made a formal offer to Canada for a new economic and political partnership, within the scope of the Bill Respecting the Future of Quebec, and of the agreement signed on June 12, 1995?

There was a record voter turnout of 94 per cent for the referendum of 30 October 1995. Yet, it was another setback for the sovereignists. In spite of the victory for the "no" side, the "yes" side managed to obtain 49.42 per cent of the vote. Parizeau resigned following his statement, on the evening of the referendum, that it was "money and the ethnic vote" that caused the defeat of the "yes" side (Cantin, 1995: A4). The leader of the BQ, Lucien Bouchard, succeeded Parizeau and in 1996 became leader of the PQ and premier.

During this period, the pro-sovereignty government of Quebec, like the other provincial governments, had to contend with the budgetary cuts adopted by the federal government. A period of tension arose between the PQ and several of its "partners for sovereignty," who felt extremely uncomfortable with the neoliberal policies of the government. The united front was over. Unions slowly left the coalition, dissociating themselves from a government with which they were increasingly in conflict over social issues. Similarly, community-based actors in the coalition gradually distanced themselves as well. The new referendum demanded by sovereignists was postponed. It seemed that the national question was no longer a priority. The *Mouvement national des Québécois* (MNQ, The National Movement of Quebeckers), which was responsible for the coalition of the "Partners for Sovereignty," found it difficult to keep together its coalition of partners, which soon lost most of its members. The years from 1995 to 2003 constituted a period of uncertainty for the sovereignty movement.

However, little by little, and under pressure from its activists, the sovereignty movement modified the terms of its social vision. Globalization, environment, sustainable development, and renewable energy emerged as topics in *péquiste* and *bloquiste* programs. Within the PQ, and especially at party conventions, the tension was palpable. On one side was the leadership, playing the game of economic pragmatism via a series of rigorous reforms while sidelining the national and linguistic questions. On the other side was the militant rank-and-file, meticulously promoting social-democratic values, increasingly receptive to the issue of "another globalization," and anxious to see if sovereignty and protection of the French language were still current concerns of the PQ.

The beginning of the new century was marked by an improvement in the financial situation of Quebec and especially of the federal government. Consequently, the sovereignist government, led by Bernard Landry, increasingly critiqued the fiscal imbalance that, it claimed, hampered their manoeuvrability.[5] It also attacked the federal spending power that, in the PQ's view, threatened provincial jurisdiction and prevented the Quebec government from reinvesting in certain social programs such as health and education. Meanwhile, the Supreme Court ruled on the question of the legitimacy of the referendum process. Based on the Court's opinion, the federal government passed the *Clarity Act* to set out the criteria for recognizing the validity of a "Yes" vote. Among other conditions, the act stated that the federal government's recognition of the result would be contingent upon the clarity of the proposed referendum question and of the result (for example, whether or not the result obtained was a clear expression of the will of the majority of voters).

Now on the defensive, the sovereignty movement was not able to mobilize around what seemed to be a challenge not only to Quebec's jurisdiction in social policy but also to the process for holding referendums on sovereignty. In 2003, after eight years in power, the PQ lost the elections to the Liberals, led by Jean Charest. Since 2003, despite support in the polls for the sovereignist cause, the sovereignty movement has not found a way to spark grassroots mobilization, although this was where their strength lay in the early 1990s. The PQ's stint as official opposition in the provincial government and the permanent opposition of the BQ at the federal level have helped the movement convey the basic thrust of Quebec's social and national demands. However, the two parties have been unable to completely eradicate the mistrust of former allies (e.g., the trade union movement and the women's movement) which, since the 1995 referendum, have been more distanced from the party, despite their support for sovereignty. This is demonstrated by the fact that these sectors have been increasingly contemplating a political future for the Quebec left beyond the confines of this movement.

Ongoing Debates: The Current State of the Sovereignty Movement

The history of the sovereignist movement reveals that, over the years, it has formed a solid support system based on joint political action and shared values. Through these actions and values, it has been able to maintain links among campaigners and among organizations, thereby creating a coherent network. The period from the second referendum to the present has been turbulent: a number of political actions and values have been challenged. In the next section, we will endeavour to define the current structure of the movement and the new social forces with which it must deal.

STRUCTURE OF THE MOVEMENT

In its current form, the sovereignty movement consists of constellations of organizations. In Figure 10.1 below, tasks are allocated within concentric circles, each of which represents one of the two principal forces of the Quebec sovereignty movement, namely, the BQ and PQ political machines.

The first circle of the sovereignty movement is made up of the two sovereignist parties, which reinforce each other. Without question, the older of the two (the PQ) plays the leading role in the electoral representation of the sovereignist movement. There was a time when it was possible to talk about PQ hegemony in defining the sovereignist agenda and sovereignist issues. It was the PQ that established the referendum agenda, strategies for achieving sovereignty, and the government's sovereignty-oriented political program. But this hegemony has now been altered by the existence of the BQ, which, as the sovereignist force at the federal level, is playing an increasingly important role in the sovereignty movement. Furthermore, its current leader, Gilles Duceppe, has been touted as a potential *péquiste* leader. In addition to its role within the movement as "leader of the forces of protest" (it is on the front line of the critique of federalism), the BQ has a role in revitalizing sovereignist leadership. Lucien Bouchard's rise to the leadership of the PQ, and the appeals made to Duceppe to become the PQ leader, illustrate the ties that link the two party structures.

The two political parties have a close relationship as they exchange programs and activists, ideas and action plans. The national conventions of

Figure 10.1: The Sovereignist Sphere of Influence in Quebec Politics

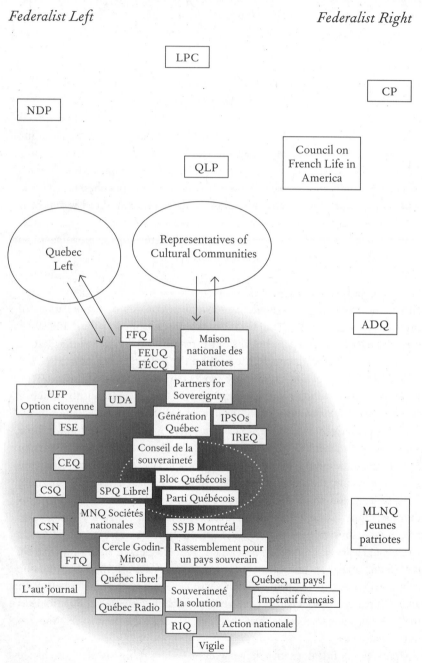

both parties welcome activists from a broad range of other social movements and provide important points of contact for sovereignists and indispensable opportunities for debate within the movement. The sovereignist political machine has extended its hand to its partners in the sovereignty movement who worked alongside the PQ during the 1995 referendum but later distanced themselves from the party. This can be seen in the interest shown by *SPQ Libre!*, an organization that brings together "union activists and progressives for a free Quebec," and in the election at the 2005 PQ convention of one of the organization's members, Monique Richard, to the position of chair of the party.

The second circle is made up of the "partners for sovereignty." The partners' organizations have very close ties to the sovereignist political parties and provide them with ongoing support. These organizations support the PQ's sovereignist strategy, whether or not the party is in power. This consists of dozens of organizations that form the nuclei of dense and specialized networks. Some of these organizations are old, while others are of a more recent vintage. They vary in size and in their stance toward PQ policies. The oldest and most active organizations are the *Société Saint-Jean Baptiste de Montréal*, the MNQ, the various regional *Sociétés nationales* and *Sociétés Saint-Jean-Baptiste* affiliated with the MNQ, and even the *Action nationale* magazine and the *Cercle Godin-Miron*. Others emerged around the 1995 referendum, either in preparation for the referendum or afterwards. These include *Génération Québec*, *Intellectuels pour la souveraineté* (Intellectuals for sovereignty), *Vigile* (an Internet site), the *Rassemblement pour l'indépendance du Québec*, *Québec, un pays!* (Quebec, a Country), *Opération Québec* (Operation Quebec), *Impératif français* (the French imperative), *Souveraineté la solution* (Sovereignty, the Solution), *Le Québécois* (the Quebecker), the *Rassemblement pour un pays souverain* (the Movement for a Sovereign Country), *SPQ Libre!* (very active in PQ and union circles), the *Conseil de la souveraineté* (the Sovereignty Council), *Québec Radio*, and the *Institut de recherche sur l'économie du Québec* (IREQ, the Research Institute on Quebec's Economy). Each of these organizations supports sovereignty in different ways: the MNQ by encouraging pride in Quebec's achievements (the organization is in charge of coordinating the activities surrounding Quebec's national holiday, the *Fête nationale du Québec*); the *Société Saint-Jean-Baptiste* by (among other things) closely following the language question and patriotic commemorations (the *Fête des Patriotes* and other themes in Quebec's history); and the *Action nationale* by serving as a forum for the exchange of ideas on the national question, including the issue of hard-line sovereignty. Other organizations, such as *Génération Québec*, *Intellectuels pour la souveraineté*, and even *SPQ Libre!* build momentum for support in specific circles (among intellectuals, "young entrepreneurs" and other business circles, and unions).

The new *Conseil de la souveraineté*, chaired by Gérald Larose (former president of the *Confédération des syndicats nationaux*—CSN, Confederation of National Trade Unions), would like to become an organization promoting sovereignty through original actions in order to maintain it on the agenda. Smaller organizations, too, have started to play an important role by taking full advantage of the Internet, circulating day-to-day sovereignist news and information on national and linguistic questions. *Internet Vigile* (Vigile, 2005) and the newspaper *Le Québécois* are leading examples of this phenomenon.

Alongside the second circle, there are the radical movements for Quebec independence. These movements have a political plan for Quebec independence, but one based on a clean break with the approach considered moderate by the PQ. For example, the *Mouvement de libération nationale du Québec*, led by Raymond Villeneuve, a former member of the FLQ, sees violence as an acceptable means of achieving its objective (the national liberation of Quebec); it also advocates a definition of the Quebec nation that is based on ethnicity. Several associations of young separatists, such as the *Mouvement des jeunes patriotes* (the "Young Patriot Movement") belong to this group. Relatively marginal, these movements and activist networks are continuing a radical tradition of separatist militancy; however, they are on the fringes of the social movement working for sovereignty.

The third circle is less *in* the movement than *on* its front step. If most organizations that belong to it may be categorized as in the sovereignist "sphere of influence," their support for the cause is sporadic and their allegiance to the PQ even more so. They are pro-sovereignty rather than actively working toward sovereignty. Their primary mission is not to defend the sovereignty option, nor have they been given a mandate to do so, even if most of them have formally supported the PQ, were clearly committed to the "Yes" side in the referendum campaigns (in particular, by contributing to the "partners for sovereignty" coalition), and from time to time still display their sympathy for the sovereignist cause. Very often, these organizations' sympathies for the sovereignist cause stem from the large number of sovereignists within their ranks. This is especially true of unions and community groups in which much of the present or former leadership is openly sovereignist, even if they are not actually *péquistes*.

Who makes up the third circle? Most of Quebec's labour confederations, including the FTQ, the CSN, the *Centrale des syndicats du Québec* (CSQ, Quebec Central Labour Body), and unions that are more sector-based, such as the *Centrale de l'enseignement du Québec* (CEQ, Quebec Teachers' Union), federations of student associations, the *Union des artistes* (UDA, Artists' Union) and the *Fédération des femmes du Québec* (FFQ, Quebec Women's Federation, the province's main coalition of women's movements). More recent networks, such as the *Réseau de vigilance* and certain networks for global social justice, recognize in a more general way the right of all peoples to political self-determination; consequently, they recognize Quebeckers as a people that have this right. However, they do not give an opinion on the validity of the Quebec sovereignty movement per se. The *Union des forces progressistes* (UFP, Union of Progressive Forces), the new political party on the left that officially came into being during the 2002 provincial elections, displays sovereignist sympathies, though it runs candidates against those of the PQ during elections. Lastly, there is a newspaper (*l'Aut'journal*—the Alternative Journal), a research institute (the *Institut du Nouveau Monde*—Institute of the New World), and a museum (*Maison nationale des patriotes*—National Patriots House).

The unions, the student movement, and the women's movement (by way of the FFQ) were active in the most recent campaign for the referendum on sovereignty. It is not unreasonable to suppose that if there is another referendum campaign, they will again provide intermittent support to the sovereignist cause. If in 2003, some of them lent explicit or implicit support to the PQ (Collombat and Gagnon, 2003: 1–14), in 2007, only the FTQ chose to support the PQ officially). Furthermore, there are quasi-structural links between the PQ and some of these organizations, which are an important source of militant *péquistes* and even *péquiste* leaders. Thus, a number of observers view the *Fédération étudiante universitaire du Québec* (FEUQ, Quebec Federation of University Students) as an organization for launching activist careers within the PQ.

The social dimensions of political debate are increasingly important for the new networks that have emerged since the early 2000s. This "social dimension" refers to the fight against poverty, the struggle for redistribution of wealth, and the general concern with social inequality and social exclusion. These forces represent a recent trend challenging the sovereignist perspective on social issues that has prevailed in Quebec since the 1970s. In the past, sovereignists on the political left argued that greater social equality would come by way of the achievement of political independence for Quebec. However, numerous activists on the critical left have raised serious questions about the division between social protest and national protest. They ask: is this division necessary or even beneficial to Quebec? This line of questioning has been taken up by a recently formed political party, the UFP, and by a young political movement, *Option citoyenne* (Citizens' Option). The latter emerged in the summer of 2004 around the figures of Françoise David, former president of the FFQ and François Saillant, former coordinator of the *Front d'action populaire en réaménagement urbain* (FRAPRU, Popular Action Front in Urban Renewal). Without necessarily challenging the objective of giving Quebec independent political status, they question the way it dominates the social project. This is also the perspective of *Option citoyenne*: "The primary concern and activity of *Option citoyenne* centres around its social project: building a Quebec based on the pursuit of the social good. The social good must be raised in conjunction with its social and political project, which must not, however, diminish the importance of the national question" (Option citoyenne, 2005).[6] Thus, this approach reverses the order of priorities: social issues have priority over national issues. This entails a complete break with the sovereignist approach to social democracy, in which social improvement depends on resolving the national question.

As marginal as it might seem from the standpoint of the sovereignist movement as a whole, this desire to reverse the "sovereignty/social project" relationship nevertheless conveys a perspective that is increasingly shared by the social forces situated on the doorstep of the sovereignist movement (the women's movement, student associations, and networks for global social justice). How did they arrive at this position?

POST-REFERENDUM TURBULENCE

Although the PQ lost the 1995 referendum and lacked the power to negotiate a constitution for a sovereign country, it remained in power and continued to manage government business. When Lucien Bouchard became premier in 1996, the third circle of social forces dissociated itself from the PQ organization for the first time. The 1996 socio-economic summits he organized aimed to build a consensus among unions, employers, and society at large regarding the importance of attaining a zero deficit in the year 2000. In spite of certain achievements in the social economy sphere, the summits failed to satisfy all demands made by student and community-based groups, which introduced a "zero poverty" plan in opposition to the proposal of the premier (Comeau *et al.*, 2002: 186–202). Moreover, over the next few years, the PQ's relationship with the women's movement deteriorated to such an extent that in 2000 Françoise David resigned as head of the FFQ. Her departure was largely related to the government's very weak response to the ten demands made by The World March of Women in 2000 (David, 2004: A7). However, the arrival in 2001 of Bernard Landry as premier helped rebuild some bridges, because he demonstrated a greater openness than did his predecessor to the issue of the war on poverty in Quebec (Dufour, 2005: 159–82).

Further political cleavage heightened the tense political atmosphere that had arisen in 1996. The Third Summit of the Americas, held in Quebec City in 2001, brought together the continent's 34 elected heads of state; its primary objective was to negotiate economic and trade issues as part of the Free Trade Area of the Americas (FTAA) agreement. It was greeted by huge demonstrations by protesters who supported alternative forms to globalization.

The summit was instrumental in restructuring the militants' sphere of action and destabilizing certain forces within the sovereignist movement. Until 2001, the PQ was more or less favourable to growth in trade relations with the other nations of the continent. It viewed these relations as an important means for supporting Quebec's economic autonomy vis-à-vis the Canadian economy and securing its future viability as a sovereign country. As social protest against free trade became better organized, it prompted Quebec's social forces to re-think their allegiance to the sovereignist movement and to build new networks of partners at the pan-Canadian and transcontinental level. With increasing clarity, Quebec's unions and leading social movements came to agree with the movement for the global social justice option, rejecting the neoliberal form of the treaties being negotiated, and gave priority to the need for solidarity over that of Quebec's political status.

When the Liberal Party came to power in Quebec in 2003, it marked the third time that the groups in the third circle of social forces distanced themselves from the sovereignist parties. These forces had surfaced during the electoral campaign and gradually formed a network of social partners (*D'abord solidaires*, Solidarity First) eager to reinsert the social agenda into the public debate. Among other objectives, the network sought to counter the rise of the ADQ, which had begun its electoral campaign with an openly neoliberal program. The first months of the Liberal government triggered further social protest. For example, a number of groups formed the *Réseau de vigilance* (a "vigilance network"), which certain labour confederations would join in the spring of 2004 at the height of their power struggle with the government. It was in the wake of these events that *Option citoyenne* was formed; meanwhile, the *Réseau de vigilance* continued its systematic opposition to those Quebec government policies it considered regressive. Gradually, Quebec's activist circles tried to formulate an alternative vision of society. In 2005, the Quebec student movement joined the general protest, launching a student strike whose scale and duration were unprecedented in Quebec. Given the virtual silence since 2002 of the PQ as an opposition party, one may ask if this ferment of social protest is moving beyond the frontiers of protest politics in order to provide the electorate with real opposition and real proposals. A brief analysis of the 2007 general elections shows that part of the protest and discontent with the PQ crystallized in votes for other parties. It remains to be seen if PQ voters defected to the ADQ, as well as supporting the new left party and the Greens.

Variations on a Sovereignist Theme

Just as in the 1980s, the PQ no longer has a monopoly on partisan representa-·tion of the sovereignty movement. Sovereignist activists, especially those on the left, now have the opportunity to channel their political energies toward new, alternative political parties and organizations that are not necessarily hostile to sovereignty. Similarly, some federalist voters in Quebec will vote for the BQ in the next federal election. The political boundary along the federalist-sovereignist divide is now blurred and intersects other political splits, especially the left-right splits, that previously played only a secondary role or were related to one's position on Quebec's political status. In sum, in the future there might be several ways of being a sovereignist. That said, what are the focal points around which today's sovereignists generally rally?

If there is one common value among all sovereignists, it is that of challenging the federal state in a fundamental way. This "shared challenge" of opposing the federal government involves both the public policies and authority of the Canadian state. It is based on the sovereignist idea that the Canadian state is not the state of Quebeckers and that the claims of Canadian "unity" that the federal government makes in Quebec about nationhood are nothing more than a myth masking a different reality. In the sovereignist view, only the Quebec government truly speaks for Quebeckers. This frontal attack is the apotheosis of the sovereignist movement's conception of Quebec's identity—based on the movement's frame of reference (values, practices, beliefs, and hopes)— and conveys its permanent disillusionment with the Canadian state's views on identity. The holding of power by the PQ ensures that this anti-establishment doctrine is communicated effectively and on a regular basis to provincial institutions. The doctrine is intended specifically for institutions under local control—such as the seat of government in Quebec, the *Fête nationale du Québec* (the holiday on June 24, also known as Saint-Jean-Baptiste Day), and the *fleur de lisé* flag—all of which have become "national" institutions. In many respects, opposition to the Canadian state continues to be important to all of the movement's partners, including its most critical elements. For example, they view the fiscal imbalance between the federal government and Quebec as undermining Quebeckers' freedom of action.

Aside from the challenge to the state, sovereignists are united behind a political option and project: the sovereignty of Quebec. It is a project built simultaneously on the assertion of national identity (preparing for sovereignty) and Quebec's independence (whose form and content they are trying to envision). This, too, involves an imperative: regardless of their activist niche, "sovereignists" believe above all in national independence and in the idea that Quebec constitutes a nation. They also believe that Quebeckers are a people, whose fulfillment and apotheosis can take only one path: the independence of Quebec and the creation of *Un pays pour le monde* ("One country for the people"), the title of the PQ program (Parti Québécois, 2001: 40). From the sovereignist standpoint, this people's presence within Canada is more of an accident of history (the Conquest) than the product of a collective and voluntary choice. The myth of Canada as consisting of two founding peoples is well and truly dead among Quebec sovereignists. Rather, it is the dream of "le Grand Soir," expressed by René Lévesque during the 1980 referendum—the very moment where Quebec will become a country. There are many different views on the method by which independence can be achieved—implementation by stages to a unilateral declaration of independence to a referendum election. There are also different views on the form that the future state would take, for example, republic versus monarchy, secularism, cultural diversity, the status of the French language, armed forces, international policy, environmental issues, and so on. Certain activists tend to pay greater attention to this second aspect of sovereignist identity, focusing less on its legitimacy than on its effectiveness. For certain left activists especially, achieving sovereignty has for too long hindered the development of a social vision for Quebec. These activists do not view a social vision as a topic for future discussion, as something that will follow later or by default once national independence has been achieved. They maintain, rather, that the movement as a whole must support it as an immediate political objective in the "here and now."

The third main line in sovereignist political identity is shared values. This includes affirming the role of the Quebec state as a key actor in Quebec society and advocating the values of social democracy by promoting a specific type of "Quebec model." Today, this aspect is very problematic for the sovereignist movement because there is no consensus on the concrete content of a political project based on social democracy. For example, would it be along the lines of Tony Blair's "Third Way," a project of the radical left, or a broadening of the specific features of the Quebec "model" of governance?

The sovereignist movement is experiencing changes that in many ways are similar to those experienced by other social movements in Canada and, indeed, throughout the world. Like the women's movement or the workers' movement, it must deal with changes in the nature of activism (actions taken for one cause are often coupled with militant actions for other causes; allegiance to an organization is no longer taken for granted, but is in constant renegotiation) and in the role of the nation-state (Quebec or Canadian). The context for these changes is twofold: (1) the globalization of trade calls for "globalized" responses on the part of social actors, and (2) the changes must be understood within the context of the crisis of the social-democratic left or, at the very least, the extreme diversity that characterizes political projects on the left.

The sovereignist movement has taken action to counter threats to its mobilization capability. Its views since the early 2000s, and especially since Jean Charest assumed the reins of power in Quebec, have became much more open to the new problems of globalization, economic equity (sustainable development, fair trade), reinvestment in the health and education sectors, and environmental issues. Nonetheless, this new openness has not been without its difficulties and has sometimes met resistance. The language question has become less and less important, though it can still generate lively verbal sparring in the workshops of PQ conventions; the openness of the PQ to "new Quebeckers" is more and more a concrete and valued practice, even if the real space allowed to these neo-Quebeckers inside the caucus is still a question (Dutrisac, 2006). In June 2005, the party undertook a consultation on the renewal of its structure and program. As a result, it has opened itself to new political groups and is much more oriented to the left side of the political arena. However, these reforms did not challenge the fundamental aims of the sovereignty movement, namely, national self-affirmation, sovereignty as a real possibility, and social democracy as a primary orientation in the party's ideology and program.

Through ongoing dialogue and confrontation with the broader network of actors in the movement, the movement's political party leaders (the PQ and the BQ) are once again reshaping the vision of Quebec sovereignty. However, the position of the movement has now become paradoxical: the BQ seems to be at its peak, while the PQ is making major internal changes, restructuring both its leadership and its program. Since 2003, coalitions of other social forces seem to have taken on the role of opposing the neoliberal policies of the Charest government. As noted previously, these forces are not the main group in the sovereignty movement, yet neither are they separate from it. The political history of Quebec has repeatedly demonstrated that the sovereignty movement cannot remain a major force without the support of the broad network of social and political actors, just as the left cannot hope to place its demands on the agenda without support from all or part of the sovereignty movement. In a sense, social democracy in Quebec has become a sovereignist value, just as sovereignty has become a social democratic value.

Achievements of the Sovereignist Movement

Although the sovereignist movement has not yet succeeded in its main goal of establishing Quebec as an independent nation-state, it has had important effects on public policy and on Quebec society. What makes the sovereignty movement unique is that it has been able to draw on a wide range of actions. As a force within the government, the movement has been able to implement linguistic and social policies through the PQ. As a social protest movement within Canada, it established a power relationship with the central government that yielded tangible results.

When the PQ came to power in 1976, it passed a range of important and progressive legislation, much of which incorporated the party's program. This legislation included the *Charter of the French Language* (Bill 101), which established the status of the French language for Quebec's businesses, workers, educational institutions, and public areas and in so doing transformed the linguistic character of the province and especially the City of Montréal. In addition, the government passed laws on abortion, the financing of political parties, and automobile insurance. Later, the area of health and social services, too, would experience strong growth, especially with the introduction of local community service centres. In the 1990s and 2000s, three sectors of public policy were particularly important for the PQ government: child care policy on young children and primary school children, economic development policy, and recognition and support for community-based actors. In these three fields, Quebec set itself apart from the other Canadian provinces through stronger government intervention in economic regulation and in its relationships with civil society.

As a force for social protest, the sovereignty movement's constant presence in the Quebec political sphere has allowed the provincial government (even when the latter was led by the Liberal Party) to establish a stronger position with the federal government and obtain specific legislative and financial benefits for Quebec. For example, if Quebec is not "a province like other provinces" in the Canadian confederation, then this is largely because the sovereignty movement and its sympathizers have for over 40 years threatened to separate Quebec from the rest of the country. Consequently, Quebec exercises broader jurisdiction than the other provinces in the areas of immigration and linguistic policy and has greater latitude in the areas of foreign policy and diplomatic representation abroad.

In addition, the existence of the sovereignty movement partially explains Quebec's distinctive form of governance. Compared to other Canadian provinces, Quebec gives social actors a greater role in the public decision-making process (this is entirely aside from the role of the so-called "Quebec model"). Thus, Quebec adopted a policy of recognition and financing of the community sector in September 2001 that has no equivalent in the rest of Canada. This policy, which is the result of years of mobilization, provides basic financing even for those groups that struggle with the government and facilitates the representation of their voices in the public debates. The connections we have described between the core of the sovereignty movement (especially the PQ) and the third circle of sovereignty supporters have played a role in establishing this particular model of governance; the fact remains that whenever the PQ was in power, it was more receptive to the demands of its social partners than were the other political parties.

On the other hand, when the PQ behaved as a monopolistic force, it forced the militant left to voice its demands more through community-based circles than through the political party. In the name of sovereignty and the need to build a consensus among progressive forces, any dissent expressed by these actors regarding the PQ's social vision was put on the back burner during elections and referendum campaigns. Since 1995, the exchange of ideas, concerns, and identities between these social forces and the PQ has slackened to the point where some observers believe that there will eventually be a split in the sovereignty movement between the PQ and its social partners.

All things considered, the sovereignty movement has played an active role in building a sense of belonging to a Quebec nation; most Quebeckers now agree that this national consciousness is a reality. When the PQ—the core of the movement—was the governing party, it helped improve Quebeckers' access to rights (social rights and representation rights as a distinct community in Canada) while strengthening political participation mechanisms for Quebec citizens. Stated differently, over the past 30 years Quebec's "citizenship regime" (Jenson, 1998: 235–62), which is different from the Canadian citizenship regime, has derived largely from the presence and political activities of the sovereignty movement.

Conclusion

By viewing the sovereignty movement as a social movement, it is possible to highlight the complex forces that have intersected it over time. Moreover, this can be accomplished without limiting the national question in Quebec to an analysis of the PQ or the BQ. For more than 40 years, the question of the political status of Quebec has constituted a central theme in Canadian and Quebec politics. It is around this question that activist identities, and identities in which the notion of citizenship is central, have been forged in Quebec and the rest of Canada.

At a minimum, three challenges must be addressed: The core of the movement, especially the PQ, must be effectively and convincingly reformed. Since it is no longer a question of ensuring Quebec's recognition within Canada but, rather, of separating Quebec from Canada, the PQ's political project must be able to express this change in a concrete way, especially through the definition of the national project. There must be a restructuring of links with the various circles of potential movement partners, especially social partners. The sovereignty movement has been based on Quebec's self-affirmation and the mobilization of two types of protest—nationalist protest and social protest. Over 30 years, sovereignty and social democracy in Quebec have fused in several ways: sovereignty has become a social democratic value, and social democracy has become a sovereignist value. It remains to be seen how long the sovereignty movement can survive the tensions stemming from the gradual retrenchment of the Quebec state, a retrenchment that will likely shatter the long-standing alliance between Quebec nationalists and social democrats. What will happen if progressive forces in Quebec life choose not to support a national project in which social democracy is no longer the main goal? Similarly, it remains to be seen if the sovereignty movement will survive the ongoing restructuring on the left, not only in Quebec but throughout western Canada and the Maritimes. The sovereignist project may very well draw on the social democratic model; however, that model is in a crisis that will directly affect the sovereignty movement. Struggles around globalization could very well become another central theme in political life.

Notes

1. We are most grateful to Denis Monière, Éric Montpetit, and Miriam Smith for their assistance and helpful comments in the preparation of this paper.

2. Jean-François Lisée is former policy advisor to Premier Lucien Bouchard.

3. Lionel Groulx (1878–1967) was one of the main intellectuals of the French-Canadian nationalists of the first half of the twentieth century. His essays and articles, published in the *Action française* and in *Action nationale*, sparked the first generation of Quebec nationalists, such as André Laurendeau (1912–68). Laurendeau, for his part, was for a long time editor of the review, the *Action nationale*, a leading Quebec journalist and co-director of the Royal Commission on Bilingualism and Biculturalism (the "B and B" Commission) (1963–69). He was a major figure in Quebec journalism and Quebec political thought before and during the Quiet Revolution. See Monière and Laurendeau (1983) and Bock (2004).

4. This anti-colonial approach, very present in some nationalists' writings such as that of Pierre Vallières (1968) and in the discourse of the FLQ, influenced Quebec nationalism, at least at the beginning. Along with this idea of "liberation" comes a change in the self-designation of people living in Quebec. From French Canadian they progressively became Quebeckers.

5. The notion of fiscal imbalance is contested in Canada. For the Quebec government, "fiscal imbalance" is used to describe the situation which Quebec and other provinces experience with regard to public finances: "given the current occupation of taxation fields, they do not have enough revenue to finance their program responsibilities whereas, conversely, the federal government has at its disposal more revenue than it needs to finance its own areas of jurisdiction" (Commission on Fiscal Imbalance, 2001: 9).

6. *Option citoyenne* and the UFP merged to form the new provincial political party, *Québec solidaire* (QS) in 2006. QS supports sovereignty but only as a tool for achieving social justice, not as an end in itself.

References and Further Reading

Anderson, Benedict. 1991. *Imagined Communities: Reflections on the Origin and Spread of Nationalism*. Rev. ed. London: Verso.

Assemblée nationale du Québec. 2003. *Résolution unanime sur la nation québécoise*. 30 October. <http://www.saic.gouv.qc.ca/publications/resolutions/20031030.pdf>.

Bloc Québécois. "Le scandale des commandites." <http://www.blocquebecois.org/fr/default.asp>.

Bloc Québécois. "Paul Martin et les paradis fiscaux." <http://www.blocquebecois.org/fr/default.asp>.

Bloc Québécois. "Pour éliminer le déséquilibre fiscal." <http://www.bloc quebecois.org/fr/default.asp>.

Bloc Québécois. "Pour faire le ménage à Ottawa." <http://www.blocquebecois.org/fr/default.asp>.

Bloc Québécois. "Pour protéger les intérêts économiques du Québec à Ottawa." <http://www.blocquebecois.org/fr/default.asp>.

Bock, Michel. 2004. *Quand la nation débordait les frontières : Les minorités françaises dans la pensée de Lionel Groulx*. Montréal: Éditions Hurtubise HMH.

Bourque, Gilles, and Jules Duchastel. 1996. *L'identité fragmentée: Nation et citoyenneté dans les débats constitutionnels canadiens 1941–1992*. Montréal: Fides.

Bourque, Gilles, and Anne Legaré. 1979. *Le Québec, La question nationale*. Paris: Petite collection Maspéro.

Cantin, Philippe. 1995. "Parizeau blame l'argent et le vote ethnique." *Le Devoir*, 31 October: A4.

Coleman, William D. 1984. *The Independence Movement in Quebec, 1945–1980*. Toronto: University of Toronto Press.

Collombat, Thomas, and Mona-Josée Gagnon. 2003. "Le syndicalisme québécois face à la résurgence d'une droite antisyndicale." *Chroniques internationales de l'IRES* 83 (July): 1–14.

Comeau, Yvan, *et al.* 2002 "L'économie sociale et le Sommet socio-économique de 1996: le bilan des acteurs sur le terrain." *Nouvelles pratiques sociales* 15(2): 186–202.

Commission on Fiscal Imbalance. 2001. *Fiscal Imbalance: Problems and Issues*. Quebec: Gouvernement du Québec.

Couture, Jocelyne, Kai Nielsen, and Michel Seymour (Eds.). 1996. *Rethinking Nationalism*. Supplementary Volume, *Canadian Journal of Philosophy*. Calgary: University of Calgary Press.

CROP. January 2006. "Sondage sur la souveraineté-partenariat." <http://www.cyberpresse.ca/article/20060202/CPACTUALITES/602020436/5358/CPPRESSE>.

David, Françoise. 2004. "Pour gouverner à gauche, il faut penser à gauche." *Le Devoir*, 29 September: A7.

Dufour, Pascale. 2005. "L'adoption du projet de loi 112 au Québec: le produit d'une mobilisation ou une simple question de conjoncture politique?" *Politique et Sociétés* 23(2/3): 159–82.

Dutrisac, Robert. 2006. "Malaise au PQ, qui perd deux dirigeants." *Le Devoir,* 12 October: A3.

Fraser, Graham. 1984. *P.Q.: René Lévesque and the Parti Québécois in Power.* Toronto: Macmillan.

Gellner, Ernest. 1989. *Nations et nationalisme.* Paris: Payot.

Jenson, Jane. 1995. "What's in a Name?" In H. Johnston and B. Klandermans (eds.), *Nationalist Movements and Public Discourse: Social Movements and Culture.* Minneapolis: University of Minnesota Press. 107–26.

Jenson, Jane. 1998. "Reconnaître les différences: sociétés distinctes, régimes de citoyenneté, partenariats." In Guy Laforest and Roger Gibbins (eds.), *Sortir de l'impasse: les voies de la reconciliation.* Montreal: IRPP. 235–62.

Jenson, Jane. 1999. "La modernité pluraliste du Québec: De la nation à la citoyenneté. Un avenir construit sur le respect des droits, la reconnaissance de la contribution de tous à l'histoire et la participation aux institutions politiques." *Le Devoir,* 31 July: A9.

Keating, Michael. 1997. *Les défis du nationalisme moderne: Québec, Catalogne, Écosse.* Montreal: Les Presses de l'Université de Montréal.

Laurendeau, André, Patricia Smart, and Dorothy Howard. 1991. *The Diary of André Laurendeau: Written during the Royal Commission on Bilingualism and Biculturalism 1964–1967.* Halifax: Lorimer.

Levine, Marc V. 1990. *The Reconquest of Montreal: Language Policy and Social Change in a Bilingual City.* Philadelphia: Temple University Press.

Lisée, Jean-François. 2005. "Des radicaux au PQ? Normal." *L'Actualité* 30(12): 44.

McRoberts, Kenneth. 1988. *Quebec: Social Change and Political Crisis.* Toronto: McClelland and Stewart.

McRoberts, Kenneth. 1997. *Misconceiving Canada: The Struggle for National Unity.* Oxford: Oxford University Press.

Monière, Denis. 1981. *Ideologies in Quebec.* Toronto: University of Toronto Press.

Monière, Denis, and André Laurendeau. 1983. *Et le destin d'un peuple.* Montreal: Québec Amériques.

Morchain, Janet Kerr, and Mason Wade. 1984. *Search for a Nation: Canada's Crises in French-English Relations, 1759–1980.* Toronto: Fitzhenry and Whiteside.

National Assembly of Québec. 2003. <http://www.saic.gouv.qc.ca/publications/resolutions/20031030.pdf>.

Option citoyenne. 2005. *Démarche d'Option citoyenne sur la question nationale et constitutionnelle.* Letter. 27 April 2005. <http://www.optioncitoyenne.ca/pivot/entry.php?id=215>.

Parti Québécois. 2001. *Un pays pour le monde, Programme du Parti Québécois, version abrégée.* Montreal: Parti Québécois.

Pinard, Maurice, Robert Bernier, and Vincent Lemieux. 1997. *Un combat inachevé.* Quebec: Presses de l'Université du Québec.

Rocher, François, and Guy Lecours. 2003. "La 'nation' ne tombe pas du ciel. Sur les rapports structurants des nationalismes en concurrence. Les cas de la Belgique et du Canada." In Raphaël Canet and Jules Duchastel (eds.), *La nation en débat. Entre modernité et postmodernité*. Montreal: Athéna. 111–33.

Rumilly, Robert. 1975. *Histoire de la Société Saint-Jean-Baptiste de Montréal*. Montreal: L'Aurore.

Ryan, Claude. 2002. *Les Valeurs libérales et le Québec moderne, une perspective historique sur l'apport du Parti libéral du Québec à l'édification du Québec d'hier et d'aujourd'hui*. Quebec: Parti libéral du Québec.

Thiesse, Anne-Marie. 1999. *La création des identités nationales, Europe XVIIIᵉ–XXᵉ siècle*. Paris: Seuil.

Traisnel, Christophe. 2004. *Le nationalisme de contestation. Le rôle des mouvements nationalistes dans la construction politique des identités wallonne et québécoise en Belgique et au Canada*. Ph.D. thesis, Université de Montréal, Université de Paris II.

Vallières, Pierre. 1968. *Nègres blancs d'Amérique*. Montreal: Parti pris.

Vallières, Pierre. 1971. *White Niggers of America*. Trans. Joan Pinkham. Toronto: McClelland and Stewart.

Vigile. 2005. <http://www.vigile.net/>.

PART FOUR
Environment, Disability, and Health

ELEVEN

The Environmental Movement in Canada: Retreat or Resurgence?

Judith I. McKenzie

In the 37 years since the first Earth Day was held in the US, there have been some profound changes to the environmental movement in North America. On that April morning in 1970, more than 20 million Americans took to the streets to celebrate nature and the environment. By all accounts, it was the largest demonstration in American history, far surpassing the biggest Vietnam War protests and Martin Luther King Jr.'s famous "March on Washington" (Mowrey and Redmond, 1993). Both Houses of Congress recessed in order to allow elected representatives to join their constituents in observing the event. At the time, it was described as a protest that caught the political establishment by total surprise. Since that time, environmentalism has waxed and waned at the national level in both Canada and the US, while local disputes have ignited activism and, on occasion, militancy. Some Canadian examples that come to mind are clear-cutting in Clayoquot Sound, direct action protests by Greenpeace, protests against Daishowa by the Lubicon, water diversion from the Great Lakes, and more recently the dispute over the Devils Lake project in North Dakota.[1]

There is general agreement that the environmental movement includes most formal and informal participation and communication organized to prevent harmful exposures to toxic substances and resource exploitation that could threaten or interfere with the health and survival of the human and non-human world. It is also a "form of collective behaviour in which leadership as well as rank and file membership tend to crystallize at some times and become amorphous or disappear altogether at other times" (Sperber, 2003: 6). There is clear evidence that some green groups in Canada, like their counterparts elsewhere, have become increasingly professionalized or institutionalized. These groups—described by Jeremy Wilson as "the majors"—include the Nature Conservancy of Canada, the Canadian Nature Federation (CNF), World Wildlife Fund (WWF) Canada, the David Suzuki Foundation, Ducks

Unlimited Canada, Greenpeace, the Canadian Parks and Wilderness Society (CPAWS), and the Sierra Club of Canada (SCC). All are hierarchical in organization with boards of directors and full-time professional staff. There also is considerable evidence that participatory protest continues to have an important presence in the environmental movement (May, 2006, 1990).

In North America, increasingly, environmental policy-making has become a shell game within an international diplomacy and trade protectionist framework. Two examples that clearly demonstrate this are the American closure of its border to Canadian beef and the softwood lumber dispute. In both cases, these decisions appear to have been driven by Canadian reticence to support American international initiatives and by the desire to shore up and protect American farm and forestry interests. In other words, trans-border and international environmental issues have become heavily politicized.

This chapter argues that the Canadian environmental movement can best be understood through the lens of social movement theory and political opportunity structure. Although there was an early wave of environmentalism that occurred prior to the 1960s, it was driven more by the idea of celebrating nature than it was by challenging the status quo and questioning the environmental degradation associated with unbridled capitalism. Since the 1960s, environmentalism in Canada has involved groups and citizens concerned about the quality of air and water and the unsustainable practices used by industry in exploiting our natural resources. These ideals and interests are often referred to as post-materialist values. Green groups have often aligned with each other in presenting a united front aimed at achieving a cultural and knowledge shift. As will be discussed later in this chapter, this is presently occurring in the field of climate change.

Although most environmental groups use conventional tactics in attempting to educate the public, some have been known to use direct action—for example, monkey-wrenching, placing oneself between a whaling ship and a pod of whales, and Greenpeace's sailing into a nuclear testing area—in order to gain publicity and garner media attention. Occasionally, green groups seize on an opportunity in order to score political points when the public's attention is focused on an environmental issue. Events such as the nuclear accident at Chernobyl or the Walkerton water contamination crisis had the effect of holding the public's attention for a prolonged period of time. Kathryn Harrison (1999: 124) claims that only when an issue can hold the attention of the public will it become an issue to which governments will respond.

Within social movement theory, environmentalism has been characterized "as a new form of decentralized, multiform, network-oriented, pervasive social movement" (Castells, 1997: 113). In the Canadian case, these collective actions have mobilized in four waves of contention, each defined by a series of different factors, including pivotal events, an inspirational writer or leader, and the presence of a collective consciousness among supporters. There is a wide array of green organizations in Canada, both formal and informal; some are driven by moderate reform environmentalism, while others are more radical, employing a diverse set of tactics and strategies to affect change. As environmental issues increasingly become international (climate change, hazardous waste storage, water shortages, to mention just a few), Canadian groups have been forced to broaden their scope and increasingly join international efforts. There are also specific issue coalitions and national and region-specific networks. Collectively, all of these groups constitute the Canadian environmental movement.

Waves of Environmentalism

FIRST-WAVE ENVIRONMENTALISM

In North America, first-wave environmentalism is largely associated with the writings of Henry David Thoreau, the wilderness movement spearheaded by John Muir, and the conservation movement led by Aldo Leopold and Robert Marshall. American transcendentalism, a liberal spinoff from Puritanism, was a nineteenth-century philosophic and literary movement centred in the Boston area (Opie, 1998). The transcendentalists expressed doubts about Enlightenment empiricism; one of its chief proponents, Ralph Waldo Emerson, wanted "nature and nature's God to enfold him in a mystical union" (Opie, 1998: 193). Transcendentalists believed that human values did not spring from man's conquest of nature; rather, they emanated from wild nature itself. They implored their political leaders to rethink the ideal of industrial progress and to follow a different path (Opie, 1998). At the time, many of these transcendentalists were dismissed as oddballs who were wildly out of touch with mainstream thinking. Interestingly enough, more than a century later, many of their works were embraced by the second-wave of the environmental movement. Thoreau, in particular, became a counterculture hero when his ideas were included in Skinner's *Walden Two* (1962 [1948]), which became the counterculture manifesto for the Woodstock generation. Written after World War II, the book chronicled a fictional experimental community premised on cooperation and sustainability rather than individualism, consumerism, competitiveness, and the pursuit of wealth; it produced its own food and governed itself through its own form of direct democracy. The transcendental ideals of a holistic and natural world, a fundamental need to remain in contact with nature, and a naturalistic ethic struck a chord with second-wave environmentalists in the 1960s and 1970s. Although transcendentalism did not predict the ruin or breakdown of society, it did raise serious questions about blind trust in science and the unfettered profit-taking of capitalism (Opie, 1998). Thoreau's musings about agriculture are credited with laying the groundwork for organic farming, and his recommendation that each New England town should preserve a primitive forest of no less than 500 acres made him a visionary for modern timber conservation (Opie, 1998).

John Muir's (1838–1914) leadership and vision led to the founding of the Sierra Club in 1892 as well as the creation of six national parks in the US. Wilderness tourism flourished, and Muir's articles and books appealed to a national audience that soon embraced wilderness protection. Historians credit his wilderness philosophy as a visionary one in which he advanced the idea that wild nature provided an escape from American urban industrial society (Opie, 1998). Like the transcendentalists before him, Muir abhorred materialistic greed and was critical of modern science. And like Thoreau, who retreated to a small cabin on Walden Pond, Muir left society behind to seek refuge in Yosemite Valley. His fame grew, and his message spread. By 1915, 335,000 visitors enjoyed the American National Park system as compared to just 69,000 in 1908 (Opie, 1998).

The conservation movement founded at the beginning of the twentieth century by Gifford Pinchot had less altruism. Unlike the wilderness movement whose vision was for improved human health as well as preserving the aesthetics of nature, the conservation movement "sought only to ensure that resources such as minerals, timber and fish were used wisely and not squandered so there would always be plenty of them to support a growing economy" (Dryzek, 2005: 14). Indeed, there are many similarities between the conservation movement of the first wave and the wise use movement[2] in the second. Nevertheless, many of these early leaders, including John Muir, Aldo Leopold, and Robert Marshall were not scientists but impassioned amateurs driven by their love of nature. They did not embrace political sensitivities and were indifferent to how their views resonated with people of money and influence (Manes, 1990).

In Canada, first-wave environmentalism was slower to take root. In 1929, a Canadian journalist offered the explanation for this relative slowness to an American conservationist: "You cannot expect from the Canadian public anything like the response ... in the United States, because ... you have suffered and lost much of your wilderness and we are merely in the process of losing it" (Killan and Warecki, 1992: 3).

Naturalist organizations, which did not become established until the early twentieth century, were inspired particularly by the nature writings of Ernest Thompson Seton, who in 1898 published *Wild Animals I Have Known*, and Charles G.D. Roberts, who published *The Kindred of the Wild* in 1902 (McKenzie, 2002). Nature writing was given a new impetus by Grey Owl, an Englishman who successfully posed as a First Nations Canadian. Also, the experiences of cottaging, canoe-tripping, and going to summer camp became an important part of the lives of many urban Canadians and strengthened their association with the land and nature. Possibly the most visible manifestations of this were the paintings of Tom Thomson and the Group of Seven. Painted after World War I, they took their inspiration "directly from the tangled disorder of black spruce, swamp, and wind-chopped northern lakes" (Macdonald, 1991: 85). The popularity of these paintings helped to foster a growing affection of city dwellers for the beauty of Canada's natural landscape.

Unlike the American first wave of environmentalism, its manifestation in Canada was distinctly different. Its message was couched in the language of the beauty of nature, not in the language of anti-establishment and counterculture. And, rather than being conveyed through philosophy, the message of the Canadian movement was conveyed through visual appeals and artistic expression.

SECOND-WAVE ENVIRONMENTALISM

New types of collective action—civil rights, peace, the women's movement, the gay and lesbian rights movement, and the second-wave environmental movement—began to appear in the early 1960s throughout North America. As outlined in the Introduction, these movements were unlike organized interest and advocacy groups in terms of their focus, in their promotion of certain values, and in the strategies and tactics used.

Given the strong social democratic tradition in northern Europe and the badly damaged infrastructure in much of Western Europe after World War II, it was widely believed that second-wave environmentalism would develop there first. However, growing concerns among Americans over the negative effects of urban and industrial forces spurred the second-wave in the US. According to Ulf Hjelmar, "The environmental movement in the 1960s pointed to the connection between these problems [including limited and contaminated water supplies and inadequate collection and disposal of waste and sewage] and the way in which industrial society in general treated nature" (Hjelmar, 1996: 125). Moreover, the US had a rich history and tradition of conservation. Coupled with the widespread skepticism about industrialization and urbanization, it provided fertile ground for the development of an environmental movement.

The very affluence that was enjoyed by middle-class young Americans brought with it a marked increase in their hopes of what their environment *should* be like. Increasingly, they were critical of the "system"—the government, the military-industrial complex, and universities. For a variety of reasons, the 1960s and 1970s spawned a significant reconsideration of the liberal democratic tradition that had dominated Western political thought for decades. For the most part, this era of general protest tended to be identified as an adjunct of the New Left, which was committed to revising socialist theory (McKenzie, 2002). However, because many of its ideas had regressive social and economic consequences—such as higher prices for commodities as a result of environmental measures as well as higher unemployment—the environmental movement was often perceived as an elitist, middle-class phenomenon that threatened the standard of living of the working class (Eckersley, 1992). Despite these criticisms, by the mid-1960s a genuine counterculture had emerged and shook the foundations of the values that North Americans had come to take for granted (Tokar, 1992). Coupled with this value change was a growing sense of urgency as air quality declined and lakes and rivers were dying after prolonged periods of uncontrolled dumping of sewage and industrial wastes.

Thus, the second-wave of the American environmental movement cannot be understood as a social movement with roots in democratic socialism, liberalism, or conservatism. Rather, it came out of the distinctive change in values that combined elements of those existing ideologies along with specific green ideals, such as sustainability, participatory democracy, social justice, peace, and communalism. As a social movement, therefore, second-wave environmentalism was driven by value change and was based on ideals and political beliefs that championed the common good rather than individual self-interest.

As Emerson and Thoreau were to American first-wave environmentalism, Rachel Carson and her book, *Silent Spring* (1962), were to the second-wave. For 31 weeks, *Silent Spring* was on the *New York Times* bestseller list. With a lifelong interest in nature, particularly the oceans, Carson sounded the alarm that synthetic poisons, particularly chlorinated hydrocarbons such as DDT, were poisoning the entire globe. For some 20 years, DDT had been seen as the saviour in the war against pests and had even won its Swiss inventor, Paul Muller, the 1948 Nobel Prize (McKenzie, 2002). What was so significant about Carson's work is that it challenged a powerful corporate member in the American economic system—the chemical industry. A diminutive, soft-spoken nature writer succeeded where many others had failed—her work raised doubts in the minds of Americans about the primary activity of large American industry. Despite personal attacks on Carson herself and on her scientific credentials, she provided a credible and compelling analysis of the dangers of common pesticides. Most important, *Silent Spring* offered a new form of criticism that deliberately combined science and advocacy on the grounds that evidence of public danger entailed a moral duty to warn about existing and potential harm. In addition, her work invoked the issue of environmental rights. As Carson's biographer pointed out: "The debate between Carson and the scientific establishment was not fundamentally over scientific fact or institutional objectivity. It was a quarrel about values, and consequently, about power" (Lear, 1997: 415).

THIRD- AND FOURTH-WAVE ENVIRONMENTALISMS

Although many environmentalists believe that the movement can best be understood as having only two waves, others believe that there have been two subsequent waves—or, at the very least, ripples—in the 1980s and 1990s. Both of these subsequent waves were much weaker than the first two, and each reflected a different perception of the environment.

Third-wave environmentalism has been characterized as having a much more conciliatory tone than the "all or nothing" rhetoric of the first two waves. While second-wavers were interested in the most rigorous standards possible and were inclined to use litigation regularly as a policy tool, third- and fourth-wavers were more flexible and recognized that any solutions to environmental problems needed to make use of the marketplace (McKenzie, 2002). To this end, there was a certain willingness on the part of some green groups to sit down with business and discuss compromises. As such, the buzzwords of third-wave environmentalism were "market-based incentive, demand side management, technological optimism, non-adversarial dialogue and regulatory flexibility" (Dowie, 1996: 105–06). This strategy alienated a number of green groups who argued that it was nothing short of a sell-out to corporate interests. In terms of tactics and strategies, the "essence of third-wave environmentalism was the shift from the court room to the boardroom" (Dowie, 1996: 106).

Fourth-wave environmentalism began in the mid-1990s and continues to this day. It has been described by Beder (1997) as a life-and-death public relations battle, in part because lobbying and public relations had become an industry in themselves both within government and outside it. Corporations took steps to give the impression that they were becoming greener and that they had become good environmental citizens. With the collapse of communism and the rhetoric and discourse that had guided politics for half a century (pitting West against East, good against evil, and capitalism against communism) a vacuum was created, which multinational corporations rushed to fill. According to Brian Tokar (1992), the last obstacle to the complete hegemony of multinational corporate capitalism has been the growth of ecological awareness in the industrialized countries. Environmental groups themselves have morphed into organizations that are competing with one another for charitable donations, and many have undergone significant changes in this competitive environment. It has been estimated that there are some 80,000 registered charities in Canada alone, and competition for donations is fierce (Reynolds, 2004). Seed money that governments had previously given to non-profits in the social sector as well as to green groups such as Pollution Probe was cut off in the mid-1990s with the resurgence of neoliberal political practices of downsizing and deregulating. In many ways, governments of the day believed that funding provided to non-profits expanded their capacity to be critical of government policies and programs. Green groups—like other charities—have adopted the language of survival, using "terms like branding, demographic shifts and target audiences" (Reynolds, 2004: 46). In other words, green groups, like others resisting corporate tie-ins and pandering to pop-cultural trends, recognize this new reality. Greenpeace, one of the most successful environmental groups in the 1970s and 1980s whose causes such as Save the Whales led to an international whaling ban in 1986, has been particularly hard hit in the early 2000s. Its American membership has been reduced by more than half, and its Canadian branch has experienced similar problems in retaining members. Other established environmental groups are struggling as well in the current competitive culture among charities and NGOs. The youth who had mobilized around environmental issues in the 1970s and 1980s now favour other causes (Reynolds, 2004: 47–48).

Environmental movement organizations (EMOs), like other social movements, are faced with choices between mass participatory or more professional forms of organization and between unconventional and conventional forms of tactics and strategies. It is clear that some of Canada's larger green organizations have become more professionalized and have adapted to a mass media age. However, the question that has emerged is "whether these adaptations ultimately weaken the capacities of EMOs to effect the mass mobilizations from which the environmental movement's power initially derived its power" (Rootes, 1999: 3). There is evidence from green groups in Europe that this professionalization—or what some term institutionalization—has become widespread in their environmental movements, causing a growing disillusionment with major EMOs as they are seen as being exclusive and paternalistic. This disillusionment has fuelled efforts to develop new forms of organizations that are sufficiently flexible to include the diversity of the environmental justice movement as well as responding to changing local circumstances (Rootes, 1999). In order to provide a united front and in order to foster solidarity, in the late 1970s green groups of all stripes and their leaders began to practice a networking strategy aimed at promoting a universal identity. Beginning with the Canadian Environmental Advisory Council under the leadership of Dr. Don Chant as Chair, the network soon was renamed the ENGO Network. Its objective was to ensure that green groups of all shapes, sizes, and capabilities would have some access to bureaucrats within Environment Canada. Renamed the Canadian Environmental Network (CEN) in 1977, this coalition of over 800 environmental groups operates through 11 regional networks, each of which has staff support.

Canadian Environmental Network (CEN)

Because of Canada's federal system, shared jurisdiction over the environment, health, agriculture, and natural resources presents challenges to green organizations in this country. As such, they are not as easily categorized as they would be in a smaller and unitary political system.

Institutionalism was a critical factor in influencing the Canadian environmental movement when the CEN was created in the late 1970s. The federal government and Environment Canada, in particular, believed they had a role to play in introducing some degree of rationality and organization to environmental policy-making. Certain high-profile green groups were assured of being given positions on government organizations, to the frustration of smaller groups that were less organized and resourced. The CEN allowed all green organizations to meet in a forum where they could search for consensus on environmental issues and share information, and it formalized the selection of which groups would participate in national and international conferences. While smaller green groups now have greater access to Environment Canada, there is no question that the democratization of the CEN has come about at a cost to some of the major professionalized green groups, who believe that government funding for its operation may have compromised its autonomy. While CEN may have some detractors, there appears to be a widespread agreement that it has been a positive development for the environmental movement in Canada. Most federal government departments now believe that the CEN is preferable to the old system because it is transparent, bilingual, and is supported by most of the environmental community.

For governments, the CEN has proven to be a central clearinghouse for environmental research. Its mandate is to protect the earth and promote ecologically sound ways of life, and its permanent staff of eight employees is located in Ottawa. It receives financial support from Environment Canada and self-describes as being independent and non-partisan. Its role is not to develop policy or take positions on environmental issues but to work directly with concerned citizens and organizations and to help organizations make connections with others who share similar concerns.

CEN consists of 11 caucuses—agriculture, atmosphere/energy, biotechnology, environmental assessment, forestry, health, mining, toxics, water, international program, and youth—each staffed by a coordinator. Each caucus is self-directing but is subject to CEN's by-laws and policies. A vacant position on a caucus is open to all CEN members in good standing. The delegate selection process is very democratic and has been designed to ensure that not just a select few from an elite group of environmental NGOs are chosen to be key players in government consultations. For example, the Agriculture Caucus consists of a caucus coordinator and representatives from such groups as the Crooked Creek Conservancy Society (Athabasca, Alberta), the SCC (Ottawa), the New Brunswick Partners in Agriculture, the Peace and Environmental Resource Centre (Ottawa), *Mouvement au courant* (Quebec), and Beyond Factory Farming (British Columbia).

Issue-Driven Alliances

On special occasions, environmental issues are so sweeping that there have been specific alliances among key groups and individuals. Two policy areas where such coalitions have formed are climate change and trade and the environment. In 1996 in response to concerns that the WTO appeared to be moving in the direction of declaring multilateral treaties on the environment (e.g., the Montreal Protocol and the Framework Convention on Climate Change) as barriers to trade, the SCC joined forces with the Council of Canadians, the Polaris Institute, and the CLC. One of Canada's leading environmental lawyers who had been active in the CUFTA debate was recruited to work with the group. These kinds of alliances mobilize in an ad hoc way in response to international initiatives or perceived crises.

Green Organizations in Canada

Ideally, a vibrant domestic environmental movement should have at least four groups of organizations: institutionalized/formal groups, informal/grass-roots groups, non-institutionalized/radical groups, and environmental justice groups. In some countries, particularly in Western Europe, such groups have forged alliances with green political parties. There will always be individuals and groups within the Canadian environmental movement who will resist the compromises implicit in institutionalization. While some established groups may be resentful of these more radical fragments, "it is often also an invaluable asset to them for it is a reminder of the conscience of the movement" (Rootes, 1999: 8). These radical elements serve also as a means of keeping in touch with grassroots opinion and can be used as "a lever which can be used in dealings with the powerful who can thus be reminded that if they too strongly resist the reasonable demands of semi-institutionalized moderates, they may fuel the altogether more disruptive demands of non-institutionalized radicals. Relations between environmental radicals and the representatives of established EMOs are, as a result, often surprisingly cordial and co-operative" (Rootes: 1999, 8).

Table 11.1 identifies these different groups and their objectives, summarizes their tactics and strategies, and lists examples.

Table 11.1: Green Group Typologies in Canada

Green Group Type	Group Objectives	Strategies and Tactics	Examples
Institutionalized/ formal groups	· Activist or advisory. · Offer membership or popular support. · Advise decision-makers on legal, technical, and scientific matters.	· Primarily use insider strategy by working closely with negotiators and governments. · May also use outsider strategy in attempting to influence public opinion.	Sierra Club, Greenpeace, WWF, and other major groups.
Informal/ grassroots groups	· Most fit into the categories of naturalist, outdoor recreation, and advocacy.	· Tend to mobilize around local issues, e.g., pesticide use in cities.	"Friends of ..." groups and "Save the ..." Groups.
Radical groups	· Highly ideological. · Embrace the ideas of deep ecology.	· Highly critical of ideas and values that underpin industrial capitalism. · May use unconventional or illegal behaviours.	Earth Liberation Front (ELF).
Environmental justice groups	· Correlate environmental harm (hazardous wastes, pesticides, and metals) with socioeconomic status and race.	· Use litigation.	Friends of the Lubicon, Port Colborne residents.
Green Party	· Has official status as a registered political party nationally and at the provincial level.	· In the 2004 and 2006 federal elections, the Green Party of Canada ran candidates in all 308 ridings.	Have yet to achieve an election breakthrough.

INSTITUTIONALIZED/FORMAL GROUPS

It is generally agreed that Pollution Probe was one of the first environmental organizations to develop in Canada. It was formed in 1969 by students and professors at the University of Toronto in "response to a Canadian Broadcasting Corporation (CBC) television documentary, *The Air of Death*, which highlighted the ongoing fluoride pollution by the Electric Reduction Company at Port Maitland, Ontario" (Read, 2003: 164). By 1970, while continuing to be Toronto-based, the organization had over 1,000 members. Shunning a hierarchical type of organization, Pollution Probe was project-oriented and could draw on the expertise of an advisory board that was composed of professors, researchers, and other influential community members. It was also heavily involved in the DDT debate, and when the Province of Ontario announced extensive restrictions on the use of DDT in 1970, the Toronto media "gave overwhelming credit to Pollution Probe" (Read, 2003: 165).

Gulbrandsen and Andresen (2004) argue that organizations are either activist or advisory in nature. Activist organizations obtain funding and legitimacy through offering membership and popular support. Advisory organizations, on the other hand "obtain funding and legitimacy through their ability to give policy recommendations and advise decision-makers on legal, technical and scientific matters" (Gulbrandsen and Andresen, 2004: 56). Green groups that choose to gain influence by working closely with negotiators and governments use an *insider strategy*. Professionalized organizations tend to favour this approach; advisory groups use it almost exclusively. Other groups that choose to put pressure on decision-makers by writing letters of protest, rallying, direct actions, and boycotts, among other behaviours, use an *outsider strategy* whose goal is to influence public opinion. The best-resourced green groups, such as Greenpeace and the WWF, are likely to pursue a *dual strategy* in that they also engage in knowledge construction through the research undertaken by scientists and analysts. As issues have become more global in scope, the dual strategy has become necessary.

Researchers such as Joann Carmin and Deborah B. Balser (2002) employ a slightly different set of terminologies in determining why some EMOs adopt different tactics and identify a number of factors that influence EMO selection of a repertoire of action. Upon undertaking a comparative analysis of Friends of the Earth and Greenpeace between 1969 and 1976, they concluded, for example, that environmental philosophy was one of several interpretive factors influencing repertoire choice. In combination, various filters "work interdependently to shape interpretations that in turn, lead to the repertoire choice." Strategies or repertoires may either be institutional—litigation, lobbying, and educational campaigns—or expressive—protests, boycotts, and street theatre (Carmin and Balser, 2002: 366–67).

As is the case with all social movement organizations, there is a continuum of strategies and tactics available to green groups ranging from conventional to more unconventional behaviours, both listed above. In addition, strategies used by green groups may also be influenced by their supporters. A number of "the majors" have yearly budgets of over $1 million, with four reporting annual expenditures during the late 1990s of over $5 million (Wilson, 2002: 47). Research suggests that different environmental philosophies attract funds from different types of donors and, once accepted, lead recipient EMOs to use tactics that are acceptable to their supporters. Carmin and Balser (2002) claim that preservationist organizations are more likely to receive funds from corporations whereas more radical groups like Earth First! and Greenpeace tend to rely on their members for support. Therefore, green groups reflect the interests of their funders, with preservationist groups generally relying on less contentious tactics, while more radical groups engage in more confrontational acts (Carmin and Balser, 2002). It has been estimated that there are up to nine different philosophical discourses that EMOs adopt, ranging from reform environmentalism to deep ecology, ecofeminism, and environmental justice.

Indeed, a number of the larger environmental organizations have always been similar to public interest lobbies with their professional staff, research capability, and governance. Many groups that used to thrive on protest mobilizations and boycotts now favour initiatives such as referendums, petitioning, and postcard campaigns as well as educational campaigns in schools (Diani and Donati, 1999). Also, as was seen earlier, national networks of groups reject professional activism in favour of voluntary, grassroots action.

INFORMAL/GRASSROOTS GROUPS

Conservative estimates are that there are between 1,500 and 2,000 environmental groups at work across Canada. There is great diversity within these less formalized groups, but most would fit into the categories of naturalist, outdoor recreation, and advocacy organizations (Wilson, 2002). For instance, of the approximately 500 groups that make up the Ontario Environmental Network, there are "16 ' Friends of ...' groups (for example Friends of Temagami and Friends of the Spit) and another five 'Save the ...' organizations (for example Save the Rouge Valley System)" (Wilson, 2002: 58). So, although the "majors" have a high profile in the Canadian environmental movement, there exists a thriving collection of smaller groups that vary in their capacity and capability to lobby and to do advocacy work.

When opposition is mobilized on a local issue, rarely is an institutionalized group initially involved. Residents who are concerned about impending issues take the initiative and form ad hoc committees and citizens' groups. For many of these citizens, it might be the first time that they have participated in this kind of struggle. Tactics are usually legitimate and may include actions such as speaking with elected officials or attending public meetings. If legitimate means fail to have an influence, more unconventional behaviours, such as a blockade or picket line, may follow. Lest we think that most environmental victories are won by institutionalized groups, we must note that a number of beneficial outcomes have been associated with the activities of grassroots organizations. For example, "local actions have contributed to cleaning contaminated sites, preventing polluting facilities from being built, forcing corporations to improve production processes, providing social support to affected individuals, influencing national attitudes toward the environment and public health, and enhancing right to know legislation and citizen participation" (Carmin, 1999: 107). These local groups may develop in several ways but generally rely on volunteers more interested in problem resolution and community ability than pursuing non-profit status or organizational survival (Carmin, 1999). In fact, once there is a resolution to an issue—either positive or negative—local groups often cease to exist.

One example where local activism has found considerable success is in the area of pesticide use in Canadian cities. In the 1990s, pesticides were singled out in scientific reports as posing risks for "birth defects, cancer, developmental delays, motor and nervous system dysfunction and immunotoxicity" (Cooper and McClenaghan, 2005: 23–24) particularly among vulnerable children. While municipalities had long been reducing pesticide use on public properties, Hudson, Quebec, was the first to ban pesticide use on private property. The 1991 by-law was appealed by two lawn care companies. Although they lost in the lower and appeal court system in Quebec, they went all the way to the Supreme Court of Canada, which, in June 2001, ruled that Hudson did, in fact, have the legal right to enforce the by-law. Since that time, some 70 pesticide by-laws are now in place in Quebec, Ontario, Nova Scotia, New Brunswick, and British Columbia (Cooper and McClenaghan, 2005).

RADICAL GROUPS

Most activists in the Canadian environmental movement would likely self-describe as moderate environmentalists. However, many would openly admit that a vital and dynamic green movement needs a radical fringe. As Rootes observes, "it is precisely the radical environmentalism which is most resistant to institutionalization which is especially valued as a source of ideas" (Rootes, 1999: 8). Environmental radicals are highly critical of both the institutions and the ideas and values that underpin industrial capitalism.

Members of radical/non-institutionalized groups embrace the ideals of deep ecology first articulated by Arne Naess in a short paper published in 1973. Deep ecology supporters argue that modest reforms to public policy are all but useless. Rather, the changes needed are "tantamount to a 'paradigm shift' from the dominant one of industrial capitalism to a new environmental or ecological paradigm" (Catton and Dunlop, 1980; Drengson, 1980). Unlike shallow or reform environmental movements that continue to emphasize sustainable economic growth for both the developed and developing world and that support evolving technologies that will ensure this sustainability, supporters of the deep ecology movement believe that there is a need to address the great disparities in opportunities of those living in the North and South (Devall, 2001). Although there is widespread agreement among "dark greens" about the relationship between deep ecology and social justice, parties of all political stripes, including green parties, have "found it difficult to integrate a deep ecology perspective and environmental justice agendas into their political agendas" (Devall, 2001: 34).

Other radical green thinkers, including Lynn White, have been highly pessimistic about democracy. White claimed that democratic culture and liberal individualism were directly related to contemporary environmental problems. The eco-apocalyptic literature of the late 1960s and 1970s often flirted with or even endorsed authoritarian political solutions to environmental crises in its critique of democracy and its related values of popular will and self-governance (Minteer and Manning, 2005).

ENVIRONMENTAL JUSTICE GROUPS

The expression "environmental justice" has been coined to encompass the concepts of environmental equity and environmental racism. In other words, "environmental justice can be achieved only when all individuals, regardless of race or socioeconomic status, are equally protected from environmental harms and their related health effects. Environmental justice advocates state that the overriding goal of the movement is the creation of a society wherein no racial or ethnic group or social class disproportionately bears the risks associated with pollution" (Lester, Allen, and Hill, 2001: 21–22). Simply stated, the environmental justice movement is concerned with the degree to which the environmental risks generated by industrial society fall most heavily on the poor and ethnic minorities. As was demonstrated in the aftermath of Hurricane Katrina, it was largely poor African Americans who were hurt the most by the storm. In the case of Canada, water contamination problems are rampant on First Nations' reserves, a fact that became evident in the evacuation of residents from Kashechewan in northern Ontario in October 2005. According to Health Canada, as of 27 October 2005, 86 First Nations communities had Boil Water Advisories (BWAs) in force. Provinces had different records of dealing with this problem, ranging from no BWAs in Quebec to 37 in Ontario and 26 in the Pacific region (CTV, 2005).

As a result of the public outcry over situations like these, more Canadians and Americans have a greater understanding of what environmental justice means and why it will likely emerge as a dominant theme within the environmental movement, especially in the US. Traditionally, issues of class and race have been ignored by mainstream environmental groups. This has led to a mobilization of green organizations dedicated to pursuing environmental justice for all racial groups. Unlike the other kinds of green groups, a defining characteristic and organizing strategy of this movement is networking across issues. For example, "activists battling computer chip plants often have to deal with not only issues of contamination, but also with the politics of public subsidies of private corporations. Organizers working on health problems of strawberry pickers in California are inevitably brought into the contested terrain of immigration law" (Schlosberg, 1999: 126–27). An important concern for organizers has been to create organizational models that are sufficient for "networking purposes and strong enough to confront issues, but yet are both flexible and diverse enough to respond to changing circumstances at the local level" (Schlosberg, 1999: 132).

The environmental justice movement has moved on a variety of fronts, including conventional litigation and lobbying as well as demonstrations, blockades, and boycotts. It has achieved many victories, such as blocking plans for noxious facilities and forcing corporations and governments to compensate victims. However, the simple presence of environmental justice organizations "is itself a significant political development, pointing to a kind of politics that is more authentically democratic and more green (in terms of green rationalism) than its mainstream alternative" (Dryzek, 2005: 224).

The environmental justice movement in the US began in 1978 when the Love Canal Homeowners' Association was organized by residents of a small working-class community near Niagara Falls, New York. Their houses and the local school had been built on top of an abandoned toxic waste dump once operated by the Hooker Chemical Company of Buffalo, New York. Over 200 toxic chemicals had leaked from drums and had begun surfacing in the school-yard and into their basements three years earlier (Livesey, 2003). Led by Lois Gibbs, this group eventually was awarded $120 million from the federal government in damages, $17 million in relocation costs for more than 900 families who lived in Love Canal, and other damages from New York State and from Occidental Petroleum to test and rehabilitate the site (Livesey, 2003). A few years later, an American study conducted on the locations of hazardous dump sites in North Carolina "determined that 3 of every 4 of the off-site hazardous waste landfills in Region 4 happened to be located in predominantly African American communities" (Bullard and Johnson, 2000: 556).

In practice, a growing body of evidence demonstrates that people of colour and low income have been exposed to greater environmental and health risks than others. This exposure occurs in their neighbourhoods, workplaces, and playgrounds (Bullard and Johnson, 2000: 558). Unlike other branches of the environmental movement, "the impetus behind the environmental justice movement did not come from within government, academia, or largely white, middle-class, nationally based environmental and conservation groups— rather the impetus for change came from people of colour, grassroots, activists and their "bottom-up" leadership approach"(Bullard and Johnson, 2000: 560). According to Dryzek, the environmental justice movement is significantly different from mainstream green groups:

> The contrast with the mainstream groups is dramatic enough for environmental justice to be styled an alternative environmental movement. The networks of this second movement can bring together otherwise very different kinds of people: for example, white suburban housewives, inner city blacks, and native Americans on reservations, united in opposition to a particular polluter or an interconnected set of environmental threats. (Dryzeck, 2005: 211)

Many environmental justice groups have become disillusioned with the mainstream environmental movement, their campaigns, and their lack of attention to the diversity of the grassroots. Moreover, they are often suspicious of the professional atmosphere of some of the larger organizations and their centralized and hierarchical structures. Ultimately, they are not convinced that these organizations are accountable to memberships or local communities (Schlosberg, 1999). In the US, more specifically, they have accused larger organizations of disregarding "the wide variety of environmental hazards faced by people of colour, a paternalistic attitude toward low income and minority communities and grass-roots groups, and the lack of attention to diversity in the memberships, staffs, and boards of the Big Ten groups" (Schlosberg, 1999: 122).

LEGAL ACTIONS AND ENVIRONMENTAL JUSTICE

In 2001, Wilfred Pearson, a resident of Port Colborne, Ontario, launched a $750 million claim against Inco, the Ontario Government, the Region of Niagara, and the City of Port Colborne, among others, for alleged community-wide pollution. Settlements were reached with all defendants except Inco in 2003 and 2004. Two lower Ontario courts ruled that while individual actions could be brought against Inco, the claims were not viewed as suitable to go forward as a class action. After hearing Pearson's appeal in May 2005, the Ontario Court of Appeal ruled in November 2005 that a class-action lawsuit can proceed. Inco has indicated that it will appeal this decision to the Supreme Court of Canada. In making the case for a class-action suit, the Environmental Commissioner of Ontario (ECO), the Canadian Environmental Law Association, and Friends of the Earth, represented by the Sierra Legal Defence Fund, were granted intervenor status on the issue of costs. In its ten-year history, this is only the second time that the ECO has intervened in a proceeding (Sierra Legal Defence Fund, 2005).

Excluding Quebec (which uses the civil rather than common law code), this is the first class action for long-term historic environmental harm in Canada. Although there have been a number of local residents who have developed cancer, the case is being fought on the basis of property devaluation. Inco operated a refinery from 1918 to 1984 in the area, and it has been estimated that the company released some 20,000 tonnes of nickel into its surroundings. Most of the metal is in the form of nickel oxide, which the federal government has classified as a carcinogen. This contamination case is an environmental justice case because, like the Love Canal community, the neighbourhood most affected by declines in real estate values live around Rodney Street, a low income community in Port Colborne and home to an estimated 1,000 residents. Prices for real estate in this area have allegedly fallen by 45 per cent (Mittelstaedt, 2005). It is difficult to predict if the Port Colborne contamination class action will succeed. However, the fact that it was allowed to proceed at all could be a watershed event for future environmental claims. This precedent-setting case reflects well the concept of political opportunity whereby the courts have provided a point of access to groups such as this to bring their cases to decision.

Canadian history is rife with examples of environmental accidents in which Aboriginal ways of life, livelihoods, and health have been altered. In the case of mercury poisoning, a disproportionate number of victims were Aboriginal people. Perhaps the best known case involves the Lubicon Cree of northern Alberta. The situation began as an oil exploitation issue, evolved into a forestry issue, and eventually emerged as an environmental health issue. The plight of the Lubicon was supported by a loose coalition of groups and individuals who launched one of the biggest boycotts ever in Canadian history.

Both the federal government and the province of Alberta argued that Aboriginal title to the Lubicon territory had been ceded by the 1899 treaty made with other Aboriginal societies in the surrounding area. Despite years of discussions with the Alberta government and the Canadian federal government to demarcate their lands, the Lubicon Cree Nation had been denied justice. Provincial officials claimed that they were "squatters" on provincial Crown land. The government reluctance to demarcate a reserve was, in part, driven by evidence of significant oil and mineral wealth in the area. In 1979, the province had completed the construction of a road to the Lubicon territory, the purpose of which was to access the oil lying under Lubicon lands "despite the unresolved issue of extant aboriginal title to the entire area" (Huff, 1999: 168). After the completion of the road, during the winter of 1979–80, dozens of transnational oil companies moved into the Lubicon territory, and over 400 oil wells were installed, all within 15 miles of the main Lubicon community of Little Buffalo.

Until the 1970s, Lubicon land provided a livelihood for its inhabitants and ensured the survival of Lubicon culture. Prior to the invasion of the oil companies, a trapper earned over $5,000 a year. By the late 1980s, this income had dropped to only $400 a year. Traditional practices were "replaced by welfare, a dramatic rise in alcoholism, domestic violence, fights, accidents, theft and suicide" (Huff, 1999: 170). In total, 95 per cent of the community survived on welfare. In addition, in 1988, of 358 people screened at Little Buffalo, 107 were put on medication for tuberculosis, making the outbreak "one of the worst in Canada since the Depression" (Goddard, 1991: 154). By 1988, with the exception of the 25 square mile portion next to Buffalo Lake, all the land was included in a timber leasing agreement. Timber extracted from the area was to supply a giant pulp mill that was to be built on the Peace River by Daishowa, Inc., a Japanese multinational paper corporation. In 1991, an Ontario organization called the Friends of the Lubicon (FOL) organized a boycott of Daishowa paper products. By 1994, approximately 50 companies representing some 4,300 retail and fast food outlets had joined in. A year later, Daishowa sued the organizers of the boycott, charging them with misrepresentation and conspiracy.

The suit was highly complex and alleged that the FOL had committed a variety of economic torts against the plaintiff including intimidation, private nuisance, and unlawful interference with economic relations. Daishowa sought an injunction that would effectively terminate the boycott and claimed damages of $5 million (Tollefson, 1996). Although Strategic Lawsuits Against Public Participation (SLAPPs) were common occurrences in the US, they have been much rarer in Canada, particularly after the entrenchment of the *Charter of Rights and Freedoms*. In May 1995, Justice Kiteley of the Ontario Court rejected Daishowa's bid for an interim injunction. In her decision, she argued that the FOL were using political expression and concluded that their predominant intention was not to harm Daishowa but rather "to support the Lubicon Cree in their struggle to obtain a land claim settlement" (Tollefson, 1996: 126). Judge Kiteley also made the critical determination that the Charter protects secondary picketing and boycotting and that these activities should not be considered illegal as they relate to private tort litigation (Tollefson, 1996: 126).

Although the judge ruled against Daishowa's request for an interim injunction of the FOL's boycott activities, she did order the FOL to refrain from using the term "genocide" in describing the situation confronting the Lubicon Cree. Daishowa appealed this decision to the Ontario Divisional Court. On 23 January 1996, the Ontario Divisional Court overturned the lower court's decision and also "rejected Kiteley J.'s conclusion that the Charter should inform the development of the common law" (Tollefson, 1996: 126). In June 1997, the Supreme Court of Canada denied the FOL's application for leave to appeal the appellate court decision that the FOL's intent was to cause economic injury through unlawful means to Daishowa. To say that this SLAPP case sent a chill through the environmental justice community is an understatement.

The fact that the Lubicon Cree Nation was unable to find any redress within the Canadian legal infrastructure was a major setback to the environmental justice movement in Canada. According to many commentators, the championing of the exploitation of natural resources over the right of the Lubicon Cree to live as an Indigenous people on their traditional lands has established a dangerous precedent (Huff, 1999).

GREEN PARTIES

In many countries of Western Europe, including Belgium, Finland, France, Germany, and Italy, green parties have been part of the electoral landscape for over a quarter of a century. In some cases, they have joined governing coalitions and provided government ministers (especially environment ministers). Although the world's first green parties were the United Tasmanian Group in Australia and New Zealand's Values Party, which both formed in 1972, the German Greens, *Die Grünen* (DG), occupy a central position as the most successful one (Dryzek, 2005). The DG was founded in 1980, and by 1983 it had captured 5.6 per cent of the national vote, which climbed to 8.6 per cent in 2002. Until the most recent election in September 2005, the DG were in a governing coalition with the social democratic party, the SPD. The objective of the DG has been to change the world through influence on public policy, not just individual consciousness (Dryzeck, 2005).

Earlier European green politics in the first half of the twentieth century tended to be located on the fascist right rather than the progressive left (Capra and Spretnak, 1984). Green parties have attempted to broaden their appeal by expanding their definition of "environmental" to include other policy stances on such issues as foreign policy and social and economic issues. At a convention held in Rome in 2004, green parties from 32 countries managed to reach a consensus among their diverse memberships to form the European Green Party. Governed by a single platform, the party managed to capture 35 seats of the 624-member European Parliament in the June 2004 election (Dobbin,

2005). While the party was not as radical as some would have liked, its policies are still socially democratic and critical of corporate globalization. In addition, "the party also calls for a guaranteed minimum income across Europe, a ban of all genetically modified organisms (GMOs), and making manufacturers responsible for the entire lifecycle of their products" (Dobbin, 2005: 42).

Canada's single member plurality electoral system is a significant barrier to Canada's Green Party in terms of winning seats. Although the Green Party of Canada (GPC) was founded in 1983, it was based out of the same office as the Green Party of Ontario and lacked its own infrastructure until 2000. However, it made a rather large breakthrough in the 2004 general election when it captured 4.3 per cent of the popular vote and ran candidates in all 308 ridings. This translated into 582,247 individual votes cast by Canadians. In the 2006 federal general election, the rate increased modestly to 4.5 per cent of the popular vote. In terms of regional support, 6.5 per cent of Alberta's voters and 5.3 per cent of Cape Breton voters voted green in 2006. Under the conservative leadership of national leader, Jim Harris, policy development of the GPC was primarily determined by the national office. Like many green parties, there is an ideological tension between "dark" and "light" green supporters. The more radical members left the governing council in 2004 and have been critical of the mainstreaming of the party. However, a number of GPC members—especially in Ontario and Alberta—supported Harris's eco-capitalist solutions. According to Murray Dobbin, "in the simplest analysis, Harris would end subsidies to polluting industries, such as tax breaks for oil companies, and redirect the money to social programs and [to] initiatives to dramatically increase energy efficiency" (Dobbin, 2005: 44). One change that has benefited the GPC is *Bill C-24* which amended the rules for fundraising by political parties. In order to receive government funding, parties must receive at least 2 per cent of the popular vote, and they will receive $1.75 per vote received in the previous election. On the basis of the 2004 election results, the GPC received $1,018,932, which allowed it to mount a more national campaign in the 2006 election.

On 26 August 2006, the GPC selected a new party leader—Elizabeth May. She is the former executive director of the SCC and is a highly regarded environmental activist. A month later, the party released its *Greenprint for the Future, GP2* (GPC, 2006), which set the foundation of the policy and platform as *tax shifting*, also described as ecological fiscal reform. While the GPC propose that some taxes be reduced (payroll and income, for example), a graduated levy will be imposed that will tax the fuel with the highest levels of greenhouse gases (that is, coal) graduated downwards to the fuel with the lowest—natural gas. This plan will serve as an incentive for consumers to make economically rational choices such as improving home insulation and buying a more fuel efficient vehicle or choosing public transit (GPC, 2006). The GPC believes that if *GP2* was implemented, the 2008–12 Kyoto target could be achieved.

When interviewed about how the GPC fits within the political spectrum, May made the following comment:

> We find in the Green Party that the political spectrum is irrelevant to our policies and our transformative brand of politics. We aren't left. We aren't right. We're about a real shift in Canadian politics that moves behind labels. We intend to take policy instruments and solutions from tool kits that might be described as left, or that might be described as right and if it works we will use it. (CBC, 2006)

Even if the GPC fails to make an electoral breakthrough in future elections, it may have the effect of forcing the established "grey" parties "and the political system as a whole, to craft responses to the green electoral threat" (Dryzek, 2005: 219). Moreover, if an environmental issue emerges that captures the attention and mood of the public, the GPC and its *GP2* may seize the political opportunity to capture more voters.

Kyoto, Climate Change, and The Clean Air Act: A Resurgence?

In January 2007, a new poll by Decima Research indicated that the environment has eclipsed health care, the war in Afghanistan, taxes, and the economy to become the most frequently mentioned preoccupation of Canadians. More importantly, 19 per cent of those polled indicated that the environment is the issue that concerns them the most, followed by health care at 13 per cent. Mentions of the environment as the top issue were up by 13 points since the same question was posed in September 2006 (Decima: 4 January 2007). What has led to this resurgence in interest? There have been several critical factors and events that have focused the public's attention on the environment. First, there has been a mobilization of opposition to the Conservatives' alternative to Canada's participation in the Kyoto Protocol. Second, in one of the most exciting Liberal leadership conventions ever, the winning candidate, Stéphane Dion, made the environment his key message and the policy priority for the Liberal Party. Third, the winter of 2007 has been characterized by severe weather variability amid news that a significant part of a northern glacier has broken away.

In October 2006, the Harper government introduced the *Clean Air Act* to a chorus of criticism from environmentalists and opposition parties. The legislation was intended to replace the Kyoto Protocol, which came into effect in 2005 with 141 countries signing on, including every industrialized country except for the US, Australia, and Monaco. Two of the world's largest polluters, India and China, did not have to sign on as both are considered developing countries and are outside the protocol's framework. In total, the US, China, and India account for an estimated half of the world's greenhouse gas emissions. In April 2005, the Liberal government pledged $10 billion over seven years to help Canada cut its average greenhouse gas emissions by 270 megatonnes a year from 2008 to 2012. This money was to be used by provinces in assisting industries, utilities, and municipal public transit systems to cut emissions. Although Ontario had negotiated a $538 million agreement with Ottawa to help close the province's coal-fired power plants, the $10 billion fund has now been reduced to $2 billion. It is not yet clear whether or not the Conservative government will honour this agreement with Ontario.

If passed, the *Clean Air Act* would require reductions in the intensity of emissions rather than absolute reductions. It does not contain any short-term targets to cut greenhouse gases, and its emissions regulations on large polluters would not take effect until 2010. The act and its accompanying regulations set a new target of 2050, which is disconcerting to many environmentalists. This timeline, it is feared, will allow greenhouse gas emissions to keep growing for years.

There are a number of indicators that green organizations are currently mobilizing in a major campaign to get the government to recommit to the Kyoto Protocol. It could be argued that because the Harper Conservatives have stalled in the polls, green groups and the environmental movement, in particular, are sensing that an opportunity to raise awareness about the environment and environmental problems has presented itself. In October 2006, a number of environmental groups sent an open letter to Stephen Harper. They represent the spectrum of green organizations from major institutionalized groups to grassroots groups, radical groups, and environmental justice groups. They presented the prime minister with a series of recommendations that they believe should be included in his much-awaited environment plan. Their first two priorities were a recommitment to the Kyoto Protocol and to improving air quality. In terms of Kyoto, the letter encouraged Harper to establish both short-term and long-term targets for reductions in greenhouse gas emissions and to publish drafts of greenhouse gas regulations under the *Canadian Environmental Protection Act* within three months (Pembina Institute, 2006).

In December 2006, the Liberal Party of Canada hosted a leadership convention in Montreal. The clear frontrunners were Michael Ignatieff and Bob

Rae. However, both candidates also had large blocks of delegates who were not comfortable with either of them. In the week leading up to the convention, it was clear that their campaigns had stalled and that the third and fourth place candidates—Gerard Kennedy and Stéphane Dion—had considerable momentum. With one-third of the delegates being under the age of 25, there was considerable talk about the new generation of Liberals. Dion's campaign differed significantly from the other candidates in how he made the environment his key priority. Since the beginning of his campaign, he had talked about climate change, environmental sustainability, and the health of the next generation. He stayed on message in his speech to the convention on the Friday evening and in his victory speech on Saturday evening.

Since the Liberals chose Dion as leader, Prime Minister Harper, the NDP, and the BQ have all been talking in language that is much greener. In the new year, Harper shuffled his cabinet by removing the embattled Environment Minister, Rona Ambrose, and replacing her with John Baird, largely seen as one of the stars in the Harper government. Moreover, on 19 January 2007, the prime minister announced more than $1.5 billion in funding for the ecoEnergy Renewable Initiative to boost Canada's renewable energy supplies. Currently, the opposition parties have all said that they will not support the *Clean Air Act*, which makes it unlikely that it will pass. By not abiding by the rules of the game that were spelled out in the Kyoto Accord, Canada has adopted an isolationist policy on climate change which has been described by one climatologist as "foolhardy and impractical" (Smit, 2006).

Conclusion

As outlined in this chapter, the environmental movement has had significant periods of retreat, particularly in challenging economic times when the public's interest was more focused on issues such as the economy and health care. Governments of the day seized the political opportunity to champion these policy areas at the cost of initiatives and programs related to the environment. Although the Canadian environmental movement has been described as having four waves of activity, green groups have had to be resilient and have had to find new ways of mobilizing. The recent mobilization of green groups that has occurred as a result of Prime Minister Harper's decision to scrap Canada's commitment to the Kyoto Accord set the tone and context for Liberal leader Stéphane Dion's emergence as the political champion of the environment. To counter this Liberal momentum, Harper has recently used the opportunity to make several significant environmental announcements including a tax credit on transit passes and the ecoEnergy Retrofit program. Tax credits on transit passes include buses, streetcars, subways, commuter trains and local ferries.

As it relates to the retrofit program, individual homeowners can receive grants of up to $5,000 if they retrofit their homes to be more energy efficient. Small and medium-sized businesses are also eligible for funding under this program.

The environmental movement in Canada has achieved some important victories over the years. The Canadian environmental movement has fallen short in its efforts to reframe the environment as a rights, justice, or health issue. In recent elections, the environment has rarely been elevated as an issue of importance by political parties or the electorate. Despite the energy blackout in Ontario in 2004, record levels of smog alerts, and soaring costs for gasoline, grey behaviours by individual consumers, corporations, and governments continue. While many green groups and organizations continue the good fight, a resurgence in the environmental movement will likely emerge only in response to a widespread and prolonged environmental crisis such as climate change. This will necessitate a sustained, high profile, and well-networked campaign by environmental groups across the country.

Notes

1. Devils Lake in North Dakota has nearly tripled in size after more than a decade of wet weather. It has gobbled up farmland and has forced people to leave their homes. A 22.5-kilometre, US $28 million outlet to divert some of the water was undertaken because Devils Lake has no natural outflow. Environmentalists in Manitoba have argued that the outlet will contaminate the Lake Winnipeg watershed with rogue marine life, salt, and farm chemicals. An American environmental group called People to Save the Sheyenne is also fighting the man-made outlet from draining water off the lake and into the Sheyenne River, then into the Red River and Lake Winnipeg. Canada pressed unsuccessfully to have the dispute heard by the International Joint Commission which oversees the Canada-US Boundary Waters Treaty. On 6 August 2005 an agreement was announced that the parties' claim provides a system of environmental safeguards. Activists and local NDP MP, Pat Martin, say the deal was little more than a face-saving measure when it became evident that nothing was going to stop the North Dakota Governor from opening the outlet. On 25 August 2006, the NAFTA Commission on Environmental Cooperation rejected a call for an independent inquiry into the enforcement of the legally binding 1909 *Boundary Waters Treaty* on the matter of the controversial Devils Lake Diversion.

2. Wise Use activists in the second-wave (according to its critics) are comprised of groups ranging from unemployed loggers, off-road motorcyclists, and rural county commissioners to the top levels of industry and government. At its core, Wise Use/Property Rights is a counterrevolutionary movement, defining itself in response to the environmental revolution of the past 30 years. See Helvarg 1994.

References and Further Reading

Beder, Sharon. 1997. *Global Spin: The Corporate Assault on Environmentalism*. UK: Green University Press.

Bullard, Robert D., and Glenn S. Johnson. 2000. "Environmental Justice: Grassroots Activism and Its Impact on Public Policy Decision Making." *Journal of Social Issues* 56(3): 555–78.

Capra, Fritjof, and Charlene Spretnak. 1984. *Green Politics*. New York: E.P. Dutton.

Carmin, Joann. 1999. "Voluntary Associations, Professional Organizations and the Environmental Movement in the United States." In Christopher Rootes (ed.), *Environmental Movements: Local, National and Global*. London and Portland: Frank Cass Publishers. 101–21.

Carmin, Joann, and Deborah B. Balser. 2002. "Selecting Repertoires of Action in Environmental Movement Organizations." *Organization & Environment* 15(4): 365–88.

Carson, Rachel. 1962. *Silent Spring*. Boston: Houghton Mifflin.

Castells, Manuel. 1997. *The Power of Identity*. Oxford: Blackwell.

Catton, William R., Jr., and Riley E. Dunlop. 1980. "A New Ecological Paradigm for Post-Exuberant Sociology." *American Behavioral Scientist* 24(1).

CBC News. 2006. "A talk with the new Green Party leader, Elizabeth May." <http://www.cbc.ca/news/background/green-party/elizabeth-may.html>.

Cooper, Kathleen, and Theresa McClenaghan. 2005. "Ban Stands." *Alternatives Journal* 31(2): 23–25.

CTV. 2004. "First Nations Communities with Boil Water Advisories (BWAs)." <http://www.ctv.ca>.

Decima Research. 2007. *In the News*. <http://www.decima.com/en/inthenews/2007-01-05>.

Devall, Bill. 2001. "The Deep, Long-Range Ecology Movement 1960–2000: A Review." *Ethics & The Environment* 6(1): 18–41.

Diani, Mario, and Paolo R. Donati. 1999. "Organizational Change in Western European Environmental Groups: A Framework for Analysis." In Christopher Rootes (ed.), *Environmental Movements: Local, National and Global*. London and Portland: Frank Cass Publishers. 13–34.

Dobbin, Murray. 2005. "Green Party Blues." *The Walrus* (July/August).

Dowie, Mark. 1996. *Losing Ground*. Cambridge, MA: MIT Press.

Drengson, Alan. 1980. "Shifting Paradigms: From the Technocratic to the Person-Planetary." *Environmental Ethics* 3: 221–40.

Dryzek, John S. 2005. *The Politics of the Earth: Environmental Discourses*. 2nd ed. Oxford: Oxford University Press.

Eckersley, Robin. 1992. *Environmentalism and Political Theory*. New York: State University of New York Press.

Goddard, John. 1991. *Last Stand of the Lubicon Cree*. Vancouver and Toronto: Douglas and McIntyre.

GPC (Green Party of Canada). 2006. *Greenprint for the Future, GP2*. <http://www.greenparty.ca/en/platform/documents/gp2>.

Gulbrandsen, Lars H., and Steinar Andresen. 2004. "NGO Influence in the Implementation of the Kyoto Protocol: Compliance, Flexibility Mechanisms, and Sinks." *Global Environmental Politics* 4(4): 54–75.

Harrison, Kathryn. 1999. "Retreat from Regulation: The Evolution of the Canadian Regulatory Regime." In Bruce Doern et al., (eds.), *Changing the Rules: Canadian Regulatory Regimes and Institutions.* Toronto: University of Toronto Press.

Helvarg, D. 1994. *The War Against the Greens.* San Francisco: Sierra Club Books.

Hjelmar, Ulf. 1996. *The Political Practice of Environmental Organizations.* Aldershot, UK: Ashgate.

Huff, Andrew. 1999. "Resource Development and Human Rights: A Look at the Case of the Lubicon Cree Indian Nation of Canada." *Colorado Journal of International Environmental Law and Policy* 10(1): 161–94.

Killan, Gerald, and George Warecki. 1992. "The Algonquin Wildlands League and the Emergence of Environmental Politics in Ontario, 1965–1974." *Environmental History Review* 16(4): 1–27.

Lear, Linda. 1997. *Rachel Carson: Witness for Nature.* New York: Henry Holt.

Lester, James P., David W. Allen, and Kelly M. Hill. 2001. *Environmental Injustice in the United States: Myths and Realities.* Boulder, CO.: Westview Press.

Livesey, Sharon M. 2003. "Organizing and Leading the Grassroots." *Organization & Environment* 16(4): 488–503.

Macdonald, Doug. 1991. *The Politics of Pollution.* Toronto: McClelland and Stewart.

Manes, Christopher. 1990. *Green Rage.* Boston: Little Brown.

May, Elizabeth. 1990. *Paradise Won: The Struggle for South Moresby.* Toronto: McClelland and Stewart.

May, Elizabeth. 2006. *How to Save the World in Your Spare Time.* Toronto: Key Porter Books.

McKenzie, Judith I. 2002. *Environmental Politics in Canada: Managing the Commons Into the Twenty-First Century.* Toronto: Oxford University Press.

Minteer, Ben A., and Robert E. Manning. 2005. "An Appraisal of the Critique of Anthropocentrism and Three Lesser Known Themes in Lynn White's 'The Historical Roots of our Ecological Crisis.'" *Organization & Environment* 18(2): 163–76.

Mittelstaedt, Martin. 2005. "Court Okays Suit Against Inco: Landmark Ruling Paves Way for Ontario's First Class Action on Environmental Issue." *Globe and Mail*, 19 November: A9.

Mowrey, Marc, and Tim Redmond. 1993. *Not in Our Backyard.* New York: William Morrow and Company.

Naess, Arne. 1973. "The Shallow and the Deep, Long-Range Ecology Movement: A Summary." *Inquiry* 16: 95–100.

Newman, Peggy. 1994. "Beyond the Neighbourhood: Women Working for Multi-Ethnic, Multi-Issue Coalitions." *The Workbook* 19(2).

Opie, John. 1998. *Nature's Nation.* Orlando, FL: Harcourt Brace.

Pembina Institute. 2006. *Letter to Prime Minister Harper Re: The Environment as a Priority—A Real Opportunity to Put Canada on Track* (4 October). <http://www.pembina.org/pubs/pub.php?id=1297\>.

Read, Jennifer. 2003. "Pollution Probe: The Emergence of the Canadian Environmental Movement." In Char Miller (ed.), *The Atlas of US and Canadian Environmental History*. New York: Routledge.

Reynolds, Cynthia. 2004. "Charity Chic." *Maclean's*, 20 December.

Rootes, Christopher. 1999. "Environmental Movements: From the Local to the Global." In Christopher Rootes (ed.), *Environmental Movements: Local, National and Global*. London and Portland: Frank Cass Publishers: 1–12.

Schlosberg, David. 1999. "Networks and Mobile Arrangements: Organizational Innovation in the US Environmental Justice Movement." In Christopher Rootes (ed.), *Environmental Movements: Local, National and Global*. London and Portland: Frank Cass Publishers: 122–48.

Sierra Legal Defence Fund. 2005. "Court of Appeal Grants Top Environmental Organizations Intervener Status in Port Colborne, Ontario Inco Case." <http://www.sierralegal.org>.

Skinner, B.F. 1962 [1948]. *Walden Two*. New York: Macmillan

Smit, Barry. 2006. "Isolationist Policy Foolhardy." *Toronto Star*, 20 October.

Smith, Miriam. 2005. *A Civil Society? Collective Actors in Canadian Political Life*. Peterborough: Broadview Press.

Sperber, Irwin. 2003. "Alienation in the Environmental Movement: Regressive Tendencies in the Struggle for Environmental Justice." *Capitalism Nature Socialism* 14(3): 1–43.

Tokar, Brian. 1992. *The Green Alternative*. San Pedro: R. and E. Miles.

Tollefson, Chris. 1996. "Strategic Lawsuits and Environmental Politics: *Daishowa Inc. v. Friends of the Lubicon*." *Journal of Canadian Studies* 31(1): 119–32.

White, Lynn, Jr. 1967. "The Historical Roots of Our Ecological Crisis." *Science* 155(3767): 1203–07.

Wilson, Jeremy. 2002. "Continuity and Change in the Environmental Movement." In Debora L. VanNijnatten and Robert Boardman (eds.), *Canadian Environmental Policy: Context and Case*. 2nd ed. Toronto: Oxford University Press. 46–63.

TWELVE

Barrier by Barrier:
The Canadian Disability Movement and the Fight for Equal Rights

Sally Chivers

"And what about in-your-face advocacy, the crawl-up-the-Capitol-steps, chain-your-wheelchair-to-the-bus variety? Do groups like ADAPT or Not Dead Yet even exist here?" "Oh, no," says Lucille Owen laughing, "We're Canadian." (Lathrop, 2000)

The above exchange between an American journalist and a Canadian disability activist is indicative of the evolution and efforts of the Canadian disability movement as a whole. Despite the faulty appeal to clichéd notions of national character—where Americans are boisterous and Canadians polite—it is the case that the American disability movement has made dramatic progress through civil disobedience arranged by two key groups (among others): ADAPT (American Disabled for Attendant Programs Today, formerly American Disabled for Accessible Public Transportation) and Not Dead Yet (an anti-euthanasia advocacy group). As this chapter will argue, the Canadian disability movement has made less dramatic but nonetheless meaningful progress by working both against and within state systems to achieve recognition of disabled people's human rights—enshrined in the *Charter of Rights and Freedoms* (the Charter)—and to argue for disabled people's rights to full citizenship. In a discussion of disability advocacy in Canada, Aldred H. Neufeldt explains, "those concerned with disability issues embraced a broader Canadian way of thinking—that negotiation and consensus seeking were preferred over what was often seen as the more confrontational styles of our American neighbours" (2003: 13–14).

While the disability movement is founded on the transformative and liberation politics of the 1960s new left movements referenced in the Introduction, many actions on the parts of Canadian disability groups rely on pluralist arguments. Because disabled people have suffered the label "special" in many contexts (particularly special education), they are in a different position from other identity-based coalitions in situating themselves as a "special" interest group. That is, it may not be in their best interests to be labelled "special." In order to effect change and resist segregation, disabled Canadians have had to argue that they merit the same rights and have the same capacities as other citizens. This argument is symbolized by the frequent choice on the part of many disability groups to prefer the terminology *people with disabilities* which puts the person ahead of the disability and emphasizes the common ground of humanity over the special needs invoked by appeals to disability. The alternate formulation, *disabled people*, makes disability an inherent part of personhood and is becoming more popular in North America as activists resist needing to pretend to be like everybody else. (It has always been the preferred nomenclature in the UK.) Disability activists have to choose whether to emphasize their similarity to all other people in order to achieve equal status or their difference from others in order to justify demands for resources and support. In Canada, the former argument—that personhood comes before disability—has been the most prominent.

In this chapter, I begin by situating disability as a socially constructed status that affects all Canadians. I then show the progression from a nascent civil rights movement to the inscription of disability rights in the Charter, the fight for which is the focus of its own section. Next, I show the effect Charter inclusion has had on the disability rights movement and suggest some directions for future action.

Defining Disability: Authority and Experience

Disability is difficult to define since many different bodily and psychiatric statuses can fit into the category. The idea that blind people, wheelchair users, psychiatric survivors, people with cerebral palsy, D/deaf people,[1] obese people, and migraine sufferers share a political purpose and can gather under the banner of disability is continually contested. Not all disability activists agree on what constitutes disability, and not all policy-makers respond equally to claims of disability. This has become particularly evident in the range of claims made under the *Americans with Disabilities Act* (ADA) south of the border; Canada currently lacks a similar federal act, though Ontario has recently succeeded in passing a provincial version as outlined below. While a federal policy would increase the political visibility of disability, its absence is a benefit because there is a more flexible set of rules at play in Canada. Differences in what constitutes a valid claim of disability appear as well in the complicated process involved when a person wants to make a claim for support through such venues as the Ontario Disability Support Program (ODSP) or Assure Income for the Severely Handicapped-Alberta (AISH). On the elementary school playground, many forms of bodily and other difference may invite social stigma, but, when money is involved, the definition of disability becomes as narrow as possible, requiring medical authority to assure that recipients of social support are entitled and not malingering. Childhood bullies may be able to spot disability easily in order to taunt those perceived as weak, but only medical practitioners are considered capable of verifying that an individual merits support for their disability. Disability activists challenge this narrow view of expertise and claim that disabled people, their families, and members of their care networks possess equally valuable knowledge through their experience.

The disability movement aims to reassign authority so that doctors and teachers are not the only people seen as capable of understanding the needs and rights of disabled people. As the Newfoundland Association for Community Living reports, this goal is shared by disabled people and by many of their family members:

> If there is one message that Roberta would like to leave with other parents of children with disabilities it is that, in her opinion, the education system in Newfoundland and Labrador is very intimidating. "They talk to you like 'they' know what is best for your child. They make parents feel belittled and intimidated every time you speak with them." (Neary, 2001: 16)

Disability activists demonstrate that people with disabilities best understand their own conditions and their living situations and that they should have full autonomy in making decisions which affect their futures. As one activist explained the necessary negotiation between support and independence,

> I am one of the founders of the People First movement, a movement that is run by people labelled developmentally handicapped. We advocate for the rights of all people with disabilities to have the right to make their own decisions and lead their own lives. That doesn't mean that we don't need support. It simply means that we shouldn't have to give up our rights in order to get the support we need. (Cited in Hillier, 2001: 30)

The issue of autonomy is different for children with disabilities than it is for adults with disabilities, especially in relation to the medical profession.

However, for both children and adults with disabilities, it can be the case that they do not always agree with family members. Thus, especially for adults with disabilities, full autonomy can require separation from family, but it is most likely that the family has been providing care without adequate state support. Proponents of the Independent and Community Living Movements try to find living situations that provide disabled adults with the care they need along with autonomy.

The Social Dynamics of Disability

The disability movement is founded on the principle that disability is not a medical issue but rather a social one. Disability rights activists argue that people with disabilities do not need cure or pity, often chanting the slogan "Piss on Pity"; instead, they require jobs and the opportunity to participate fully in society. The problems faced by people with disabilities are created by barriers and not by physical or cognitive differences. Some of these barriers are physical, such as stairs, small print, and narrow doorways; others are attitudinal, such as prejudice, pity, and charity. This position is known as the social model of disability, which locates the discrimination faced by disabled people in social dimensions—physical and attitudinal—rather than in bodily differences. Activists assert that disability is not necessarily negative. Catherine Frazee explains this complicated relationship to living disabled in Canada:

> The simple arithmetic of it is that my disability has brought me smartly to all of the things I value—my career, my friendships, my creative life, my skills, my tenacity, my intimate partner, my world view. And there is no logical reason to believe that this will not continue to be the case for as long as I remain alive. (2000: 40)

Instead of accepting the broad social view that disability *necessarily* entails disadvantage, disability activists argue that the widespread social opinion that disability is bad and that disabled people are deficient *creates* the disadvantages that often accompany disability. As Frazee goes on to say: "let me be very clear: stigma, barriers, and exclusion are the enemy—not my disability" (2000: 40).

Disability activists call the widespread negative social opinion about disability and its accompanying prejudices *ableism*, an inelegant but helpful term in pinpointing pervasive and persistent injustice towards people with disabilities. Members of the disability movement argue that if we imagined a world that included people with disabilities—the way we imagine a world that includes women—then people with disabilities would have access to meaningful employment and greatly improved quality of life. If we continue to segregate people with disabilities—in separate classrooms, outside the workplace, and absent from popular media—discrimination is bound to continue. Many disability activists argue that disability is a unique and often positive way to experience the world that enriches rather than impoverishes existence and that everybody would benefit if disability were a fully integrated part of everyday life.[2] As a result, like the women's movement and the lesbian and gay movement, they draw heavily on the idea that the "personal is political" and fight against attempts to keep disabled people out of the public view (through institutionalization and refusal of employment supports).

To illustrate that the popular imagination does not typically consider disability as part of everyday lived experience, disability activists often draw on the example of the arbitrary choice to build stairs rather than ramps at the entrances of public and private buildings (and in countless other locations). The choice is supposedly aesthetic, but it is not at all clear on what basis steps are more beautiful than slopes. The tangible difference is, in fact, functional: a person who uses a wheelchair can enter a building only if there is a ramp and will most likely be kept out of a building accessible only by stairs. The opposite choice to build ramps rather than stairs would eliminate the disadvantage for that person and allow fuller and more equal access to the building. From a disability perspective, architecture is intentional and reflects a broad societal intention to prevent disabled people from social inclusion (Titchkosky, 2003: 113–14).

Since it is rare that disabled people choose to live in an institutional setting, de-institutionalization is a key disability issue that even more than ramps illustrates a need for social inclusion. Disability advocates work to free others from nursing homes, favouring support programs that allow them to live and work in the community. The focus on consumer advocacy comes from the argument that disability is best lived in relation to services not charity. In keeping with what Harriet McBryde Johnson (2003) has called the "disability gulag,"[3] the Canadian Association for Community Living (CACL) and People First especially refer to "the continued and unacceptable incarceration of persons with intellectual disabilities in institutions" (CACL, 2005a). They argue that this is a citizenship issue, as it quite clearly bars people labelled as having intellectual disabilities from full social participation. Disability activists prioritize this because they see it as intricately tied to the other issues that claim centrality in the disability agenda and because it crystallizes the thinking behind ableism. As CACL (2005a) explains, "Continued warehousing of individuals in institutions is a national disgrace and, until corrected, makes meaningless much of the language surrounding the disability movement in this country that speaks of rights, independence and freedom." Most disability groups would like to see the closing of all institutions for the intellectually disabled.

The line between disabled people and non-disabled people is not as clear as mainstream society would like to think, and the segregation of "severely" disabled people into living spaces separate from mainstream society does not help to clarify it. Some people in the disability movement seek to demonstrate that the line is blurred and remove it altogether. Disability activists frequently remind others that "if you live long enough" you will almost certainly live with a disability. Indeed, the 2001 census provided data indicating that 14.6 per cent of Canadians between the ages of 15 and 44 live with disabilities, 16.7 per cent of Canadians between the ages of 45 and 64 live with disabilities, and 40.5 per cent of Canadians over the age of 65 live with disabilities (quoted in Prince, 2004: 61). This shows an increase with age of reporting living with activity limitations (the Census definition of disability).

In addition to this increasing likelihood of personally experiencing disability, almost all Canadians have family members and friends who live with disabilities. While women are more likely than men to take on caregiving roles, many Canadians will live long enough to interact with and understand disability in their private lives. Accordingly, disability activists argue that disability ought to concern everybody and should be central in social and political decision-making as well as in the popular imagination. Having disabled people living in the community rather than in institutions supports this thinking. This perspective would reframe disability policy debates from a perspective of helping those in need to a perspective of supporting all Canadians equally.

Like other social movements, the disability movement has challenged stigma and marginalization by mobilizing a politicized sense of collective identity. The social model of disability is predicated upon a political identity that mobilizes the movement, its activists, and its organizations. By asserting that disability is socially and politically constructed, disability activists challenge the dominant codes of society with respect to what is normal. In fact, the most radical disability activists argue against normalcy as a viable concept in any sense. The Deaf community in particular makes a clear argument against forcing children to speak verbal English as opposed to American Sign language, and they would argue that the latter language is more "normal" than spoken language for some people. As James Roots explains,

> Since hearing and speaking hardly come naturally to children who are congenitally incapable of doing so due to deafness, the "normalization" process takes a pedagogic form. There is nothing natural about educators, parents, and therapists spending hours every day drilling an unhearing child to attempt to simulate

the mouth-shapes, breath-patterns, and throat and cheek throb-bings involved in enunciating a word-sound. It is, instead, a very deliberate and structured training regime. (2003: 75)

Although disability activists have long fought for important policy changes as well as legally based human rights protections, they have also devoted considerable efforts to upsetting the deceptively neat dichotomy between able bodied and disabled people. Disability activists often call the supposedly non-disabled "temporarily able-bodied" (TAB for short), and this label reinforces the idea that disability is part of human experience rather than a unique state of abnormalcy. Activists seek to reframe approaches to disability so that they require disability experience and disability knowledge for their success. The slogan "Nothing about us without us" emerges as crucial to understanding what disability activists want—they want to be at the table making decisions about their own lives.

Disability in and of itself, then, does not have to prevent people from full participation in society, but social and physical barriers can and usually do. Eyeglasses provide another common example to illustrate the arbitrariness of what obtains the label disability. Social acceptance, even to the extent of clear, separately named "vision care" provisions in extended health care coverage, indicates that it is worthy of support, and even normal, to wear prostheses in the form of prescription lenses, without which many people would be severely limited in their daily lives, not being able to drive, read, or work. However, similar social acceptance, and clearly demarcated health coverage, does not apply to wearing an artificial limb or walking with a cane. While such pros-theses are often covered by employee benefits, they are grouped together with temporary aids, indicating that the need for them is not normalized in the way that the need for eyeglasses is.

The two examples of eyeglasses and ramps are very useful in illustrating the central tenets of the international disability movement; however, they also create a problem for disability advocates. Each of them focuses on physical disability, but disability can take many forms, including mental disability. This problem is further highlighted by the supposedly universal symbol for disability of a static wheelchair (usually in white on a blue background). The idea that a disabled person will have a very visible mark of difference causes difficulties for those with invisible disabilities or conditions less obviously ac-cepted as disability. This raises a thorny question about who fits under the category "disabled," a point raised by Canadian policy-makers in resistance to disabled activists' efforts to achieve equal rights status as discussed in the final section of this chapter.

Because disabled people have to navigate an environment full of barriers, they require an inordinate amount of specialized information not only about their physical, mental, and social needs, but also about how to handle Byzantine social support systems. As a result, much of disability activists' collective work involves gathering and providing access to information. The time, expense, and effort that these groups and individuals give to this one aspect of struggling against disability discrimination demonstrates that education is an important means for achieving social inclusion. If the disability community were to achieve their goal of increasing awareness of an overall social responsibility and involvement in disability issues leading to a reframing of disability policy issues, its members would have considerably more time, energy, and money to devote to concrete improvements in the social and physical conditions of people with disabilities.

Developing a Framework for Action: From Charity to Rights

A powerful and cohesive—if diverse—union of voices and actors, the Canadian disability movement has developed from smaller groups arranged around types of disability (such as the Canadian National Institute for the Blind, the CNIB) and around local communities (especially in the prairies) (Driedger, 1993; Crichton and Jongbloed, 1998; Kitchin and Wilton, 2003). While many credit action on the part of disabled veterans for current disability supports, most point to the successful struggle to add disability to the list of equality rights in the Charter as the galvanizing moment for the Canadian disability movement (Peters, 2003; Rioux and Frazee, 1999). As Prince points out, though the Standing Committee on Human Rights and the Status of Disabled Persons attributes the inclusion of disability in the Charter to federal and provincial governments, "in fact, the authors of the achievement were disability groups" (2004: 64). For many social and national movements in Canada, including the ethnocultural, women's, Aboriginal, and lesbian and gay movements, constitutional politics provided an unparalleled political opportunity to assert the political and social rights of those who had traditionally been marginalized in Canadian society. As for other movements, the late 1970s and early 1980s was the key moment when the Canadian disability movement came together. As Yvonne Peters explains, disability organizations and activists shifted from an attempt to gain adequate services to an insistence on the appropriate and rightful place of disabled people in society: "At the heart of the disability rights movement was the desire to transform disability from a concept of charity to a concept of rights" (2003: 123).

To be clear, there was activism in the name of disability before the charter era. Building on the work of Canadian WWII veterans, in the 1950s, disability activists fought for education of the general public about the status and needs of disabled citizens (Tremblay, 2003). The still active CACL, which supports people with intellectual disabilities, was founded as the CAMR in 1958. The 1960s saw an increase in awareness of social issues and interest in social justice, especially in Quebec. As Boucher *et al.* point out,

> In the beginning of the 1960s, Quebec society was animated by a vast and deep social change movement, a process of political modernization that led to a redefinition of its mode of social organization. The state then became the main force around which this new organization of social forces took shape. It was then that society discovered the reality of people with disabilities in all its complexity. (2003: 139)

This 1960s basis laid the groundwork for serious change across Canada for disabled people.

In the 1970s, the Canadian disability movement began to articulate its social model position that disability is not a medical issue and that disabled people are not passive, helpless individuals (Kitchin and Wilton, 2003; Peters, 2003). Neufeldt explains,

> Beginning in the early 1970s, in parallel with the broadening civil rights revolution then under way, and with a much better educated population comfortable with developing new meanings for old words in rapidly changing social contexts, some disability organizations began casting themselves as advocacy organizations, in distinction to organizations devoted to service delivery. (2003: 14)

Accordingly, the movement's focus on services continued, but shifted to the community level. Influenced by the emergence of a strong American disability movement, the fledgling Independent Living Movement embraced this social model position, especially in relation to the living conditions of people with disabilities. For those working in the Independent Living Movement, this commitment based on a concept of civil rights to moving people with disabilities into the community sometimes meant supporting new forms of service delivery that, ironically, disability activists now fight against, such as sheltered workshops, special schools, and special classes.

In 1973 and 1974, to argue for self-advocacy and the expertise of people with disabilities about disability issues, People First was formed after a meeting of people labeled as mentally handicapped. As a group promoting self-advocacy, they are the most lucid of all Canadian disability groups about what constitutes their membership, and their focus is on "people who have been labelled." This mandate reveals their knowledge of the damage and importance of the process of labeling practices undertaken by medical practitioners and policy-makers. Their insistence on "self-naming," which Jane Jenson (1995) argues is crucial to the ability of social movements to reconfigure the "political opportunity structure" shifts the domain of disability from that of the medical to that of the social so that the resistance to labeling (from the outside or the inside) is an argument for the equality and even equivalence of people who have been labeled with people who have not yet been labeled.

With a similar disability-centred mandate of being run by people with disabilities instead of support workers or other allies, the current Council of Canadians with Disabilities (CCD) was begun in Alberta, Manitoba, and Saskatchewan in the early 1970s; formed as the Coalition of Provincial Organizations of the Handicapped (COPOH) in 1976; and represented the beginnings of a shift from local organizing to national organizing.

In 1979, a group of disabled activists organized a protest on Parliament Hill to underscore how inaccessible the halls of Canadian government were to its disabled citizens. In one of the most confrontational protests in Canadian disability history, participants climbed and leapt out of their wheelchairs onto the steps and across the entranceways of the buildings. The protest was successful in that affected MPs helped to carry the protesters into Parliament where they passed a new resolution about accessibility on the very day of the event (Valentine, cited in Lathrop, 2000). However, the first paraplegic MP was elected only in 2004, and he is only guaranteed not to be a backbencher by virtue of the fact that the back benches of Canadian Parliament are still not wheelchair accessible.[4] The 1979 protest was only partly successful then, as demonstrated by the election 25 years later of a disabled politician being remarkable and newsworthy rather than commonplace. The protest—though perhaps foreshadowing Charter inclusion—also lost momentum because of a political shift in the decade that followed from support for collective action to admiration of individual achievement.

Not surprisingly, the neoliberal 1980s saw the societal value of the individual and individualism translate into arguments for individualized services for disabled Canadians, alongside arguments for human rights and inclusion. The Canadian Association of Mental Retardation's (CAMR) name change in 1986 to Canadian Association for Community Living (CACL) reflected this change in values and goals from looking after disabled people to supporting disabled people in their social integration. As Peter Park of People First explains of the name change,

We are asking for very little, and it's time you stopped and *listened*! We are asking for the name of the Association to be changed to a non-labelling name, whatever that name. We are proposing "Community Living."

Everyone across Canada was saying the same thing. It brought people from all walks of life together. People got together and said, "Hey, we want this." We no longer want to be told, "Oh go to the back of the bus." We want our rights. We want to be able to exercise our rights. We want to be just people. Our handicap happens to come in there but it is secondary. (Cited in Park *et al.*, 2003: 189)

The 1980s saw the solidification of an effective but divisive focus for the disability movement on advocacy and especially self-advocacy, rather than service. The focus on advocacy was not as tangible at the level of local organizations, and so numbers of volunteers decreased and the local groups diminished in impact. Provincial disability movements, however, benefited greatly from the efficacy of an advocacy approach to disability issues. People First formed its first provincial groups in the 1980s and clearly articulated its self-advocacy goals.

This was a decade of enormous change for disability activism motivated by tangible results in the Charter. Neufeldt explains the reasons for the surge in action: "Three different phenomena coalesced to shape this wave. One had to do with the inherently limiting nature of aging systems; a second with growing resistance to the use of 'pity' and 'sickness' images of disability; and the third with the disability rights revolution" (2003: 22). The actions of disability activists that arose from these motivations were the beginning of major involvement by the disability movement in political processes (Boucher *et al.*, 2003: 152).

Changing the Charter: Mental and Physical Disability Rights

The first major success of the Canadian disability movement, as mentioned above, was the fight to have disability included in the list of rights included in the Charter. Not only was this successful, but disability was the only right added to the Charter in parliamentary debate.[5] The disability movement was inexperienced, under-resourced, and learning how to create powerful and effective coalitions through the process of lobbying for inclusion. As David Lepofsky explains,

Disability activists were inexperienced at national lobbying. We had no faxes for instant communication, for example. I, along with Ontario's disability organizations, was preoccupied with lobbying the provincial Conservative government to include disability in Ontario's Human Rights Code. There was no time to coordinate a national strategy. (Cited in Lathrop, 2000)

As a result, different groups approached the issue simultaneously, drawing on their connections and methods in order to receive hearings and due attention.

The movement was helped by the timing of the Charter. While there had been previous attempts at arguing for disability rights and improved access in Canada, the early 1980s was the first time disabled activists gathered publicly and collectively demanded their rights. As Yvonne Peters explains, speaking of a COPOH arranged demonstration which took place on 3 November 1980: "From my perspective, the demonstration on Parliament Hill signified a historical turning point; an emergence of people with disabilities as a political force in Canadian democracy" (2003: 122). The Charter was debated and passed well into 1981, the UN's International Year of the Disabled (a declaration that Canada had co-sponsored).

Disability advocates applied all the types of political pressure they could, and their eventual success appears to have come from the effectiveness of their coalition, even though it was not a fully coordinated strategy. David Lepofsky, then "constitutional spokesman" of the CNIB (a position that was hastily created for the purpose of campaigning for disability inclusion), argued for a chance to speak at a constitutional hearing. He was eventually invited, but with only 36 hours notice. As he explains, although this put remarkable pressure on him (he was a law student at the time),

> Arguments made by various organizations before the parliamentary committee and elsewhere in 1980 were simple: If the Charter is to guarantee equal rights, it must include equality for all, including persons with disabilities, not just equality for some. (Cited in Lathrop, 2000)

Despite this straightforward argument and the concerted efforts on the part of many groups, then Justice Minister Jean Chrétien initially and continually rejected efforts on the parts of disability activists on the following grounds:

> Since an entrenched Charter is by its very nature a generalized document which does not lend itself to detailed qualifications and limitations, it was ultimately decided to limit the grounds of non-

discrimination to those few which have long been recognized and which do not require substantial qualification. Unfortunately such is not yet the case with respect to those who *suffer physical handicaps* and consequently provision has not been made in the Charter for this ground. (Cited in Peters, 2003: 124–25; emphasis added)

As the language makes clear, those in Chrétien's office did not understand the terms of the disability movement. They were not listening to disabled Canadians' arguments since the idea of "suffering" a "physical handicap" rather than celebrating a difference contradicts their fundamental arguments. Further, that terminology supports the long-standing idea that disability is only a medical condition rather than a socially produced stigma. Chrétien's statement also ignores the existence of mental disability. The basic conflict is between the disability movement's insistence on equality rights and the policy focus on "special projects" that do nothing to address the systemic problems facing disabled Canadians. The COPOH targeted exactly this misunderstanding as it developed a Charter strategy at the Winnipeg World Congress of Rehabilitation International (a gathering that also needed to be convinced of the social dimensions of disability). COPOH coordinator Jim Derksen became a member of the newly struck Obstacles Committee (a Parliamentary Special Committee on the Disabled and the Handicapped) putting him in a position to push from the inside for what his fellow disability advocates were pushing for from the outside.

It is not fully known what resulted in the eventual change of heart on the part of policy-makers—the lobbying from within, the protests outside, the infallible argument presented, the threat of large numbers of disabled people descending en masse onto Parliament Hill, widespread political pressure, fear of international censure. Nonetheless, the term "disability" was added to section 15 of the Charter.

After the Charter: Breaking the Barriers

The Charter inclusion of both physical and mental disability has provided the basis for some interesting and important moments of disability activism and legal challenges and clarifications. In the early 1990s, Canadians with psychiatric and mental disabilities were granted the vote, and polling centres were required to become physically accessible so that people with mobility and sensory impairments would be able to act on a right that had always been legally, but not practically, theirs. In appeals of the initial decision in *Eldridge vs. British Columbia*, the Supreme Court of Canada ruled that Deaf Canadians had the Charter right to sign language interpretation in medical encounters in order to prevent misdiagnosis and other forms of malpractice. These battles, as well as the fight against legalizing euthanasia discussed below, have been relatively successful, but they are lengthy and the outcomes are not always predictable or obviously binding, especially with regards to future policy. As a CCD (1999) publication makes clear, the *Eldridge* decision, which should guarantee equal access to public *and private* programs and services, was important for the disability community but has been ignored by governments who refuse to legislate accessibility. Though a clear success on the part of disability activists, the inclusion of physical and mental disability in the Charter is only one necessary gesture towards full citizenship for Canadians with disabilities.

The 1990s saw the promotion of important notions of community participation, full citizenship, and the development of support programs that would better allow disabled people to gain full employment and therefore have full value in a capitalist social system. COPOH changed its name to the Council of Canadians with Disabilities (CCD) in 1994 to reflect that its members were Canadian citizens primarily. This more national slant was reinforced by the founding of People First of Canada to supplement the existing local and then provincial units (beginning in Alberta) of People First. However, there was a sense that an attempt at a National Strategy for the Integration of Disabled Persons was not cohesive nor comprehensive and that, despite Charter inclusion, there was no clear social justice approach to disability in Canada (Prince, 2004: 65).

In the mid 1990s, a group of Ontario disability advocates began to work together towards the goal of meaningful legislation to ensure full citizenship for Ontarians with disabilities. With the goal of a barrier-free society, the *Ontarians with Disabilities Act* (ODA) committee worked with the ADA as a model. The work for this ODA at first took place under the banner of the provincial Ministry of Citizenship and Immigration, sending the message that full access to society was a matter of belonging, rights, and responsibilities rather than a medical issue. However, recently, the portfolio has been changed to the provincial ministry of social services, sending a very different message about the meaning of the legislation, a message that results from the misunderstanding of an outsider perspective—that disabled people need help more than equality.

Named with explicit reference to the ADA, the ODA came about directly as the result of concerted and consistent lobbying and organizing on the part of disability activists. The push for meaningful legislation aimed at the elimination of physical and social barriers in the public and private sector, in the form of a provincial act, began most notably in Toronto, though other Ontario disability groups had similar goals. With initial support from the NDP government in the mid 1990s, the group made small but insufficient progress. The ODA Action committee was formed as a result and had greater success through lobbying all provincial parties during election time. Each party agreed to support a barrier-removal-focused legislation if elected.

The ODA Action committee grew beyond its Toronto base and functioned through a consultation process which ensured the representation of a wide range of localized concerns (Kitchin and Wilton, 2003). The first ODA (*Bill 83*) was tabled in November 1998. The ODA Action committee was critical of that bill's failure to be comprehensive or to include the private sector. The second ODA (*Bill 125*) from 2001 was slightly improved but still failed to include the private sector in its scope. It was also unclear what the ramifications for public sector organizations would be if they failed to meet the standards it mandated. The third ODA (*Bill 118*), passed in 2005, has a disappointing time frame but includes both physical and social barriers and governs the private and public sectors. It mandates removal of all barriers by the year 2025, which is not really a meaningful or helpful deadline for Canadians with disabilities trying to negotiate everyday life until that date. Nonetheless, the *Access for Ontarians with Disabilities Act* marks a major success based on the actions of the ODA Action committee which, like the groups who fought for inclusion in the Charter, worked both within and outside the legislative process. As Lepofsky (2002) explains,

> Litigating Charter claims, one barrier at a time, costs too much and takes too long. That's why many worked so hard over the past seven years to get Ontario's Conservatives to fulfil their promises to enact and implement an effective Ontarians with Disabilities Act.

Killing Me Softly: Preventing and Removing Disability

The Charter success also led to a flare in the always controversial euthanasia domain in Canada. Euthanasia is the most dramatic means of keeping disabled people out of the mainstream but is seen by radical activists as a similar practice to that of segregated education systems (including special education classrooms). In 1992 Sue Rodriguez decided to fight for access to legal physician-assisted suicide. She and her legal team used the Charter to support her right to what they claimed was an equal rights and access issue. Her lawyer argued that section 241 of the Criminal Code goes "against rights enshrined in the Charter of Rights, including those that prevent discrimination against disabled people. Able-bodied persons can commit suicide on their own" (cited in *Hamilton Spectator*, 1992). While Rodriguez and her legal team were unsuccessful in changing the Criminal Code, the people present at her eventual suicide (including MP Svend Robinson) were never prosecuted. Disability groups tried to support Rodriguez's desire to die with dignity because of their principles of autonomy in decision-making, but they expressed their support carefully so as not to seem to argue that death was always or even often an appropriate choice for disabled Canadians. They faced the dilemma of how to support the autonomy of a disabled person to choose her own life and death situation while also trying to demonstrate publicly that disabled life is well worth living and that disabled people deserve the same rights and freedoms as all Canadians. The BC Coalition of People with Disabilities made clear that they "supported Rodriguez, in public and in court," stating that the coalition "doesn't favor or promote suicide but people should have the right to 'exercise individual autonomy by making significant personal decisions' a right that must extend to the decision to die" (Watts, 1994).

When Robert Latimer murdered his daughter, Tracy, the disability movement took a very clear position against his action that it maintains to this day. Mary Williams, then President of the BC Coalition of Persons with Disabilities, wrote an editorial in which she clearly states,

> Tracy Latimer and Sue Rodriguez were alike in that they were both profoundly disabled. With that, the similarity ends. Sue Rodriguez was a mentally competent adult who made an informed choice to end her own life. Tracy Latimer was a child who had her life terminated without her consent. The BC Coalition of Persons with Disabilities supported and continues to support Sue Rodriguez and her informed choice to end her own life. The coalition does not support Robert Latimer and his actions. (1994: A16)

This stance demonstrates that children with disabilities, whose voices are even less likely to be understood as autonomous, may require advocacy not only from their family members but also from a group of disabled people who have shared their experiences. When Latimer's legal team set out to appeal his conviction, disability advocates[6] received intervenor status, claiming that "the disabled would feel threatened by a reduced sentence" (*Ottawa Citizen*, 1995). Latimer's appeal was unsuccessful, and he is currently serving a 25-year sentence for his crime.

The disability movement is by no means unified on the issue of physician-assisted suicide, but all members are well aware of the dangerous argument that can make the choice of one legal euthanasia lead to a widespread policy, and they feel threatened by that. The spectre of eugenics looms large again at the present moment because of advances in medical technology that allow for genetic prenatal testing that could lead potential parents to decide to discontinue pregnancies if they were at "risk" of giving birth to a disabled child. Disability activists evaluate and educate about the ethics of such genetic testing. The prospect of designer babies could not only result in an overabundance of tall, blond, blue-eyed boys, but also in the elimination of congenital disability. The disability movement does not think of this as a social good, and this is an important way in which their perspective differs markedly from a medical view of disability that would advocate the elimination of disability. As Sophia Isako Wong puts it:

> Until we live in a society where people with Down syndrome are fully integrated into our lives, I do not think that we can know the extent and quality of their contributions. This is why I oppose the use of selective abortion to reduce the number of people born with Down syndrome, just as I oppose the use of sex selection to reduce the number of women in this world. (2002: 102)

Conclusion

Canada may not have witnessed as many in-your-face actions as the US has in the fight for disability equality, but the progress that Canadian disability activists have made is impressive and perhaps more meaningful. While it may seem that the ODA is merely a copycat version of what the US put into place at the national level over a decade ago, it is not only relatively stronger legislation, but it is also based on a constitutional understanding of the equality and social importance of people with both physical and mental disabilities. Disability activists in Canada have made momentous progress, but there is still much work to be done in educating other Canadians about the rights, place, and value of disabled citizens. Despite their many successes, Prince argues that

> A strong and widespread sense of frustration persists within the disability community in Canada, based on personal experience and engagement with authorities, that the political will to act by the federal and provincial governments, while evident at times through the 1980s and 1990s, has, for the most part, been haphazard. (2004: 77)

Prince contends that the process of challenging for, developing, and implementing disability policy is cyclical, at times frustratingly so. He has named this "the déjà vu discourse of disability" within which he includes "the official declaration of plans and promises by governments and other public authorities, followed by external reviews of the record, and then official responses with a reiteration of previously stated plans and promises" (2004: 66). The discourse, as he describes it, tends to be superficial and not attentive to structural change, limited in action, refusing a human rights approach, and limited in scope with vague future promises (2004: 69).

Disability is an issue that affects everyone, and the number of Canadians it affects in terms of personal experience is only set to grow in the coming decades. As Prince explains, the oft-cited advanced age of the baby boomer population will lead to an increase in disability (since disability rates are currently more than double in the seniors' population) (2004: 61). This is an increasingly pressing issue for an aging movement, and there are possibilities for alliances with groups, such as the Raging Grannies, that draw on the limited powers offered to them as venerated older members of the population to take political action. However, the disability movement also needs to attract the attention of younger generations if it is to continue to build on its successes.

Disability is a multi-faceted and highly variable identity and state. This variability results in coalitions of people working collectively for rights under a banner that is tenuously inclusive. Other social movements could benefit from the understanding disability necessitates of the fluidity of identity. Whether as the result of an accident, illness, or change in policy definition, most people will live to experience disability personally. All activists, then, whether disabled or not, have a personal stake in the movement, and should take notice of disabled Canadians in their actions. As Kimberlé Crenshaw has demonstrated, "The problem with identity politics is not that it fails to transcend difference, as some critics charge, but rather the opposite—that it frequently conflates or ignores intra group differences" (1994: 93). She focuses on the relationship between sexism and racism, which often occur simultaneously and cannot be resisted in isolation from each other. Similarly, ableism often occurs in sexist and racist contexts. The DisAbled Women's Network of Ontario (DAWN) demonstrates the importance of intersectionality to the entire spectrum of social movements, arguing that women with disabilities "have needs which are different from men with disabilities" (DAWN, 2005). However, racism is another issue that intersects with disability, as do many gay, lesbian, and transgender issues. As yet, there has not been enough activism in Canada exploring these conjunctions, despite clear indications that Aboriginal peoples in Canada have the highest rate of disability of any group and experience discrimination on a number of fronts. There is still much to be done to achieve full citizenship for all disabled Canadians, and the limits of a rights-based approach, which can elide important and valuable differences, may push the disability movement in exciting and radical new directions.

Notes

1. Deaf refers to people who consider themselves to be part of a cultural community with a shared language, history, and culture. The term deaf refers to the medical condition more commonly understood. D/deaf, then, is an inclusive term referring to culturally Deaf and medically deaf people.

2. Sarah Triano has recently initiated the Disability Pride movement, modeled on other pride movements, particularly gay pride. She explains:

> Disability Pride represents a rejection of the notion that our physical, sensory, mental, and cognitive differences from the non-disabled standard are wrong or bad in any way, and is a statement of our self-acceptance, dignity and pride. It is a public expression of our belief that our disabilities are a natural part of human diversity, a celebration of our heritage and culture, and a validation of our experience. Disability Pride is an integral part of movement building, and a direct challenge to systemic ableism and stigmatizing definitions of disability. It is a militant act of self-definition, a purposive valuing of that which is socially devalued, and an attempt to untangle ourselves from the complex matrix of negative beliefs, attitudes, and feelings that grow from the dominant group's assumption that there is something inherently wrong with our disabilities and identity. (Triano, 2005)

3. Johnson calls institutions housing disabled people and older people (in the American context) the "gulag," saying, "Today's gulag characterizes isolation and control as care and protection, and the disappearances are often called voluntary placements. However, you don't vanish because that's what you want or need. You vanish because that's what the state offers. You make your choice from an array of one" (2003: 58).

4. The physicality of the protest led to some awareness of visible physical disabilities, but mental and invisible disabilities are not addressed in this instance. This is an ongoing concern for the disability movement.

5. While the women's movement and a number of ethno-cultural groups were mobilized and tried to shape the Charter through protest and debate (with some success), Lepofsky makes clear that equality for persons with disabilities was "the only right explicitly added to [the Charter] in the parliamentary debates" (2002).

6. Particularly the Saskatchewan Voice of the Handicapped and the Council of Canadians with Disabilities.

Case

Eldridge vs. British Columbia (Attorney General) [1997] 3 S.C.R. 624.

References and Further Reading

Boucher, Norman, Patrick Fougeyrollas, and Charles Gaucher. 2003. "Development and Transformation of Advocacy in the Disability Movement of Quebec." In Deborah Stienstra and Aileen Wight-Felske (eds.), *Making Equality: History of Advocacy and Persons with Disabilities in Canada.* Concord: Captus Press. 137–62.

CACL (Canadian Association for Community Living). 2005a. "Deinstitutionalization." <http://www.cacl.ca/english/priorityresouces/deinstitution/index.html>.

CACL. 2005b. "Our Values and Beliefs." <http://www.cacl.ca/english/aboutus/valuesbeliefs.html>.

Canadian Association of the Deaf. 2005. "Projects." <http://www.cad.ca/index.php?lid=e&cid=2&pid=0>.

Canadian Council of the Blind. 2005. <http://www.ccbnational.net>.

Canadian Mental Health Association. 2005. "Routes to Work." <http://www.cmha.ca/bins/content_page.asp?cid=7-13-716&lang=1>.

Canadian Mortgage and Housing Commission. 2005. "FlexHousing Adapts to Life's Changes." *Abilities: Canada's Lifestyle Magazine for People with Disabilities* 65 (Winter): 42–43.

CCD (Council of Canadians with Disabilities). 1999. "A Work In Progress: A National Strategy for Persons with Disabilities: The Community Definition." Law Reform: Analysis. <http://www.ccdonline.ca/law-reform/analysis/natstategy.htm>.

CCD. 2005. "About Us." <http://www.ccdonline.ca/about-us/index.htm>.

Crenshaw, Kimberlé Williams. 1994. "Mapping the Margins: Intersectionality, Identity Politics, and Violence against Women of Colour." In Martha Albertson Fineman and Roxanne Mykitiuk (eds.), *The Public Nature of Private Violence.* New York: Routledge. 93–118.

Crichton, Anne, and Lynne Jongbloed. 1998. *Disability and Social Policy in Canada.* Concord: Captus Press.

DAWN (DisAbled Women's Network of Ontario). 2005. "Who We Are." <http://dawn.thot.net/who.html>.

Doe, Tanis. 1994. "Looking for Solidarity in the Margins." *Canadian Congress for Learning Opportunities for Women.* <http://www.nald.ca/cclow/search/details.asp?id=5853>.

Doe, Tanis. 1997. "How Katie Baker Changed My Mind: Second Thoughts on the Slippery Slope." *Herizons* 11(3): 21.

Driedger, Diane. 1993. "Discovering Disabled Women's History." In Linda Carty (ed.), *And Still We Rise: Feminist Political Mobilizing in Canada.* Toronto: Women's Press. 173–87.

Fraser, John, Cynthia Wilkey, and JoAnne Frenschkowksi. 2003. "Denial by Design: The Ontario Disability Support Program." Income Security Advocacy Centre. <http://www.incomesecurity.org/publications.html>.

Frazee, Catherine. 2000. "Body Politics: As a Child, I Had Only One Wish: To Be Able to Walk. At Forty-six, Would I Still Make the Same Wish?" *Saturday Night*, 2 September: 40.

Frazee, Catherine. 2002. "Intersections: Race, Disability, and Activist Culture at Ryerson." *Abilities* 51 (Summer): 39.

Gullison, Line. 2003. "Examining the Housing Choices of Individuals with Disabilities." *Research Highlights: Canadian Housing and Mortgage Corporation* July: 1–4.

Hamilton Spectator. 1992. "Woman Wants Her Suicide Fight to be Heard in BC Courtroom." 4 December: A10.

Hillier, Derek. 2001. "Legal Notes." *Gateway* (Winter): 28–31.

Jenson, Jane. 1995. "'What's in a Name?': Nationalist Movements and Public Discourse." In Hank Johnston and Bert Klandermans (eds.), *Social Movements and Culture*. Minneapolis: University of Minnesota Press. 107–26.

Johnson, Harriet McBryde. 2003. "Disability Gulag." *New York Times Magazine*, 23 November: 58–64.

Kitchin, Rob, and Robert Wilton. 2003. "Disability Activism and the Politics of Scale." *Canadian Geographer* 47(2): 97–115.

Lathrop, Douglas. 2000. "O Canada—The Disability Movement North of the Border." *New Mobility* (September). <http://www.cailc.ca/CAILC/text/illibrary/ocanada/movement_e.html>.

Lepofsky, David. 2002. "How Disabled Won Place in Charter." 17 April. <http://www.odacommittee.net/20years-charter.html>.

Neary, Michele. 2001. "Parents Helping Parents." *Gateway* (Winter): 13–16.

Neufeldt, Aldred. 2003. "Growth and Evolution of Disability Advocacy in Canada." In Deborah Stienstra and Aileen Wight-Felske (eds.), *Making Equality: History of Advocacy and Persons with Disabilities in Canada*. Concord: Captus Press. 11–32.

Ottawa Citizen. 1995. "Three Groups Want Voice at Appeal for Man Who Killed Disabled Child; Farmer Says Daughter Saved from Life of Pain." 18 February: A5.

Panitch, Melanie. 2004. "Vision. Passion. Action. Launching an Activist Poster." *Abilities* (Fall): 47.

Park, Peter, Althea Monteiro, and Bruce Kappel. 2003. "People First: The History and the Dream." In Deborah Stienstra and Aileen Wight-Felske (eds.), *Making Equality: History of Advocacy and Persons with Disabilities in Canada*. Concord: Captus Press. 183–96.

Peters, Yvonne. 2003. "From Charity to Equality: Canadians with Disabilities Take Their Rightful Place in Canada's Constitution." In Deborah Stienstra and Aileen Wight-Felske (eds.), *Making Equality: History of Advocacy and Persons with Disabilities in Canada*. Concord: Captus Press. 119–26.

Prince, Michael. 2004. "Canadian Disability Policy: Still a Hit and Miss Affair." *Canadian Journal of Sociology* 29(1): 59–82.

Rae, John. 2005. "President's Report: Celebrating Our Future." May. <http://www.blindcanadians.ca>.

Rioux, Marcia, and Catherine Frazee. 1999. "The Canadian Framework for Disability Equality Rights." In Melinda Jones and Lee Ann A. Basser Marks (eds.), *Disability, Diversability and Legal Change*. Boston: Martinus Nijhoff Publishers. 171–88.

Roots, James. 2003. "Deaf Education and Advocacy: A Short History of the Canadian Association of the Deaf." In Deborah Stienstra and Aileen Wight-Felske (eds.), *Making Equality: History of Advocacy and Persons with Disabilities in Canada*. Concord: Captus Press. 73–86.

Titchkosky, Tanya. 2001. "Disability: A Rose by Any Other Name? 'People-First' Language in Canadian Society." *Canadian Review of Sociology and Anthropology* 38(2): 125–41.

Titchkosky, Tanya. 2003. *Disability, Self, and Society*. Toronto: University of Toronto Press.

Tremblay, Mary. 2003. "Lieutenant John Counsell and the Development of Medical Rehabilitation and Disability Policy in Canada." In Deborah Stienstra and Aileen Wight-Felske (eds.), *Making Equality: History of Advocacy and Persons with Disabilities in Canada*. Concord: Captus Press. 51–72.

Triano, Sarah. 2005. "Disability Pride." In Gary L. Albrecht (ed.), *Encyclopedia of Disability*. London: Sage.

Valentine, Fraser. 1996. "Taking Policy to Task: Disability Community is Monitoring Federal Task Force on Disability Issues." *Abilities* (Fall): 41.

Valentine, Fraser. 2002. "A National Social Policy Model: Making it Accessible and Empowering for Canadians with Disabilities." *Abilities* 52 (Fall): 53.

Valentine, Fraser. 2005. "From 'Lunatics' to Citizens: Tracing the Emergence and Growth of Disability Politics in Ontario." *Abilities* (Fall): 24.

Vickers, Jill, and Fraser Valentine. 1996. "'Released from the Yoke of Paternalism and Charity': Citizenship and the Rights of Canadians with Disabilities." *International Journal of Canadian Studies* 14: 155–78.

Watts, R. 1994. "Police Probe Quiet Death of Rodriguez." *Victoria Times-Colonist*, 13 February: 1.

Wendell, Susan. 1996. *The Rejected Body: Feminist Philosophical Reflections on Disability*. New York: Routledge.

Williams, M. 1994. "Tracy Latimer Case Not Comparable to Death of Sue Rodriguez." *The Vancouver Sun*, 23 November: A16.

Wong, Sophia Isako. 2002. "At Home with Down Syndrome and Gender." *Hypatia* 17(3): 89–117.

THIRTEEN

Health Social Movements: The Next Wave in Contentious Politics?[1]

Michael Orsini

From breast cancer activism to the struggle of people with AIDS to the recent mobilization of persons suffering from environmental illness, the last few decades have been witness to a flurry of social movement activity targeting health. This chapter provides a glimpse into the brave new world of social movement politics through the lens of three health social movements: AIDS, environmental illness (specifically, Multiple Chemical Sensitivity), and asthma. I am interested in exploring whether health social movements represent the next wave in contentious politics. While we have witnessed waves of protest organized around recognition struggles from, for instance, feminists, LGBT (lesbian, gay, bisexual and transgender) citizens and racial minorities (see Hobson, 2005), and global counter movements against the deleterious effects of globalization and neoliberal policies, I ask whether health is emerging as a "master frame" around which an array of movements is organizing or whether health is simply another way to frame underlying questions of injustice.

Admittedly, this chapter can only begin to scratch the surface of these diverse and heterogeneous movements, each of which merits its own treatment. I have chosen these three to illustrate my contention that such movements throw up at least two new challenges not addressed by many traditional social movements. First, they simultaneously critique and engage with science, as is the case with people suffering from environmental illnesses and AIDS activists, and trouble our common understanding of expert knowledge. Second, they reflect, albeit in new ways, some of the traditional political cleavages that have animated the social movement landscape for decades, namely, gender and racial oppression and class inequalities. What is novel about these movements is how they are able to reconstruct or re-imagine already existing grievances with respect to, for instance, racial oppression or gender oppression, through the lens of health. A good example of this is "asthma activists" in the US who have joined forces with civil rights leaders and environmentalists in mobilizing racialized communities to take ownership of asthma. Activists charge that members of minority communities are disproportionately affected by asthma because, among other things, their physical environment places them at greater risk of being exposed to pollutants, especially in the inner cities of key American states. This debate is especially charged as asthma is increasingly being diagnosed in children; at least 12 per cent of Canadian children have asthma (Asthma Society, 2006).

Not all of the movements mentioned here are particularly active in the Canadian context. Asthma activism, for instance, has taken root in major American urban centres such as Detroit, which is marked by a large African-American underclass, but has not taken hold in the Canadian context—at least not yet. Other movements, however, such as the one advocating on behalf of persons suffering from environmental illness, have had surprising success in cities like Halifax, which recently instituted a scent-free policy to respond to demands from persons who claim to be seriously affected by exposure to, among other chemicals, artificial scents that are found in many products from household cleaners to soap to perfumes.

As is the case with many social movements, contentious politics is marked by its refusal to respect national borders (see Keck and Sikkink, 1998; Tarrow, 2005). Therefore, what is occurring in different national contexts can, and often does, have important effects on how other movements frame their demands and on how they adopt or adapt the templates or "master frames" present in other societies to shape their own collective responses. As outlined in the Introduction, social movement literature draws our attention to the importance of "political opportunity structures"—features of the external political environment that affect the ability of movements to challenge authorities (see Tarrow, 1994: 18). While much has been made of the domestic opportunity structures that influence movement politics, attention has turned recently to expanding this to contention that occurs outside of domestic or national contexts (see Tarrow, 2005). Movements in different territorial contexts may not only provide windows of opportunity for similar or like-minded movement activity to emerge, they may also provide important impetus to a host of challengers or counter movements (Meyer and Staggenborg, 1996).

The chapter begins by introducing the "health social movement" (HSM) concept, which is fairly recent in its formulation, even though scholars have been studying them for several decades. I ask why HSMs should command the attention of scholars and students of Canadian politics and public policy and argue that they provide us with an opportunity to examine the cross-cutting issues of race, gender, and sexuality that have animated traditional social movements. In addition, they are particularly useful in locating debates about the use and dominance of expert knowledge in our society. Second, I provide brief vignettes of three HSMs, each of which reveals an important aspect of the new terrain of collective action. Third, I ask whether new theoretical tools and approaches are required to capture the dynamics of collective action in the field of health.

What Are Health Social Movements?

Health social movements (HSMs) are "collective challenges to medical policy and politics, belief systems, research and practice that include an array of formal and informal organizations, supporters, networks of co-operation and media" (Brown *et al.*, 2004: 52). They are particularly interested in contesting power and authority, be it in the realm of science, medicine, or politics. In addition, HSMs challenge how we understand individual and collective identity. While some might assume that the primary challenge for some HSMs, especially those representing persons living with stigmatizing conditions, might be to mobilize supporters in the first place, one of the more interesting features of such movements has been their ability not only to do so but also to include interested people who are not actually affected by the condition or illness. One important example of the latter has been the ability of the breast cancer movement, especially some of its radical offshoots which target the environmental causes of breast cancer, to mobilize women who are not living with breast cancer to get involved (see Klawiter, 2004). Moreover, it is important to stress here that in addition to the regular obstacles movement actors might face, many HSM activists face the added problem of being ill, which can compromise their ability to mobilize. Seemingly mundane things—such as attending a demonstration in blistering heat—can be especially taxing for someone who is ill.

It is also important to note that the processes of contestation are not uniform when one surveys a range of HSMs. For some movements, the primary struggle is to move scientifically legitimate conditions, which are not the subject of contestation within official circles, onto the political stage (Brown *et al.*, 2004). Asthma is a useful example, since activists need not spend time convincing others that it is a legitimate condition; instead, asthma offers an opportunity to mount wider challenges around environmental issues such as transit pollution, which activists claim disproportionately affects people living with asthma. Asthma has also become racialized in the US, as it is has become known that the overwhelming majority of new cases occur in economically disadvantaged urban communities in which there are significant numbers of African Americans. In addition, some members of HSMs face a greater uphill battle in convincing the public and authorities that their condition is legitimate in the first place, as is amply demonstrated by the case of environmental illness.

Much energy is devoted to convincing naysayers that the symptoms they are experiencing are indeed real and that these symptoms can be linked directly to their exposure to consumer items that many of us take for granted.

Following Brown *et al.* (2004), I divide HSMs in three categories: *health access*, *constituency based*, and *embodied* health movements. First, health access movements, as their name implies, are primarily interested in "equitable access to health care and improved provision of health-care services" (Brown *et al.*, 2004: 52). Constituency based health movements are interested in redressing health inequalities that may be based on race, ethnicity, gender, class, and/or sexuality differences. The third type, embodied health movements, "address disease, disability or illness experience by challenging science on etiology, diagnosis, treatment and prevention" (Brown *et al.*, 2004: 52).

Embodied health movements are identified by three characteristics (Brown *et al.*, 2004). First, they place the "biological bodies" of people who are experiencing the disease at the centre of their efforts. Second, they often contest existing scientific or medical knowledge and practice. As Epstein (1995) has said of the AIDS movement, they challenge "science as industry" and "science as procedures." In the case of AIDS, for instance, activists have contested the role of the pharmaceutical industry with respect to the availability and affordability of AIDS drugs (science as industry), but they also insinuated themselves into debates about the appropriate conduct of science, including the use of clinical trials (science as procedures). Third, movement actors often find themselves collaborating with scientists and other health professionals in working to raise the profile of the disease/illness in question, whether that be advocating for increased funding for research, treatment issues, or prevention efforts. These three features, taken together, allow Brown *et al.* to position embodied health movements as "boundary movements." They use this term to underline their contention that these movements blur the lines between the state and civil society, between what is considered expert knowledge and experiential or lay knowledge (Brown *et al.*, 2004: 54). Moreover, these movements borrow liberally from other social movements (e.g., the feminist and environmental movements), which complicates efforts to study them in isolation without paying attention to their forerunners.

Given the range of movements that merit scholarly attention, why, one might ask, is it useful to throw the spotlight on HSMs? First, the attainment of health is becoming a dominant theme in society and thus is on the minds of policy-makers interested in reflecting back citizens' priorities. Some scholars view this as part of a broader trend toward "healthism," a twenty-first-century ideology based on the primacy of health and wellness (Marsh, 2001). Why is health so important to us today? The answers are varied. One might argue, for instance, that rapid progress and the speed of changes associated with globalization have ushered in an era in which our environment, both physical and social, may be placing our collective health at risk. German sociologist Ulrich Beck famously coined the term "risk society" to characterize an era in which we are increasingly less capable of shielding ourselves from all manner of risk (Beck, 1992). Others speculate that health is emerging as an important political/social cleavage in its own right because people's sense of spiritual and material alienation forces them to find some comfort in assuming a "sick role"; they are able to find, as it were, an identity through illness. Sociologist Frank Furedi (2005: 2) has argued that society is becoming obsessed with sickness to the extent that "being ill is seen as a normal state, possibly even more normal than being healthy. We are all now seen as being potentially ill; that is the default state we live in today." One can claim a middle ground, however, between a focus on the individual and a broader focus on the external world; such a perspective would view health and contestation around health as intersubjectively created and produced through subjects who make choices in a context that is not necessarily of their own making.

AIDS Activism and the Social Construction of Knowledge

Although we are only a quarter century into the AIDS epidemic, much has happened in the world of AIDS activism since the early 1980s when the disease first struck the gay community in North America. AIDS activism has moved from the very margins of society to occupying a central place in understanding the response to the epidemic. Kinsman was correct to suggest that the AIDS movement has become "one of the most profound social movements ever to emerge around health issues" (1992: 217). The biennial International Conference on AIDS attracts more than 15,000 of the world's leading researchers, scientists, and advocates in the field. After much agitation, this meeting of distinguished experts carved out an important space for the "other" experts: patients themselves and groups representing them.

When AIDS activists adopted the Holocaust slogan "Silence=Death" to characterize government inaction on AIDS, they probably had no idea how these simple words would burn in the memory of generations of activists. The slogan was the brainchild of ACT UP (AIDS Coalition to Unleash Power), one of the high profile AIDS activist organizations to emerge on the international scene. Formed in New York City in 1987, it retains several chapters in major North American and European cities. Two Canadian chapters, one in Montreal and another in Vancouver, had been in the forefront of radical AIDS activism in Canada, but have since disbanded. ACT UP made an important splash at the International Conference on AIDS when it was held in Vancouver in 1996. Spurred on by ACT UP, thousands of delegates at the conference stood and turned their backs on then federal Health Minister David Dingwall for the duration of his speech to protest against the government's plan to cancel the National AIDS Strategy, a program that funds a range of community-based prevention initiatives across the country. This symbolic action, reported by the international media, illustrates the importance of the media in the framing of issues. Although many of the foreign delegates attending the conference were unaware of the controversy regarding the renewal of the National AIDS Strategy, the impression left by the "action" was that all AIDS activists and AIDS researchers were united in their opposition to the Canadian government's attempts to renege on its funding commitment to AIDS. (The federal government decided in the end not to cancel the strategy.) As Gusfield notes, "mass media do more than monitor: They dramatize. They create vivid images, impute leadership, and heighten the sense of conflict between movements and the institutions of society" (1994: 71).

ACT UP redefined public protest in several key respects. For example, it staged "die-ins," during which activists drew police-style chalk outlines around each other's dead bodies. Its most popular symbol, Silence=Death, is emblazoned beneath a pink triangle, the Nazi emblem for gay men. As Gamson explains, "ACT UP takes a symbol used to mark people for death and reclaims it. They reclaim, in fact, control over defining a cause of death; the banner connects gay action to gay survival, on the one hand, and homophobia to death from AIDS, on the other" (1989: 361). ACT UP's enemy, Gamson explains, is not the state per se, but is "invisible, disembodied, ubiquitous: it is the very process of normalization through labelling in which everyone except one's own community of the de-normalized (and its supporters) is involved" (1989: 357).

Much activist energy is spent trying to resist the language commonly summoned to explain disease, and the AIDS movement is no exception. One of its early demands was that the term "AIDS victim" be replaced by "People with AIDS." The Denver Principles, the manifesto of the National Association of People with AIDS in the US, opens with this statement regarding naming: "We condemn attempts to label us as 'victims,' which implies defeat, and we are only occasionally 'patients,' which implies passivity, helplessness, and dependence upon the care of others. We are 'people with AIDS'" (quoted in Navarre, 1993: 148). Of course, the legacy of this shift in thinking about illness has spread beyond AIDS. Radical breast cancer activists, for instance, have publicly acknowledged the AIDS movement as inspiring their unique brand of activism.

One of the more contentious issues with respect to AIDS activism relates to the ability of AIDS activists to maintain an autonomous voice in the face of increased reliance on state support and creeping bureaucratization. More than a decade ago, government funding of AIDS groups had "created rather than eliminated the room to generate radical criticism of state policies" (Rayside and Lindquist, 1992: 69). It is not clear, however, whether the same holds true today. Rayside and Lindquist suggested at the time that the general suspicion with which lesbian and gay activists viewed the state provided a healthy buffer against co-optation. That said, they did warn of the potential that AIDS issues might become overly institutionalized, "tailored to fit pre-existent bureaucratic policies and agendas, and distorted in a way that depoliticizes them" (Rayside and Lindquist 1992: 70). Today, AIDS advocacy is channelled largely through institutionalized groups seeking public or community support for the delivery of programs and services, such as the Canadian AIDS Society, the national umbrella organization that represents about 125 community groups throughout the country. The radical activist politics associated with organizations such as ACT UP appears to have disappeared from the Canadian political landscape, although traces of this in-your-face brand of activism can be found in the Toronto-based group AIDS Action Now!

Finally, as alluded to earlier, much of the anger expressed by AIDS activists in general has been directed, not surprisingly, against the twin pillars of science and medicine. The case of the neglect of women is an important example in that it also illustrates how movements organized to challenge stigmatization (in this case of gay men with AIDS) can reproduce stigma of their own. For more than a decade, the Centers for Disease Control (CDC) in the US (not to mention its Canadian counterpart, which often follows the CDC's lead) was loath to represent women in epidemiological understandings of AIDS. The CDC's original definition of AIDS, produced in 1987, required HIV infection along with specific opportunistic infections or cancers (such as *Pneumocystis carinii* pneumonia or Kaposi's sarcoma, a skin cancer). The list was developed when AIDS affected mainly gay males. In women, the early stages of HIV infection produce different symptoms (such as persistent gynecological infections and cervical cancer) than those in the CDC definition. The new, expanded definition includes HIV-positive people with CD4-counts of less than 200 per milliliter and, in response to pressure from women AIDS activists, a list of HIV-related illnesses, including the gynecological abnormalities and cancers from which women had suffered or died. Since the medical conditions experienced by many HIV-infected women were not included in the CDC's AIDS definition until late 1993, women often were diagnosed and treated later than men. This was connected to broader issues of treatment, since up until recently many women did not qualify for benefit payments because their symptoms differed from men's. The sentiment of women AIDS activists was best expressed in their placard: "Women don't get AIDS; they just die from it." While waging a war of recognition of women's unique experiences with HIV, activists for women with HIV nonetheless challenged the scientific establishment on a more pragmatic front to include more women in clinical trials—to, in other words, engage with science rather than solely criticize its gender-biased practices. Several reasons were offered to explain women's underrepresentation in clinical trials of AIDS drugs: (1) they may be excluded because they are either potentially or actually pregnant; (2) they are members of minority groups and lack access to the health care system in general and to research in particular; (3) they are drug users and are presumed to be noncompliant subjects; and (4) most of the trials focused on AIDS itself, not solely HIV infection, and many women did not fit the clinical definition of AIDS (Johnson, 1992: 3).

The AIDS movement is a potent example of how individual citizens can challenge society and the state to become credible experts in their own right and confront the stigma that surrounds an HIV diagnosis. The next movement we will examine, while still in its infancy, is also interested in challenging the dominance of science and medicine. Unlike the AIDS movement, however, the main challenge posed by people suffering from environmental illness involves getting others to take the disease seriously in the first place.

Multiple Chemical Sensitivity Syndrome: Scents and Sensibilities

The number of people coming forward to claim that their health is being harmed by exposure to small amounts of chemicals and toxic products has been on the increase in the last few decades. Multiple Chemical Sensitivity (MCS) is also referred to more broadly as environmental illness. It usually denotes a reaction to chemical substances well below what would be considered normal. Those affected can be sensitive to a number of scented products—cleaning products, detergents, paints, pesticides, moulds, or food. Depending on the severity, a person may become isolated if they are unable to tolerate their workplace, school, or home. In extreme cases, this might require a visit to a "safe" place where an individual can restore their environmental health. Nova Scotia was the first province in the country to set up such a place, the Nova Scotia Environmental Health Centre. This self-described oasis provides shelter to the environmentally sensitive and acts as a place for patients seeking emotional support and various forms of treatment for their condition. The Centre takes its mission very seriously. Visitors are warned that they should arrive free of any scented products (deodorants, shampoos, perfumes, tobacco smoke) and free of clothing that has been dry cleaned. If they are found to be in violation of this policy, they "will have the option of showering and changing into Centre scrubs or making another appointment" (Nova Scotia Environmental Health Centre, 2006).

It is, perhaps, not surprising, that those advocating on behalf of the environmentally ill are often dismissed as extreme, even Draconian, in their efforts to protect themselves from an environment they perceive as encroaching on their health and well-being. While one may quibble over the extent to which society should bend in accommodating their needs, it is evident that the experiences of the environmentally ill throw up a range of interesting policy challenges not always easily accommodated by policy-makers and society more broadly. At one level, they are demanding to be viewed as legitimately disabled, which can have repercussions for how we measure and compensate suffering. If MCS is not recognized by one's physician, how, for instance, can a patient rightfully claim to be disabled or to be unable to work and thus be eligible to receive social assistance or to request permission to be on paid sick leave from her/his employer? In addition, they are asking governments and societies more broadly to introduce policies banning the use of scented products in public bathrooms, regulating the use of certain chemicals in consumer products, etc. And, in order to press their case and potentially exaggerate their "injustice frame," activists often liken their experiences with their enemies in the chemical industry— including the manufacturers of pesticides, fragrances, cosmetics, and toiletries—to the tobacco industry's attempts to deny the link between smoking and cancer. The chemical lobby, they claim, devotes much of its efforts to questioning the existence of chemical sensitivity, attacking its sufferers as well as any sympathetic researchers who have studied its prevalence, instead of asking the tough questions about the links between these chemicals and a host of illnesses.

Not surprisingly, Halifax's decision to go scent-free has sparked a flurry of responses, from support to outright condemnation. Organizations supported by the fragrance industry, for instance, have attacked the scientific basis for the claim that scented products are the culprit. American conservative critic Michael Fumento, who once wrote about the "myth of heterosexual AIDS," has lashed out at the City of Halifax for caving in to the "fragrance fighters." In one article, he quotes a researcher who suggests that the overwhelming majority of people who claim to be environmentally ill are more than likely suffering from mental illness (Fumento, 2000).

As Kroll-Smith and Floyd (2000) explain, the challenges mounted by people who claim to be environmentally ill are not benign; they require those who are not affected to alter their behaviours to accommodate those who may be potentially harmed by exposure. Those who choose to ignore the plight of the environmentally ill are "implicated in the exacerbation" of their illness. Consider this revealing anecdote. Kroll-Smith and Floyd interviewed "Jack," who claimed to be suffering from environmental illness. The interviewer was seated 20 feet from the individual, and came to the interview having respected the wishes of the interviewee: he showered without using soap, wore all cotton clothing, did not wear any scented products, and made sure his clothes were washed without the use of a fabric softener.

> Shortly after starting the interview, Jack became visibly agitated, lifting himself from side to side and up and down in his chair ... He explained that he was reacting to something new in his house ... His symptoms were increasing in severity. He looked at my pen and asked if it contained a soy based ink. I told him I bought it at a bookstore without checking the chemical composition of the ink. He smiled knowingly and asked me to put the ink pen outside. Within a few minutes his symptoms subsided. (Kroll-Smith and Floyd, 2000: 83)

While such examples may seem extreme indeed, other groups suggest that we should not underestimate the extent to which we are exposed to harmful chemicals in our everyday lives. Environmental Defence, a Toronto-based organization, released a much-publicized report in 2005 called *Toxic Nation*, which revealed the results of testing 11 Canadians from across the country for a range of chemicals. The study found that the participants tested positive for 60 of 88 chemicals, including 18 heavy metals and 14 PCBs (Toxic Nation, 2006). What's more, a person's place of residence did not seem to affect the level of exposure. Indeed, one of the study participants, a First Nations leader from Northern Quebec, which is fairly distant from most point sources of pollution, showed the highest levels of mercury and persistent organic pollutants in his system. Renowned wildlife artist Robert Bateman, who lives on idyllic Salt Spring Island, British Columbia, was not spared, either. He tested positive for 48 of the 88 chemicals, including 32 cancer-causing chemicals. As the organization's executive director put it bluntly, "If you can walk, talk and breathe, you're contaminated" (Environmental Defence, Press Release, 9 November 2005).

While there is greater acceptance of the health problems posed by our immediate environment, people suffering from environmental illness (especially MCS) must confront suggestions that the source of their ill health resides somewhere outside of their immediate environment. This, no doubt, frustrates their attempts to be seen as credible actors on the political stage.

The final movement we will discuss is also connected to the environment, but it differs from environmental illness in that the main source of contestation does not concern the legitimacy of the illness per se; rather, it focuses on the intersection of environmental and justice concerns, specifically the claim that poverty and race place certain individuals at greater risk of developing asthma than others.

Asthma Activism: Race, Class, and the Politics of Disease

Asthma may seem to be an unlikely candidate for a discussion of HSMs. For the most part, it would seem, asthma advocates eschew the type of activities normally adopted by social movement adherents. People suffering from asthma are not typically marching in the streets or agitating governments for social change. Increasingly, however, asthma has become politicized. While organizations representing people with asthma are interested typically in raising awareness of the societal costs of this condition and of the need for prevention, greater attention is shifting to explaining the underlying environmental conditions that place people at greater risk of acquiring asthma in the first place or, at the very least, of triggering symptoms. While advocates for asthma have long emphasized a need to control indoor environmental triggers (e.g., pets in a home, mould, dust mites), increasingly they are focusing attention on outdoor triggers, such as air pollution. In the case of one's indoor environment, there is a greater focus on individual responsibility; parents, for instance, are cautioned to take greater care in ensuring that their child's home is as safe as possible. When one shifts the focus to the external environment, however, suddenly the field expands considerably. Not surprisingly, this new focus has found the agenda of asthma activists overlapping significantly with the concerns of the environmental justice movement. In the US, for instance, community organizations are mobilizing people with asthma not only to manage their condition, but to "see themselves as part of a collective of people with asthma who understand the importance of external factors beyond their individual homes" (Brown *et al.*, 2003: 461). Such consciousness-raising teaches people with asthma to link their bodily experiences (wheezing, coughing) to factors in their immediate environment: "They cannot think about their inhalers without thinking about the excess of bus depots and trash incinerators located in their neighborhoods" (Brown *et al.*, 2003: 461). One Boston-area organization that targets transit issues such as the idling of diesel buses has been successful in claiming that residents of the neighbourhoods in question are victims of "transit racism" (Brown *et al.*, 2003: 458). They argued that bus riders were being discriminated against when government money that could have gone to purchase newer, less pollution-causing buses was instead given over to a major highway project.

This "politicized illness experience" takes as its starting point the subjective experience of dealing with an illness and grafts that onto a wider critique of society and politics. A key turning point for individuals, then, is to recognize that they are not helpless victims of an unfortunate condition but can be active agents mobilizing fellow sufferers and policy-makers, as well as community leaders, to take collective responsibility for health and environment issues.

Viewing the importance of outdoor environmental factors has a ricochet effect in that it allows people with asthma to recognize that the poor quality of their indoor environment is not entirely within their control but rather is linked to wider social structural problems, which force families to live in squalid conditions that might exacerbate asthma triggers (e.g., cockroach infested quarters). Cleaning up one's own household is only part of the solution. In addition, for some activists, asthma is a master key that connects the dots among a number of policy problems, from educational attainment to the role of the pharmaceutical industry, which benefits from the large market demand for prescription drugs (e.g., inhalers or "puffers") among asthmatics. As one California activist explains, "Asthma is a hub in a large net of issues that bring us together" (Winant, 2004: 1).

It is interesting to note, however, that in Canada, the main national asthma advocacy organization, the Asthma Society of Canada, does not offer much in the way of information on the social justice dimensions of asthma. While the organization's website mentions that air pollution can worsen the symptoms of asthmatic persons, it also notes that "air pollution as a cause of asthma has not been verified" (see Asthma Society of Canada, www.asthma.ca/adults/lifestyle/outdoor.php). The major focus of the organization is on individual self control—asthma patients are counselled to take responsibility by limiting their exposure to factors that might harm or trigger an asthmatic episode. Under the heading, "Taking Control," patients are told that "Asthma doesn't have to control your life. Instead, you can control your asthma ..." (Asthma Society, 2006). This hyper individuality is not unique to asthma, however. Under the guise of empowering the patient consumer, a range of illnesses/conditions are reframed as challenges to be overcome through proper lifestyle management, from diabetes to coronary heart disease to obesity.

In contrast, in the US the California chapter of the American Lung Association is supporting clean air initiatives in low-income communities of colour and using the language of the environmental justice movement to anchor its advocacy. It is responding to the fact that in California many low-income families live near refineries, petroleum tank farms, and hazardous waste disposal sites. In some neighbourhoods, as many as one in six children has asthma (see American Lung Association of California). Even the American Environmental Protection Agency has entered the fray, calling for increased asthma education and prevention to achieve environmental justice.

Having surveyed these three HSMs, each of which provides a distinctive prism through which to examine health-related contestation, I next ask whether we have the proper analytical tools to capture this newly emerging and dynamic field of social movement activism.

Desperately Seeking a Theoretical Framework

There has been much debate in the social movement literature on the choice of theoretical approach; much of this debate, however, has generated more heat than light. While it is not necessary to replay the academic jousting matches that have occurred, it is important to summarize briefly the two paradigms normally summoned to explain social movement activity and ask whether we need to adapt these approaches to the new realities of social movements. As discussed in the Introduction of this book, the first approach, Resource Mobilization Theory (RMT) is more state-centred in its approach and, hence, more akin to traditional notions of interest-group lobbying rooted in access to resources. It emphasizes the historical continuities of movements. The second, new social movement (NSM) theory, defines movements in a wider context and emphasizes goals such as identity and autonomy. Civil society, not the state, is the main unit of analysis. Of course, these strict categorizations do not sufficiently explain the processes of collective action. Identity and autonomy may be bound up with competition for resources; conversely, access to resources is often tied to larger political issues, such as autonomy. Each approach reveals only one part of the story, however. RMT theorists assert that "social movement activities are not spontaneous and disorganized and that social movement participants are not irrational" (Ferree, 1992: 29). Their strategic approach to the study of social movements is a direct response to previous theories of collective behaviour, which reduced political action to irrational outbursts of time and place (see Kornhauser, 1959; Smelser, 1962). Emerging in the US in the 1970s, RMT derived intellectual support from, among others, Mancur Olson's *The Logic of Collective Action* (1965). An economist, Olson challenged the notion that groups, much like individuals, act in their own self-interest. Indeed, according to Olson, the rational actor will pursue collective action only if the benefits of doing so outweigh the costs involved. The problem, however, is that individuals may reap the rewards of collective action regardless of their involvement—the so-called "free-rider" problem.

Resource mobilization scholars have been accused of "normalizing' collective protest. Piven and Cloward assert that RMT's focus on the similarities between conventional and protest action muddies the understanding of social movement behaviour: "Blurring the distinction between normative and non-normative forms of collective action is the most fundamental expression of this tendency, as if rule-conforming and rule-violating collective action are of a piece" (Piven and Cloward, 1995: 137). They contend that RMT theorists mistakenly lump together all collective action, regardless of whether it is in fact peaceful or violent.

If RMT responds to the "how" of social movement action, social movement theory stresses the "why"—meaning displaces structure as the foundational logic of social movements. For NSM theorists, issues of collective identity are central to the creation of social movement organizations. A key distinguishing feature of such movements is that they do not rally around class as a defining issue: "new" social movements are presumably postmodern, postmaterial, or uninterested in the economy or the state (Offe, 1985; Touraine, 1988; Cohen, 1985). It is argued that NSM actors enter the political arena to defend not their economic interests but their collective identities. Collective identity is understood here as "nothing else than a shared definition of the field of opportunities and constraints offered to collective action: 'shared' means constructed and negotiated through a repeated process of 'activation' of social relationships connecting through the actors" (Melucci, 1985: 793). Collective identity formation is an all-encompassing process through which actors produce cognitive frameworks that enable them to survey their immediate environment and to assess the costs and benefits of their actions. NSM theorists use the term "framing" to refer to "the conscious strategic efforts by groups of people to fashion shared understandings of the world and of themselves that legitimate and motivate collective action" (McAdam *et al.*, 1996: 6). As Goffman famously wrote of framing, "There is a sense in which what is play for the golfer is work for the caddy" (cited in Gusfield, 1997: 202). Movements frame the problems/issues they seek to address and the nature/substance of their claims. Collective action frames "underscore and embellish the seriousness and injustice of a particular social condition or redefine as unjust and immoral what was previously seen as unfortunate but perhaps tolerable" (Benford, 1997: 416).

Several theorists assert that the two paradigms may actually complement one another, that each can make important contributions to the study of social movements. McClurg Mueller (1992: 50) asserts that "one paradigm does not necessarily supersede the other, but rather affords a figure/ground shift in what is considered problematic." Canel (1992) suggests that social movements must be understood with reference to six factors, loosely grouped under two headings: macro-processes and micro-processes. The first set of factors includes three related concerns: systemic explanations of the rise of new social actors, an elucidation of the relationship between the state and civil society, and the process of collective identity formation. The second includes "the dynamics of mobilization, organizational dynamics, and social networks" (Canel, 1992: 50). For Canel, NSM theorists are well-equipped to address the first set of factors, while RMT theorists are adequately placed to deal with the second. Cohen and Arato (1994: 509) stress that students of social movements should "view civil society as the target as well as the terrain of collective action" and examine the processes through which "collective actors create the identities and solidarities they defend."

While Tarrow's influential work on political opportunity structures has been helpful in informing debates about the ebb and flow of collective action, it has been less useful in probing issues related to collective identity formation. Moreover, the focus on structure has tended to exaggerate the differences between the state and society. Rather than thinking in terms of movements against states, it may be more useful to recognize that the two categories can bleed into one another. Protest and contention can move inside institutions (Katzenstein, 1998); organizations can work collaboratively with state actors to bring about policy change. The focus of social movement theorists on issues of collective identity, on the other hand, sheds necessary light on issues that transcend resource attainment. This is especially relevant in the case of HSMs, since although political battles ensue over funding of scientific and medical research, a significant component of HSM activism is devoted to overturning "meanings" affixed to disease/illness generally and the role of citizens in these processes.

One promising area of research in the study of social movements has been the adoption of narrative approaches (see Polletta, 1998). There are important links between the study of narrative in social movement theory and the study of narrative in the fields of medical sociology and medical anthropology that can be exploited. As Polletta explains, subsuming narrative under the broader category of frame, however, obscures some of the real differences between the two. What makes a frame successful "is clear specification not only of the injustice against which protest must be mounted but the agents and likely efficacy of the protest. People must be shown that deliberate action will have its intended effect." Narrative, on the other hand, succeeds by what it doesn't convey: "Narrative necessitates our interpretive participation, requires that we struggle to fill in the gaps and resolve the ambiguities. We struggle because the story's end is consequential—not only as the outcome but as the moral of the events which precede it" (Polletta 1998: 141). Marrying narrative and social movement approaches to health can be useful in uncovering the embodied nature of illness; that is, understanding how people experience or make sense of illness in their everyday lives can shed light on potential strategies to reduce the incidence of disease and embrace prevention strategies. Moreover, a focus on the situated knowledge of persons living with illness can allow us to understand the dynamic processes of politicization that accompany some illnesses and not others. For instance, narratives of blame can partly help to explain why persons living with a stigmatizing illness might choose to suffer in silence; this may be compounded in instances where the ill person is already on the margins of society (see Orsini and Scala, 2006).

Conclusion

This chapter has introduced the reader to a range of HSMs that dot the Canadian political landscape—and beyond. The three movements chosen— HIV/AIDS, environmental illness, and asthma—are all engaged in efforts to deconstruct (and reconstruct) how we understand health. The AIDS movement has been instrumental in challenging the notion that the only credible experts on the epidemic are scientists or medical doctors. The lay expertise of people with AIDS has permanently marked our understanding of the disease and has influenced many HSMs formed in the wake of the epidemic. While it is fashionable to decry the mainstreaming of AIDS and the "selling out" of AIDS activists, they deserve credit for resurrecting the patient from his/her sick role—and sick bed. An interesting question that flows from this idea is whether the image of the angry, defiant, placard-waving person with AIDS has become the standard by which all people with AIDS are judged and whether there is any discursive space for people with AIDS who eschew participation in activist organizations and who prefer to live out their illness behind closed doors.

The second movement, organized around the notion of environmental illness, is less mature in Canada, but there are indications that a number of disparate organizations are beginning to make their voices heard. I chose to feature MCS because it raises a set of perplexing questions for students of social movements centred on the notion of the body itself as a site of contestation. Persons claiming to be environmentally ill use their biological bodies to contest biomedicine's claims that there is no sound science demonstrating a causal link between MCS and environmental triggers. What is particularly interesting about these processes of contestation, however, is that victims are "linking their somatic disorders to rational explanations borrowed from the profession of biomedicine" (Kroll-Smith and Floyd, 2000: 83).

The third movement we examined, asthma activism, is useful in highlighting how hitherto depoliticized illnesses can acquire a contentious dimension, especially when movements can borrow from the scripts of other movements, including in this case the environmental justice (see Chapter 11, this volume) and civil rights movements. It was noted, however, that in Canada, asthma advocacy remains tied to the notion of empowering the individual asthma sufferer to take charge of their condition.

Finally, I asked at the outset whether the proliferation of HSMs is reflective of a wider shift in the terrain of collective action. Is health emerging as a dominant cleavage in Canadian society, eclipsing other cleavages that have animated politics in the past? Is our health status becoming a currency we trade in the political marketplace, or is it, rather, another way of expressing deeply felt grievances related to other forms of oppression, such as those linked to race, gender, and sexuality? The answers to these questions are not readily available. There are certainly examples of health social movements that are new, such as MCS, in the sense that they are viewed as the product of the proliferation of chemicals and toxins in our environment. In the case of asthma, there are increasing attempts to frame this public health problem in the language of social justice. It might be best, however, to heed Melucci's suggestion that "movements no longer operate as characters but as signs" (1988: 249). In challenging the dominant "cultural codes" in society, HSMs force us to rethink how we understand the connection between our bodies and our environments.

Note

1. Part of this research was made possible by a grant from the Canadian Institutes of Health Research, which funded my research on Hepatitis C and allowed me to develop further my interest in health social movements. In addition, a grant from the University of Ottawa's Faculty of Social Sciences allowed me to hire Lee Weiler, whose research assistance is gratefully acknowledged. My thanks to Miriam Smith and to the anonymous reviewers for helpful comments.

References and Further Reading

American Lung Association of California.<http://www.californialung.org>.
Aronowitz, Stanley. 1995. "Against the Liberal State: ACT UP and the Emergence of Postmodern Politics." In Linda Nicholson and Steven Seidman (eds.), *Social Postmodernism: Beyond Identity Politics*. Cambridge: Cambridge University Press.
Asthma Society of Canada. 2006. Adults. <http://www.asthma.ca>.
Beck, Ulrich. 1992. *Risk Society: Towards a New Modernity*. Trans. Mark Ritter. London: Sage.
Benford, Robert. 1997. "An Insider's Critique of the Social Movement Framing Perspective." *Sociological Inquiry* 67(4): 409–30.
Brown, Phil, Stephen Zavestoski, Theo Luebke, Joshua Mandelbaum, Sabrina McCormick, and Brian Mayer. 2003. "The Health Politics of Asthma: Environmental Justice and the Collective Illness Experience in the United States." *Social Science and Medicine* 57: 453–64.
Brown, Phil, Stephen Zavestoski, Sabrina McCormick, Brian Mayer, Rachel Morello-Frosch, and Rebecca Gasior Altman. 2004. "Embodied Health Movements: New Approaches to Social Movements in Health." *Sociology of Health and Illness* 26(1): 50–80.
Canel, Eduardo. 1992. "New Social Movement Theory and Resource Mobilization: The Need for Integration." In William K. Carroll (ed.), *Organizing Dissent:*

Contemporary Social Movements in Theory and Practice. Toronto: Garamond Press.

Cohen, Jean L. 1985. "Strategy or Identity: New Theoretical Paradigms and Contemporary Social Movements." *Social Research* 52(4): 663–716.

Cohen, Jean L., and Andrew Arato. 1994. *Civil Society and Political Theory.* Cambridge: MIT Press.

Crimp, Douglas, and Adam Rolston. 1990. *AIDS Demo Graphics.* Seattle: Bay Press.

Environmental Defence. 2005. "Harmful Toxic Chemicals Pollute Blood of Canadians." <http://www.environmentaldefence.ca/pressroom/releases/20051109.htm>.

Epstein, Steven. 1995. "The Construction of Lay Expertise: AIDS Activism and the Forging of Credibility in the Reform of Clinical Trials." *Science, Technology, and Human Values* 20(4): 408–37.

Epstein, Steven. 1996. *Impure Science: AIDS, Activism, and the Construction of Knowledge.* Berkeley: University of California Press.

Ferree, Myra Mark. 1992. "The Political Context of Rationality: Rational Choice Theory and Resource Mobilization." In Aldon D. Morris and Carol McClurg Mueller (eds.), *Frontiers in Social Movement Theory.* New Haven and London: Yale University Press.

Fumento, Michael. 2000. "Scents and Senselessness." *The American Spectator* (April). <http://www.fumento.com/scents.html>.

Furedi, Frank. 2005. "Our Unhealthy Obsession with Sickness." <http://spiked-online.com/Printable/0000000CA958htm>.

Gamson, Josh. 1989. "Silence, Death, and the Invisible Enemy: AIDS Activism and Social Movement 'Newness.'" *Social Problems* 36(4): 351–67.

Gusfield, Joseph. 1994. "The Reflexivity of Social Movements: Collective Behaviour and Mass Society Theory Revisited." In Enrique Laraña, Hank Johnston, and Joseph R. Gusfield (eds.), *New Social Movements: From Ideology to Identity.* Philadelphia: Temple University Press.

Gusfield, Joseph. 1997. "The Culture of Public Problems: Drinking-Driving and the Symbolic Order." In Allan M. Brandt and Paul Rozin (eds.), *Morality and Health.* New York and London: Routledge.

Hobson, Barbara (Ed.). 2005. *Recognition Struggles and Social Movements.* Cambridge: Cambridge University Press.

Jenson, Jane. 1995. "What's in a Name? Nationalist Movements and Public Discourse." In Hank Johnston and Bert Klandermans (eds.), *Social Movements and Culture.* London: UCL Press.

Johnson, Judith A. 1992. *Women With HIV Infection.* Washington: Congressional Research Service, Library of Congress.

Katzenstein, Mary Fainsod. 1998. *Faithful and Fearless: Moving Feminist Protest inside the Church and Military.* Princeton, NJ: Princeton University Press.

Keck, Margaret, and Kathryn Sikkink. 1998. *Activists Beyond Borders: Advocacy Networks in International Politics.* Ithaca: Cornell University Press.

Kinsman, Gary. 1992. "Managing AIDS Organizing: 'Consultation,' 'Partnership,' and the National AIDS Strategy." In William K. Carroll (ed.), *Organizing*

Dissent: Contemporary Social Movements in Theory and Practice. Toronto: Garamond.

Klawiter, Maren. 2004. "Breast Cancer in Two Regimes: The Impact of Social Movements on Illness Experience." *Sociology of Health and Illness* 26(6): 845–74.

Kornhauser, William. 1959. *The Politics of Mass Society.* Glencoe: The Free Press.

Kroll-Smith, Steve, and Hugh Floyd. 2000. "Environmental Illness as a Practical Epistemology and a Source of Professional Confusion." In Steve Kroll-Smith, Phil Brown, and Valerie Gunter (eds.), *Illness and the Environment: A Reader in Contested Medicine.* New York: New York University Press.

Marsh, Peter. 2001. "In Praise of Bad Habits." 22 November. <http://www.spiked-online.com/Printable/00000002D2E7.htm>.

McAdam, Doug, John D. McCarthy, and Mayer N. Zald (Eds.). 1996. *Comparative Perspectives on Social Movements: Political Opportunities, Mobilizing Structures, and Cultural Framings.* Cambridge: Cambridge University Press.

McClurg Mueller, Carol. 1992. "Building Social Movement Theory." In Aldon D. Morris and Carol McClurg Mueller (eds.), *Frontiers in Social Movement Theory.* New Haven and London: Yale University Press.

McLaren, Leah. 2000. "Halifax Hysteria." *The Globe and Mail,* 29 April.

Melucci, Alberto. 1985. "The Symbolic Challenge of Contemporary Movements." *Social Research* 52: 789–816.

Melucci, Alberto. 1988. "Social Movements and the Democratization of Everyday Life." In J. Keane (ed.), *Civil Society and the State.* London: Verso.

Melucci, Alberto. 1996. *Challenging Codes: Collective Action in the Information Age.* Cambridge: Cambridge University Press.

Meyer, David, and Nancy Whittier. 1994. "Social Movement Spillover." *Social Problems* 41: 277–98.

Meyer, David S., and Suzanne Staggenborg. 1996. "Movements, Counter-movements, and the Structure of Political Opportunity." *American Journal of Sociology* 101(6): 1628–60.

Mooers, Colin, and Alan Sears. 1992. "The 'New Social Movements' and the Withering Away of State Theory." In William Carroll (ed.), *Organizing Dissent: Contemporary Social Movements in Theory and Practice.* Toronto: Garamond.

Navarre, Max. 1993. "Fighting the Victim Label." In Douglas Crimp (ed.), *AIDS: Cultural Analysis/Cultural Activism.* Cambridge and London: The MIT Press.

Nova Scotia Environmental Health Centre. 2006. *Facilities.* <http://www.cdha.nshealth.ca/facilities/nsehc/>.

Offe, Claus. 1985. "New Social Movements: Challenging the Boundaries of Institutional Politics." *Social Research* 52(4): 817–68.

Olson, Mancur. 1965. *The Logic of Collective Action.* Cambridge, MA: Harvard University Press.

Orsini, Michael, and Francesca Scala. 2006. "Every Virus Tells A Story: Toward a Narrative Centred Approach to Health Policy." *Policy and Society* 25(2): 125–50.

Piven, Frances Fox, and Richard A. Cloward. 1995. "Collective Protest: A Critique of Resource-Mobilization Theory." In Stanford A. Lyman (ed.), *Social Movements: Critiques, Concepts, Case-studies*. New York: New York University Press.

Polletta, Francesca. 1998. "'It Was Like a Fever ...' Narrative and Identity in Social Protest." *Social Problems* 45(2): 137–59.

Rayside, David M., and Evert A. Lindquist. 1992. "AIDS Activism and the State in Canada." *Studies in Political Economy* 39 (Autumn): 37–76.

Smelser, Neil J. 1962. *Theory of Collective Behavior*. New York: The Free Press.

Smith, Miriam. 2005. *A Civil Society? Collective Actors in Canadian Political Life*. Peterborough: Broadview.

Tarrow, Sidney. 1994. *Power in Movement: Social Movements, Collective Action, and Politics*. Cambridge: Cambridge University Press.

Tarrow, Sidney. 2005. *The New Transnational Activism*. New York: Cambridge University Press.

Touraine, Alain. 1988. *Return of the Actor: Social Theory in Postindustrial Society*. Minneapolis: University of Minnesota Press.

Toxic Nation. 2006. <http://www.toxicnation.ca>.

Weir, Lorna. 1993. "The Limitations of New Social Movement Analysis." *Studies in Political Economy* 40 (Spring): 73–103.

Winant, Terry. 2004. "Reflections on Asthma Activism." *Fresno Metro Ministry, News and Views*, August.

Zavestoski, Stephen, Phil Brown, Sabrina McCormick, Brian Mayer, Jaime Lucove, and Maryhelen D'Ottavi. 2004. "Patient Activism and the Struggle for Diagnosis: Gulf War Illness and Other Medically Unexplained Physical Symptoms in the US." *Social Science & Medicine* 58: 161–75.

Zavestoski, Stephen, Rachel Morello-Frosch, Phil Brown, Brian Mayer, Sabrina McCormick, and Rebecca Gasior Altman. 2004. "Embodied Health Movements and Challenges to the Dominant Epidemiological Paradigm." *Research in Social Movements, Conflict and Change* 25: 253–78.

Notes on Contributors

DAVID CAMFIELD is Assistant Professor in the Labour Studies program at the University of Manitoba. His areas of interest include public sector unions in Canada, working-class movements, labour and globalization, and social and political theory. His work has appeared in *Labour/Le Travail* and *Studies in Political Economy*.

SALLY CHIVERS is Associate Professor in Canadian Studies and English at Trent University. Her work focuses on the interdisciplinary study of the relationship between aging and disability in the Canadian public sphere, linking an interest in how artistic forms (especially literature and film) contribute to critical thought and social movements. Among other works, she is the author of *From Old Woman to Older Women: Contemporary Culture and Women's Narratives* (Ohio State University Press, 2003).

PETER CLANCY is Professor in the Department of Political Science at St. Francis Xavier University. His areas of interest are political development in the Canadian north, business politics, and economic policy. He has recently published *Micro-Politics and Canadian Business: Paper, Steel, and the Airlines* (Broadview Press, 2004).

ALEXANDRA DOBROWOLSKY is Associate Professor in the Department of Political Science at Saint Mary's University. Her main fields are Canadian politics, comparative politics, and women and politics, with a focus on issues of democratic reform, representation, social policy, and citizenship in Canada and Britain. She is the author of *The Politics of Pragmatism: Women, Representation, and Constitutionalism in Canada* (Oxford, 2000) and co-editor of *Women Making Constitutions: New Politics and Comparative Perspectives* (Palgrave, 2003) and *Women, Migration, and Citizenship: Making Local, National, and Transnational Connections* (Ashgate, 2006).

PASCALE DUFOUR is Assistant Professor in the Department of Political Science at the University of Montreal. Her areas of interest are social movements and globalization and the politics of representation in Canada and France. Her work has appeared in the *Canadian Journal of Political Science*, *Politique et Sociétés*, and *Lien social et Politiques*.

JONATHAN GREENE is Assistant Professor in Politics and Canadian Studies at Trent University. His interests include comparative political economy, social movements, poverty, and homelessness. His recent work has appeared in the journal *Studies in Political Economy*.

TREVOR HARRISON is Professor and Chair of the Department of Sociology at the University of Lethbridge. His interests include political sociology and public policy. He is author or editor of six books on Canadian society and politics, notably *Of Passionate Intensity: Right-Wing Populism and the Reform Party of Canada* (University of Toronto Press, 1995) and *The Return of the Trojan Horse: Alberta and the New World (Dis)Order* (Black Rose and the Parkland Institute, 2005).

AUDREY KOBAYASHI is Professor in the Department of Geography at Queen's University. Her work focuses on how processes of human differentiation—race, class, gender, ability, national identity—emerge in a range of landscapes and how these processes are shaped by public policy and legal and normative frameworks. She has a long-standing interest in the history of Japanese-Canadian communities. Among others, her work has appeared in *Gender, Place and Culture*, *The Professional Geographer*, *The Canadian Geographer*, and *Canadian Ethnic Studies*.

KIERA L. LADNER is Canada Research Chair in Indigenous Politics in the Department of Political Studies at the University of Manitoba. Her areas of interest are Indigenous politics, constitutional politics, social movements, and decolonization. Her work has appeared in *Studies in Political Economy* and the *Canadian Journal of Political Science*.

JUDITH MCKENZIE is Associate Professor in the Department of Political Science at Guelph University. Her areas of interest include environmental politics, public policy, women and politics, and social justice issues in Canada. She is the author of *Environmental Politics in Canada* (Oxford, 2002) and *Pauline Jewett* (McGill-Queen's University Press, 1999). Her work has also appeared in the *International Journal of Environment and Pollution* and the *Journal of Legislative Studies*.

MICHAEL ORSINI is Associate Professor in the School of Political Studies at the University of Ottawa. His areas of interest are health politics and policy, social movements, and public policy. He is the co-editor of *Critical Policy Studies* (University of British Columbia Press, 2007) and his work has also appeared in the *Canadian Journal of Political Science, Social Policy and Administration,* and the *Canadian Journal of Urban Research.*

MIRIAM SMITH is Professor in the School of Public Policy and Public Administration at York University. Her areas of interest are Canadian and comparative politics and public policy, in particular, public law, social movements, and the lesbian, gay, bisexual and transgender movements in Canada. She is the author of *Lesbian and Gay Rights in Canada: Social Movements and Equality-Seeking, 1971–1995* (University of Toronto Press, 1999), co-editor with François Rocher of *New Trends in Canadian Federalism,* 2nd ed. (Broadview Press, 2003), author of *A Civil Society?* (Broadview Press, 2005), and co-editor of *Critical Policy Studies* (University of British Columbia Press, 2007).

CHRISTOPHE TRAÏSNEL is researcher at the Canadian Institute for Research on Linguistic Minorities, Moncton. His areas of interest are comparative politics, nationalism, and protest in Canada and Belgium; social movements; and French-speaking communities. His recent work has been published in *Lien Social et Politiques* (2005). He is also the author of *Francophonie, francophonisme: Groupe d'aspiration et formes d'engagement* (LGDJ, 1998).

CHARLOTTE YATES is Professor in the Department of Political Science at McMaster University. Her areas of interest include union renewal and union organizing in the Anglo-American democracies, political economy of political parties and interest groups, organized labour and the state, and globalization and social cohesion. She is the author of *From Plant to Politics: Autoworkers in Postwar Canada, 1936–90* (Temple University Press, 1993) and co-editor of *Trade Unions in Renewal: A Comparative Study* (Continuum Books, 2003).

Index